JOE WILKINSON

MY AUTOBIOGRAPHY

WWW.PENGUIN.CO.UK

ALSO BY JOE WILKINSON

THE BEGINNER'S GUIDE TO ARMED SCRUMPING

THE COOK, THE THIEF, THE WIFE AND HER NIT NURSE

HOW TO GET AHEAD IN BUSINESS
(DON'T PUT YOUR FIST IN YOUR MOUTH)

TRAINSPOTTER SPOTTER'S LOG BOOK: AN ENTHUSIAST'S RECORD
OF NAMES AND THEIR PARKA JACKETS

THE 12 STEPS OF AAA (ALIENS' ALCOHOLICS ANONYMOUS)

THE JOY OF SEX WITH DINNER LADIES

HOW TO BE A HAPPY MUM (CO-WRITTEN WITH THE 1975
WOLVERHAMPTON WANDERERS FOOTBALL TEAM)

FIBREGLASS AND COMPOSITE MATERIALS: A GUIDE
TO HIGH-PERFORMANCE NON-METALLIC MATERIALS

JOE AND THE BOG-STANDARD CHOCOLATE FACTORY

THE DOS AND DON'TS OF CLONING YOURSELF
(PAMPHLET)

JOE WILKINSON

MY AUTOBIOGRAPHY

ILLUSTRATED BY HENRY PAKER

bantam

TRANSWORLD PUBLISHERS
PENGUIN RANDOM HOUSE, ONE EMBASSY GARDENS, 8 VIADUCT GARDENS,
LONDON SW11 7BW
WWW.PENGUIN.CO.UK

TRANSWORLD IS PART OF THE PENGUIN RANDOM HOUSE GROUP OF COMPANIES
WHOSE ADDRESSES CAN BE FOUND AT GLOBAL.PENGUINRANDOMHOUSE.COM

Penguin
Random House
UK

FIRST PUBLISHED IN GREAT BRITAIN IN 2023 BY BANTAM
AN IMPRINT OF TRANSWORLD PUBLISHERS

A CIP CATALOGUE RECORD FOR THIS BOOK
IS AVAILABLE FROM THE BRITISH LIBRARY.

ISBN 9781787630819

TYPESET IN BACK ISSUES 9PT BY HENRY PAKER
PRINTED IN ITALY.

THE AUTHORIZED REPRESENTATIVE IN THE EEA IS PENGUIN RANDOM HOUSE IRELAND,
MORRISON CHAMBERS, 32 NASSAU STREET, DUBLIN D02 YH68.

PENGUIN RANDOM HOUSE IS COMMITTED TO A SUSTAINABLE
FUTURE FOR OUR BUSINESS, OUR READERS AND OUR PLANET.
THIS BOOK IS MADE FROM FOREST STEWARDSHIP COUNCIL® CERTIFIED PAPER.

FSC
www.fsc.org
MIX
Paper | Supporting
responsible forestry
FSC® C018179

THIS BOOK IS DEDICATED TO MY EIGHTEEN ALSATIANS.

DRAGØR
MINTY
FOXY LADY
THE ANGLE GRINDER
RITA
SUE
BOB
MIKE PATTERSON
TURPS
BATTERY ACID
BIG VAL
MERTHYR TYDFIL
LUCIFER
GUNPOWDER
BERNIE NOLAN
DASHER
COURTNEY
THE MUSCLES FROM BRUSSELS

...YOU COMPLETE ME

CONTENTS (OF MY FRIDGE)

MARGARINE

CONTENTS (OF MY BOOK)

PROLOGUE

I DON'T KNOW WHAT A PROLOGUE IS, SO INSTEAD I'VE STUCK IN THE CRAWLEY/REDHILL BUS TIMETABLE.

420

460

Crawley/Redhill - Reigate - Tadworth - Epsom/Sutton

Crawley
Gatwick
Whitebushes
East Surrey Hospital
Redhill
Reigate
Lower Kingswood
Tadworth
Preston
Banstead
Belmont
Sutton
Sutton Bus Garage
420
Crawley
Gatwick
Whitebushes
East Surrey Hospital
Redhill
Reigate
Lower Kingswood
Walton-on-the-Hill
Tadworth
Preston
Tattenham Corner
Epsom
460

Talking bus

Daily from 16th January 2021
Inc. journeys on Service **820** Mon-Fri only

Mondays to Fridays

Service	460	460	420	460	420	460	460	420	460	420	420	460	420	460	420	460	420	460
Crawley Bus Station Stop I ◎	....	....	....	....	....	0601	....	....	0645	....	....	0749	....	0901	....	1001	....	....
Gatwick Road North	....	....	....	....	....	0609	....	....	0654	....	....	0758	....	0910	....	1010	....	....
Gatwick South Terminal ◎	0450	0532	....	0548	....	0613	0630	....	0658	....	....	0803	....	0915	....	1015	....	....
Horley Lumley Road, A23	0454	0536	....	0552	....	0618	0635	....	0703	....	....	0808	....	0920	....	1020	....	....
Salfords Church ◎	0458	0540	....	0556	....	0623	0640	....	0709	....	....	0814	....	0926	....	1026	....	....
Whitebushes Spencer Way	0503	0545	....	0601	....	0629	0646	....	0716	....	....	0821	0902	0933	1002	1033	1102	....
East Surrey Hospital	0505	0547	....	0603	....	0631	0648	....	0719	....	....	0824	0904	0936	1004	1036	1104	....
Redhill Bus Station (arr) ◎	0512	0554	....	0610	....	0638	0655	....	0727	....	....	0834	0912	0945	1012	1045	1112	....
Redhill Bus Station (dep) ◎	0514	0556	0558	0612	....	0641	0658	0703	0731	....	0812	0838	0916	0949	1016	1049	1116	....
Reigate Bell Street	0521	0604	0606	0620	0647	0650	0708	0713	0743	....	0827	0850	0928	1001	1028	1101	1128	1143
Lower Kingswood Fox	0529	0612	0615	0629	0656	0659	0718b	0725	0753b	....	0842	0901b	0938	1011	1038	1111	1138	1153b
Walton Oaks (see note 'b')	↓	↓	↓	↓	↓	↓	0729	↓	0805	0813	↓	0911	↓	↓	↓	↓	↓	1200
Walton-on-the-Hill Howard Close	↓	↓	↓	0638	↓	↓	↓	↓	0809	↓	↓	0915	↓	1021	↓	1121	↓	↓
Tadworth Station ◎	0535	0619	0622	0643	0706	0709	0737	0739	0815	0819	0852	0921	0946	1027	1046	1127	1146	1206
Merland Rise Sports Centre	↓	↓	0625	↓	0710	↓	↓	0746	↓	0823	0856	↓	0950	↓	1050	↓	1150	↓
Marbles Way, Merefield Gardens	0541	0625	↓	0649	↓	0715	0743	↓	0821	↓	↓	0927	↓	1033	↓	1133	↓	1212
Tattenham Corner Station ◎	0545	0630	↓	0654	↓	0720	0748	↓	0826	↓	↓	0932	↓	1038	↓	1138	↓	1217
Epsom High Street Stop K	0553	0638	↓	0703	↓	0729	0757	↓	0835	↓	↓	0941	↓	1047	↓	1147	↓	1226
Tattenham Way Reigate Road	....	....	0630	....	0716	....	....	0753	....	0829	0902	....	0956	....	1056	....	1156	....
Banstead Marks & Spencer	....	....	0635	....	0722	....	....	0759	....	0835	0908	....	1002	....	1102	....	1202	....
Belmont Downs Road	....	....	0640	....	0728	....	....	0805	....	0841	0914	....	1008	....	1108	....	1208	....
Sutton Station ◎	....	....	0644	....	0734	....	....	0811	....	0847	0920	....	1014	....	1114	....	1214	....
Sutton Bus Garage	....	....	0649	....	....	....	....	....	....	....	0926	....	1020	....	1120	....	1220	....

Mondays to Fridays cont...

Service	460	820	420	460	420	460	420	460	420	820	460	420	420	460	420	460	420	460	460
Crawley Bus Stn, Stop I ◎	1101	....	....	1201	....	1305	....	1408	....	....	1513	....	....	1621	....	1730	....	1830	....
Gatwick Road North	1110	....	....	1210	....	1314	....	1417	....	....	1522	....	....	1630	....	1739	....	1839	....
Gatwick South Terminal ◎	1115	....	....	1215	....	1319	....	1422	....	....	1527	....	....	1635	....	1744	....	1844	....
Horley Lumley Road, A23	1120	....	....	1220	....	1324	....	1427	....	....	1532	....	....	1640	....	1749	....	1849	....
Salfords Church ◎	1126	....	....	1226	....	1330	....	1433	....	....	1538	....	....	1646	....	1755	....	1854	....
Whitebushes Spencer Way	1133	....	1202	1233	1302	1337	1402	1440	1509	....	1545	1616	....	1653	1731	1802	1833	1900	....
East Surrey Hospital	1136	....	1204	1236	1304	1340	1404	1443	1511	....	1548	1618	....	1656	1733	1805	1835	1902	....
Redhill Bus Station (arr) ◎	1145	....	1212	1245	1312	1349	1412	1452	1519	....	1557	1626	....	1706	1741	1814	1844	1912	....
Redhill Bus Station (dep) ◎	1149	....	1216	1249	1316	1353	1416	1457	1524	1551	1602	1630	....	1711	1746	1818	1848	1916	1934
Reigate Bell Street	1201	....	1228	1301	1328	1405	1428	1509	1536	1603	1614	1642	....	1723	1758	1830	1859	1926	1943
Lower Kingswood Fox	1211	....	1238	1311	1338	1415	1438	1519	1546b	1613	1624b	1654b	....	1733b	1810b	1840	1909	1934	1951
Walton Oaks (see note b)	↓	1248	↓	↓	↓	↓	↓	↓	1555	1630*	1633	1703	1730	1743	1819	↓	↓	↓	↓
Walton-on-the-Hill Howard Cl.	1221	y	↓	1321	↓	1425	↓	1529	↓	1623	1637	↓	↓	1747	↓	1850	↓	1943	↓
Tadworth Station ◎	1227	↓	1246	1327	1346	1431	1446	1535	1601	y	1643	1710	1736	1753	1826	1855	1916	1948	1958
Merland Rise Sports Centre	↓	↓	1250	↓	1350	↓	1450	↓	1605	↓	↓	1714	1740	↓	1830	↓	1920	↓	↓
Marbles Way, Merefield Gdns.	1233	↓	↓	1333	↓	1437	↓	1541	↓	↓	1649	↓	↓	1759	↓	1900	↓	1953	2003
Tattenham Corner Stn. ◎	1238	↓	↓	1338	↓	1442	↓	1546	↓	↓	1654	↓	↓	1803	↓	1904	↓	1957	2007
Epsom High Street, Stop K.	1247	↓	↓	1347	↓	1451	↓	1555	↓	↓	1703	↓	↓	1812	↓	1911	↓	2004	2013
Tattenham Way Reigate Rd.	....	↓	1256	....	1356	....	1456	....	1611	↓	....	1720	1745	....	1835	....	1924	....	....
Banstead Marks & Spencer	....	1300	1302	....	1402	....	1502	....	1617	1645	....	1726	1752	....	1840	....	1929	....	....
Belmont Downs Road	....	1306	1308	....	1408	....	1508	....	1623	1651	....	1732	1758	....	1846	....	1934	....	....
Sutton Station ◎	....	1311	1314	....	1414	....	1514	....	1628	1657	....	1738	1804	....	1852	....	1939	....	....
Sutton Bus Garage	....	....	1320	....	1420	....	1520	....	1634	....	....	1744	1809	....	1857	....	1944	....	....

CODE: ◎ Rail Station nearby. **SDO** Schooldays only. **NSD** Non-Schooldays. y Via A217 Burgh Heath.
b Does not serve the Mill Road bus stop, or the Tadworth Court, Tadorne Road and The Lye bus stops on Tadworth Street. * **820** serves Walton Oaks after Walton-on-the-Hill.

Partly supported by SURREY

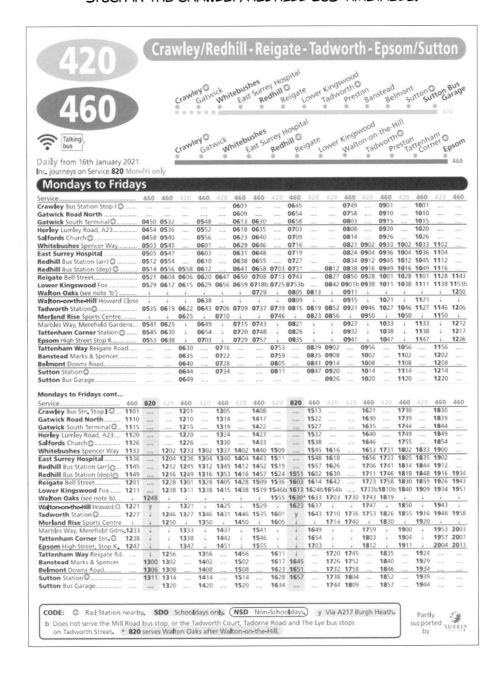

INTRODUCTION

I MUST REMEMBER TO FILL THIS BIT OUT, AND FOR
SHIT'S SAKE DON'T SWEAR ON THE FIRST PAGE.

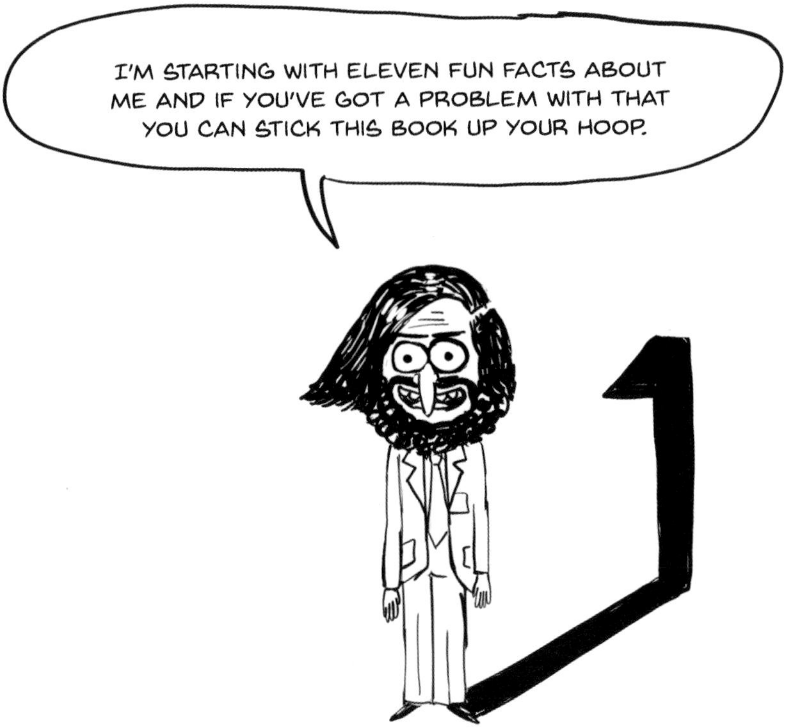
I'M STARTING WITH ELEVEN FUN FACTS ABOUT ME AND IF YOU'VE GOT A PROBLEM WITH THAT YOU CAN STICK THIS BOOK UP YOUR HOOP.

THIS IS ME

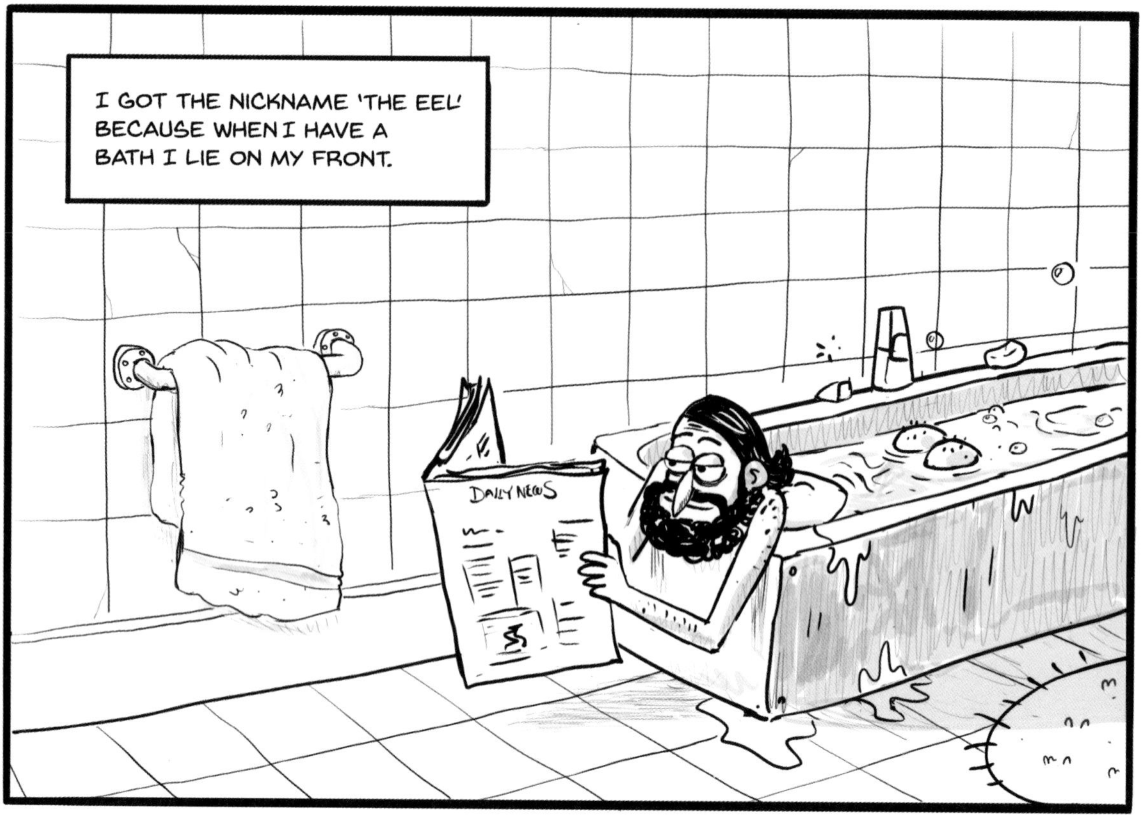
I GOT THE NICKNAME 'THE EEL' BECAUSE WHEN I HAVE A BATH I LIE ON MY FRONT.
DAILY NEWS

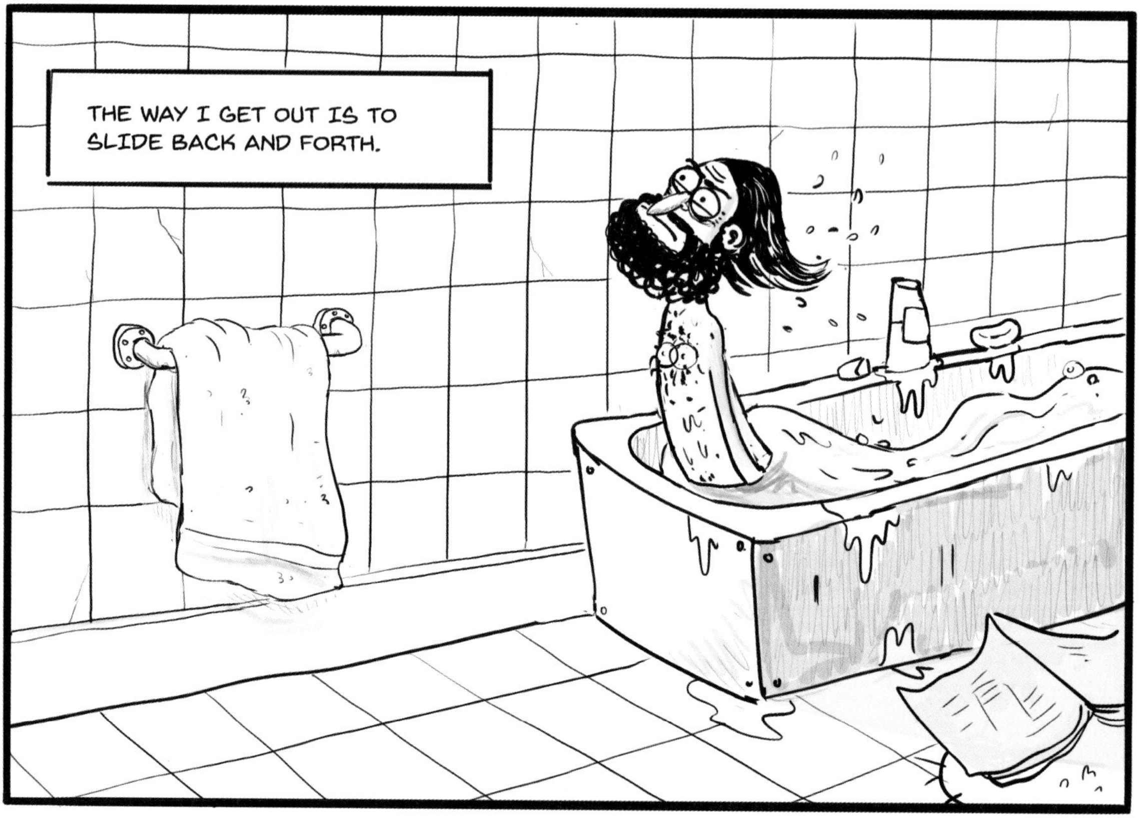
THE WAY I GET OUT IS TO SLIDE BACK AND FORTH.

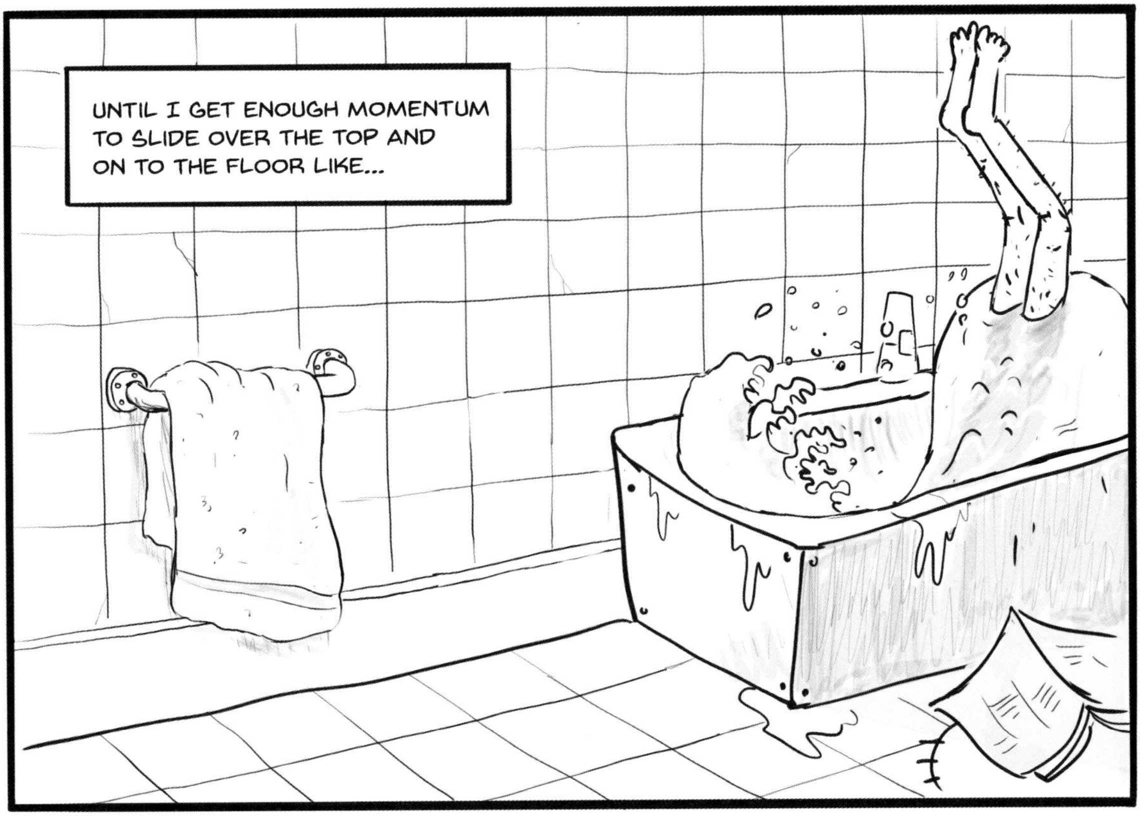
UNTIL I GET ENOUGH MOMENTUM TO SLIDE OVER THE TOP AND ON TO THE FLOOR LIKE...

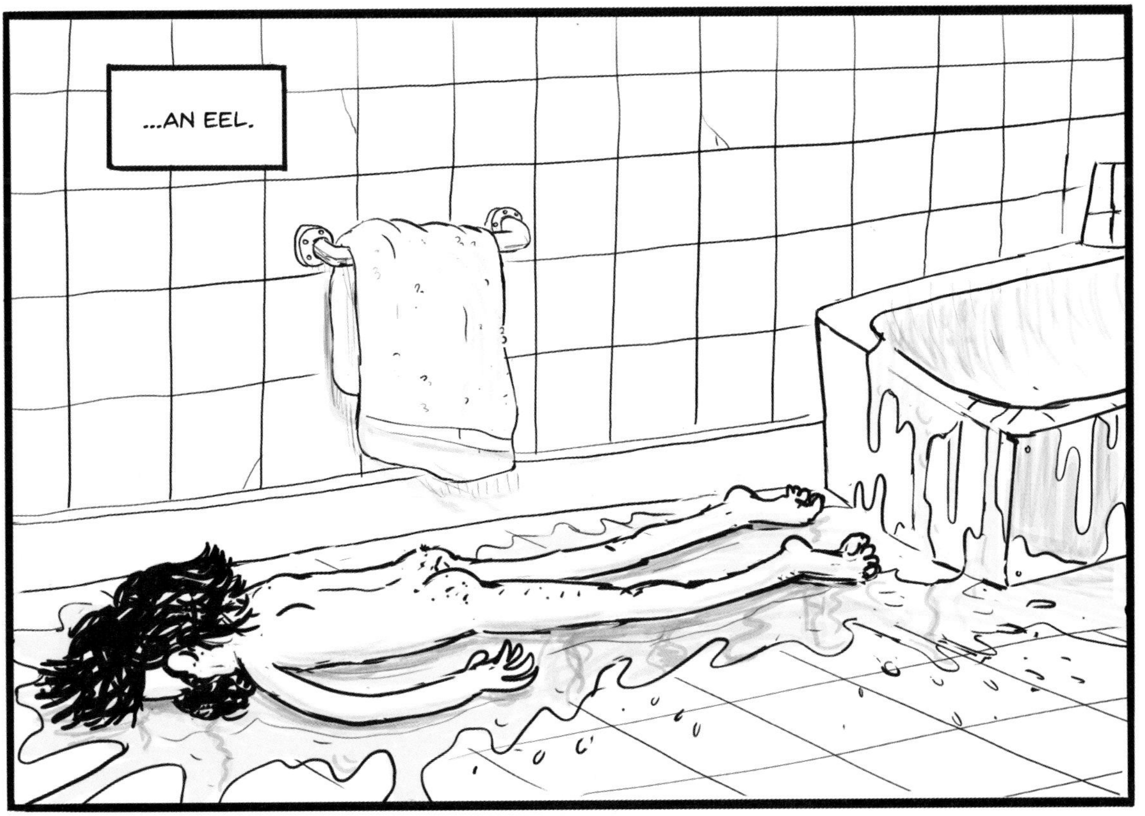
...AN EEL.

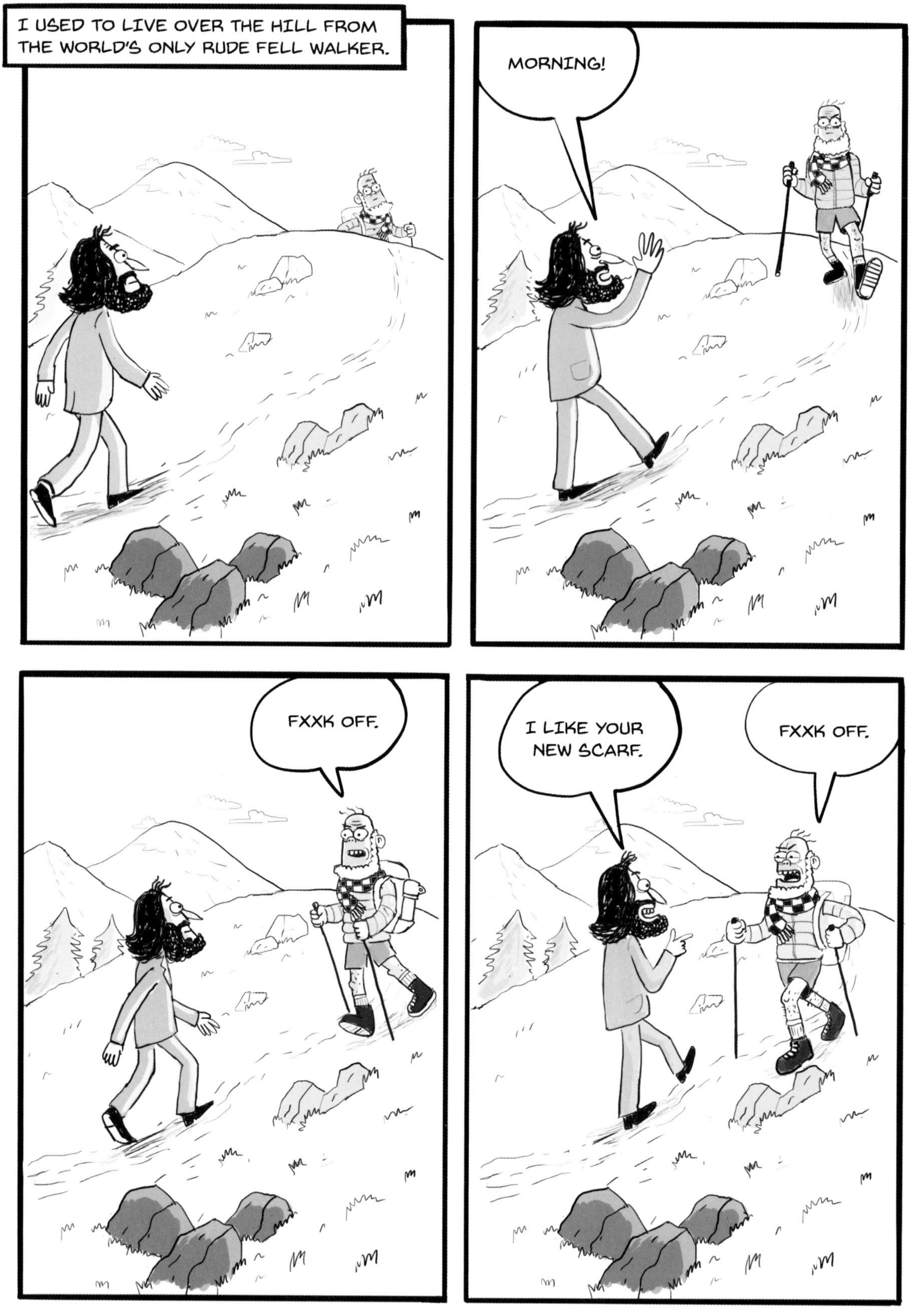
I USED TO LIVE OVER THE HILL FROM THE WORLD'S ONLY RUDE FELL WALKER.
MORNING!
FXXK OFF.
I LIKE YOUR NEW SCARF.
FXXK OFF.

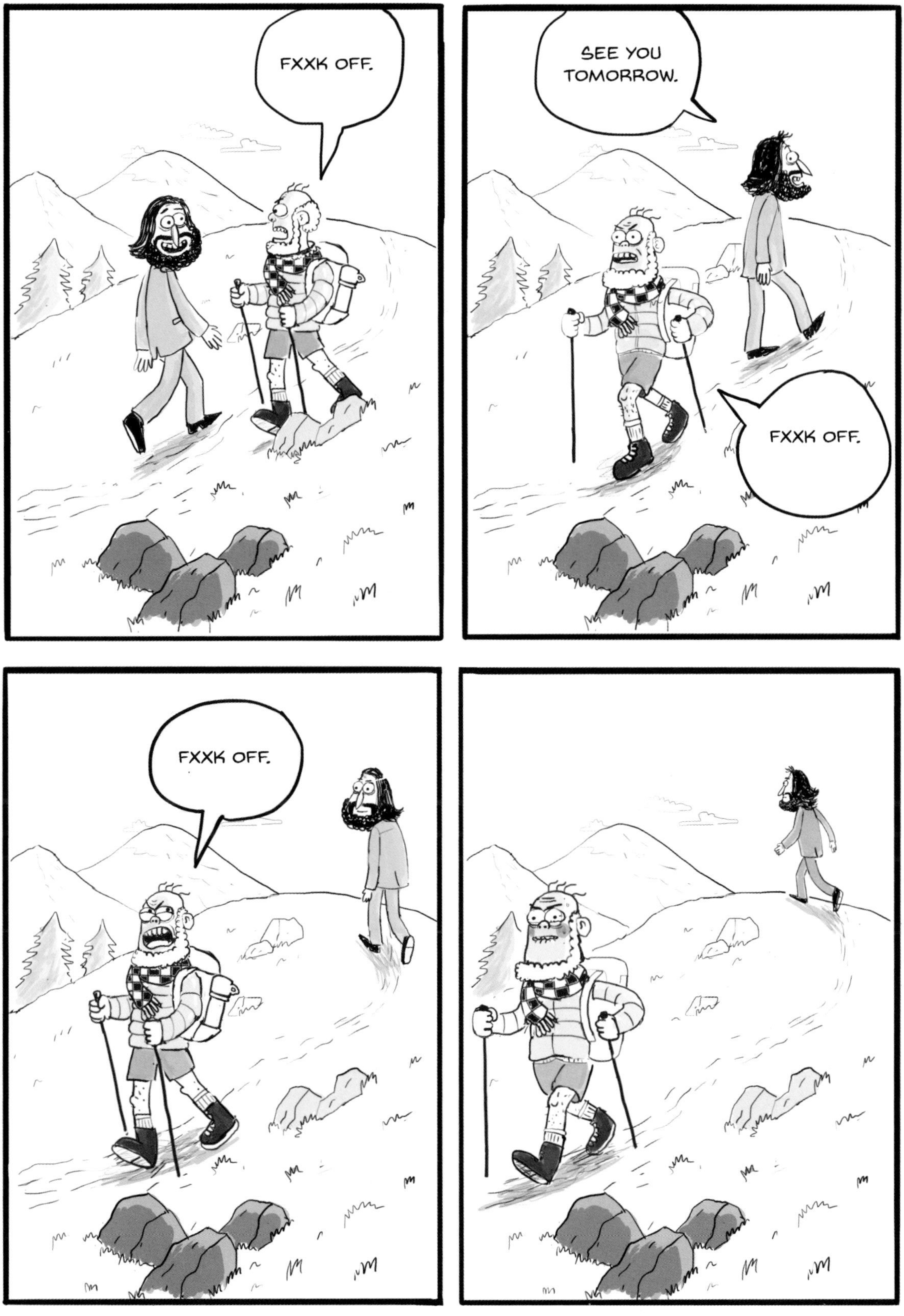
FXXK OFF.
SEE YOU TOMORROW.
FXXK OFF.
FXXK OFF.

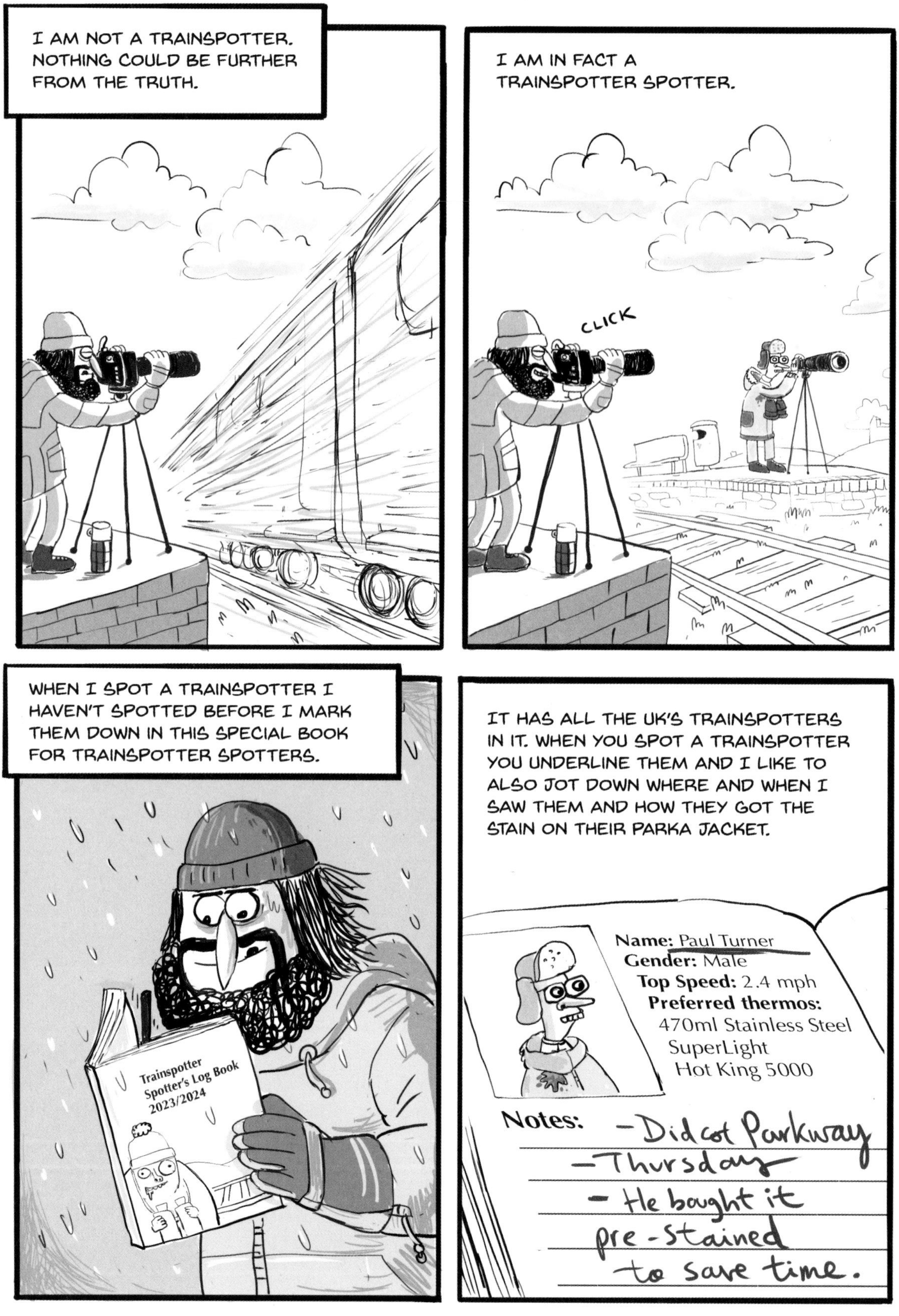
I AM NOT A TRAINSPOTTER. NOTHING COULD BE FURTHER FROM THE TRUTH.
I AM IN FACT A TRAINSPOTTER SPOTTER.
CLICK
WHEN I SPOT A TRAINSPOTTER I HAVEN'T SPOTTED BEFORE I MARK THEM DOWN IN THIS SPECIAL BOOK FOR TRAINSPOTTER SPOTTERS.
Trainspotter Spotter's Log Book 2023/2024
IT HAS ALL THE UK'S TRAINSPOTTERS IN IT. WHEN YOU SPOT A TRAINSPOTTER YOU UNDERLINE THEM AND I LIKE TO ALSO JOT DOWN WHERE AND WHEN I SAW THEM AND HOW THEY GOT THE STAIN ON THEIR PARKA JACKET.
Name: Paul Turner
Gender: Male
Top Speed: 2.4 mph
Preferred thermos: 470ml Stainless Steel SuperLight Hot King 5000
Notes: – Didcot Parkway
– Thursday
– He bought it pre-stained to save time.

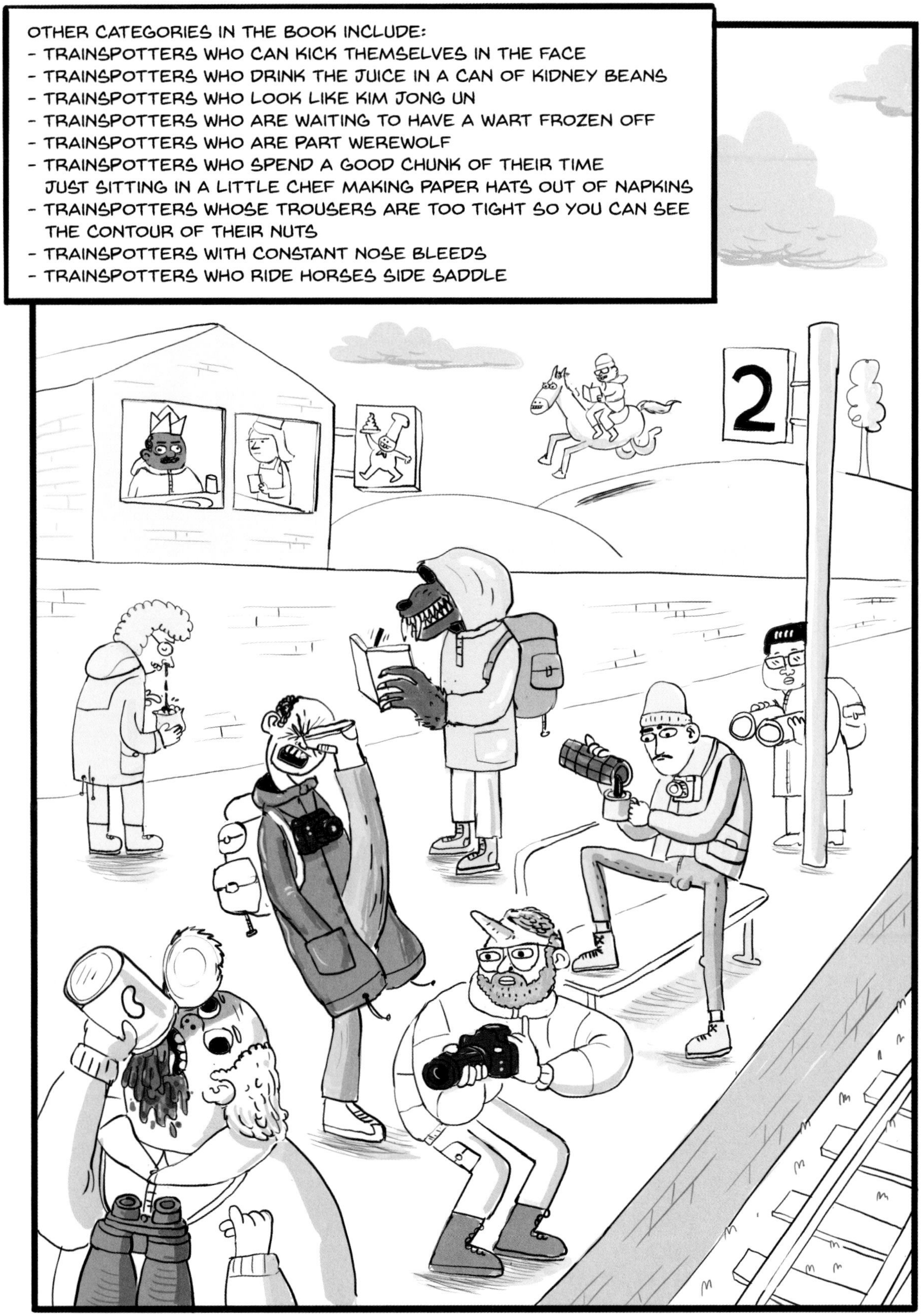
OTHER CATEGORIES IN THE BOOK INCLUDE:
- TRAINSPOTTERS WHO CAN KICK THEMSELVES IN THE FACE
- TRAINSPOTTERS WHO DRINK THE JUICE IN A CAN OF KIDNEY BEANS
- TRAINSPOTTERS WHO LOOK LIKE KIM JONG UN
- TRAINSPOTTERS WHO ARE WAITING TO HAVE A WART FROZEN OFF
- TRAINSPOTTERS WHO ARE PART WEREWOLF
- TRAINSPOTTERS WHO SPEND A GOOD CHUNK OF THEIR TIME JUST SITTING IN A LITTLE CHEF MAKING PAPER HATS OUT OF NAPKINS
- TRAINSPOTTERS WHOSE TROUSERS ARE TOO TIGHT SO YOU CAN SEE THE CONTOUR OF THEIR NUTS
- TRAINSPOTTERS WITH CONSTANT NOSE BLEEDS
- TRAINSPOTTERS WHO RIDE HORSES SIDE SADDLE
2

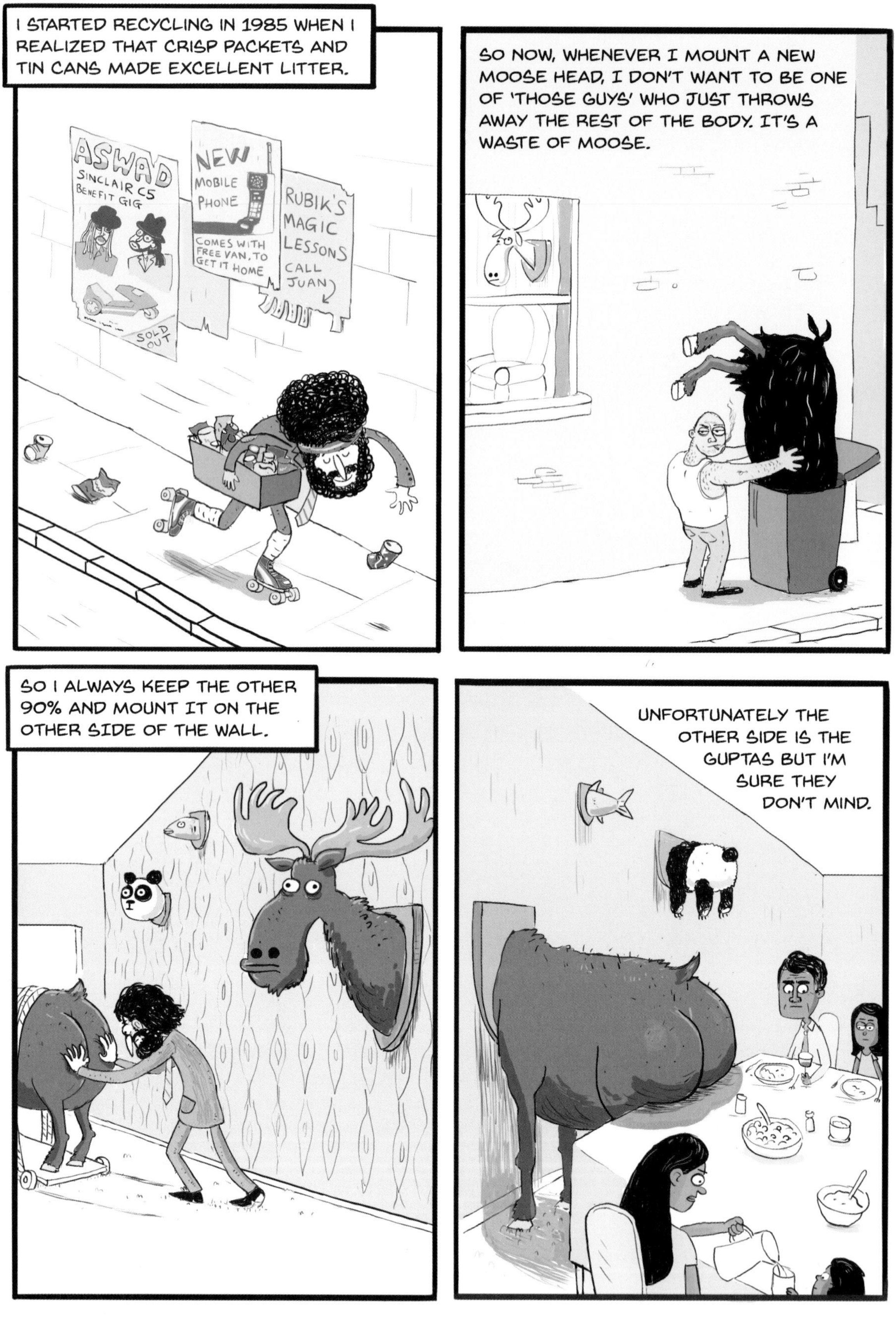
I STARTED RECYCLING IN 1985 WHEN I REALIZED THAT CRISP PACKETS AND TIN CANS MADE EXCELLENT LITTER.
ASWAD
SINCLAIR C5 BENEFIT GIG
SOLD OUT
NEW
MOBILE PHONE
COMES WITH FREE VAN, TO GET IT HOME
RUBIK'S MAGIC LESSONS
CALL JUAN
SO NOW, WHENEVER I MOUNT A NEW MOOSE HEAD, I DON'T WANT TO BE ONE OF 'THOSE GUYS' WHO JUST THROWS AWAY THE REST OF THE BODY. IT'S A WASTE OF MOOSE.
SO I ALWAYS KEEP THE OTHER 90% AND MOUNT IT ON THE OTHER SIDE OF THE WALL.
UNFORTUNATELY THE OTHER SIDE IS THE GUPTAS BUT I'M SURE THEY DON'T MIND.

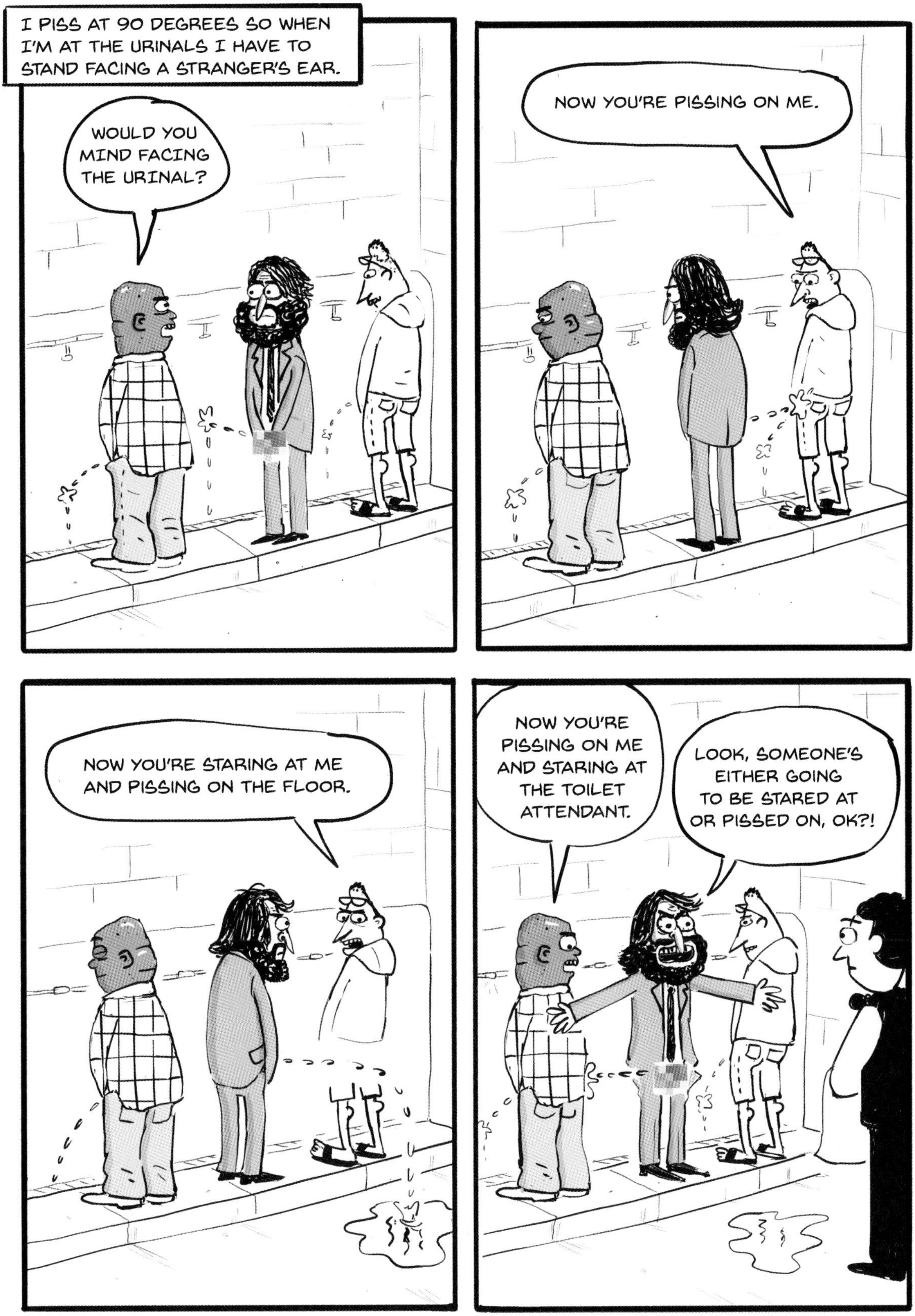
I PISS AT 90 DEGREES SO WHEN I'M AT THE URINALS I HAVE TO STAND FACING A STRANGER'S EAR.
WOULD YOU MIND FACING THE URINAL?
NOW YOU'RE PISSING ON ME.
NOW YOU'RE STARING AT ME AND PISSING ON THE FLOOR.
NOW YOU'RE PISSING ON ME AND STARING AT THE TOILET ATTENDANT.
LOOK, SOMEONE'S EITHER GOING TO BE STARED AT OR PISSED ON, OK?!

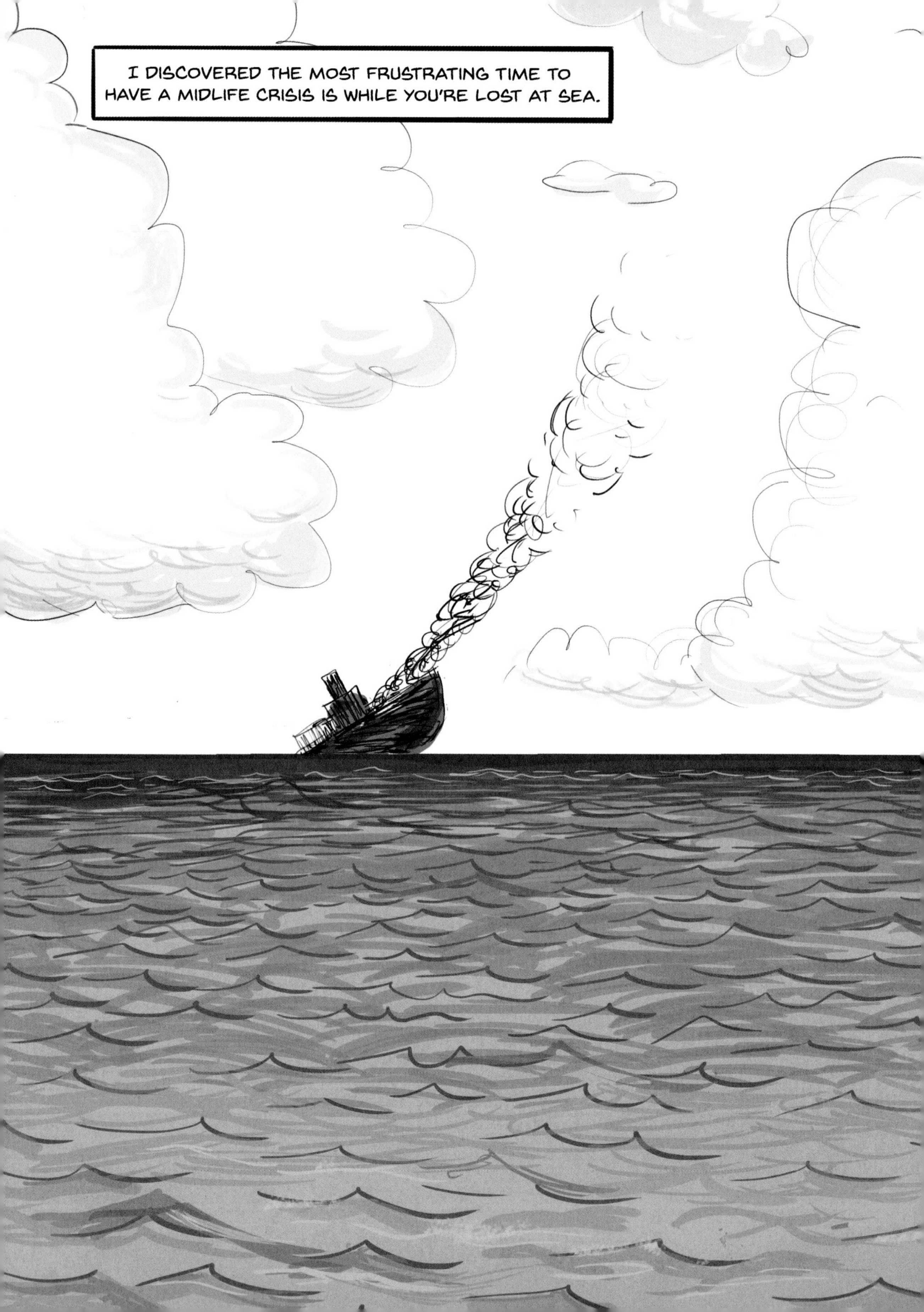
I DISCOVERED THE MOST FRUSTRATING TIME TO HAVE A MIDLIFE CRISIS IS WHILE YOU'RE LOST AT SEA.

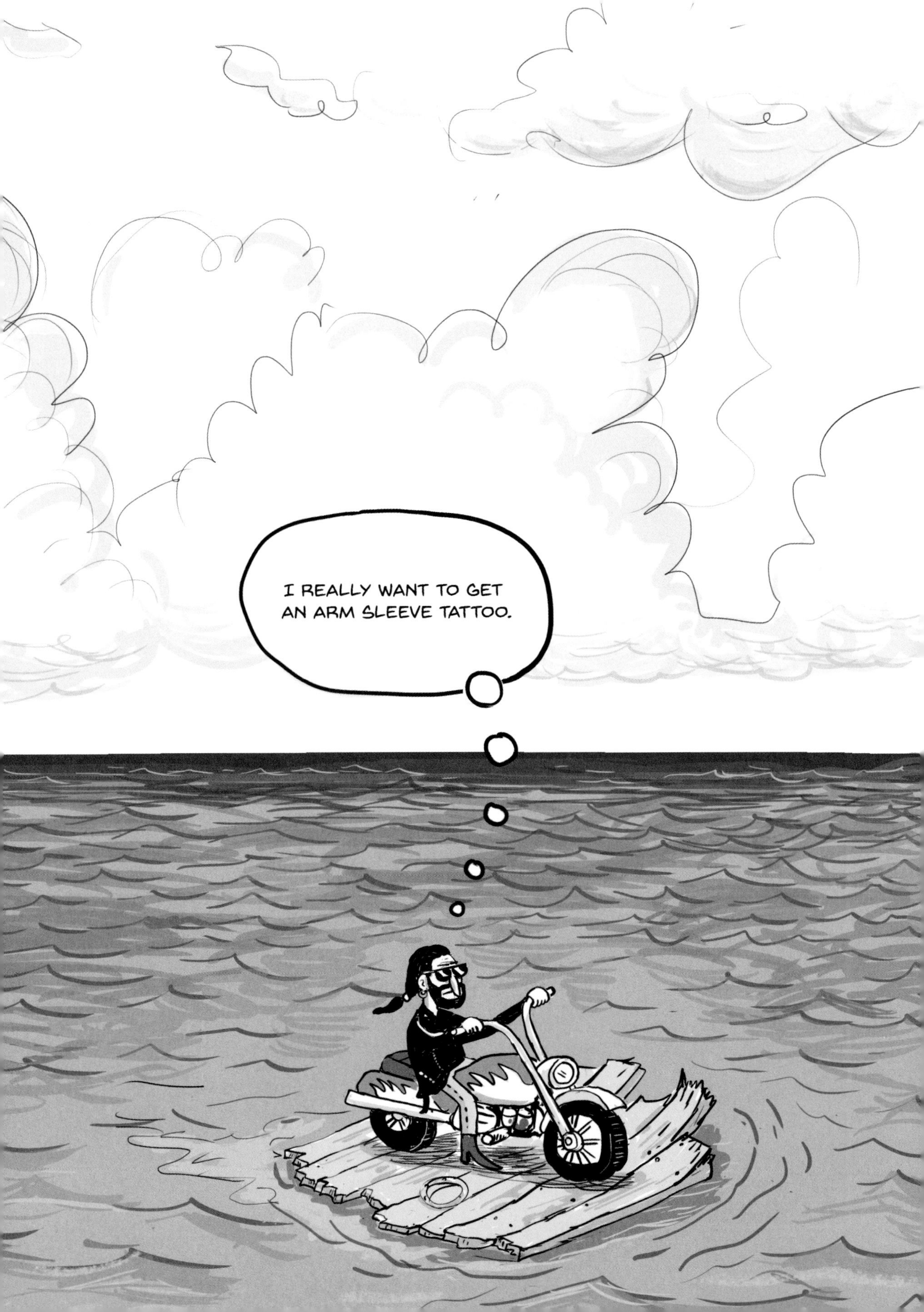
I REALLY WANT TO GET AN ARM SLEEVE TATTOO.

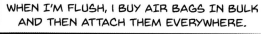

WHEN I'M FLUSH, I BUY AIR BAGS IN BULK AND THEN ATTACH THEM EVERYWHERE.

THERE WAS ONLY ONE PLACE I FORGOT TO PUT ONE.

BALLS.

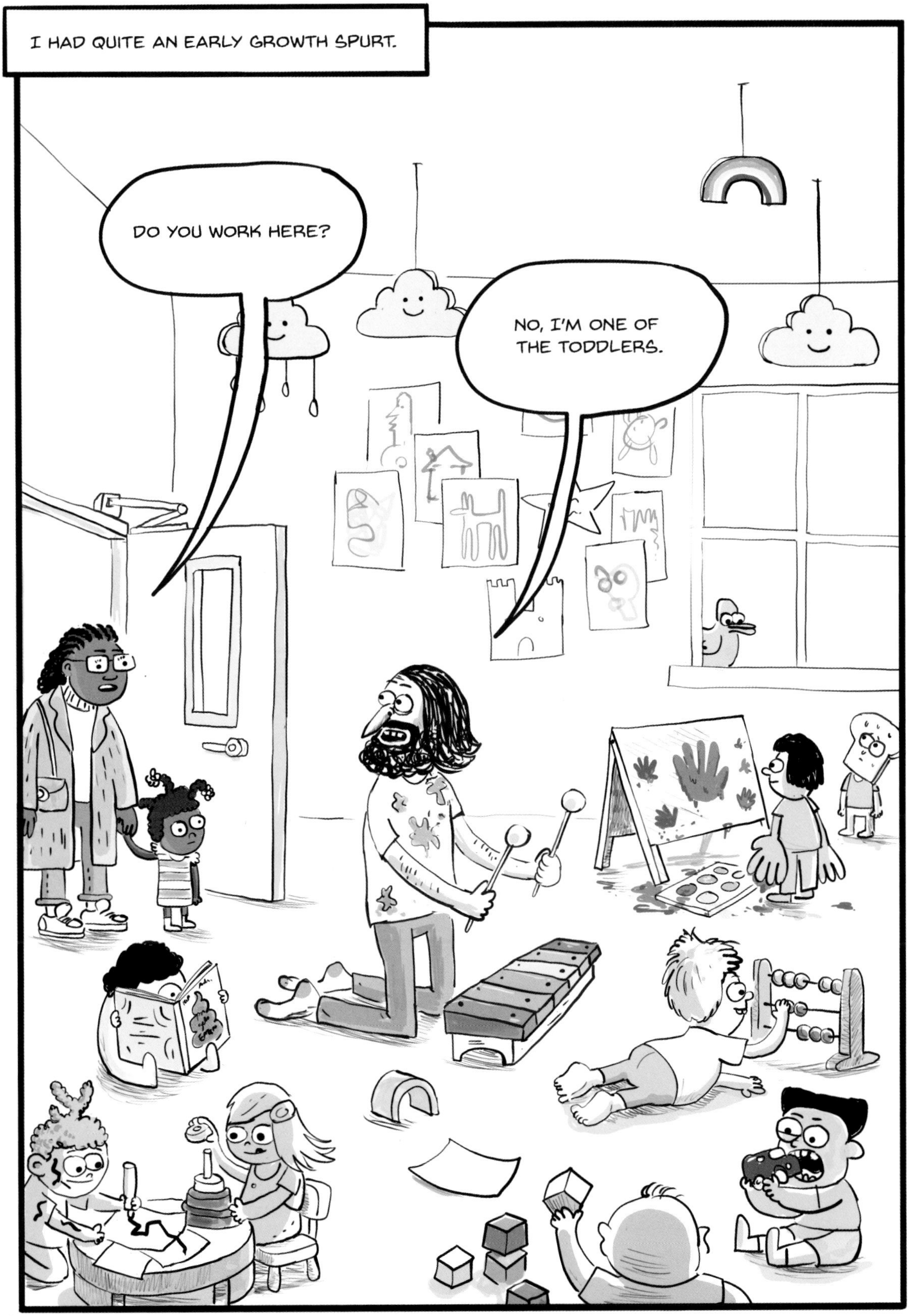
I HAD QUITE AN EARLY GROWTH SPURT.
DO YOU WORK HERE?
NO, I'M ONE OF THE TODDLERS.

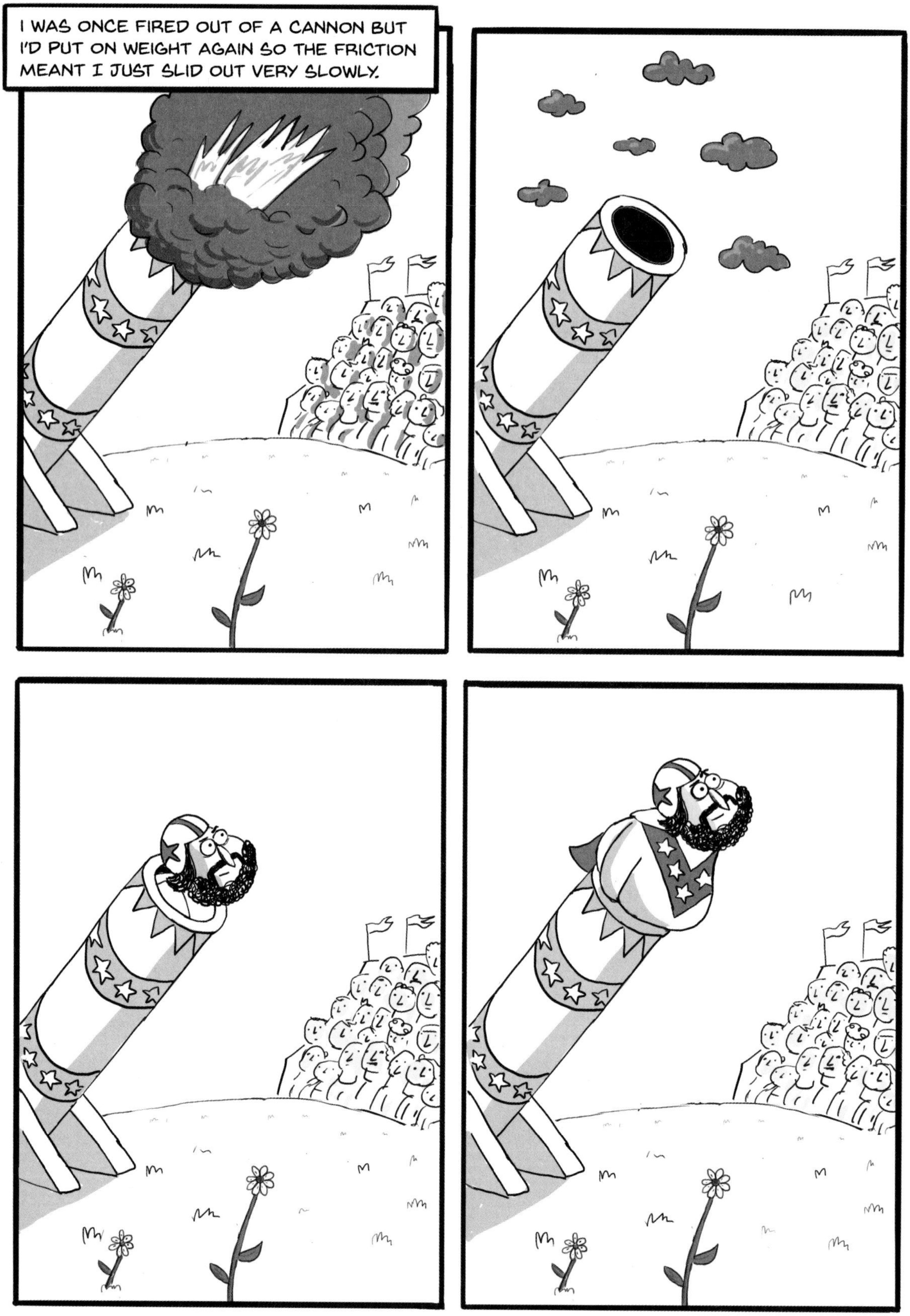
I WAS ONCE FIRED OUT OF A CANNON BUT I'D PUT ON WEIGHT AGAIN SO THE FRICTION MEANT I JUST SLID OUT VERY SLOWLY.

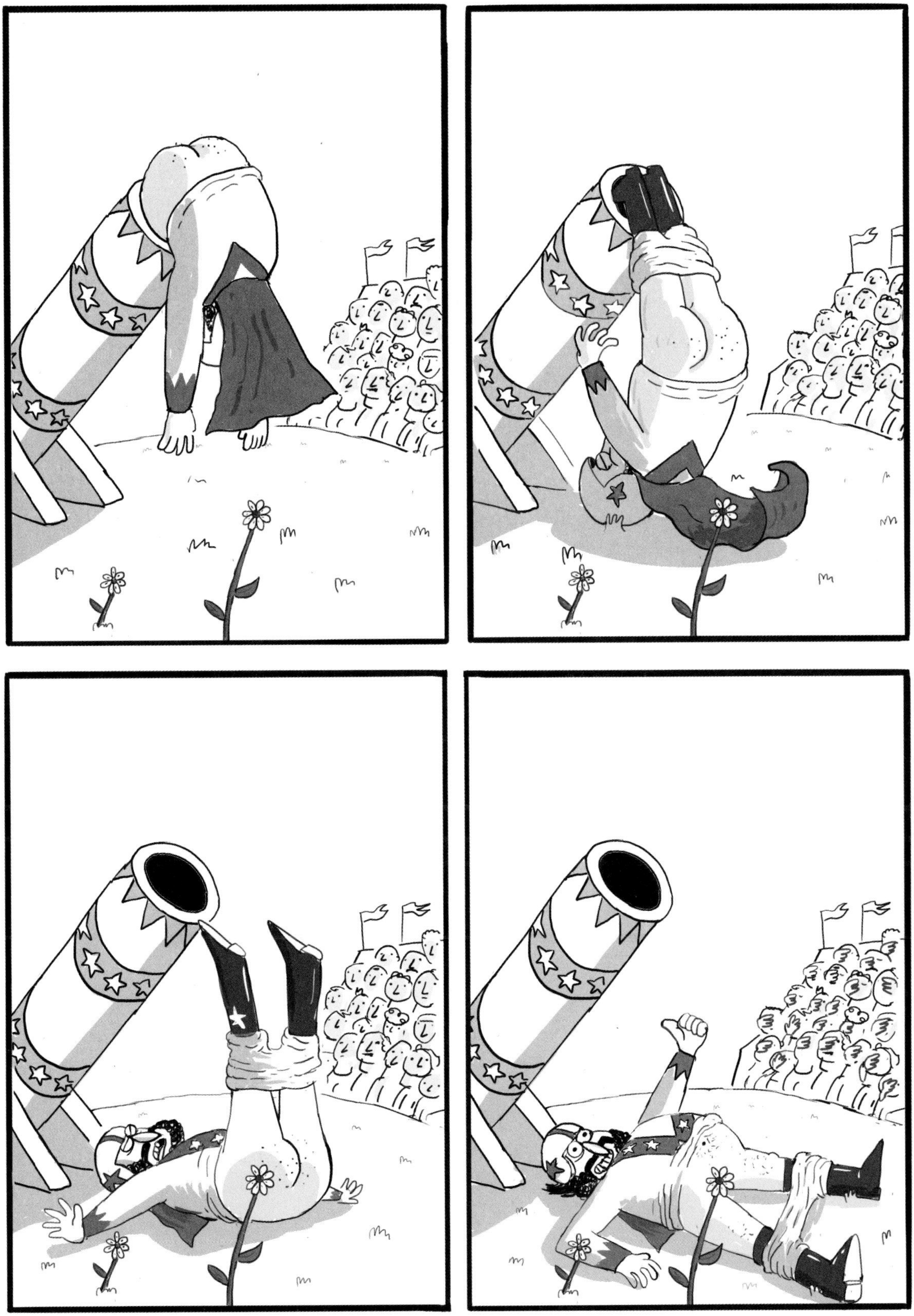

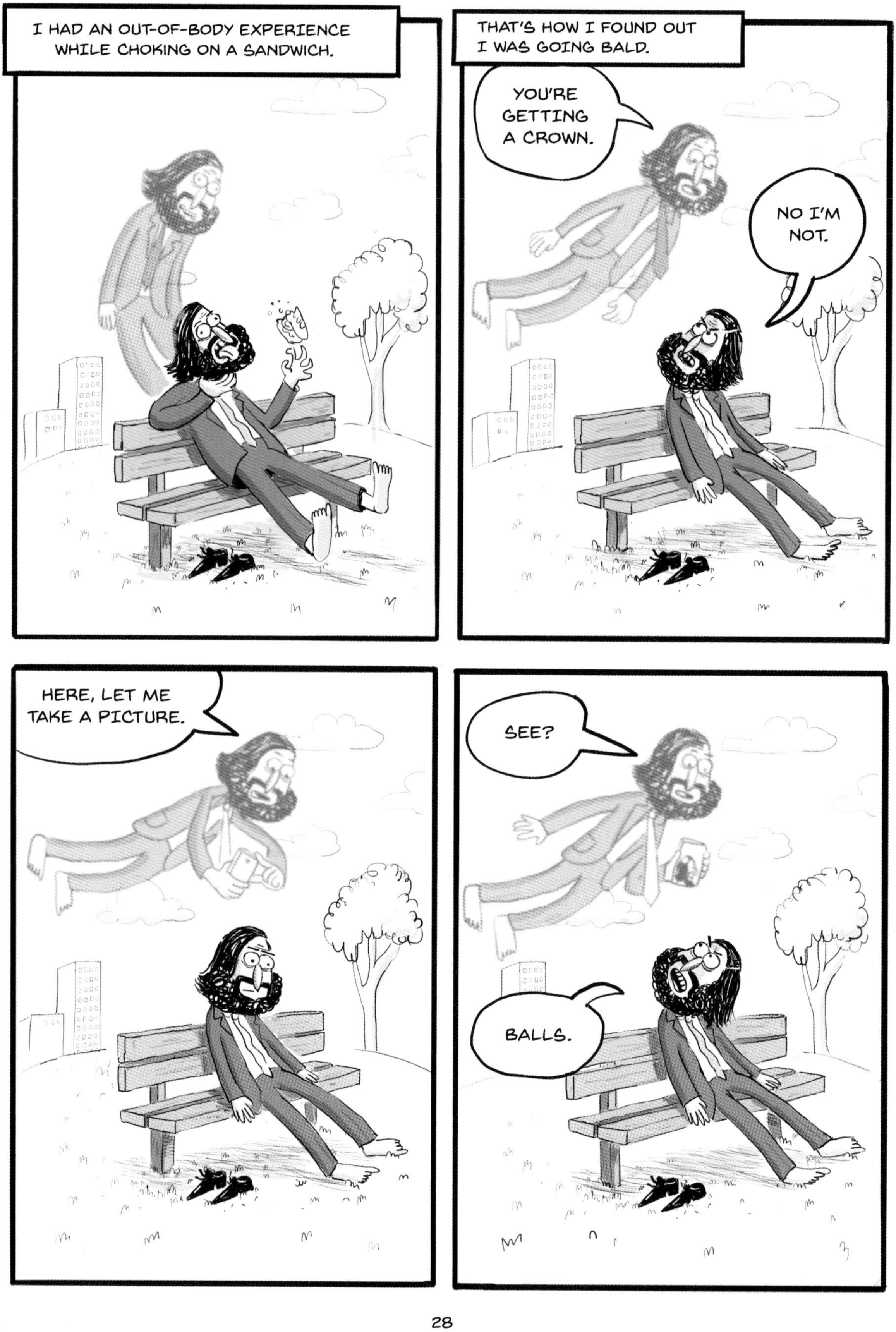
I HAD AN OUT-OF-BODY EXPERIENCE
WHILE CHOKING ON A SANDWICH.
THAT'S HOW I FOUND OUT
I WAS GOING BALD.
YOU'RE GETTING A CROWN.
NO I'M NOT.
HERE, LET ME TAKE A PICTURE.
SEE?
BALLS.

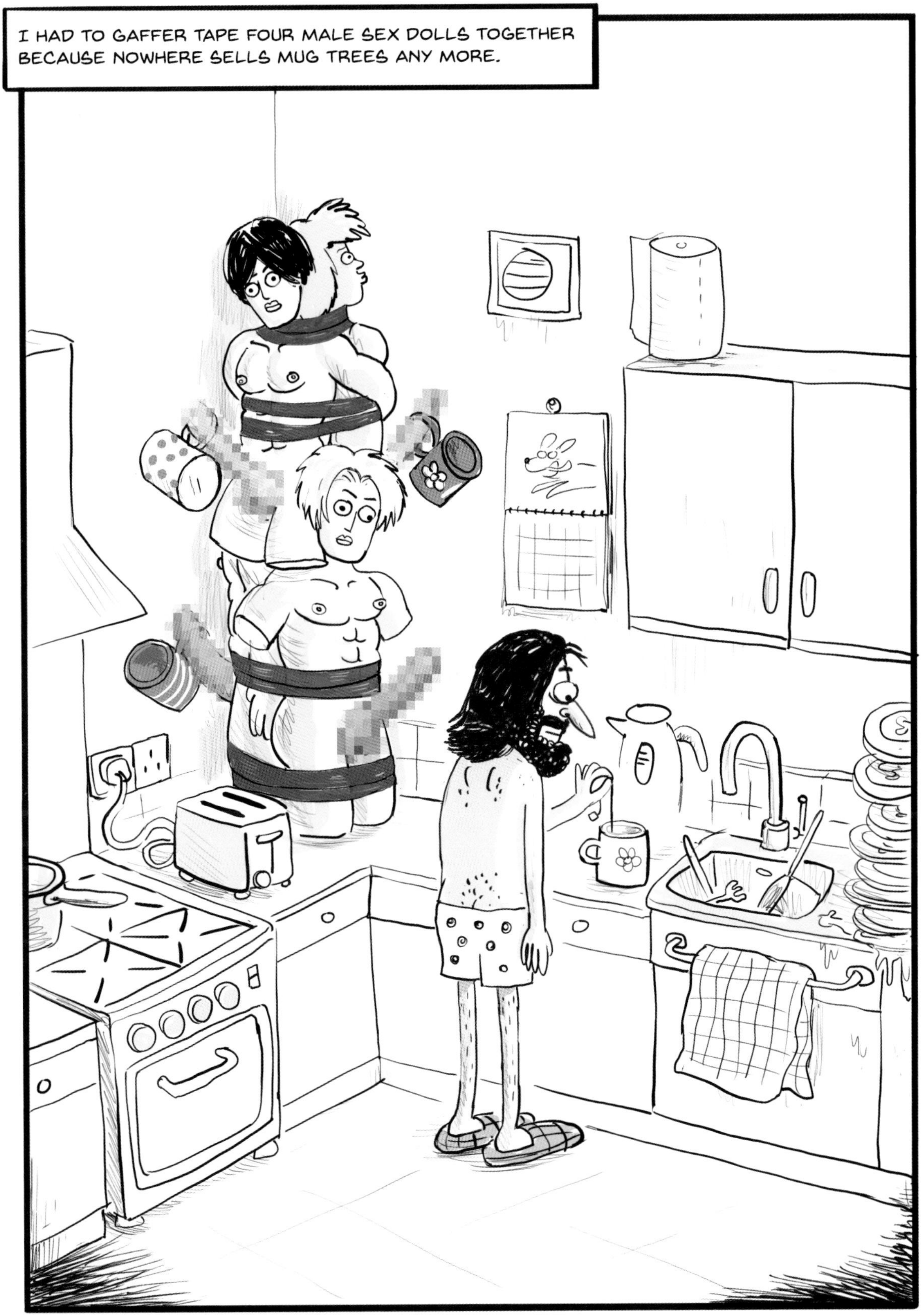
I HAD TO GAFFER TAPE FOUR MALE SEX DOLLS TOGETHER BECAUSE NOWHERE SELLS MUG TREES ANY MORE.

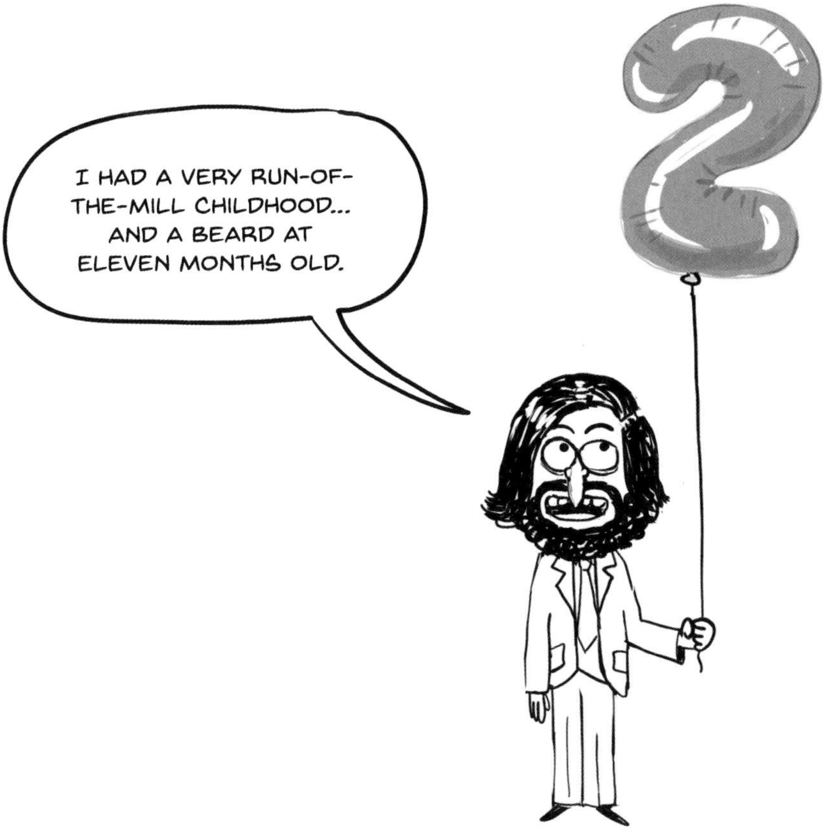
I HAD A VERY RUN-OF-THE-MILL CHILDHOOD... AND A BEARD AT ELEVEN MONTHS OLD.

THE EARLY DAYS

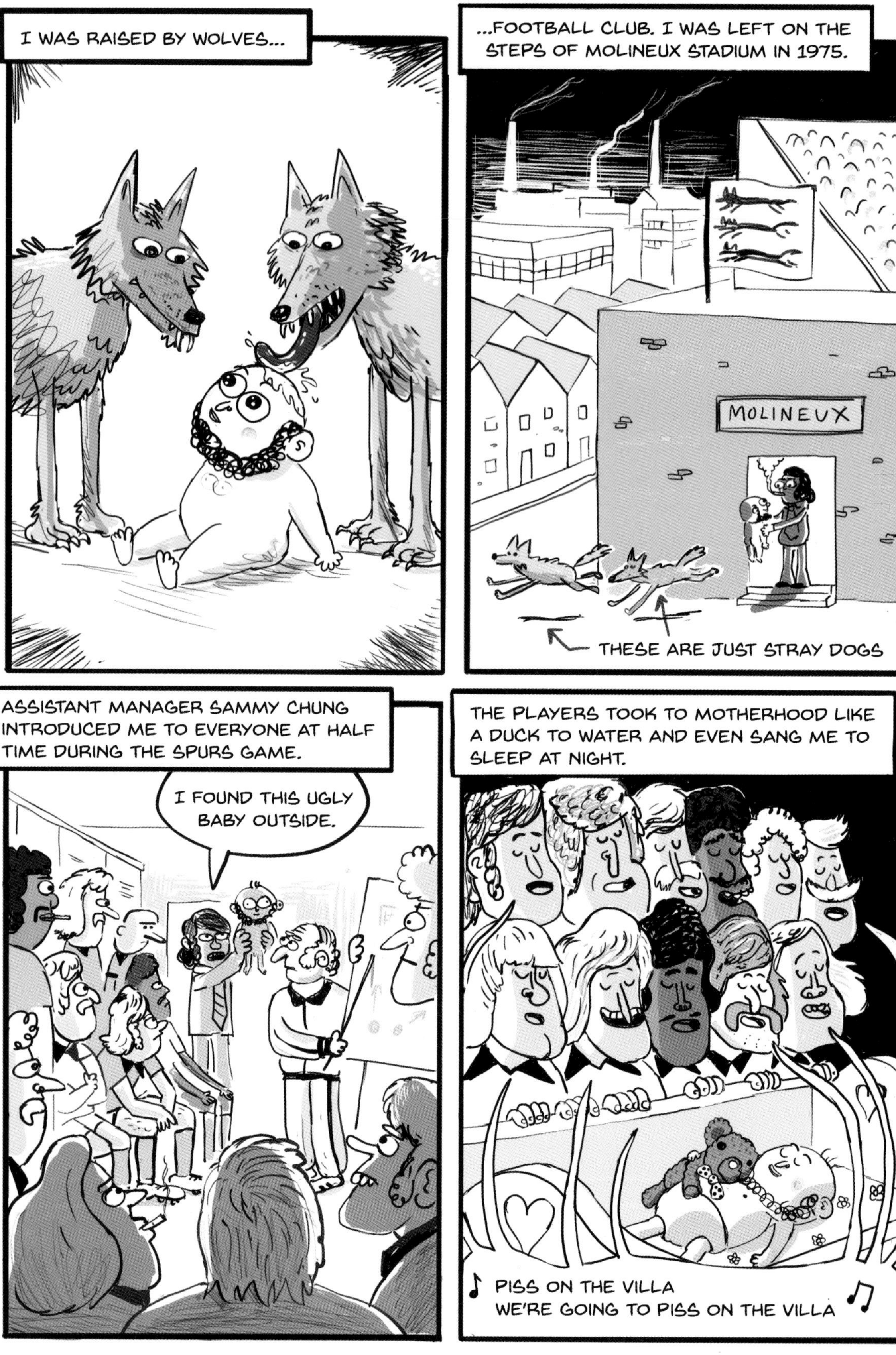
I WAS RAISED BY WOLVES...
...FOOTBALL CLUB. I WAS LEFT ON THE STEPS OF MOLINEUX STADIUM IN 1975.
MOLINEUX
THESE ARE JUST STRAY DOGS
ASSISTANT MANAGER SAMMY CHUNG INTRODUCED ME TO EVERYONE AT HALF TIME DURING THE SPURS GAME.
I FOUND THIS UGLY BABY OUTSIDE.
THE PLAYERS TOOK TO MOTHERHOOD LIKE A DUCK TO WATER AND EVEN SANG ME TO SLEEP AT NIGHT.
PISS ON THE VILLA
WE'RE GOING TO PISS ON THE VILLA

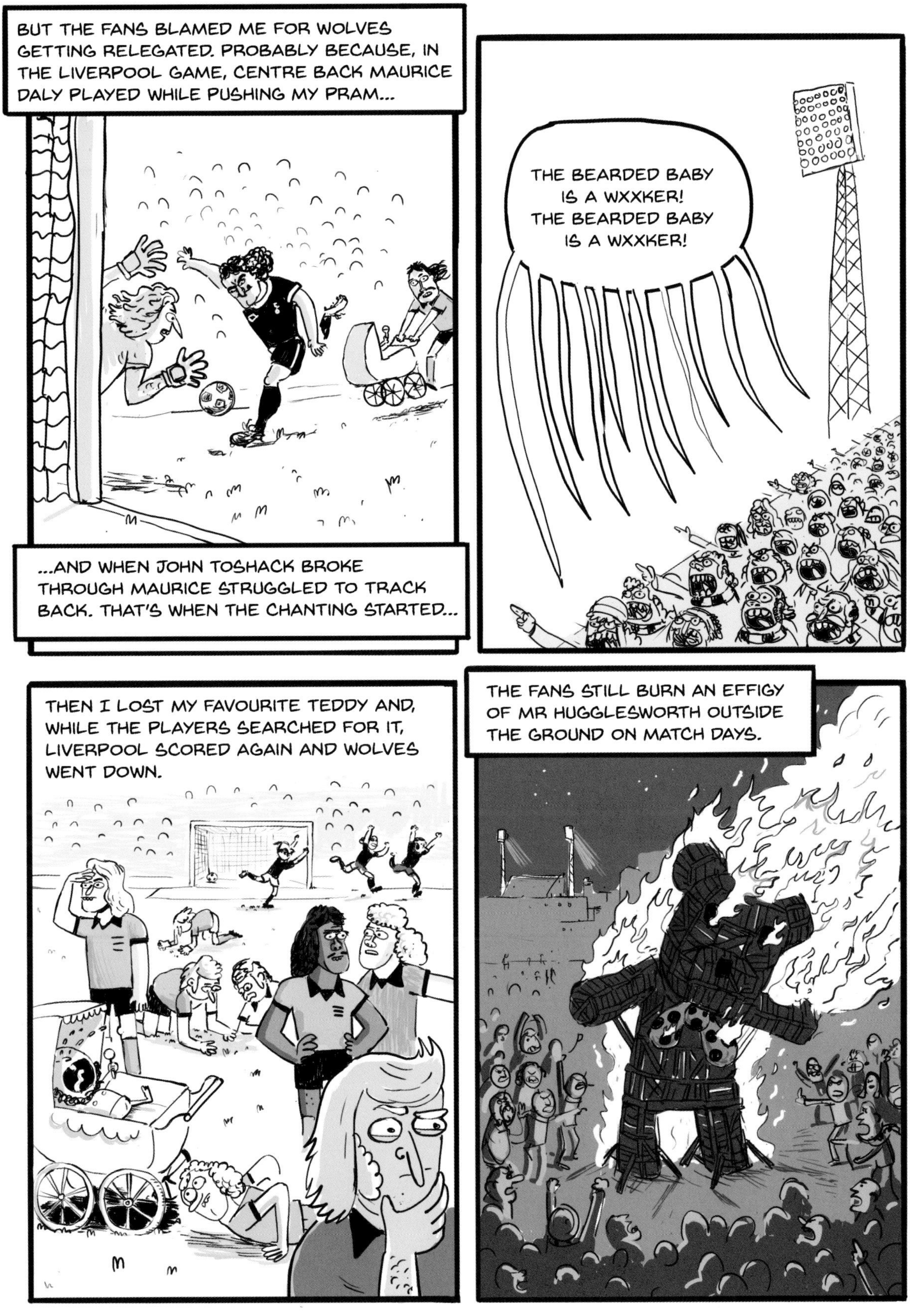

BUT THE FANS BLAMED ME FOR WOLVES GETTING RELEGATED. PROBABLY BECAUSE, IN THE LIVERPOOL GAME, CENTRE BACK MAURICE DALY PLAYED WHILE PUSHING MY PRAM...
...AND WHEN JOHN TOSHACK BROKE THROUGH MAURICE STRUGGLED TO TRACK BACK. THAT'S WHEN THE CHANTING STARTED...
THE BEARDED BABY IS A WXXKER! THE BEARDED BABY IS A WXXKER!
THEN I LOST MY FAVOURITE TEDDY AND, WHILE THE PLAYERS SEARCHED FOR IT, LIVERPOOL SCORED AGAIN AND WOLVES WENT DOWN.
THE FANS STILL BURN AN EFFIGY OF MR HUGGLESWORTH OUTSIDE THE GROUND ON MATCH DAYS.

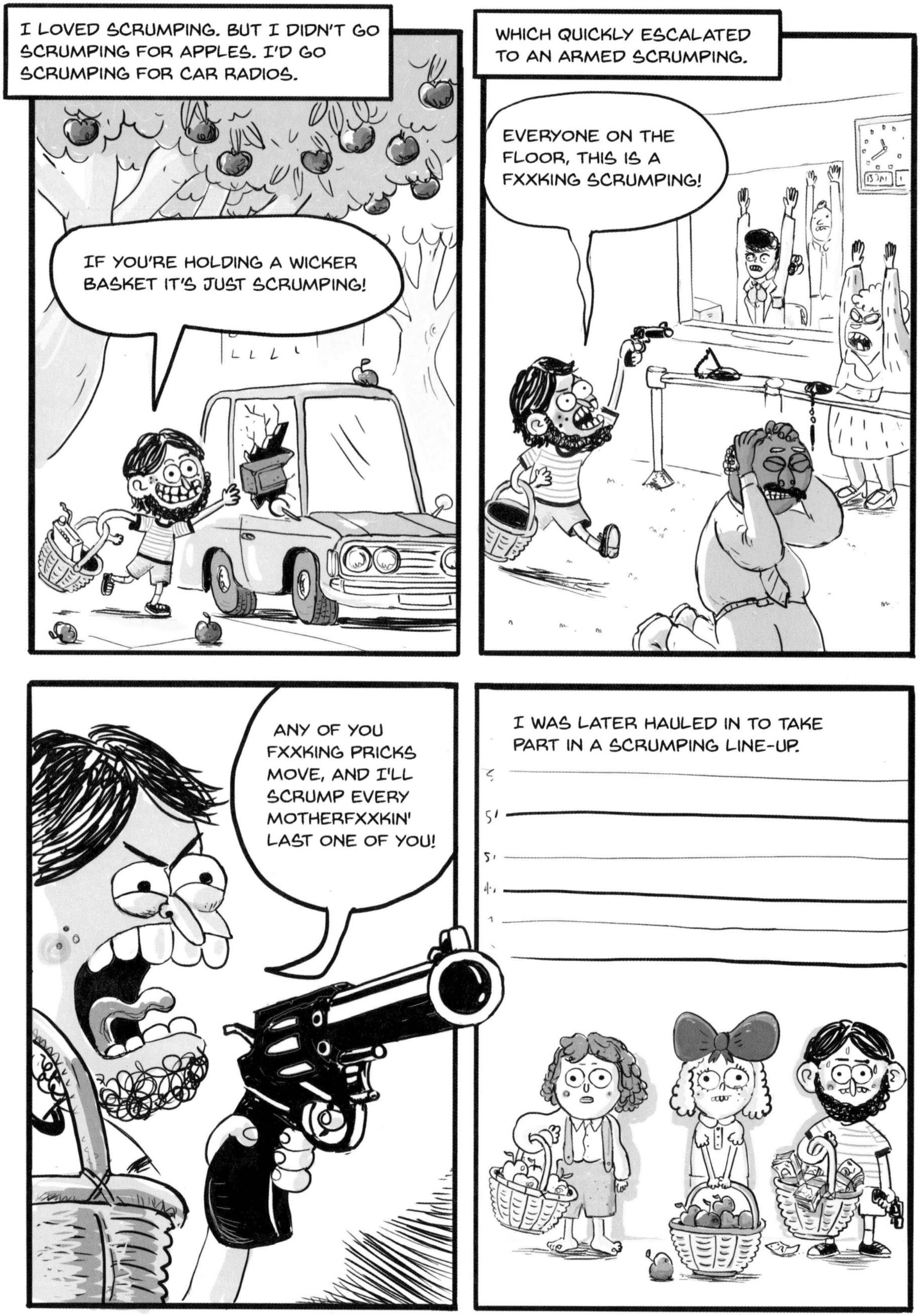
I LOVED SCRUMPING. BUT I DIDN'T GO SCRUMPING FOR APPLES. I'D GO SCRUMPING FOR CAR RADIOS.
IF YOU'RE HOLDING A WICKER BASKET IT'S JUST SCRUMPING!
WHICH QUICKLY ESCALATED TO AN ARMED SCRUMPING.
EVERYONE ON THE FLOOR, THIS IS A FXXKING SCRUMPING!
ANY OF YOU FXXKING PRICKS MOVE, AND I'LL SCRUMP EVERY MOTHERFXXKIN' LAST ONE OF YOU!
I WAS LATER HAULED IN TO TAKE PART IN A SCRUMPING LINE-UP.

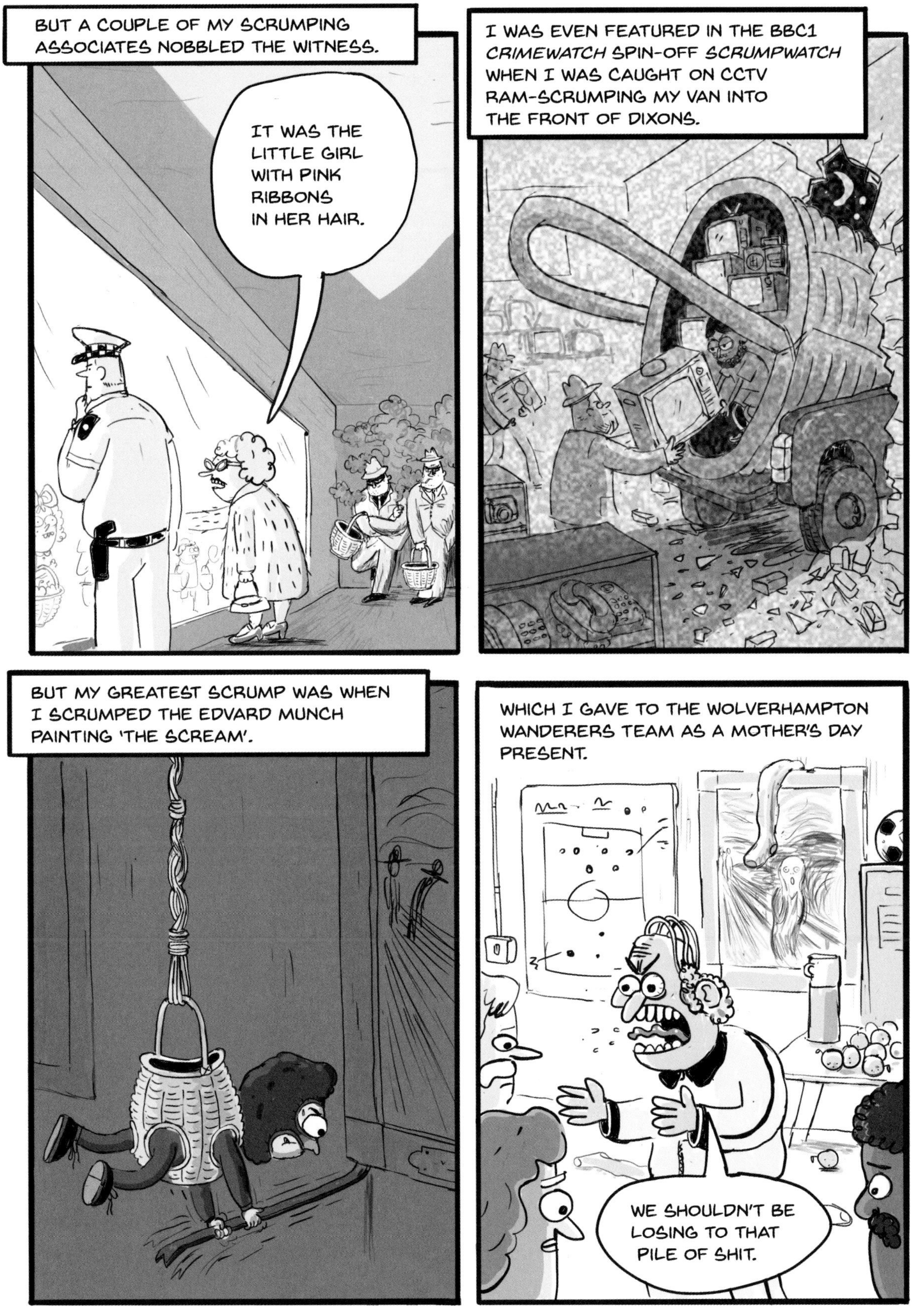
BUT A COUPLE OF MY SCRUMPING ASSOCIATES NOBBLED THE WITNESS.
IT WAS THE LITTLE GIRL WITH PINK RIBBONS IN HER HAIR.
I WAS EVEN FEATURED IN THE BBC1 *CRIMEWATCH* SPIN-OFF *SCRUMPWATCH* WHEN I WAS CAUGHT ON CCTV RAM-SCRUMPING MY VAN INTO THE FRONT OF DIXONS.
BUT MY GREATEST SCRUMP WAS WHEN I SCRUMPED THE EDVARD MUNCH PAINTING 'THE SCREAM'.
WHICH I GAVE TO THE WOLVERHAMPTON WANDERERS TEAM AS A MOTHER'S DAY PRESENT.
WE SHOULDN'T BE LOSING TO THAT PILE OF SHIT.

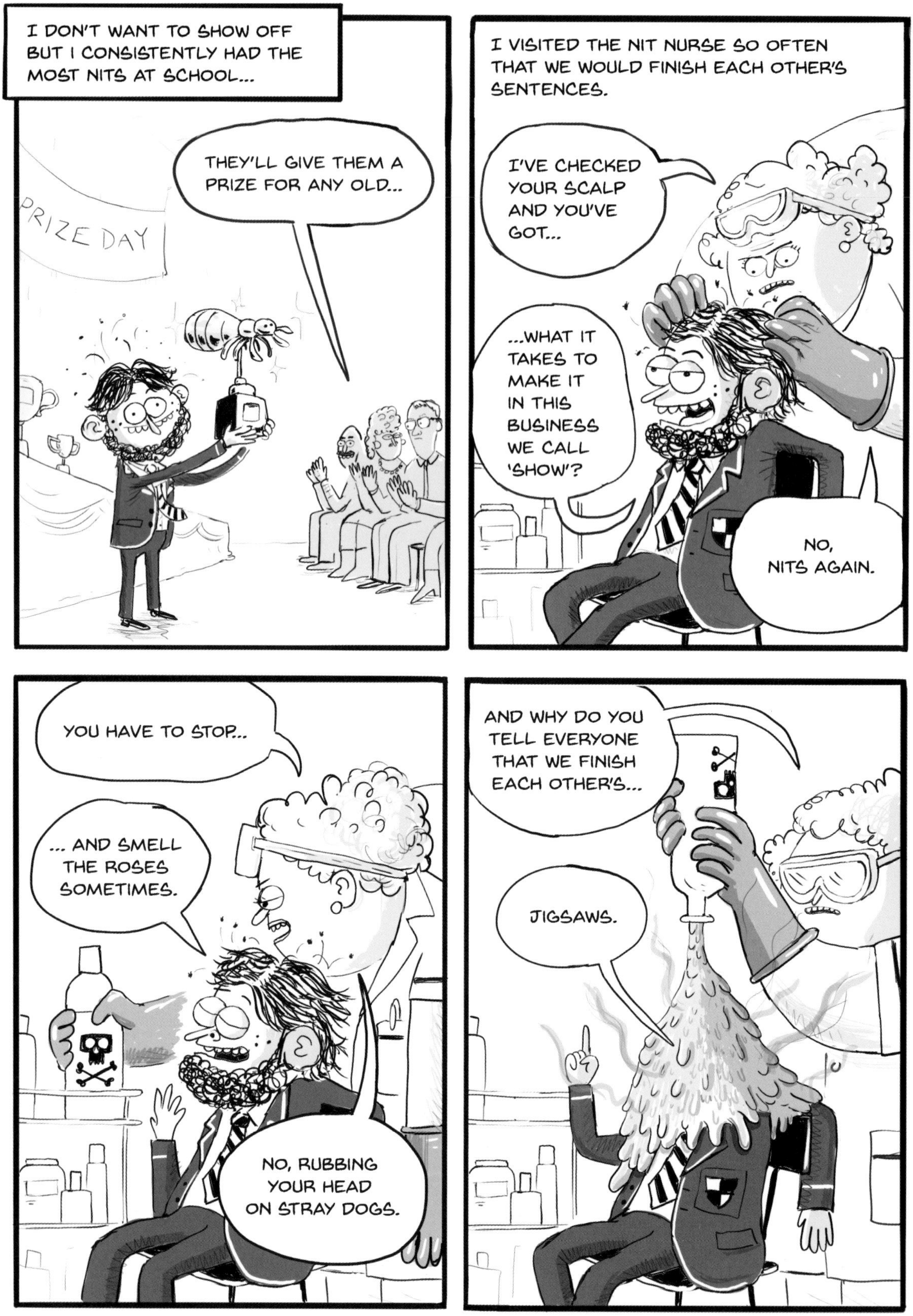
I DON'T WANT TO SHOW OFF BUT I CONSISTENTLY HAD THE MOST NITS AT SCHOOL...
PRIZE DAY
THEY'LL GIVE THEM A PRIZE FOR ANY OLD...
I VISITED THE NIT NURSE SO OFTEN THAT WE WOULD FINISH EACH OTHER'S SENTENCES.
I'VE CHECKED YOUR SCALP AND YOU'VE GOT...
...WHAT IT TAKES TO MAKE IT IN THIS BUSINESS WE CALL 'SHOW'?
NO, NITS AGAIN.
YOU HAVE TO STOP...
... AND SMELL THE ROSES SOMETIMES.
NO, RUBBING YOUR HEAD ON STRAY DOGS.
AND WHY DO YOU TELL EVERYONE THAT WE FINISH EACH OTHER'S...
JIGSAWS.

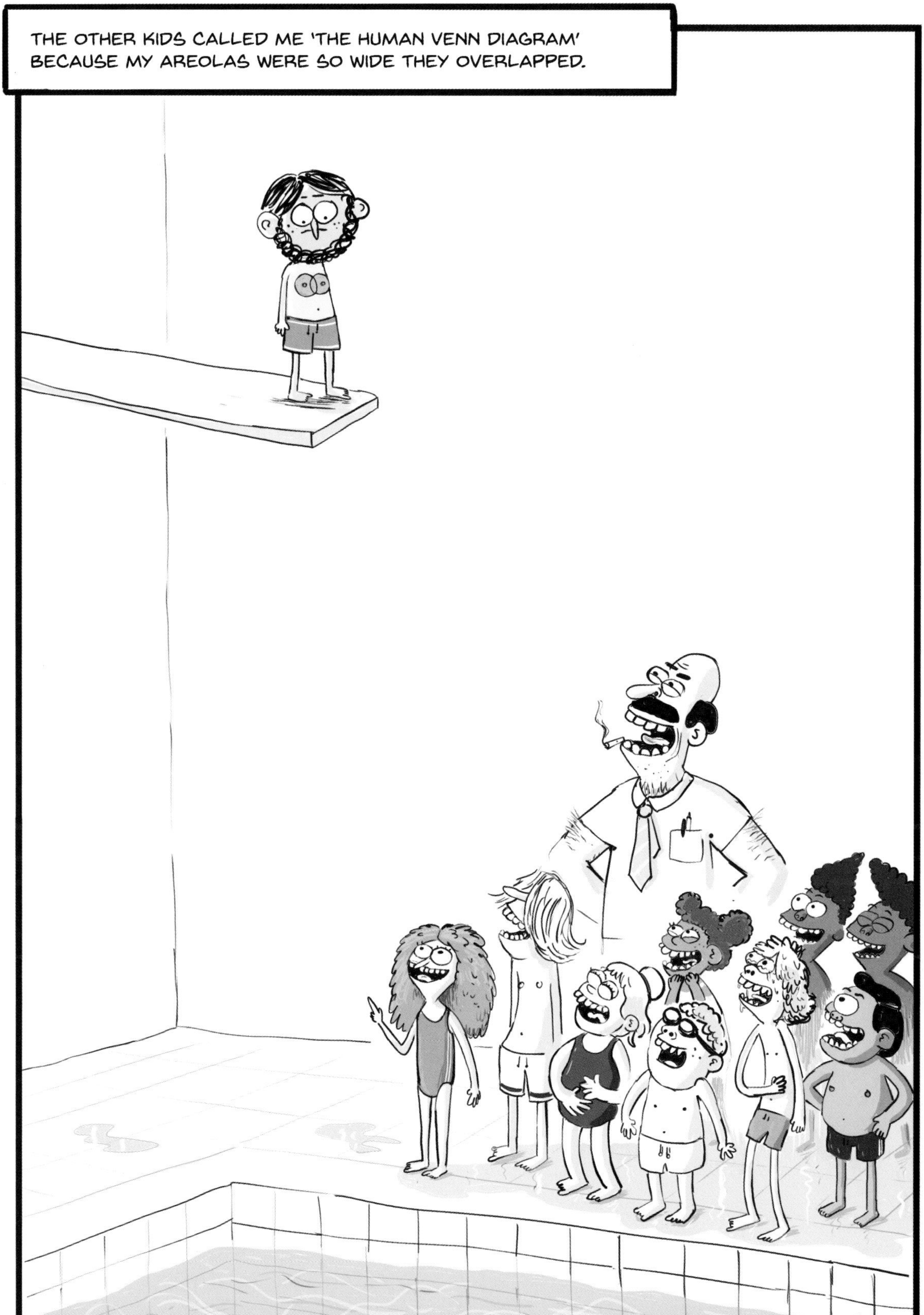
THE OTHER KIDS CALLED ME 'THE HUMAN VENN DIAGRAM' BECAUSE MY AREOLAS WERE SO WIDE THEY OVERLAPPED.

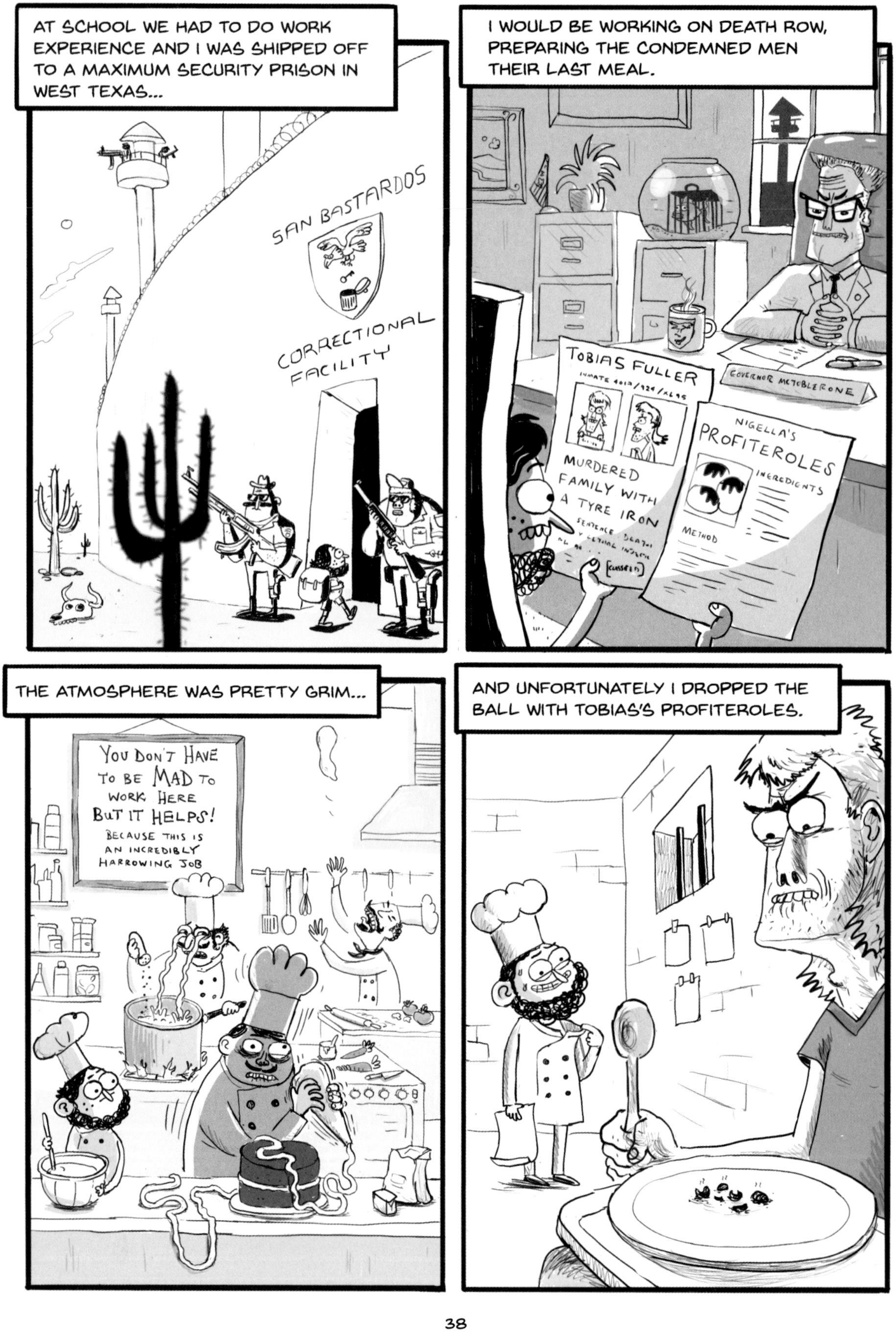
AT SCHOOL WE HAD TO DO WORK EXPERIENCE AND I WAS SHIPPED OFF TO A MAXIMUM SECURITY PRISON IN WEST TEXAS...
SAN BASTARDOS
CORRECTIONAL FACILITY
I WOULD BE WORKING ON DEATH ROW, PREPARING THE CONDEMNED MEN THEIR LAST MEAL.
TOBIAS FULLER
MURDERED FAMILY WITH A TYRE IRON
GOVERNOR MCTOBLERONE
NIGELLA'S PROFITEROLES
INGREDIENTS
METHOD
THE ATMOSPHERE WAS PRETTY GRIM...
YOU DON'T HAVE TO BE MAD TO WORK HERE BUT IT HELPS!
BECAUSE THIS IS AN INCREDIBLY HARROWING JOB
AND UNFORTUNATELY I DROPPED THE BALL WITH TOBIAS'S PROFITEROLES.

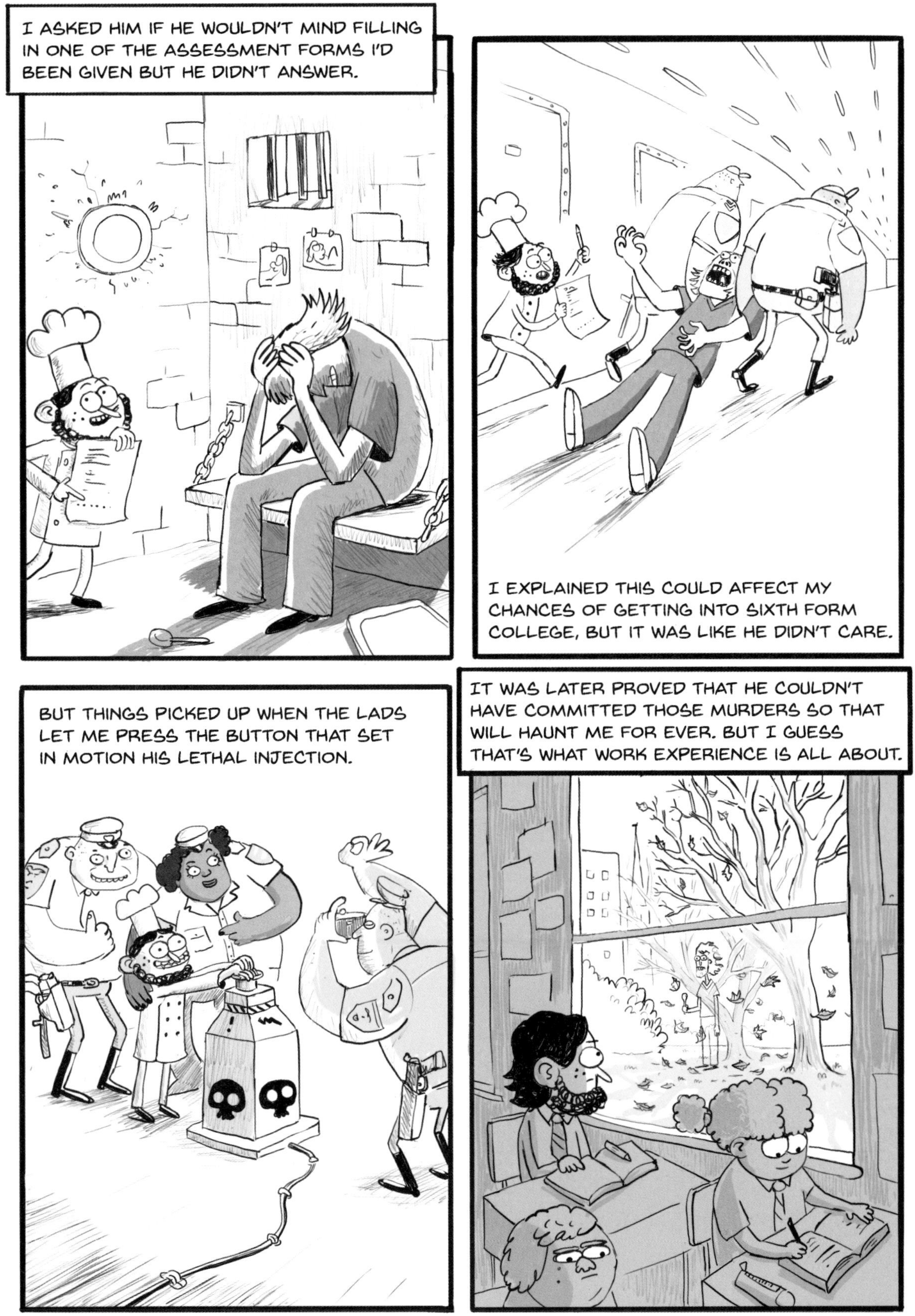
I ASKED HIM IF HE WOULDN'T MIND FILLING IN ONE OF THE ASSESSMENT FORMS I'D BEEN GIVEN BUT HE DIDN'T ANSWER.
I EXPLAINED THIS COULD AFFECT MY CHANCES OF GETTING INTO SIXTH FORM COLLEGE, BUT IT WAS LIKE HE DIDN'T CARE.
BUT THINGS PICKED UP WHEN THE LADS LET ME PRESS THE BUTTON THAT SET IN MOTION HIS LETHAL INJECTION.
IT WAS LATER PROVED THAT HE COULDN'T HAVE COMMITTED THOSE MURDERS SO THAT WILL HAUNT ME FOR EVER. BUT I GUESS THAT'S WHAT WORK EXPERIENCE IS ALL ABOUT.

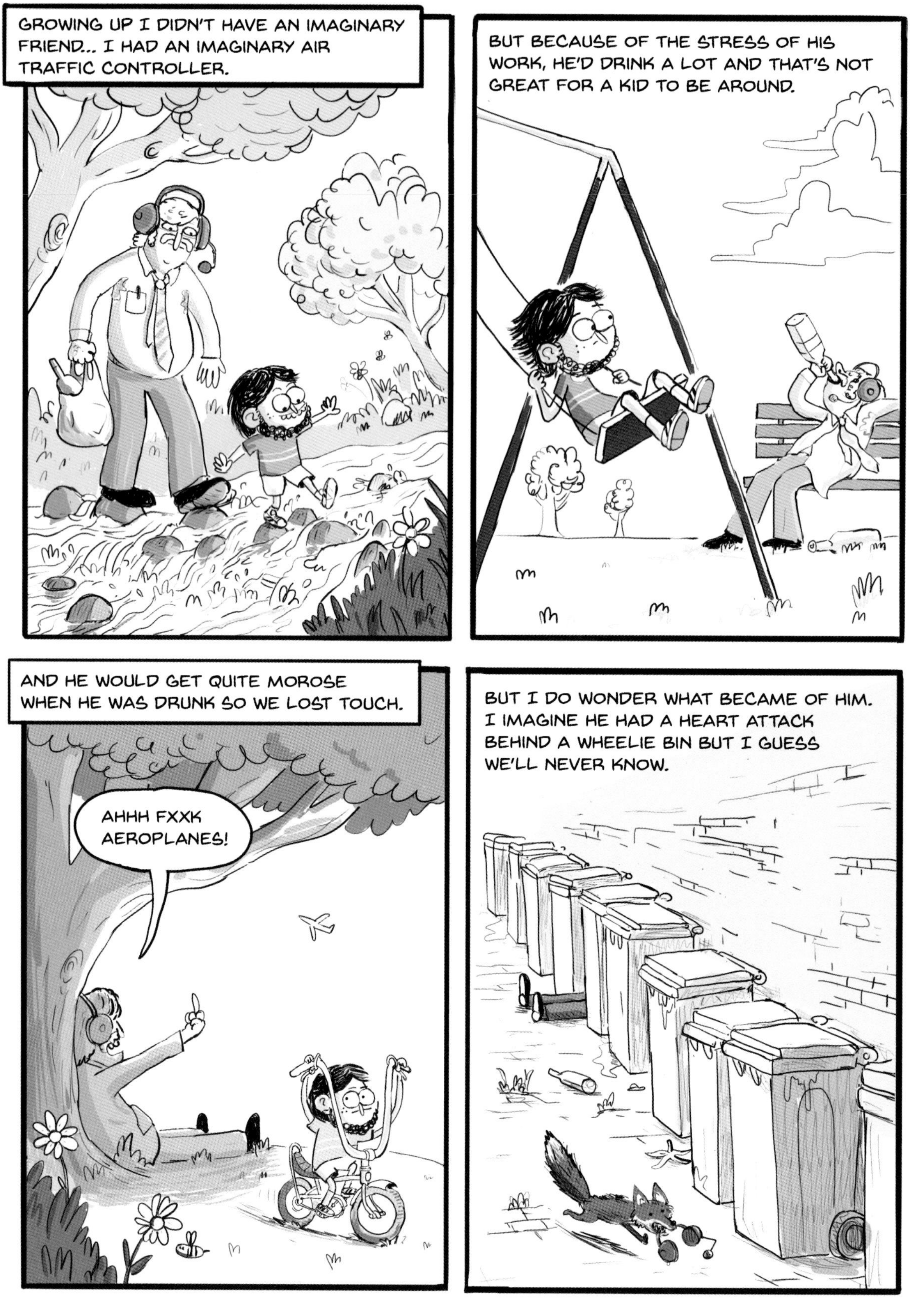
GROWING UP I DIDN'T HAVE AN IMAGINARY FRIEND... I HAD AN IMAGINARY AIR TRAFFIC CONTROLLER.
BUT BECAUSE OF THE STRESS OF HIS WORK, HE'D DRINK A LOT AND THAT'S NOT GREAT FOR A KID TO BE AROUND.
AND HE WOULD GET QUITE MOROSE WHEN HE WAS DRUNK SO WE LOST TOUCH.
AHHH FXXK AEROPLANES!
BUT I DO WONDER WHAT BECAME OF HIM. I IMAGINE HE HAD A HEART ATTACK BEHIND A WHEELIE BIN BUT I GUESS WE'LL NEVER KNOW.

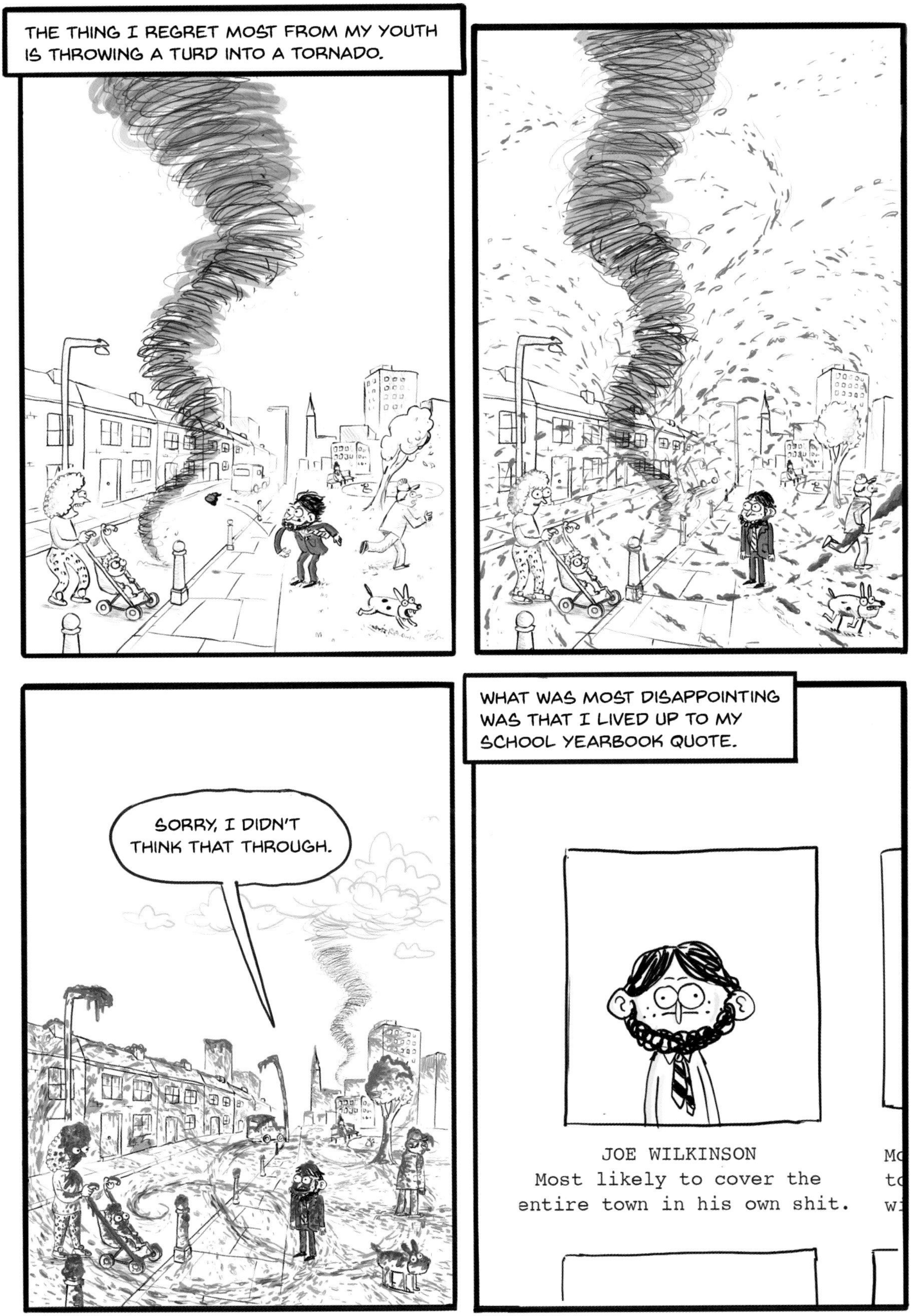
THE THING I REGRET MOST FROM MY YOUTH IS THROWING A TURD INTO A TORNADO.
SORRY, I DIDN'T THINK THAT THROUGH.
WHAT WAS MOST DISAPPOINTING WAS THAT I LIVED UP TO MY SCHOOL YEARBOOK QUOTE.
JOE WILKINSON
Most likely to cover the entire town in his own shit.

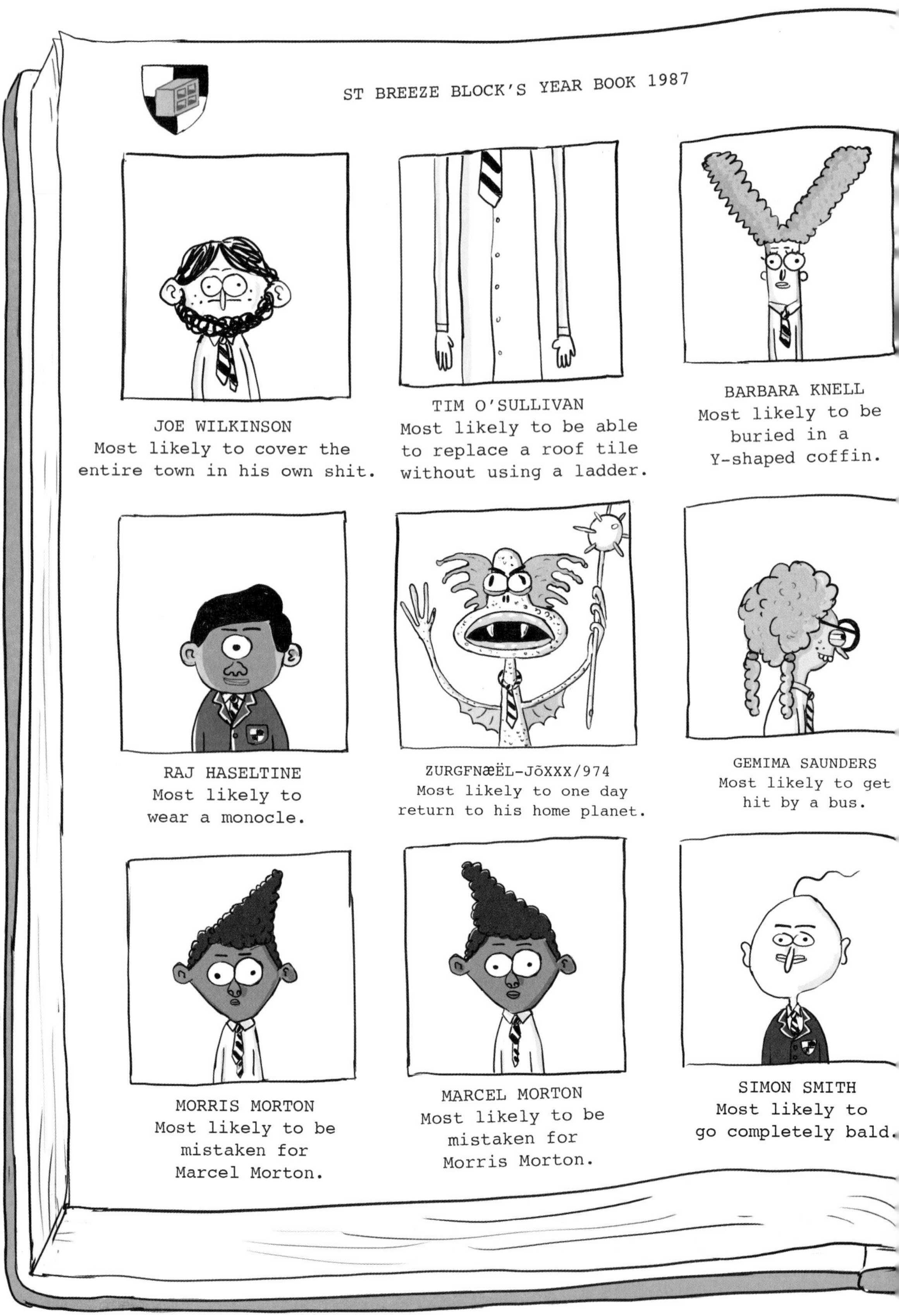

ST BREEZE BLOCK'S YEAR BOOK 1987
JOE WILKINSON
Most likely to cover the entire town in his own shit.
TIM O'SULLIVAN
Most likely to be able to replace a roof tile without using a ladder.
BARBARA KNELL
Most likely to be buried in a Y-shaped coffin.
RAJ HASELTINE
Most likely to wear a monocle.
ZURGFNæËL-JõXXX/974
Most likely to one day return to his home planet.
GEMIMA SAUNDERS
Most likely to get hit by a bus.
MORRIS MORTON
Most likely to be mistaken for Marcel Morton.
MARCEL MORTON
Most likely to be mistaken for Morris Morton.
SIMON SMITH
Most likely to go completely bald.

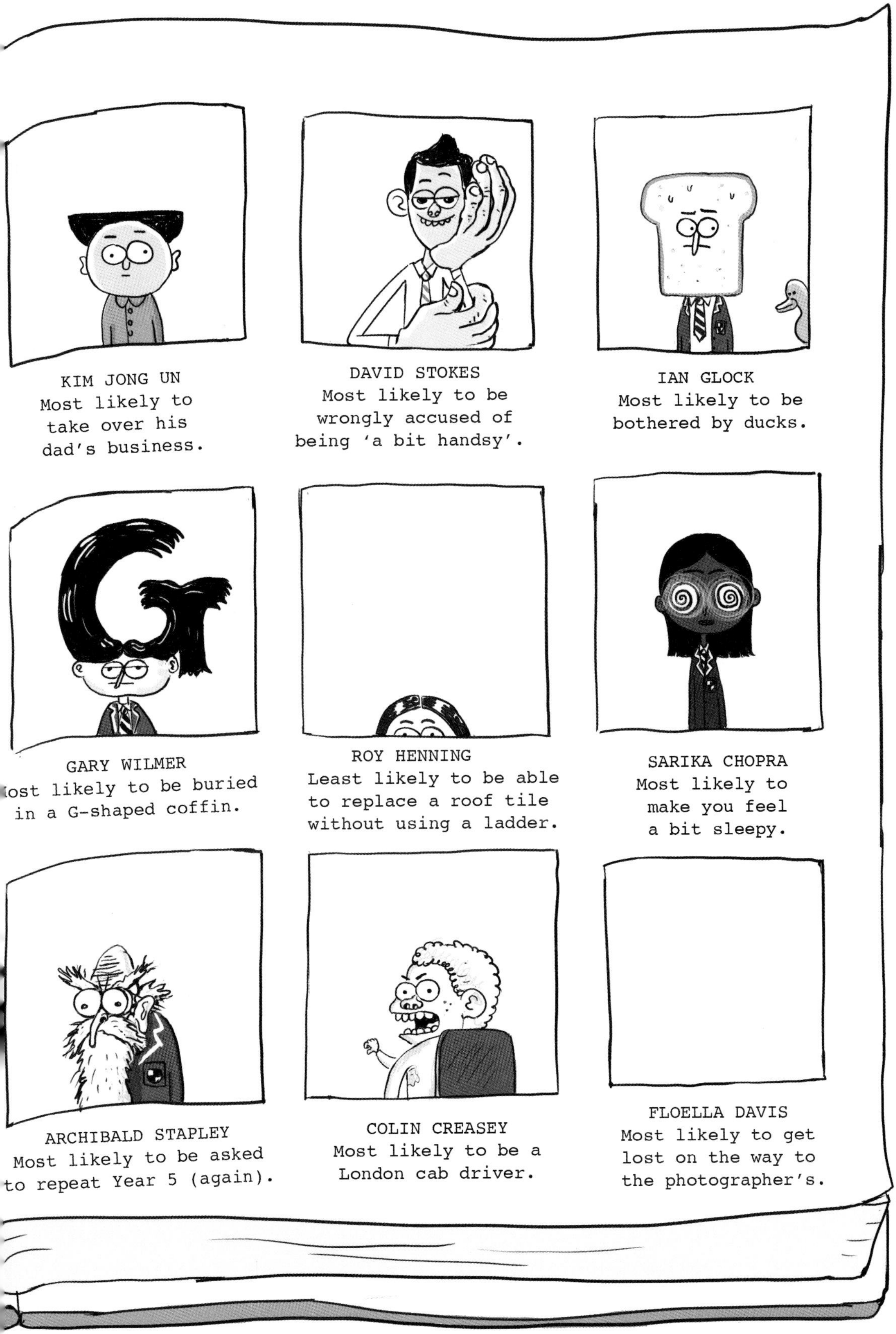
KIM JONG UN
Most likely to
take over his
dad's business.
DAVID STOKES
Most likely to be
wrongly accused of
being 'a bit handsy'.
IAN GLOCK
Most likely to be
bothered by ducks.
GARY WILMER
ost likely to be buried
in a G-shaped coffin.
ROY HENNING
Least likely to be able
to replace a roof tile
without using a ladder.
SARIKA CHOPRA
Most likely to
make you feel
a bit sleepy.
ARCHIBALD STAPLEY
Most likely to be asked
to repeat Year 5 (again).
COLIN CREASEY
Most likely to be a
London cab driver.
FLOELLA DAVIS
Most likely to get
lost on the way to
the photographer's.

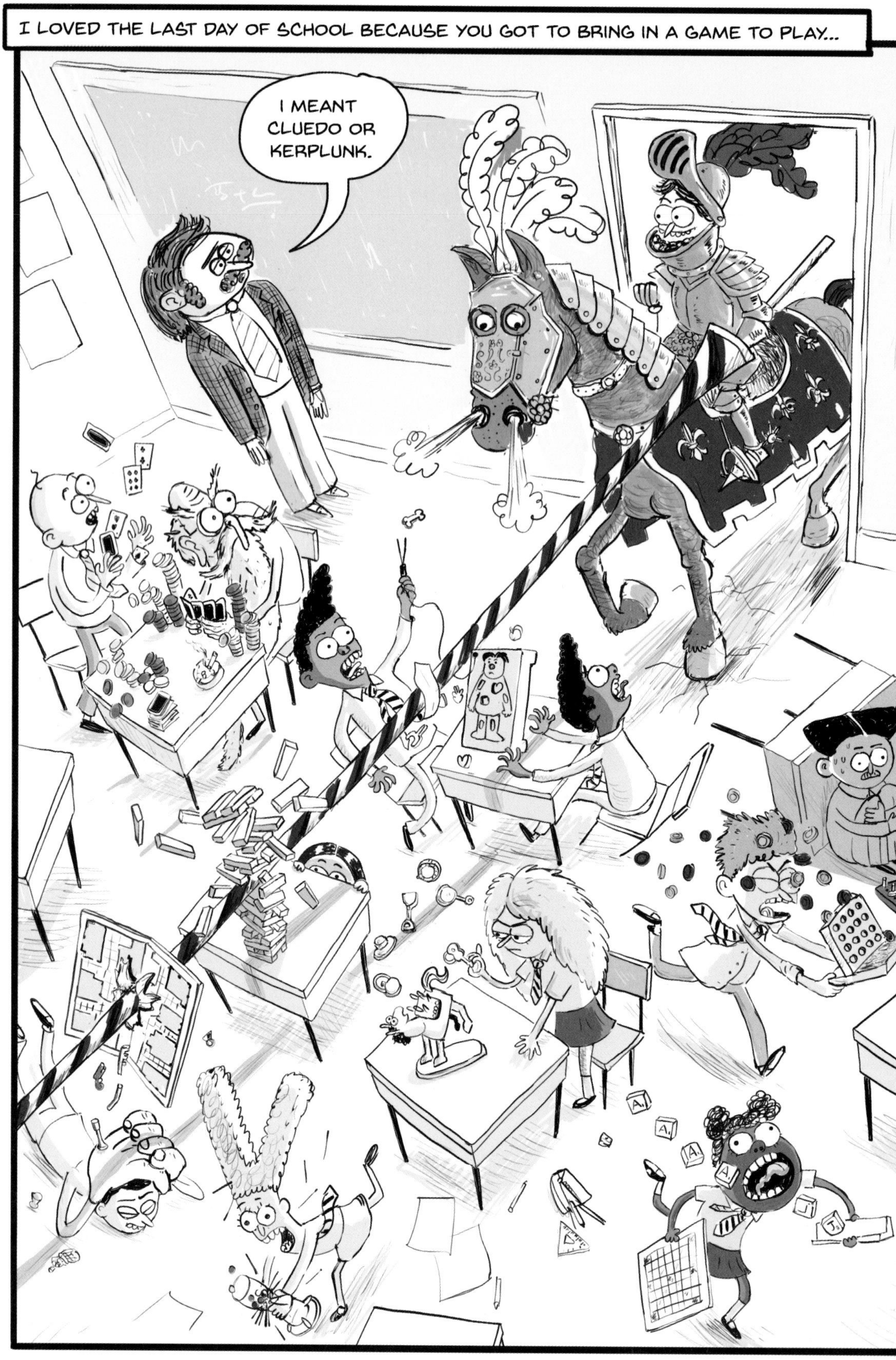
I LOVED THE LAST DAY OF SCHOOL BECAUSE YOU GOT TO BRING IN A GAME TO PLAY...
I MEANT CLUEDO OR KERPLUNK.

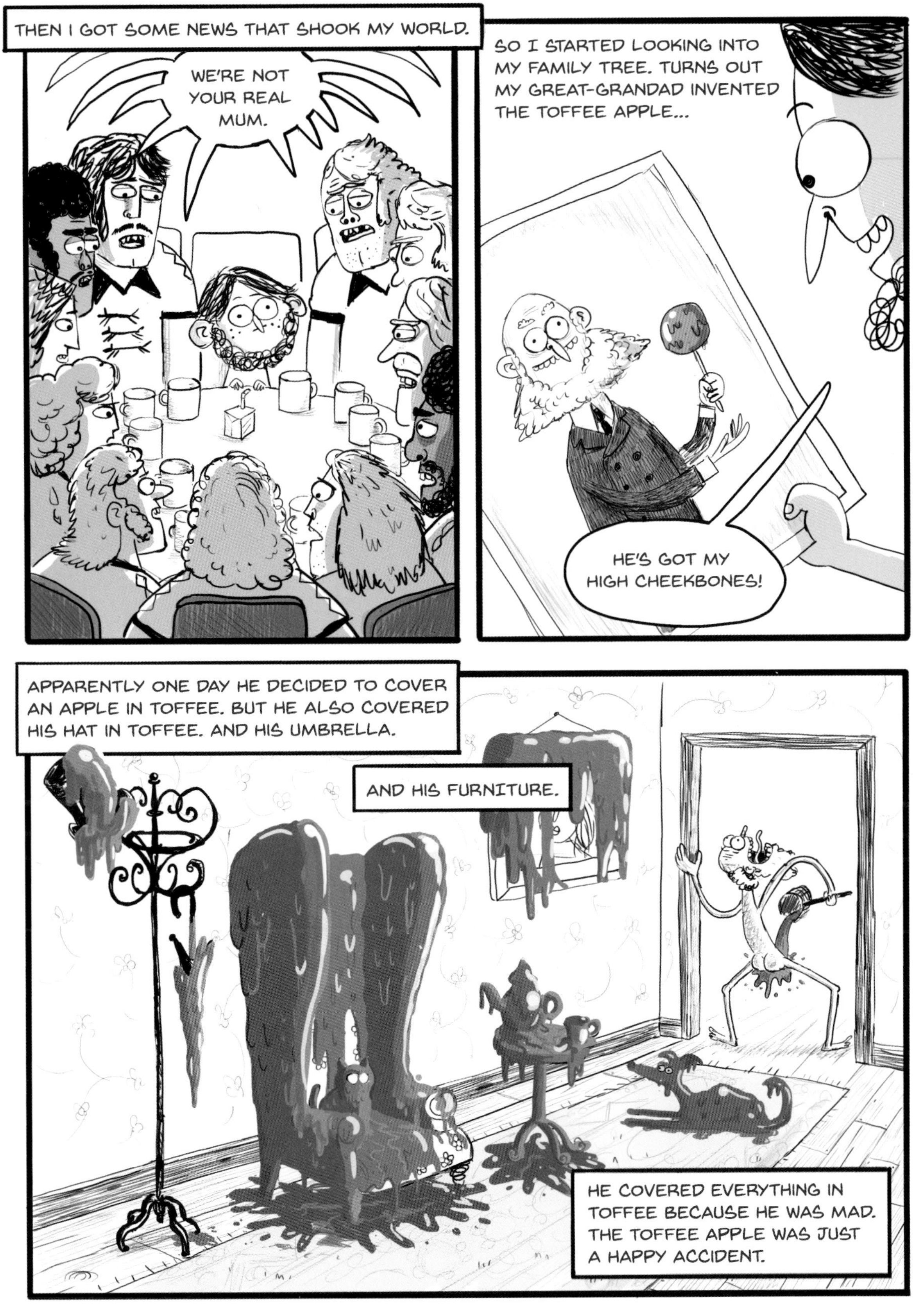

THEN I GOT SOME NEWS THAT SHOOK MY WORLD.
WE'RE NOT YOUR REAL MUM.
SO I STARTED LOOKING INTO MY FAMILY TREE. TURNS OUT MY GREAT-GRANDAD INVENTED THE TOFFEE APPLE...
HE'S GOT MY HIGH CHEEKBONES!
APPARENTLY ONE DAY HE DECIDED TO COVER AN APPLE IN TOFFEE. BUT HE ALSO COVERED HIS HAT IN TOFFEE. AND HIS UMBRELLA.
AND HIS FURNITURE.
HE COVERED EVERYTHING IN TOFFEE BECAUSE HE WAS MAD. THE TOFFEE APPLE WAS JUST A HAPPY ACCIDENT.

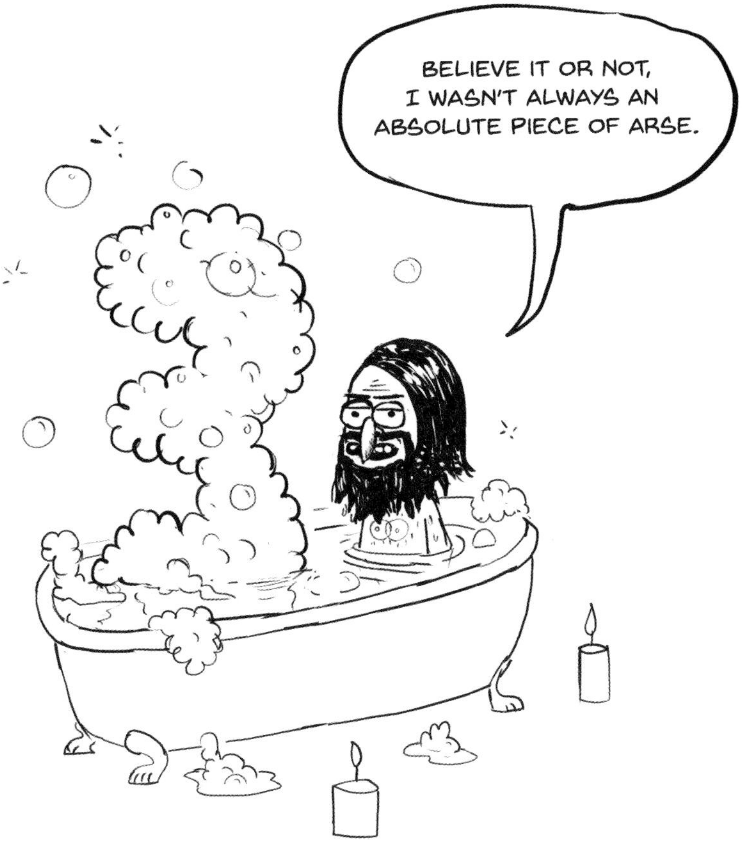
BELIEVE IT OR NOT, I WASN'T ALWAYS AN ABSOLUTE PIECE OF ARSE.

THE DATING SCENE

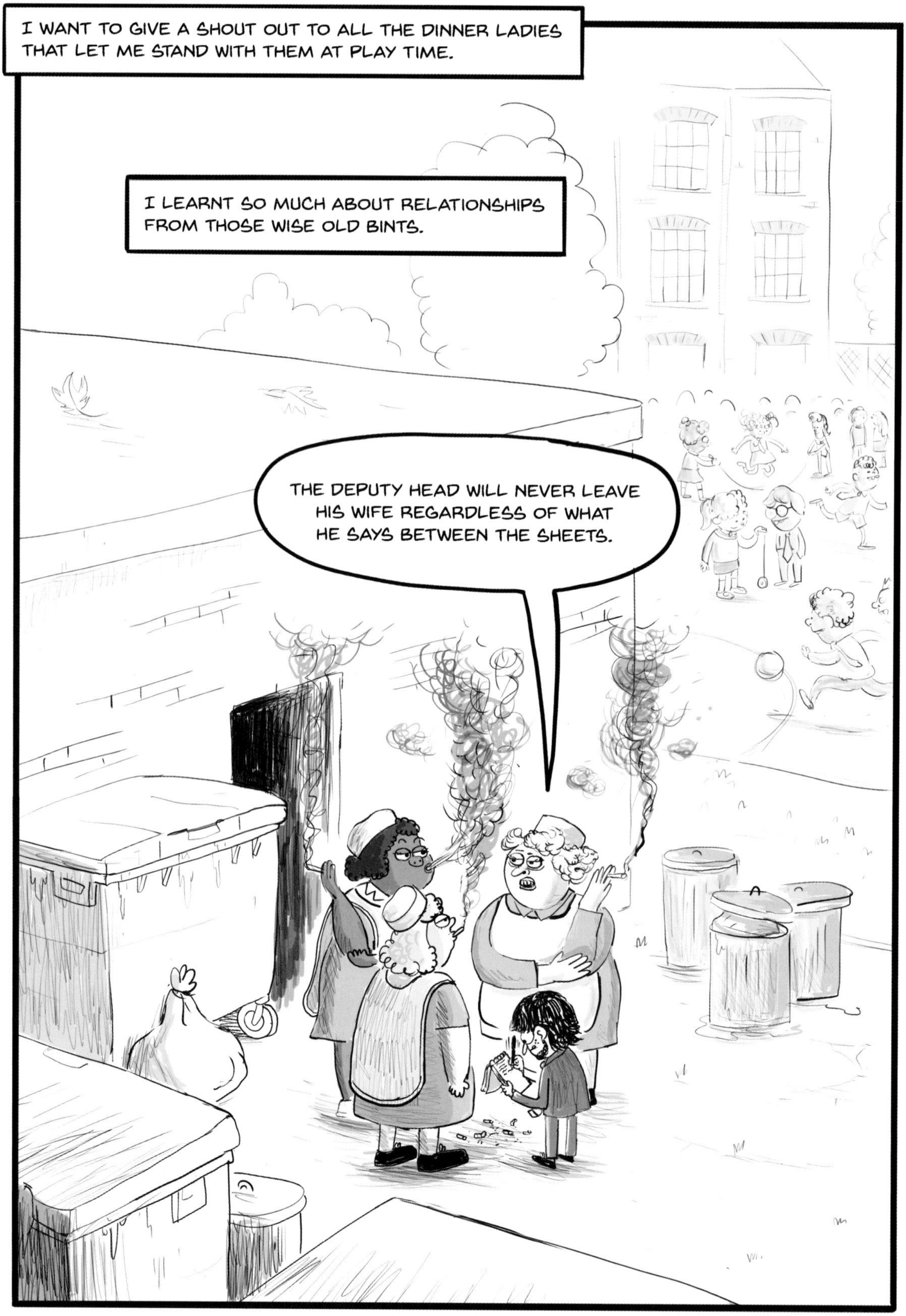
I WANT TO GIVE A SHOUT OUT TO ALL THE DINNER LADIES THAT LET ME STAND WITH THEM AT PLAY TIME.
I LEARNT SO MUCH ABOUT RELATIONSHIPS FROM THOSE WISE OLD BINTS.
THE DEPUTY HEAD WILL NEVER LEAVE HIS WIFE REGARDLESS OF WHAT HE SAYS BETWEEN THE SHEETS.

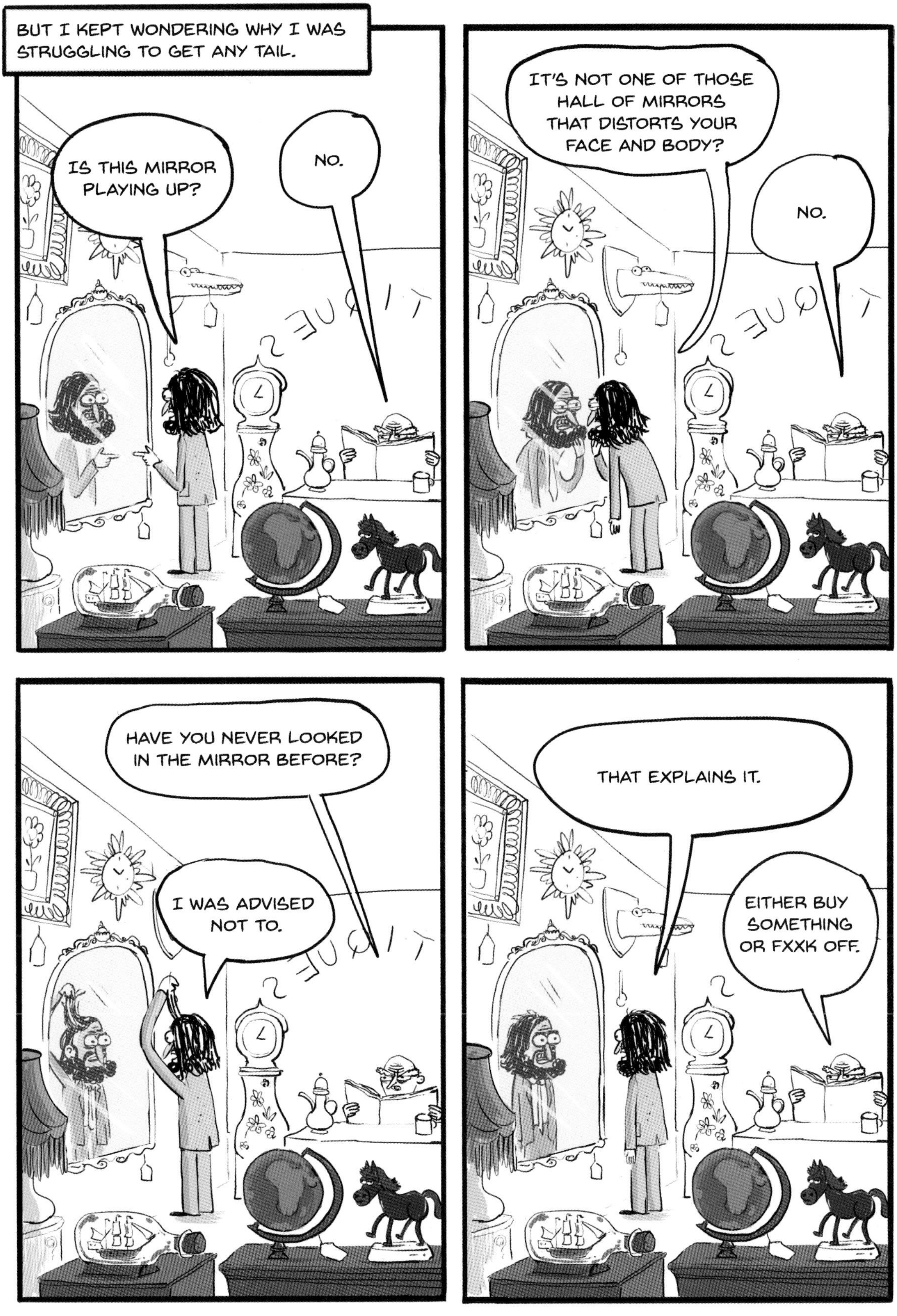

BUT I KEPT WONDERING WHY I WAS STRUGGLING TO GET ANY TAIL.
IS THIS MIRROR PLAYING UP?
NO.
IT'S NOT ONE OF THOSE HALL OF MIRRORS THAT DISTORTS YOUR FACE AND BODY?
NO.
HAVE YOU NEVER LOOKED IN THE MIRROR BEFORE?
I WAS ADVISED NOT TO.
THAT EXPLAINS IT.
EITHER BUY SOMETHING OR FXXK OFF.

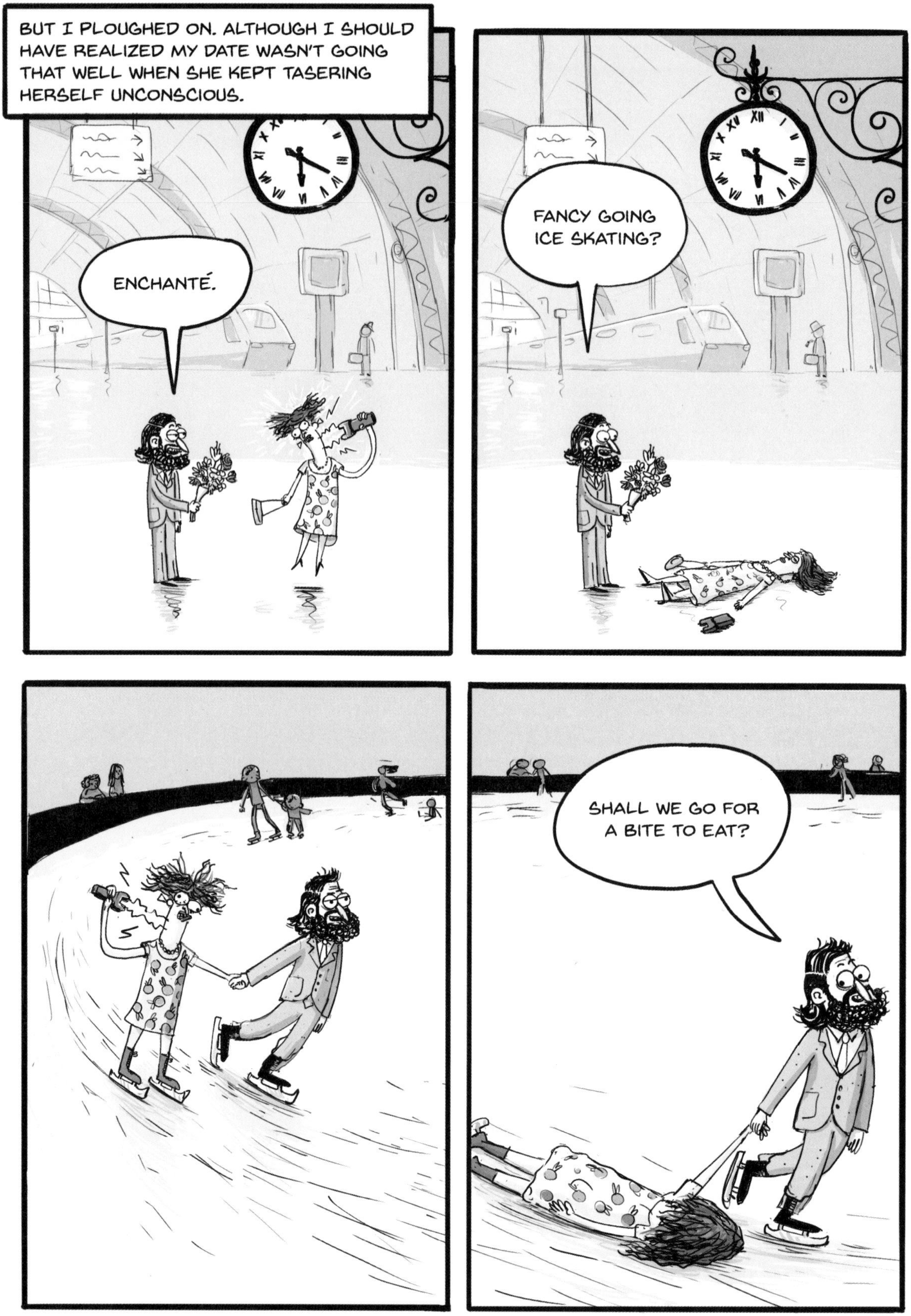
BUT I PLOUGHED ON. ALTHOUGH I SHOULD HAVE REALIZED MY DATE WASN'T GOING THAT WELL WHEN SHE KEPT TASERING HERSELF UNCONSCIOUS.
ENCHANTÉ.
FANCY GOING ICE SKATING?
SHALL WE GO FOR A BITE TO EAT?

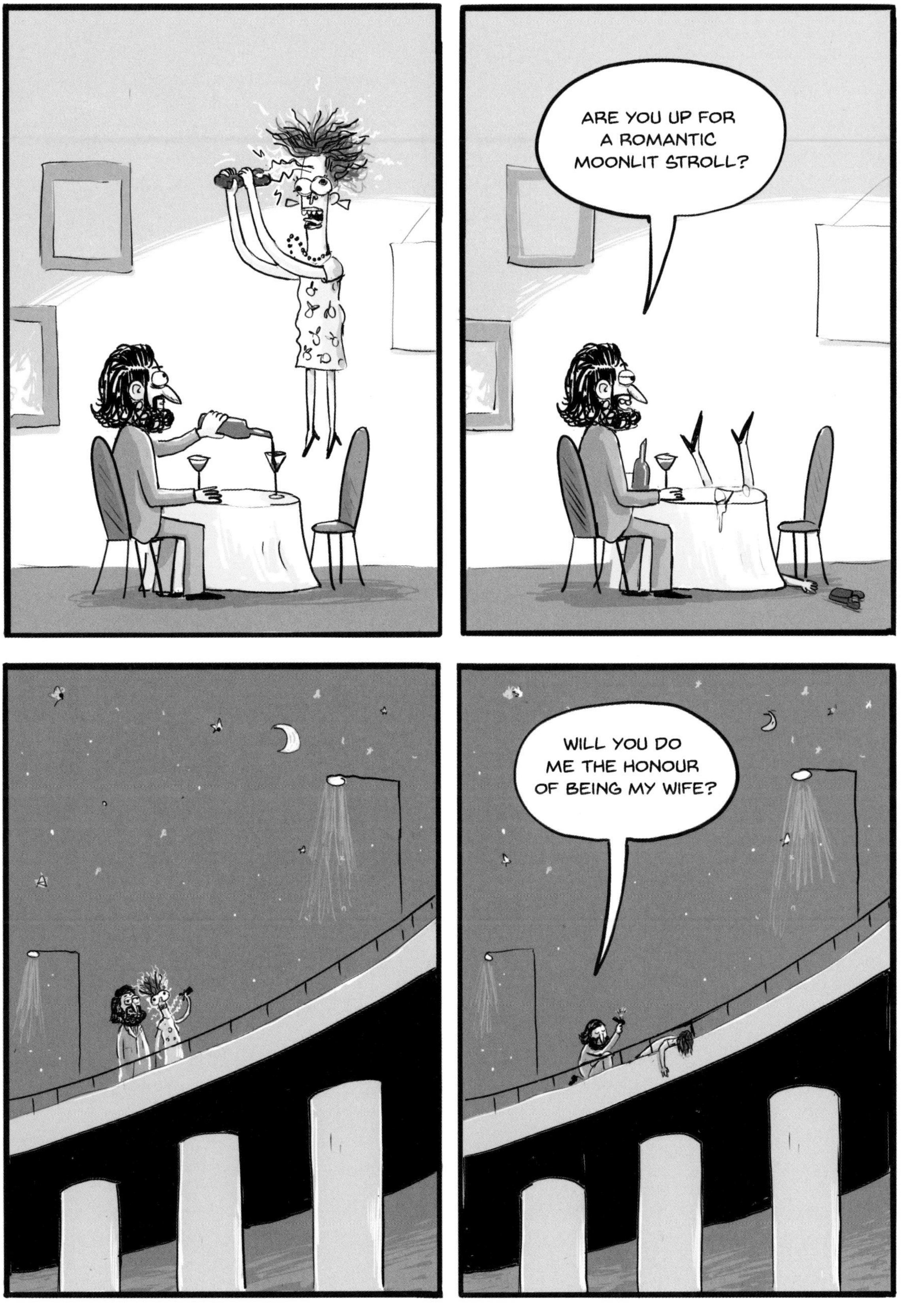
ARE YOU UP FOR A ROMANTIC MOONLIT STROLL?
WILL YOU DO ME THE HONOUR OF BEING MY WIFE?

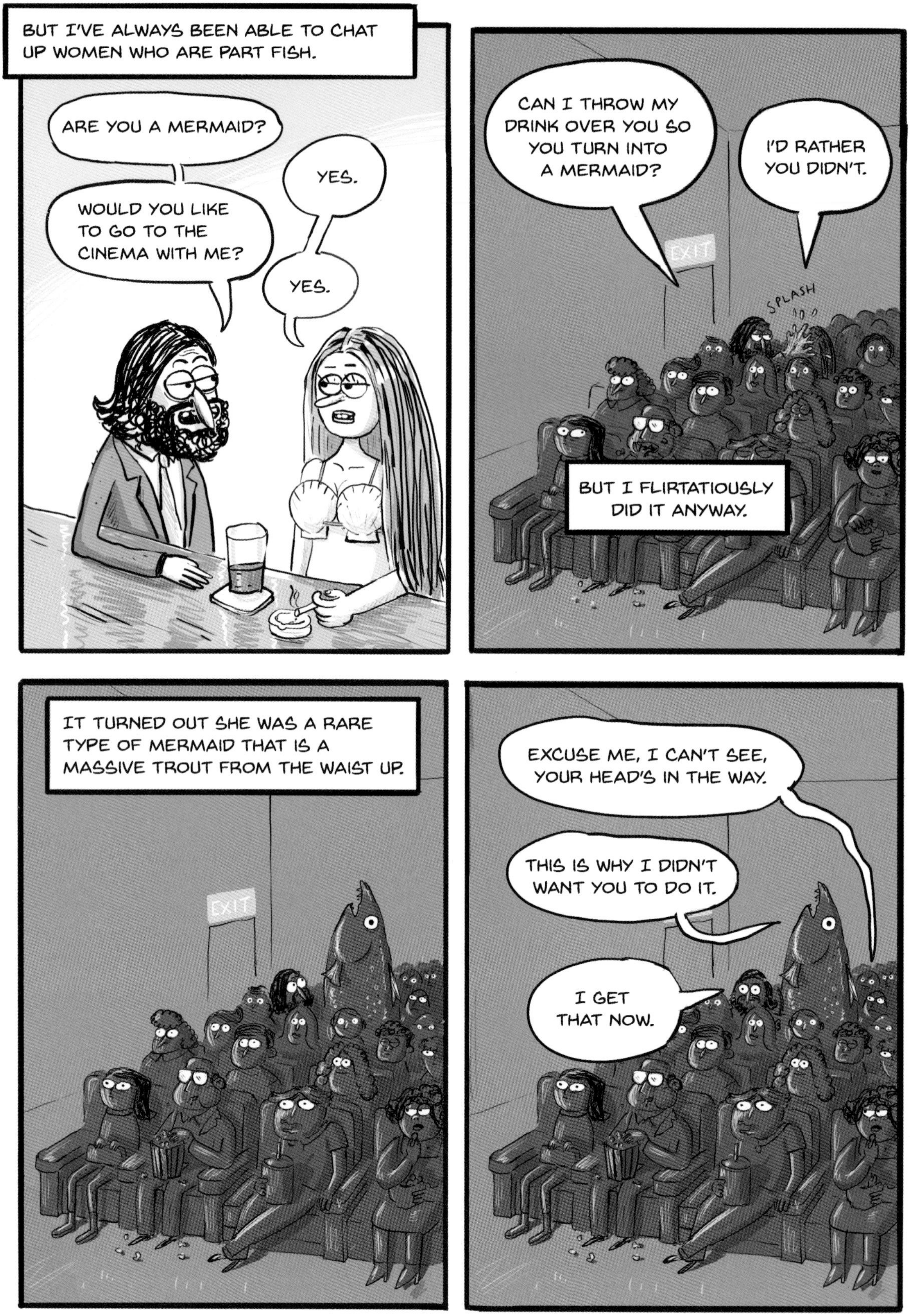
BUT I'VE ALWAYS BEEN ABLE TO CHAT UP WOMEN WHO ARE PART FISH.
ARE YOU A MERMAID?
YES.
WOULD YOU LIKE TO GO TO THE CINEMA WITH ME?
YES.
CAN I THROW MY DRINK OVER YOU SO YOU TURN INTO A MERMAID?
I'D RATHER YOU DIDN'T.
EXIT
SPLASH
BUT I FLIRTATIOUSLY DID IT ANYWAY.
IT TURNED OUT SHE WAS A RARE TYPE OF MERMAID THAT IS A MASSIVE TROUT FROM THE WAIST UP.
EXIT
EXCUSE ME, I CAN'T SEE, YOUR HEAD'S IN THE WAY.
THIS IS WHY I DIDN'T WANT YOU TO DO IT.
I GET THAT NOW.

THEN I THOUGHT I'D GO ON A DOUBLE DATE BUT
I COULDN'T FIND THREE OTHER PEOPLE TO GO WITH ME.

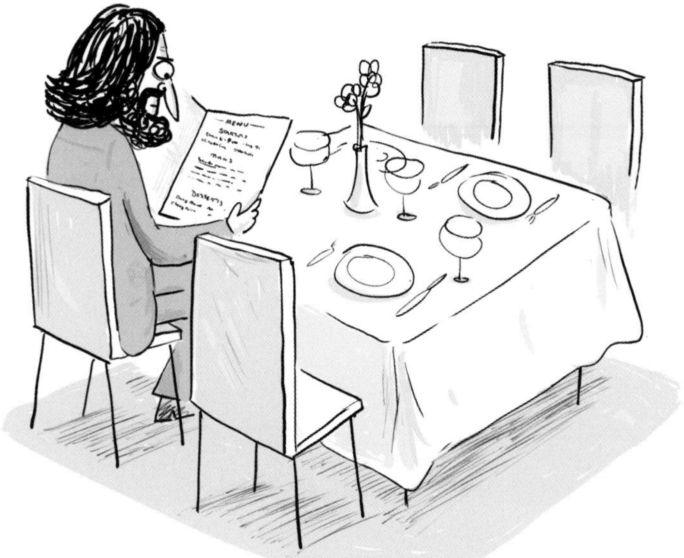
MENU

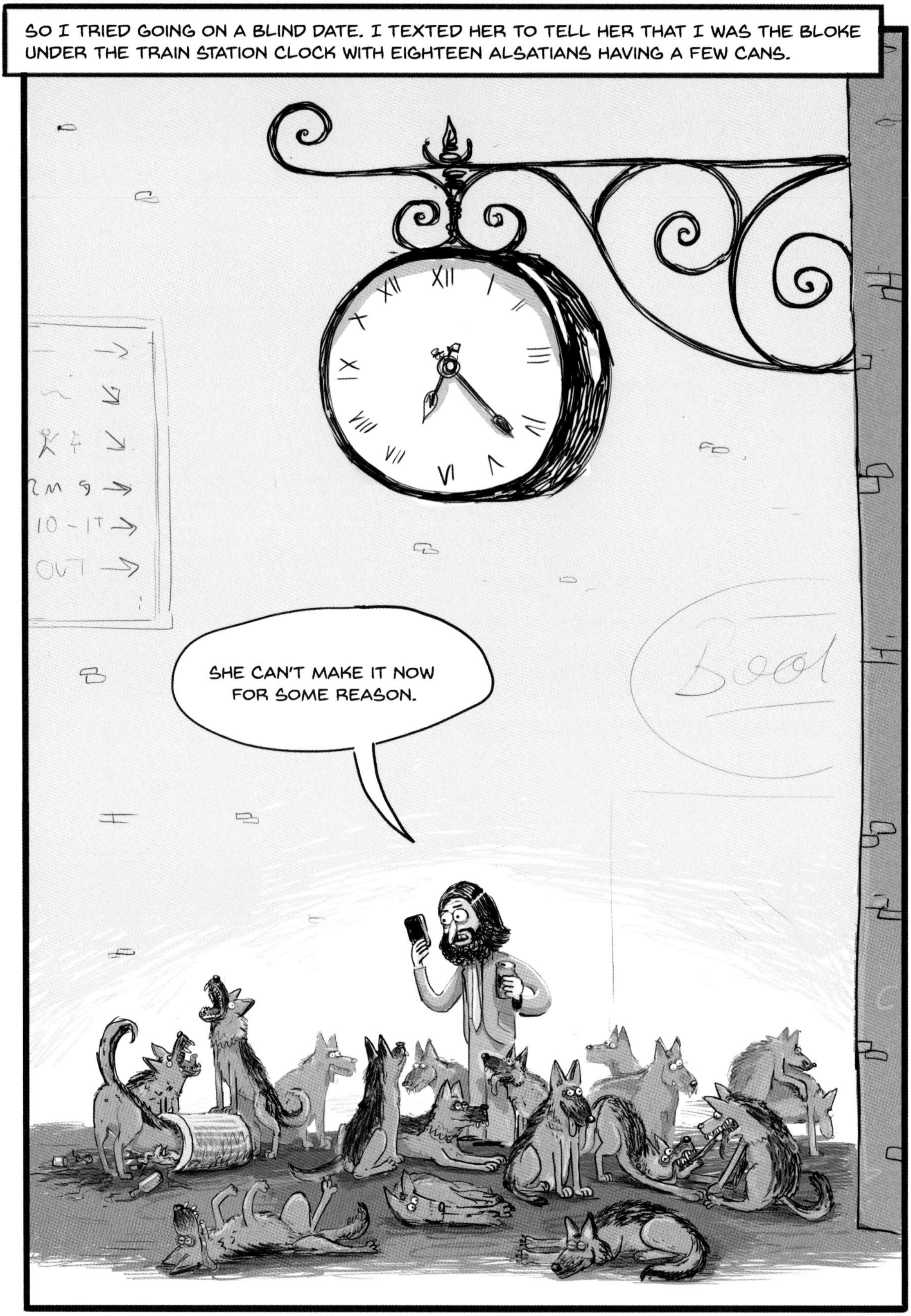
SO I TRIED GOING ON A BLIND DATE. I TEXTED HER TO TELL HER THAT I WAS THE BLOKE UNDER THE TRAIN STATION CLOCK WITH EIGHTEEN ALSATIANS HAVING A FEW CANS.
SHE CAN'T MAKE IT NOW FOR SOME REASON.

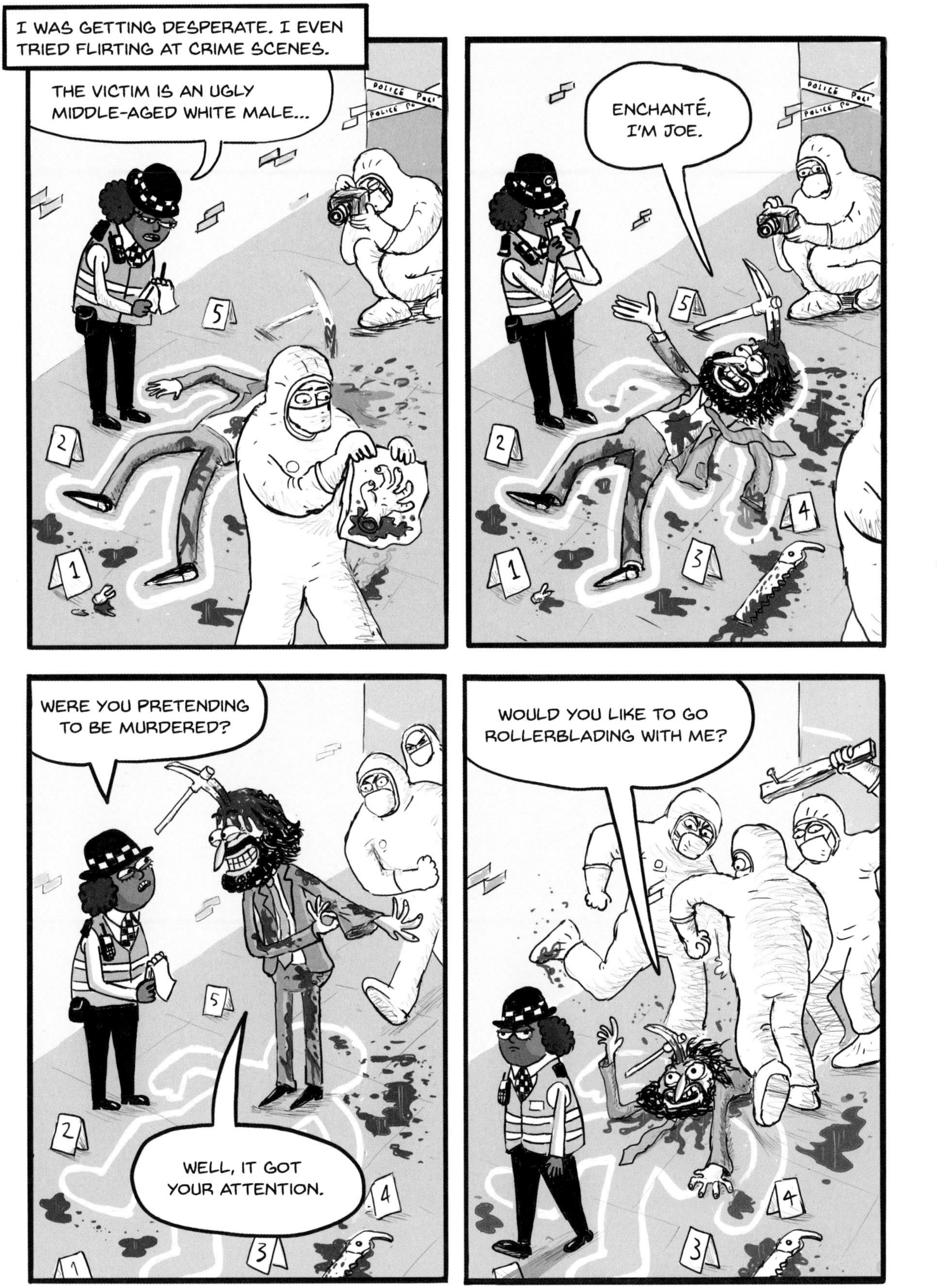
I WAS GETTING DESPERATE. I EVEN TRIED FLIRTING AT CRIME SCENES.
THE VICTIM IS AN UGLY MIDDLE-AGED WHITE MALE...
ENCHANTÉ, I'M JOE.
WERE YOU PRETENDING TO BE MURDERED?
WELL, IT GOT YOUR ATTENTION.
WOULD YOU LIKE TO GO ROLLERBLADING WITH ME?

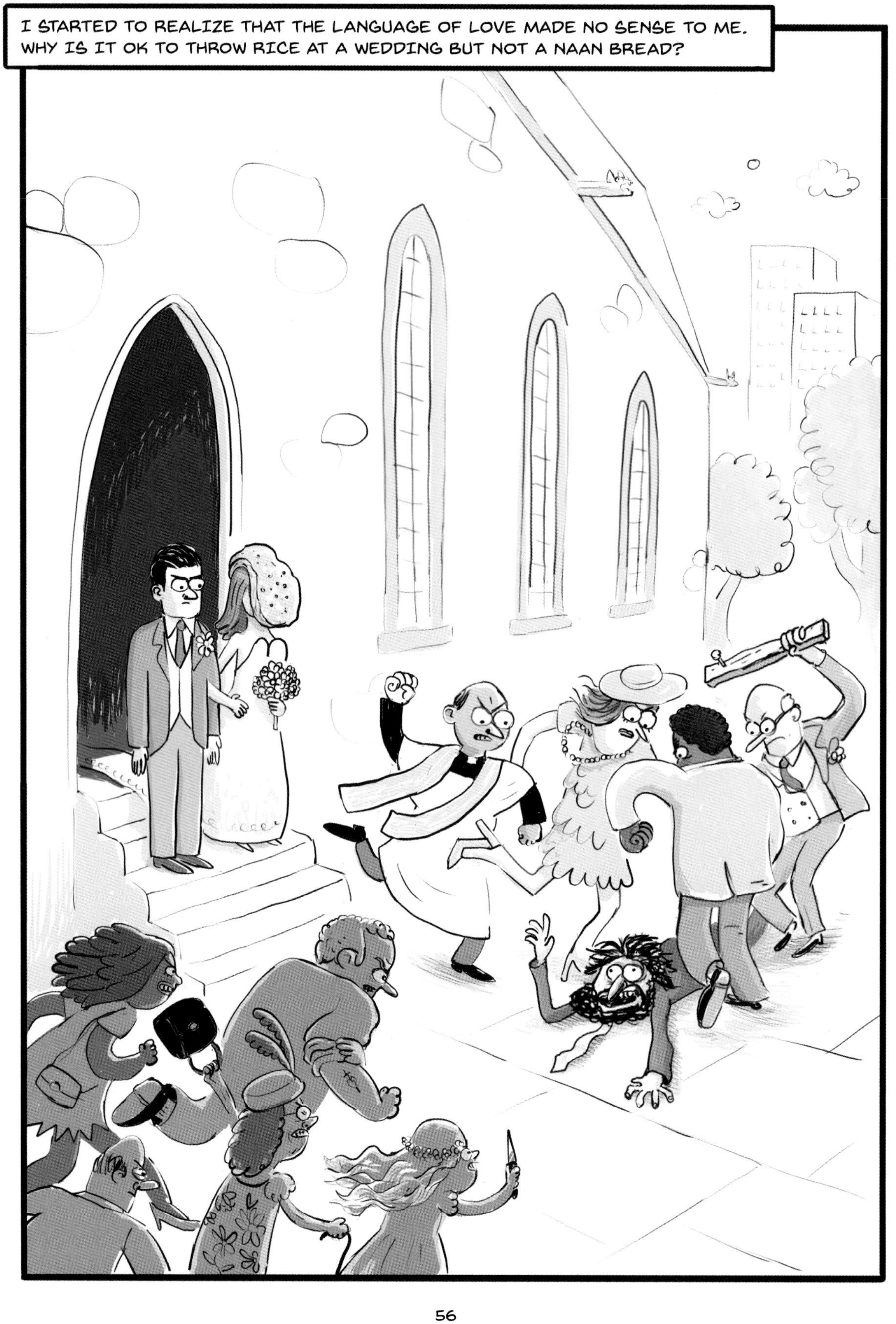
I STARTED TO REALIZE THAT THE LANGUAGE OF LOVE MADE NO SENSE TO ME.
WHY IS IT OK TO THROW RICE AT A WEDDING BUT NOT A NAAN BREAD?

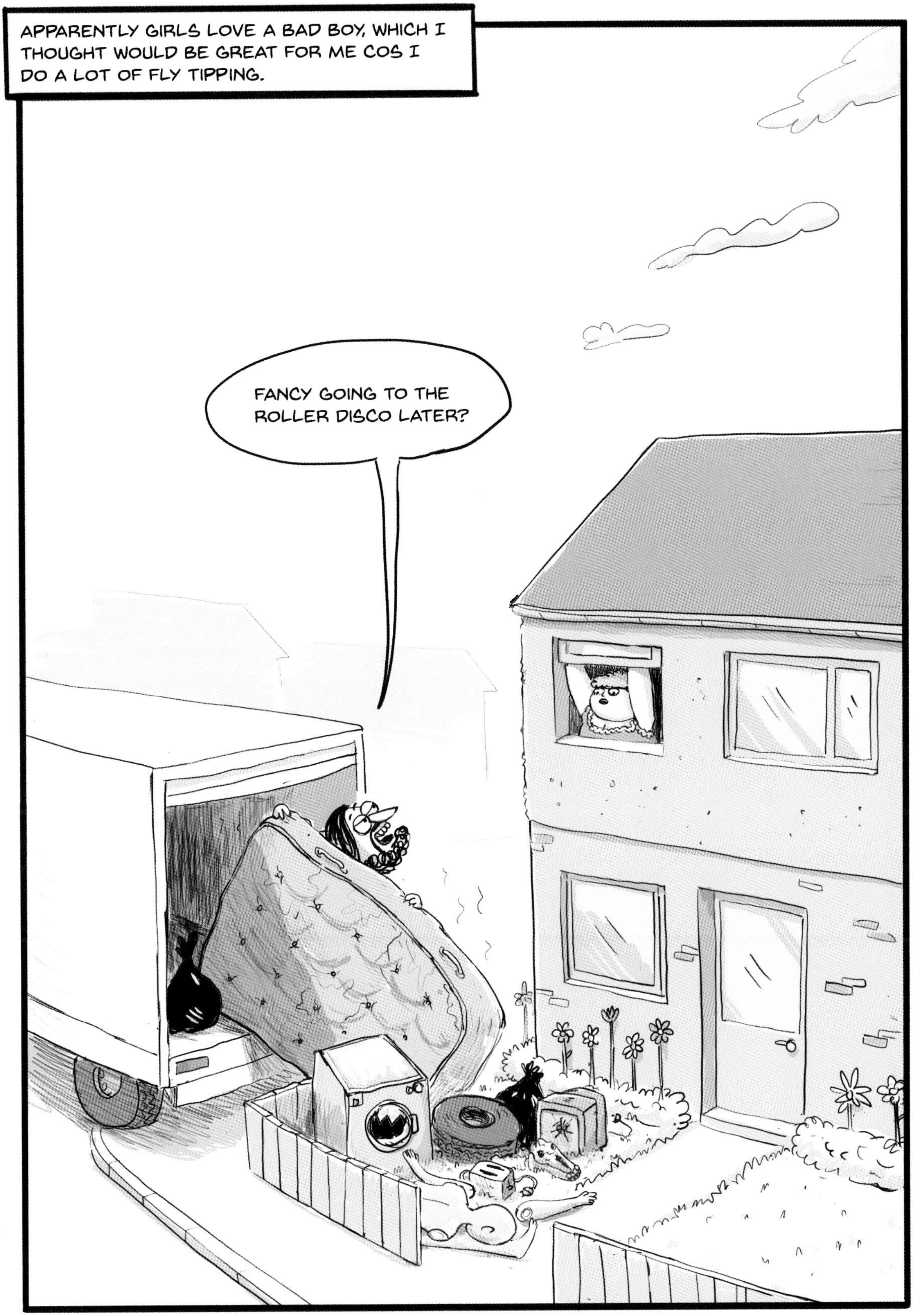
APPARENTLY GIRLS LOVE A BAD BOY, WHICH I THOUGHT WOULD BE GREAT FOR ME COS I DO A LOT OF FLY TIPPING.
FANCY GOING TO THE ROLLER DISCO LATER?

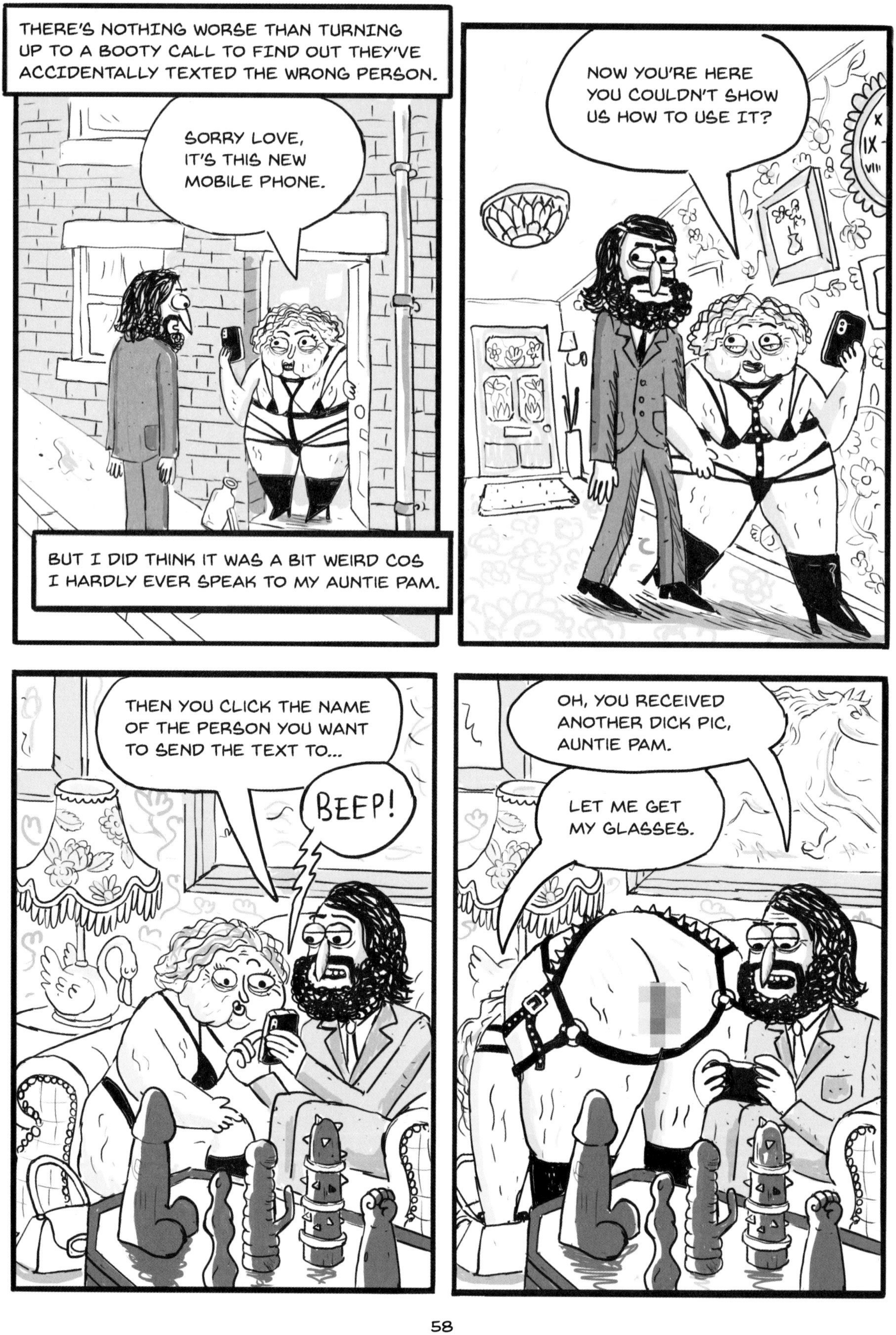
THERE'S NOTHING WORSE THAN TURNING UP TO A BOOTY CALL TO FIND OUT THEY'VE ACCIDENTALLY TEXTED THE WRONG PERSON.
SORRY LOVE, IT'S THIS NEW MOBILE PHONE.
BUT I DID THINK IT WAS A BIT WEIRD COS I HARDLY EVER SPEAK TO MY AUNTIE PAM.
NOW YOU'RE HERE YOU COULDN'T SHOW US HOW TO USE IT?
THEN YOU CLICK THE NAME OF THE PERSON YOU WANT TO SEND THE TEXT TO...
BEEP!
OH, YOU RECEIVED ANOTHER DICK PIC, AUNTIE PAM.
LET ME GET MY GLASSES.

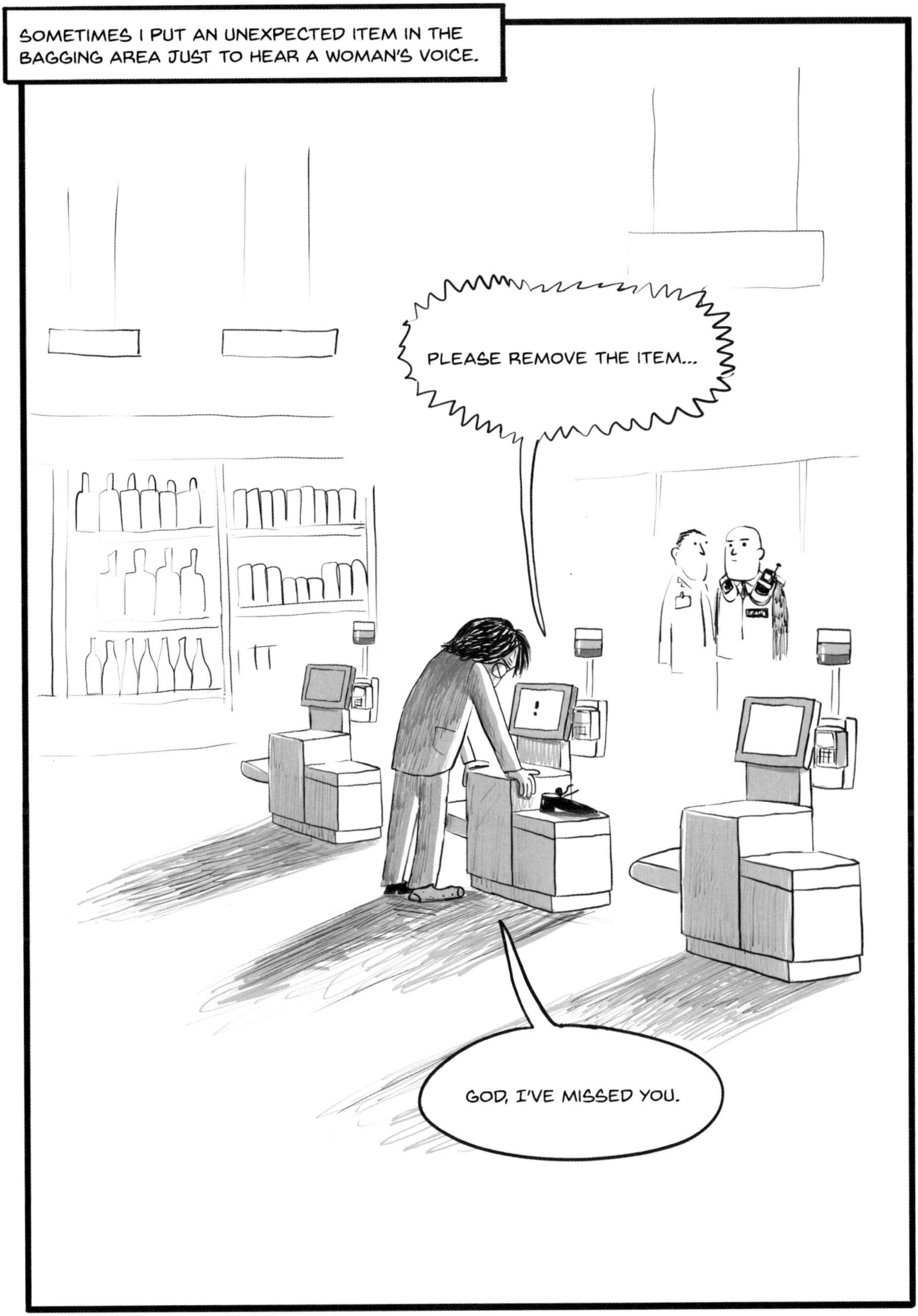
SOMETIMES I PUT AN UNEXPECTED ITEM IN THE BAGGING AREA JUST TO HEAR A WOMAN'S VOICE.
PLEASE REMOVE THE ITEM...
GOD, I'VE MISSED YOU.

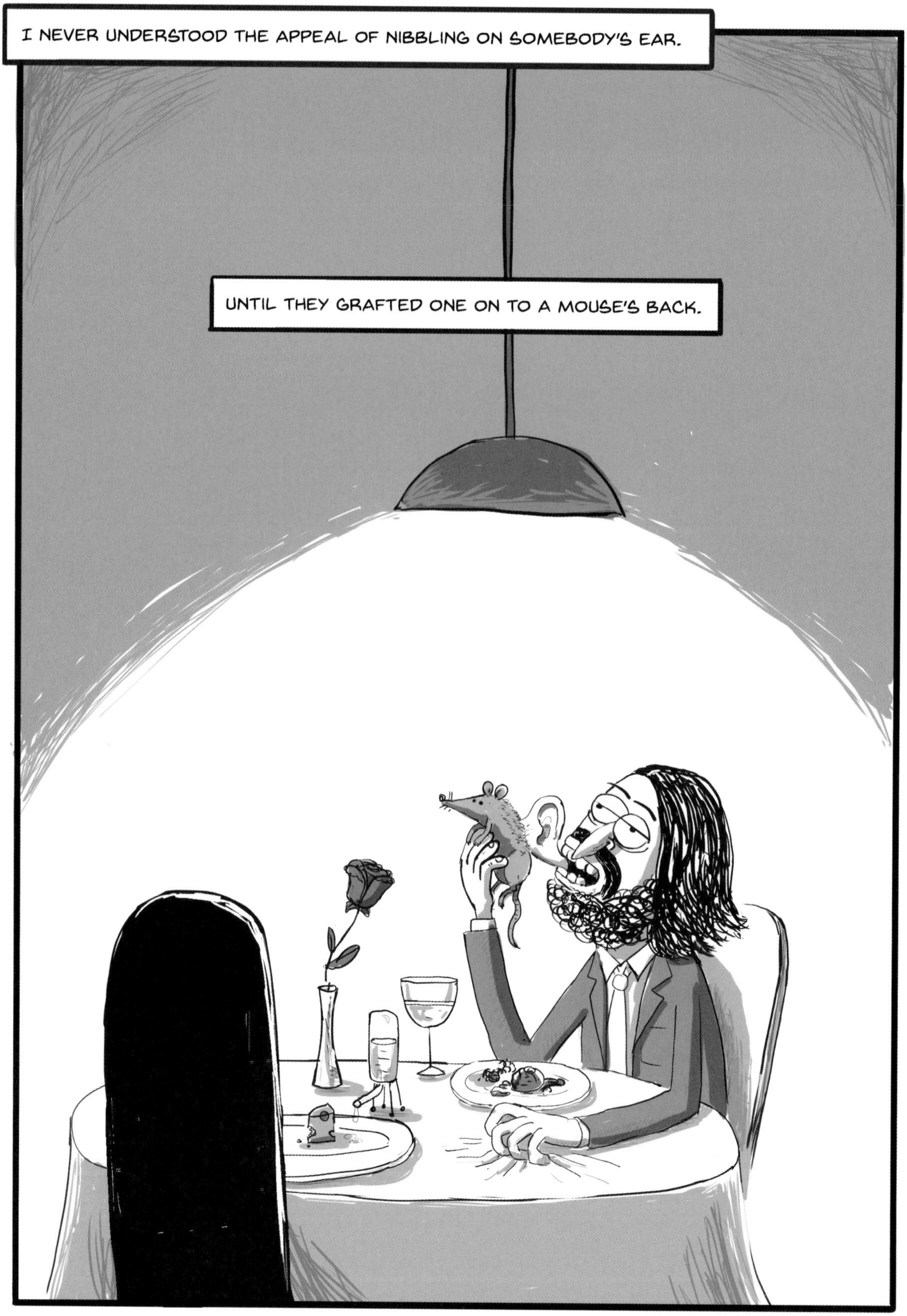
I NEVER UNDERSTOOD THE APPEAL OF NIBBLING ON SOMEBODY'S EAR.
UNTIL THEY GRAFTED ONE ON TO A MOUSE'S BACK.

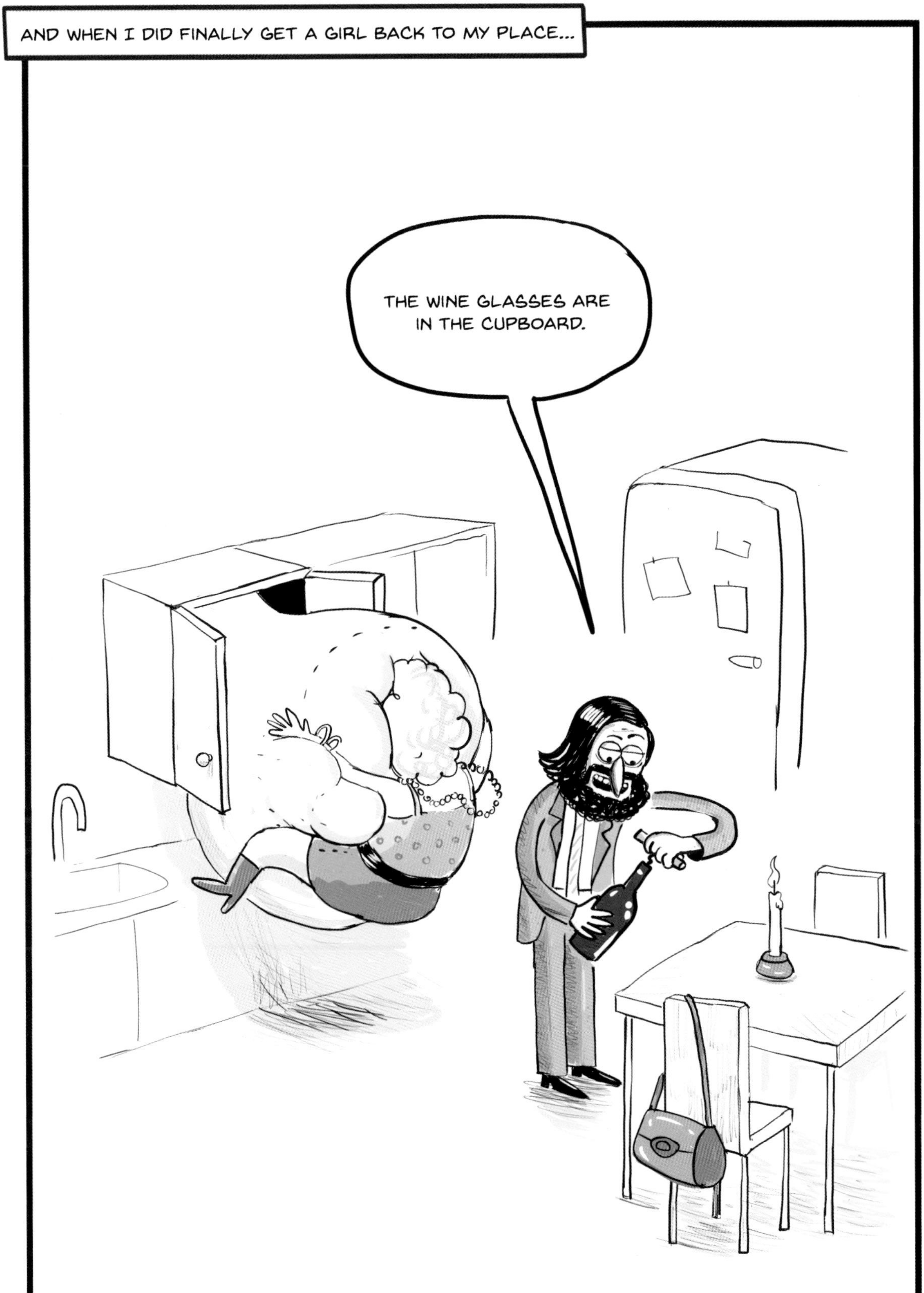
AND WHEN I DID FINALLY GET A GIRL BACK TO MY PLACE...
THE WINE GLASSES ARE IN THE CUPBOARD.

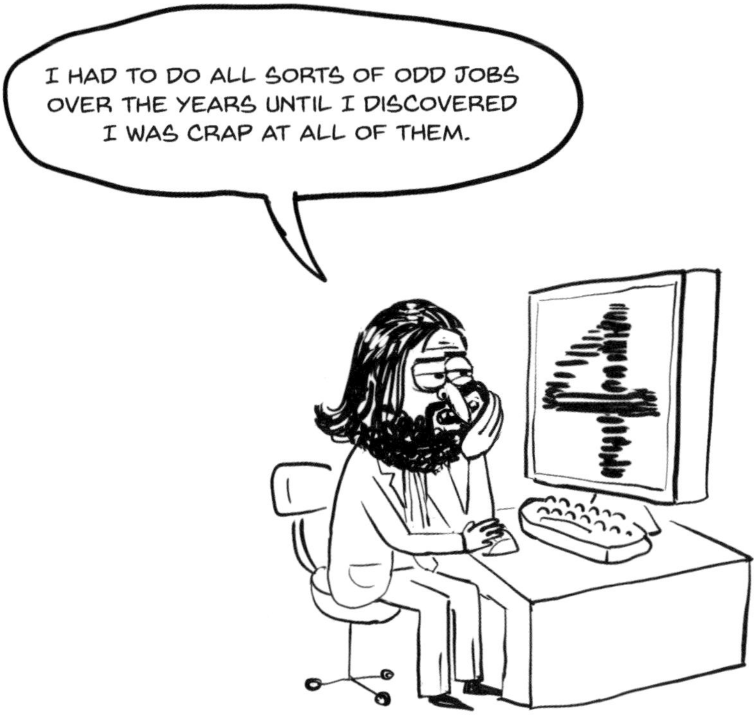
I HAD TO DO ALL SORTS OF ODD JOBS OVER THE YEARS UNTIL I DISCOVERED I WAS CRAP AT ALL OF THEM.

WORKING FOR THE MAN

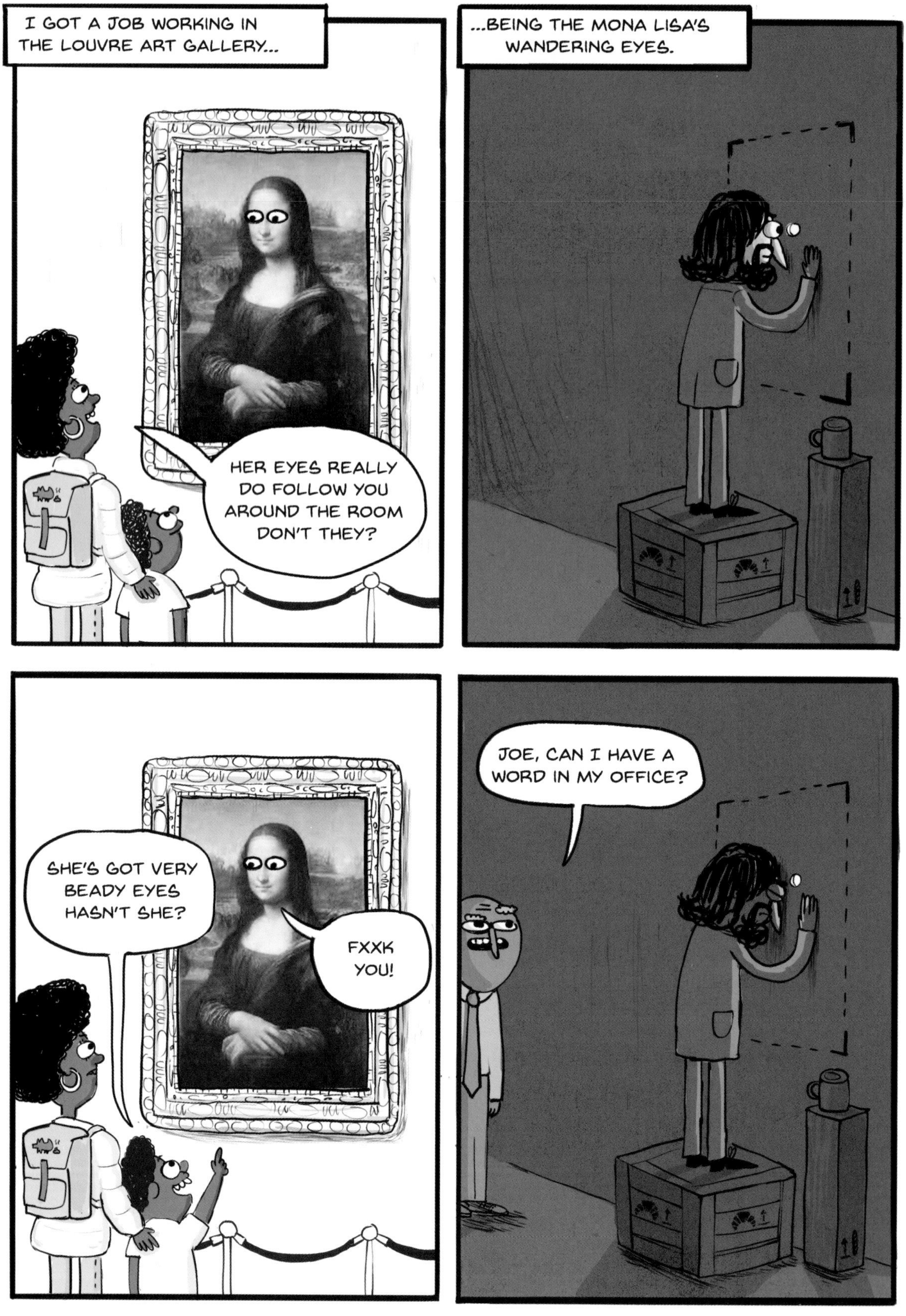
I GOT A JOB WORKING IN THE LOUVRE ART GALLERY...
HER EYES REALLY DO FOLLOW YOU AROUND THE ROOM DON'T THEY?
...BEING THE MONA LISA'S WANDERING EYES.
SHE'S GOT VERY BEADY EYES HASN'T SHE?
FXXK YOU!
JOE, CAN I HAVE A WORD IN MY OFFICE?

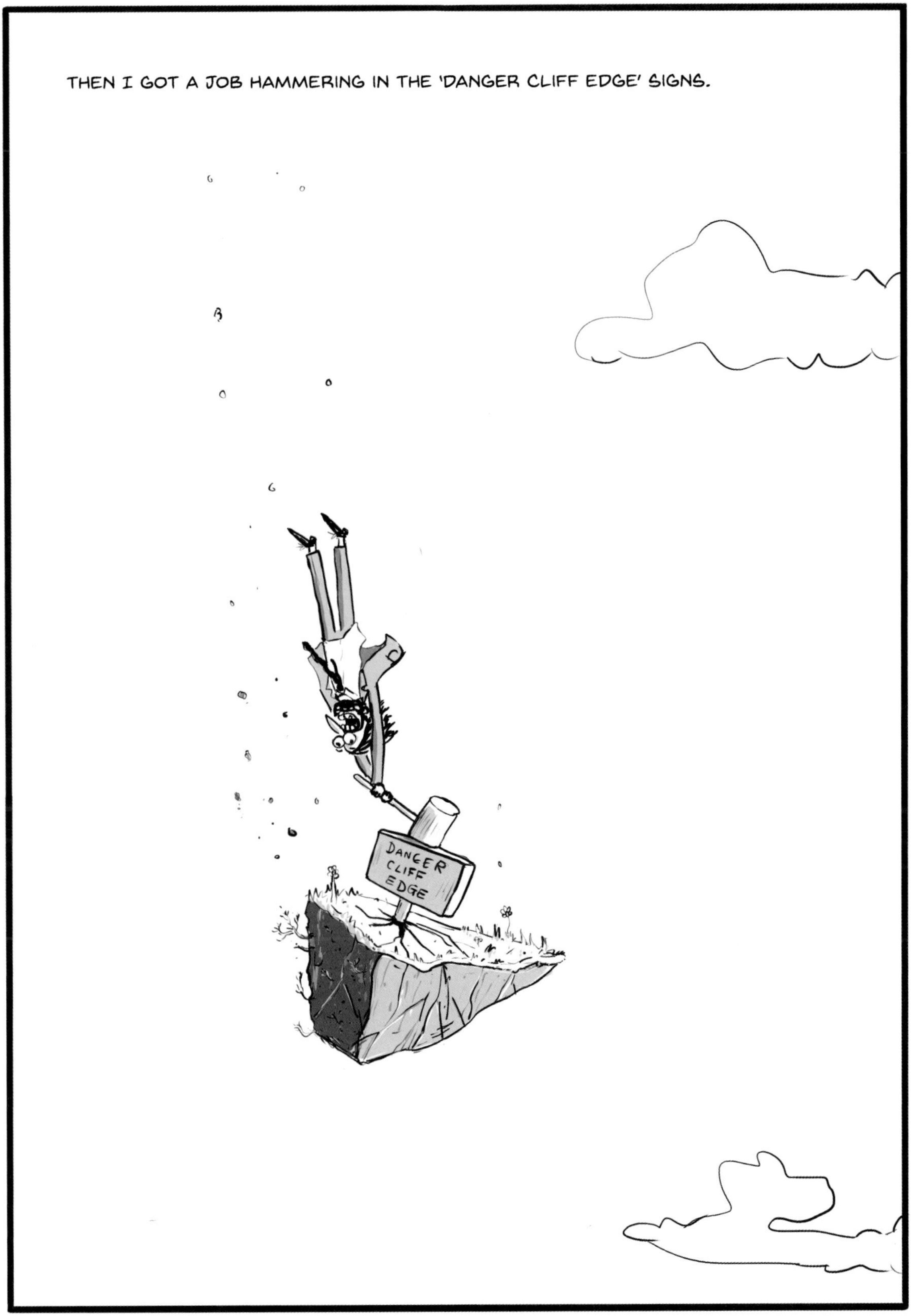
THEN I GOT A JOB HAMMERING IN THE 'DANGER CLIFF EDGE' SIGNS.
DANGER
CLIFF
EDGE

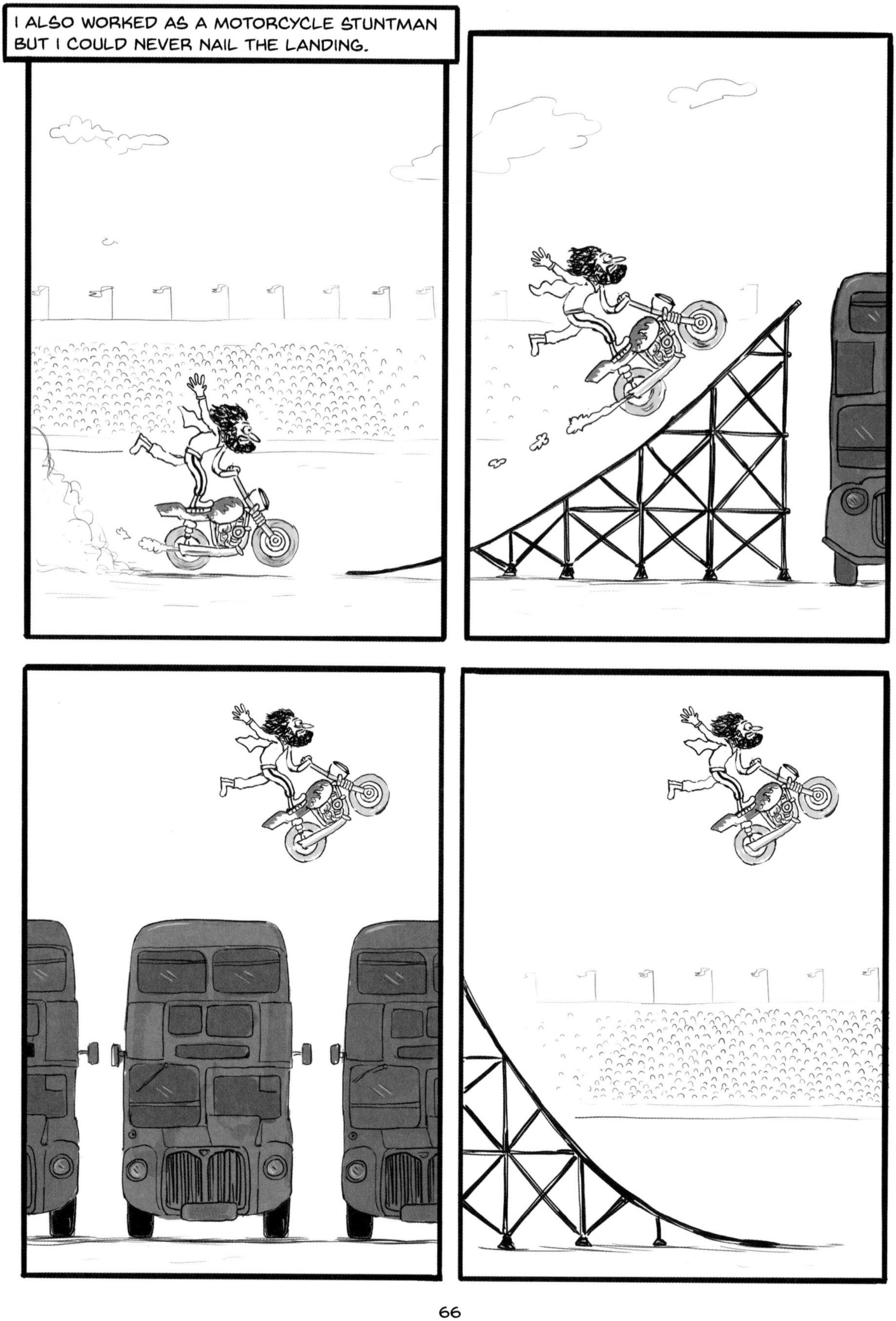
I ALSO WORKED AS A MOTORCYCLE STUNTMAN
BUT I COULD NEVER NAIL THE LANDING.

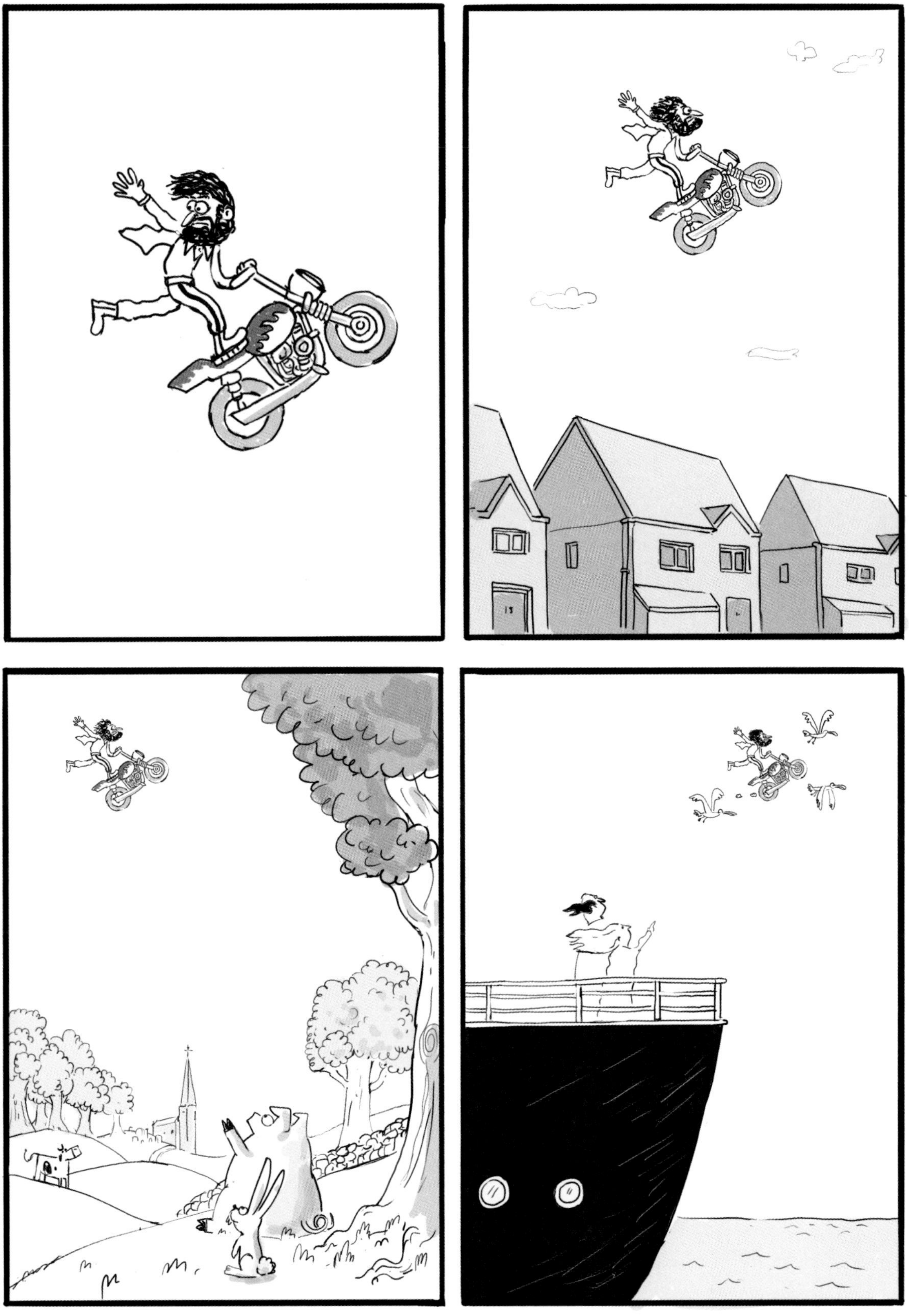

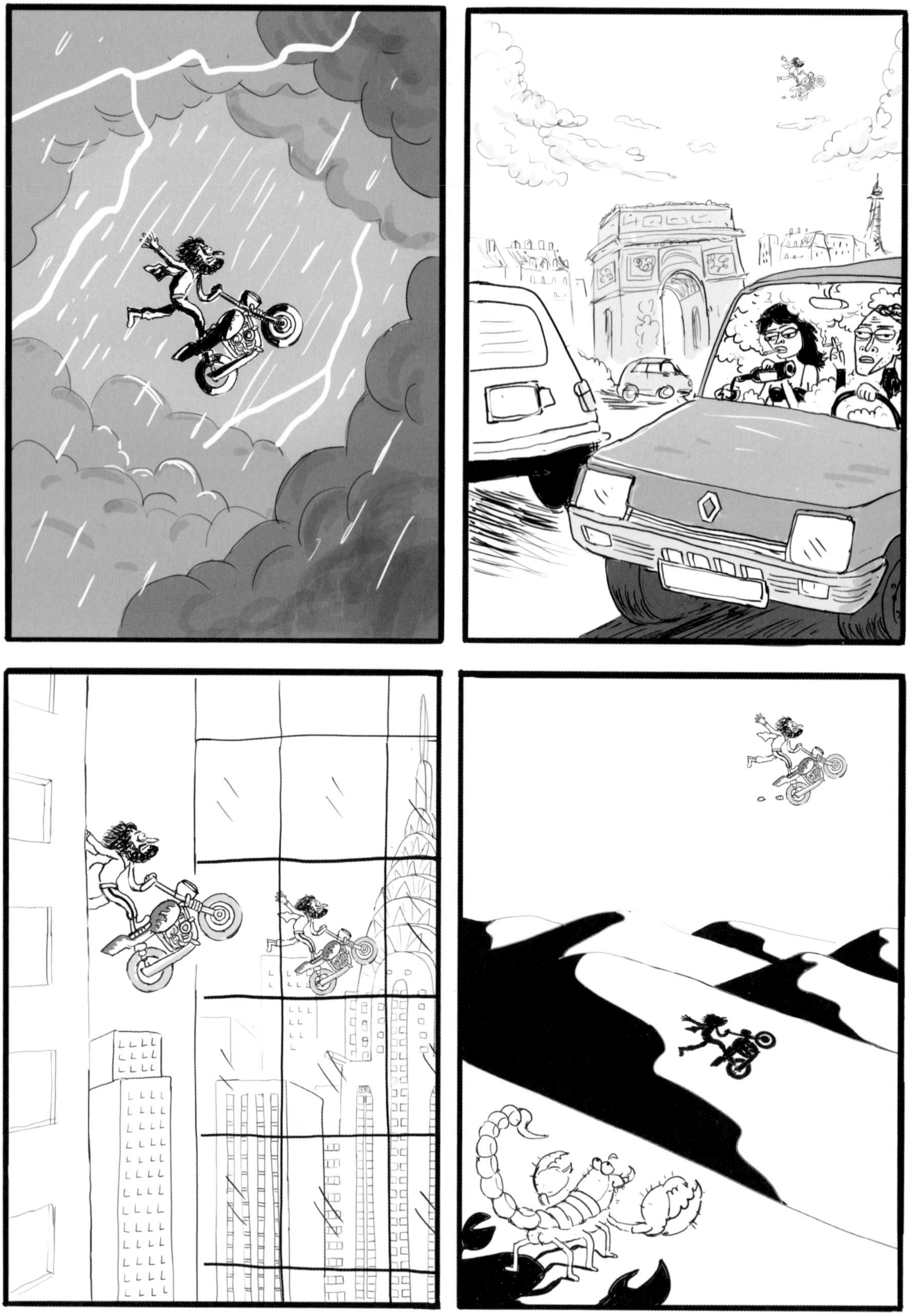

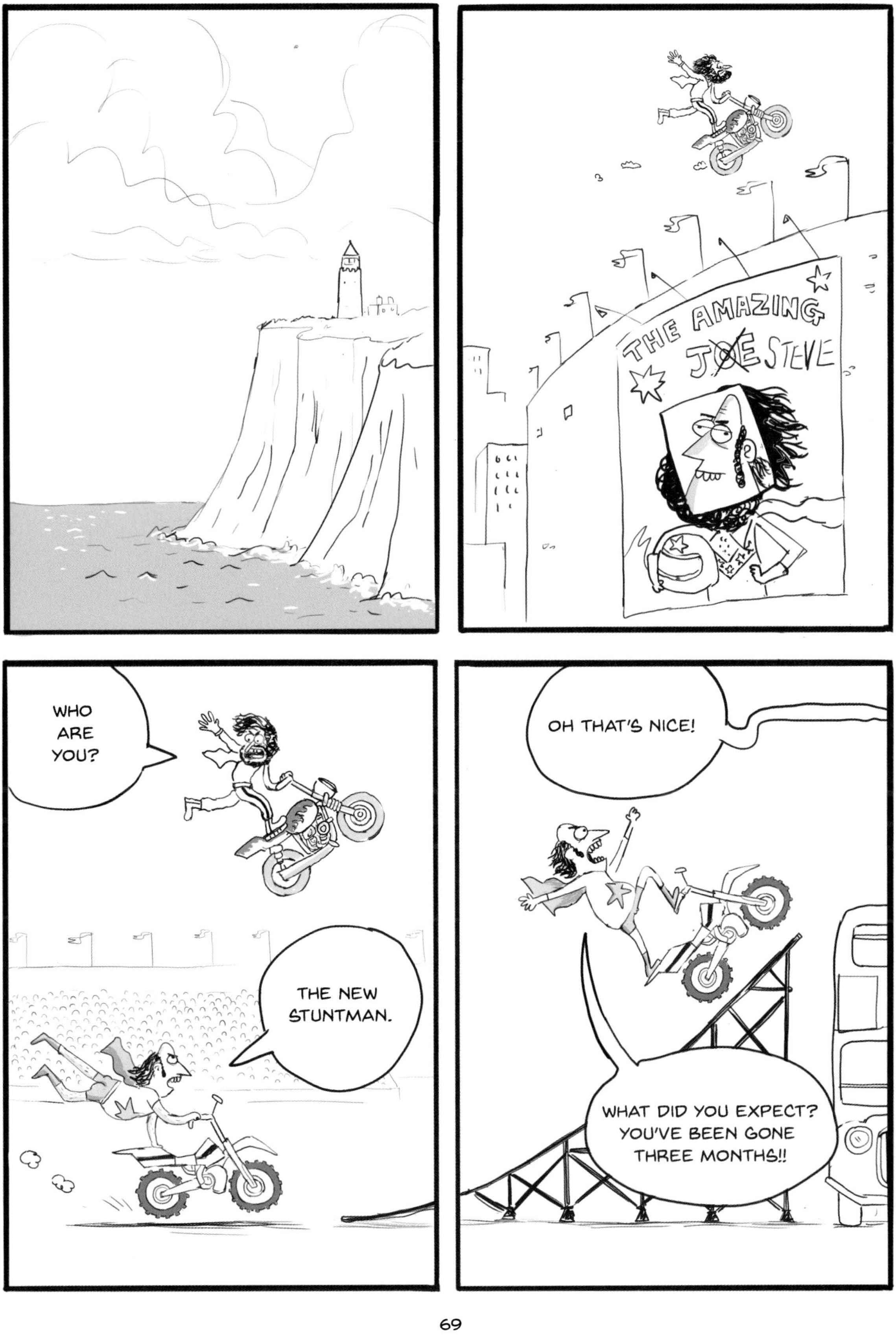
THE AMAZING JOE STEVE
WHO ARE YOU?
THE NEW STUNTMAN.
OH THAT'S NICE!
WHAT DID YOU EXPECT? YOU'VE BEEN GONE THREE MONTHS!!

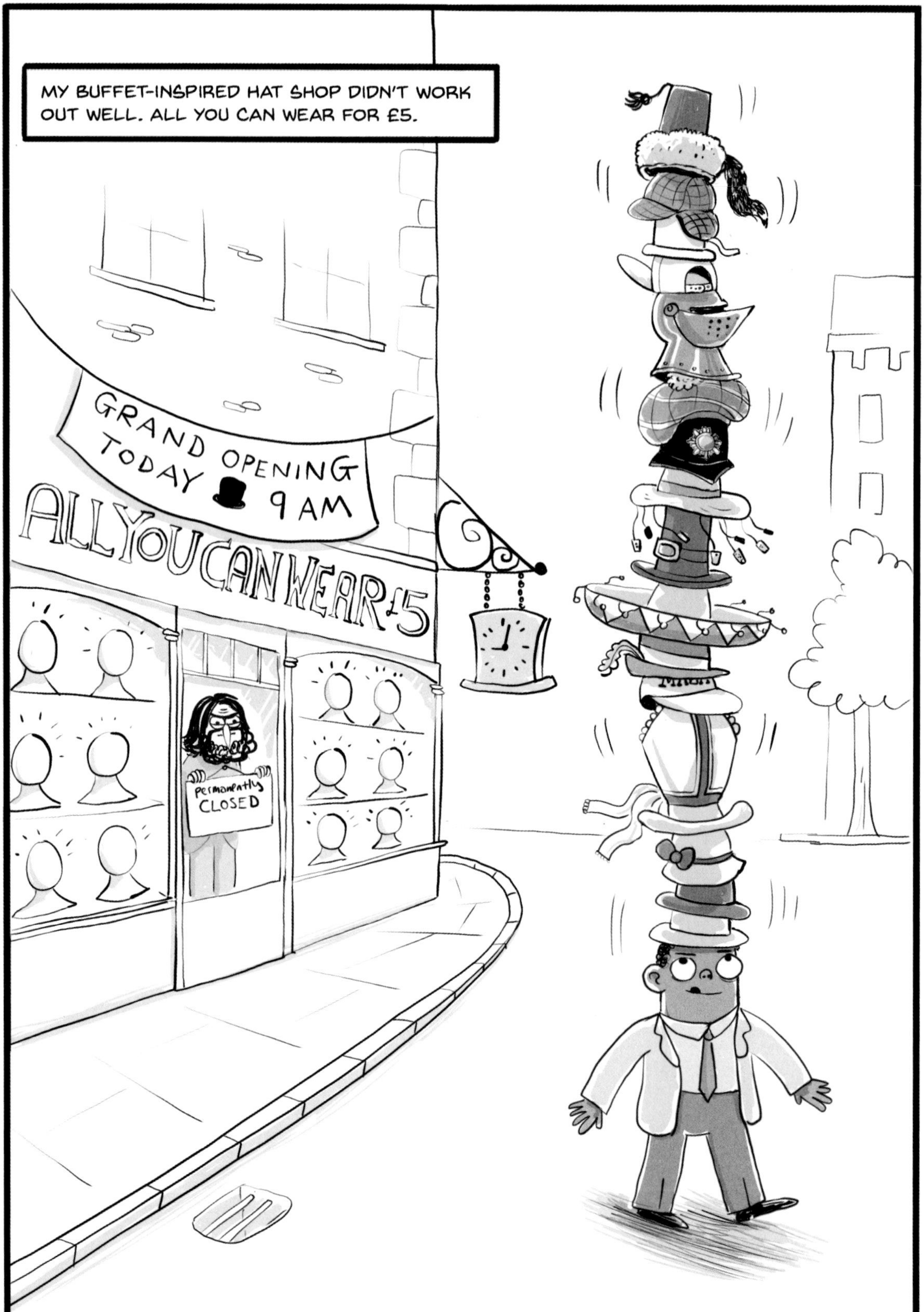
MY BUFFET-INSPIRED HAT SHOP DIDN'T WORK OUT WELL. ALL YOU CAN WEAR FOR £5.
GRAND OPENING TODAY 9 AM
ALL YOU CAN WEAR £5
Permanently CLOSED

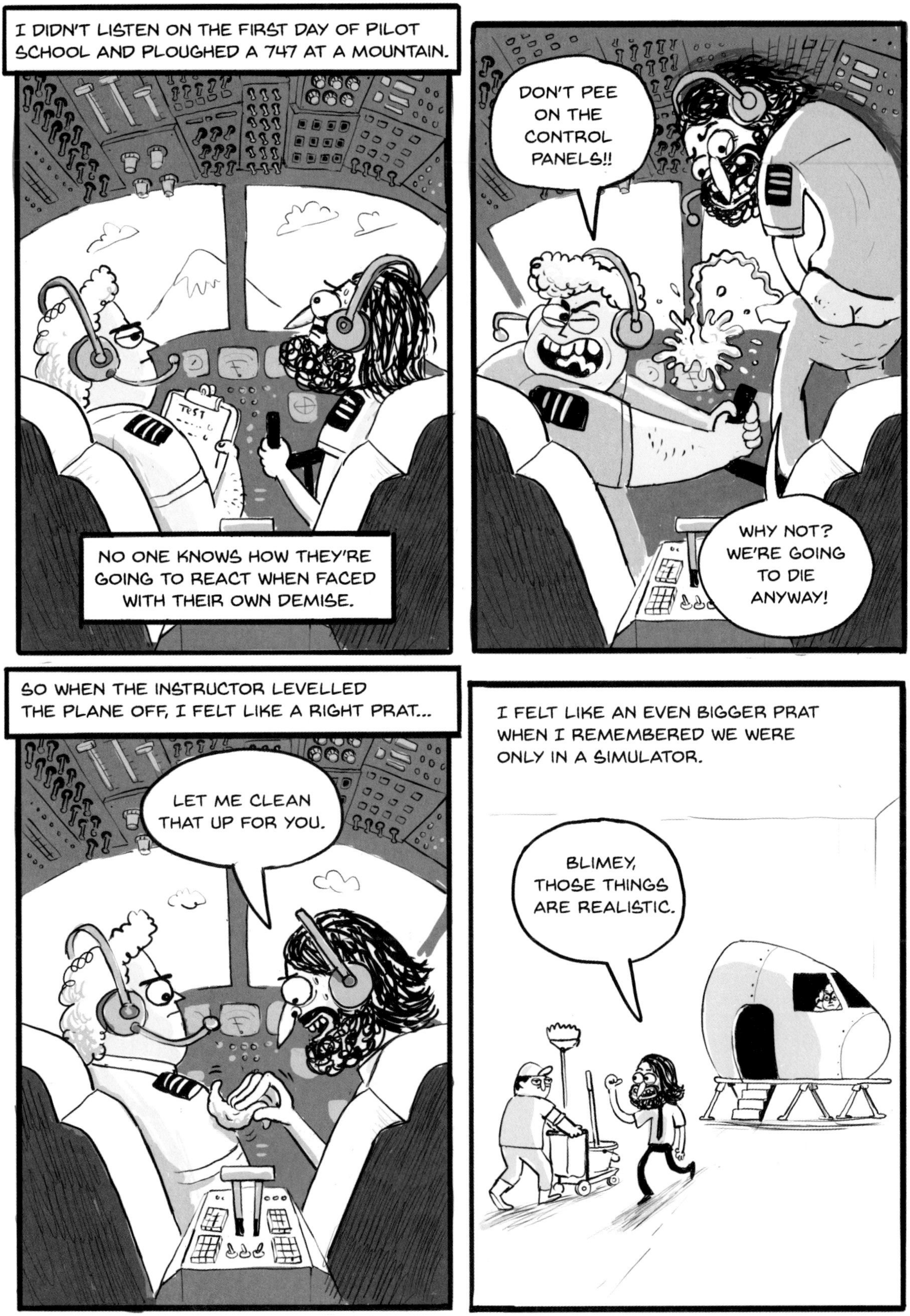
I DIDN'T LISTEN ON THE FIRST DAY OF PILOT SCHOOL AND PLOUGHED A 747 AT A MOUNTAIN.
TEST
NO ONE KNOWS HOW THEY'RE GOING TO REACT WHEN FACED WITH THEIR OWN DEMISE.
DON'T PEE ON THE CONTROL PANELS!!
WHY NOT? WE'RE GOING TO DIE ANYWAY!
SO WHEN THE INSTRUCTOR LEVELLED THE PLANE OFF, I FELT LIKE A RIGHT PRAT...
LET ME CLEAN THAT UP FOR YOU.
I FELT LIKE AN EVEN BIGGER PRAT WHEN I REMEMBERED WE WERE ONLY IN A SIMULATOR.
BLIMEY, THOSE THINGS ARE REALISTIC.

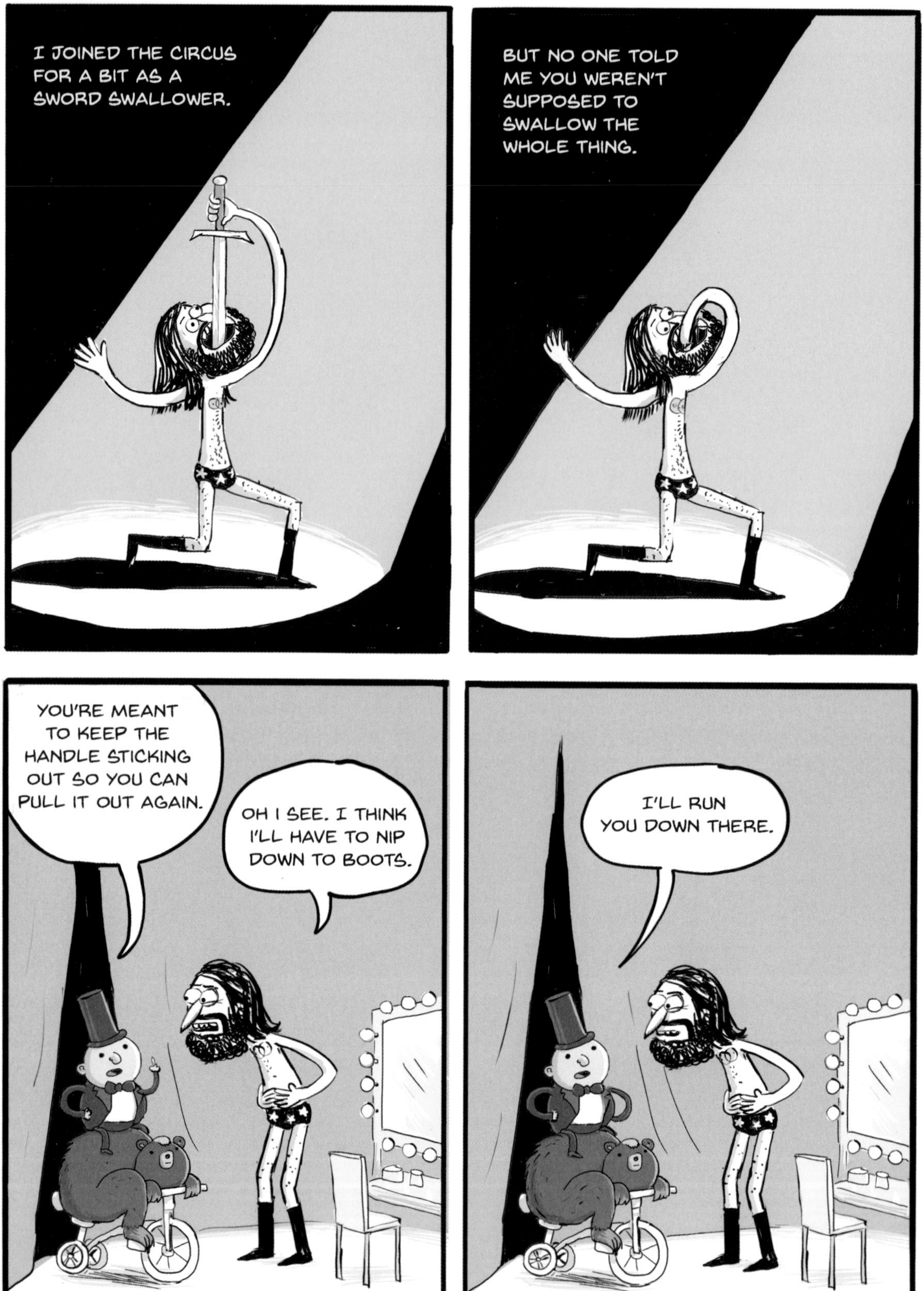
I JOINED THE CIRCUS FOR A BIT AS A SWORD SWALLOWER.
BUT NO ONE TOLD ME YOU WEREN'T SUPPOSED TO SWALLOW THE WHOLE THING.
YOU'RE MEANT TO KEEP THE HANDLE STICKING OUT SO YOU CAN PULL IT OUT AGAIN.
OH I SEE. I THINK I'LL HAVE TO NIP DOWN TO BOOTS.
I'LL RUN YOU DOWN THERE.

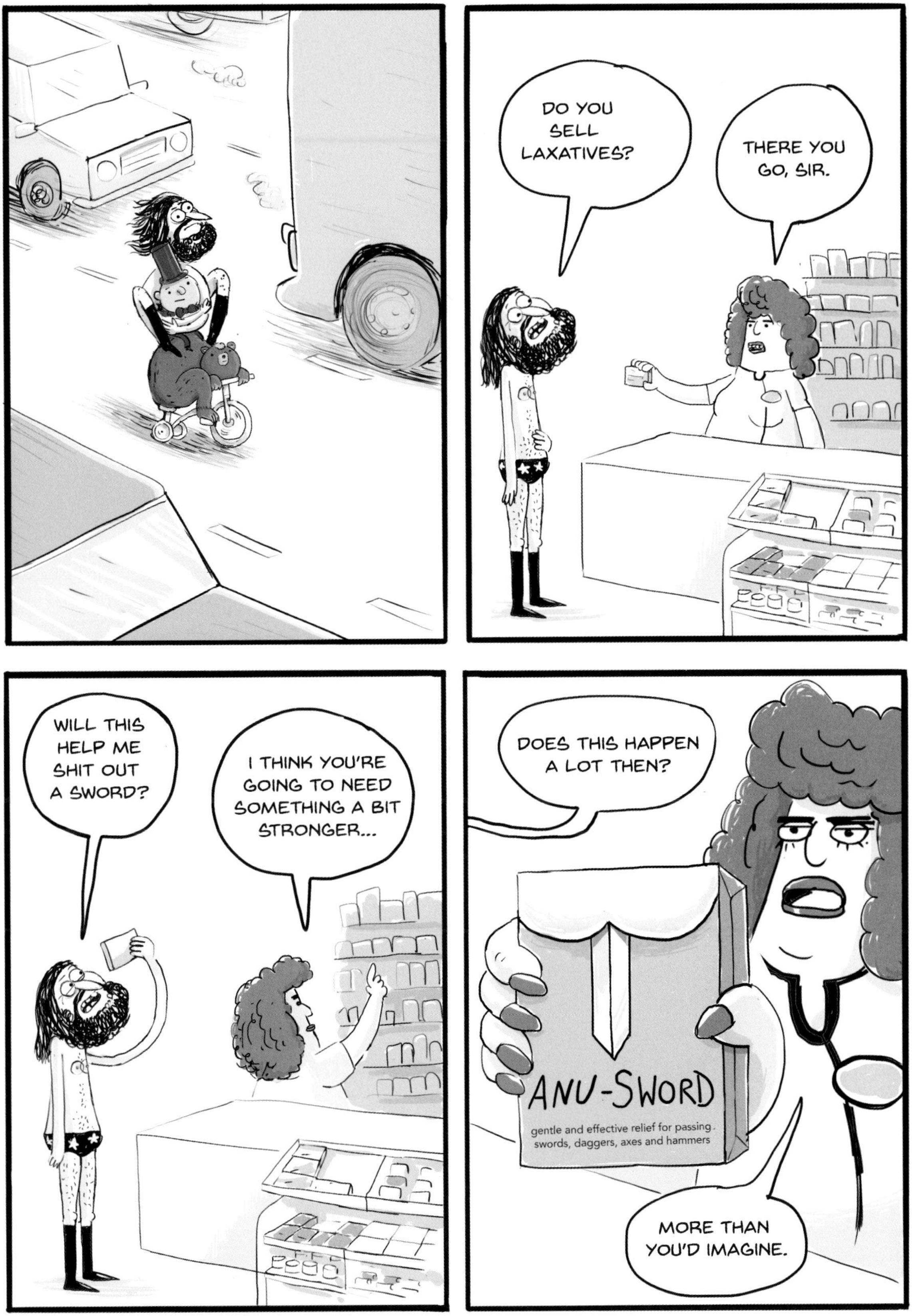
DO YOU SELL LAXATIVES?
THERE YOU GO, SIR.
WILL THIS HELP ME SHIT OUT A SWORD?
I THINK YOU'RE GOING TO NEED SOMETHING A BIT STRONGER...
DOES THIS HAPPEN A LOT THEN?
ANU-SWORD
gentle and effective relief for passing swords, daggers, axes and hammers
MORE THAN YOU'D IMAGINE.

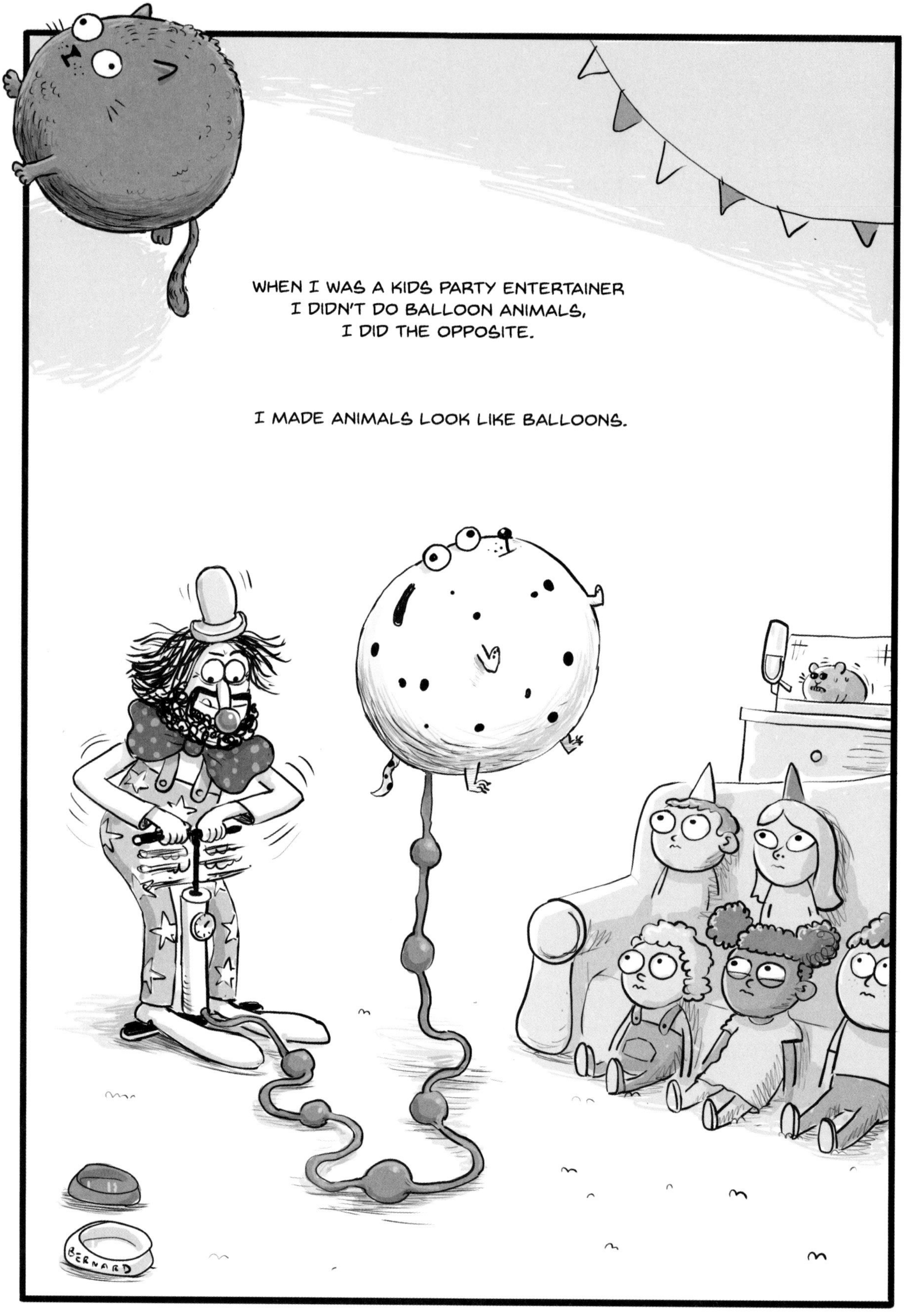
WHEN I WAS A KIDS PARTY ENTERTAINER
I DIDN'T DO BALLOON ANIMALS,
I DID THE OPPOSITE.
I MADE ANIMALS LOOK LIKE BALLOONS.
BERNARD

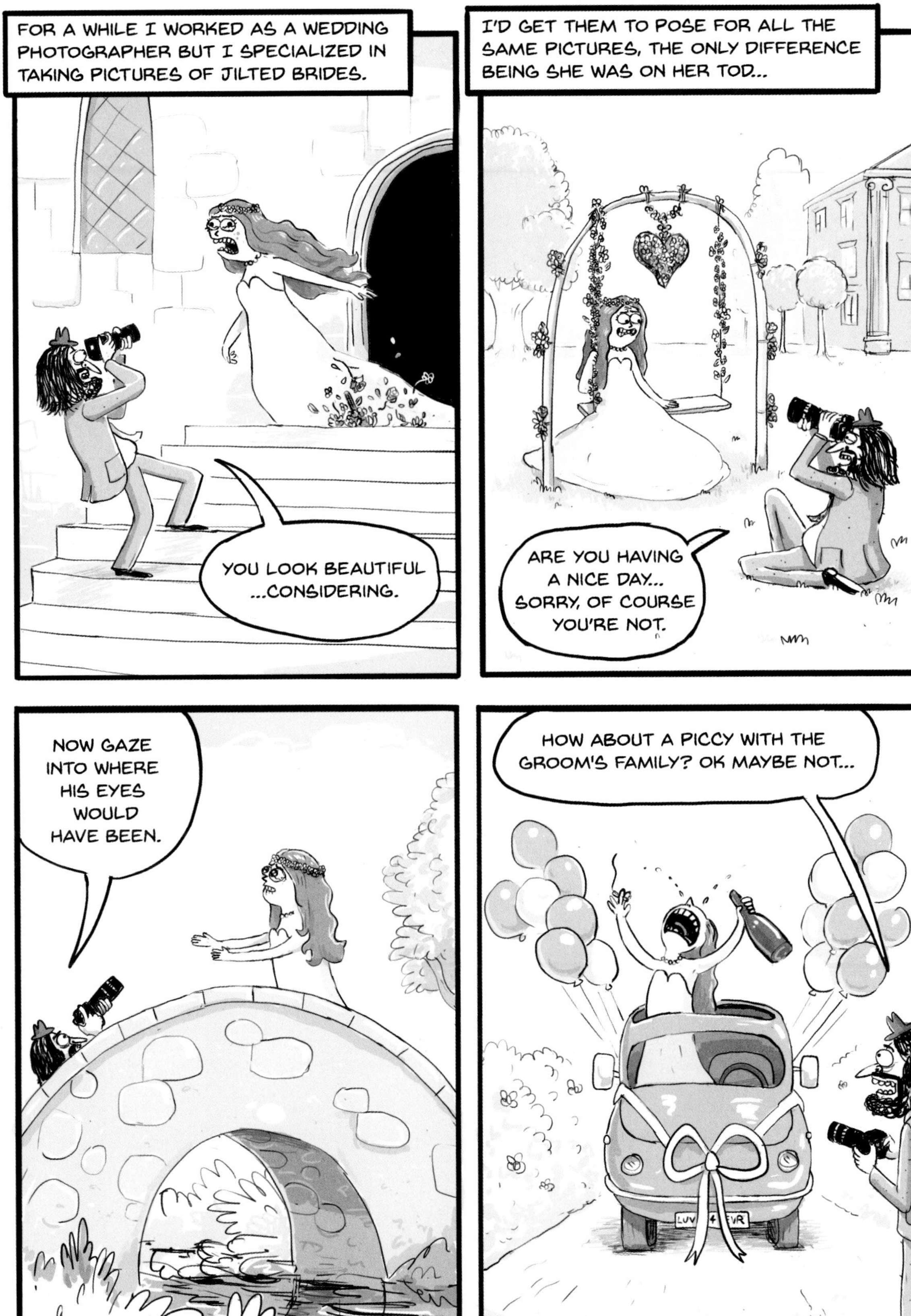
FOR A WHILE I WORKED AS A WEDDING PHOTOGRAPHER BUT I SPECIALIZED IN TAKING PICTURES OF JILTED BRIDES.
YOU LOOK BEAUTIFUL ...CONSIDERING.
I'D GET THEM TO POSE FOR ALL THE SAME PICTURES, THE ONLY DIFFERENCE BEING SHE WAS ON HER TOD...
ARE YOU HAVING A NICE DAY... SORRY, OF COURSE YOU'RE NOT.
NOW GAZE INTO WHERE HIS EYES WOULD HAVE BEEN.
HOW ABOUT A PICCY WITH THE GROOM'S FAMILY? OK MAYBE NOT...
LUV 4 EVR

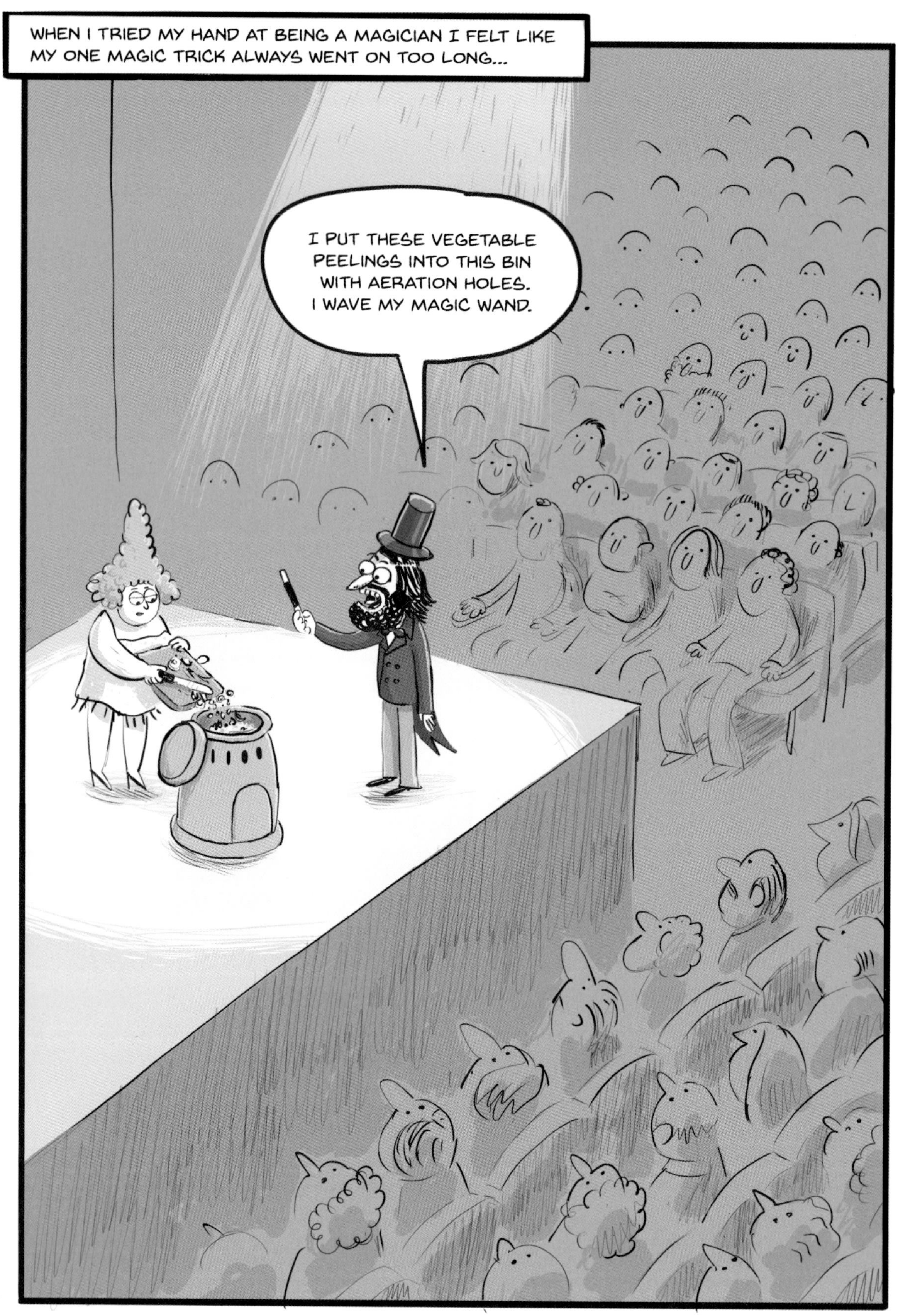
WHEN I TRIED MY HAND AT BEING A MAGICIAN I FELT LIKE MY ONE MAGIC TRICK ALWAYS WENT ON TOO LONG...
I PUT THESE VEGETABLE PEELINGS INTO THIS BIN WITH AERATION HOLES. I WAVE MY MAGIC WAND.

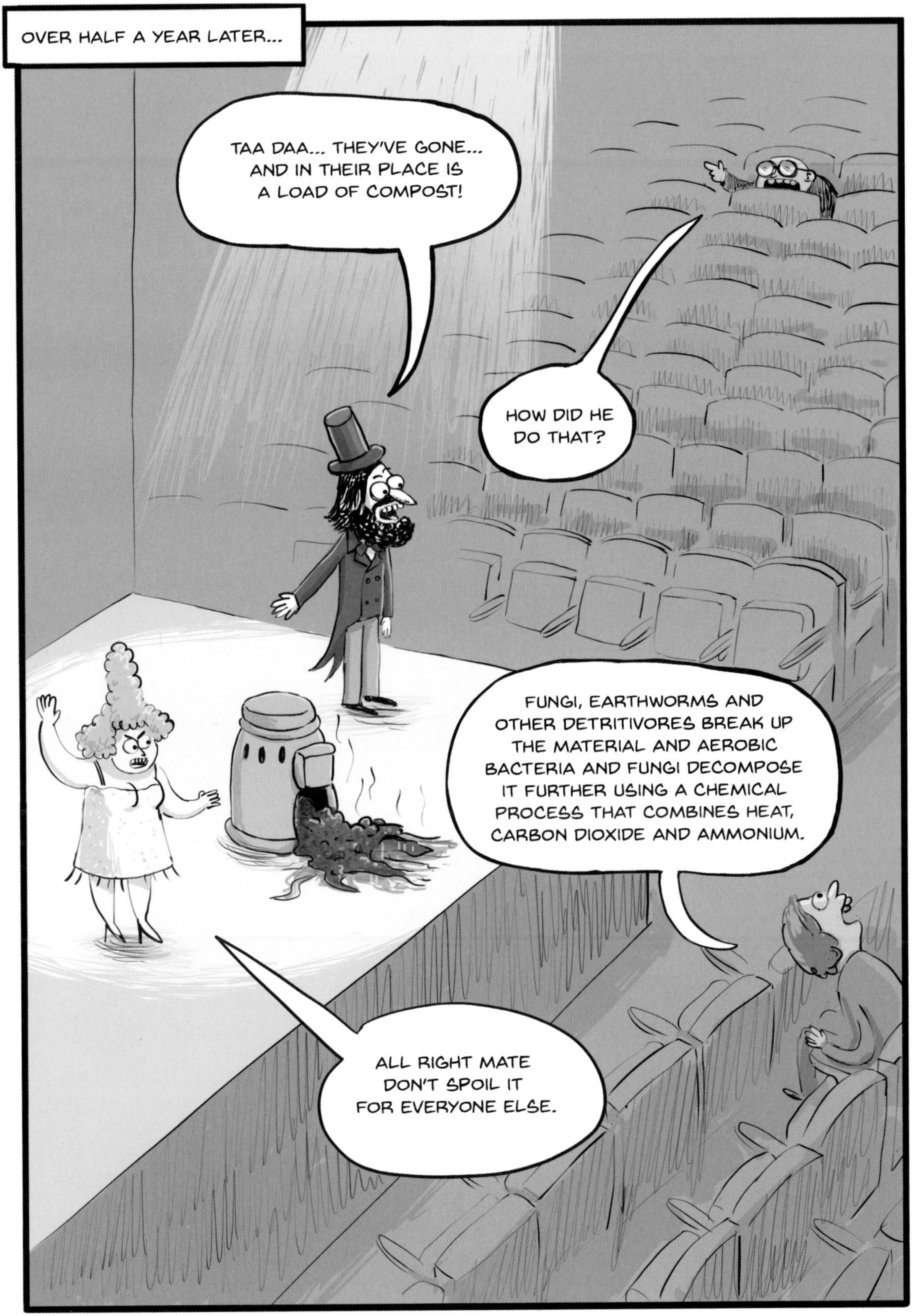
OVER HALF A YEAR LATER...
TAA DAA... THEY'VE GONE... AND IN THEIR PLACE IS A LOAD OF COMPOST!
HOW DID HE DO THAT?
FUNGI, EARTHWORMS AND OTHER DETRITIVORES BREAK UP THE MATERIAL AND AEROBIC BACTERIA AND FUNGI DECOMPOSE IT FURTHER USING A CHEMICAL PROCESS THAT COMBINES HEAT, CARBON DIOXIDE AND AMMONIUM.
ALL RIGHT MATE DON'T SPOIL IT FOR EVERYONE ELSE.

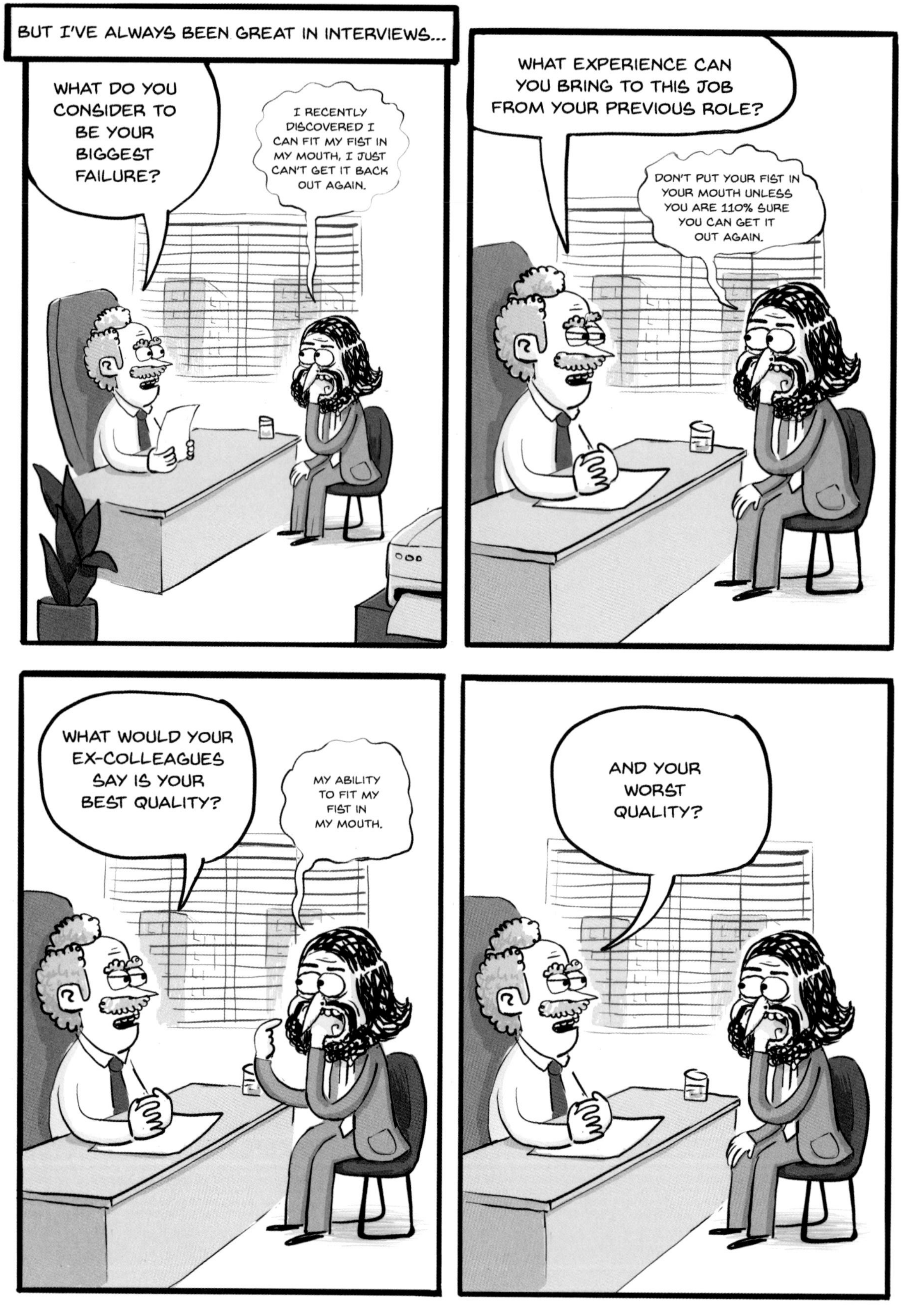
BUT I'VE ALWAYS BEEN GREAT IN INTERVIEWS...
WHAT DO YOU CONSIDER TO BE YOUR BIGGEST FAILURE?
I RECENTLY DISCOVERED I CAN FIT MY FIST IN MY MOUTH, I JUST CAN'T GET IT BACK OUT AGAIN.
WHAT EXPERIENCE CAN YOU BRING TO THIS JOB FROM YOUR PREVIOUS ROLE?
DON'T PUT YOUR FIST IN YOUR MOUTH UNLESS YOU ARE 110% SURE YOU CAN GET IT OUT AGAIN.
WHAT WOULD YOUR EX-COLLEAGUES SAY IS YOUR BEST QUALITY?
MY ABILITY TO FIT MY FIST IN MY MOUTH.
AND YOUR WORST QUALITY?

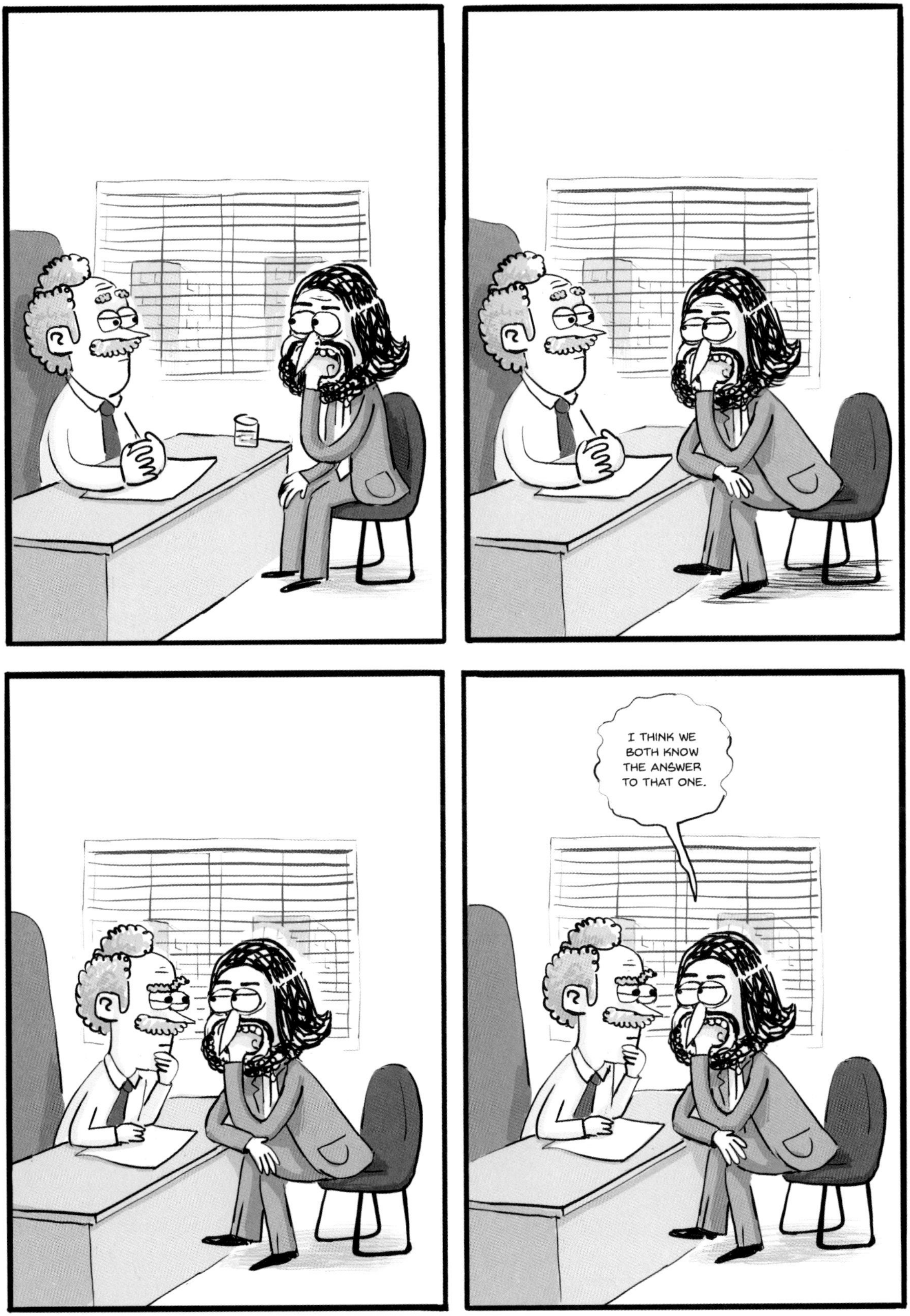
I THINK WE BOTH KNOW THE ANSWER TO THAT ONE.

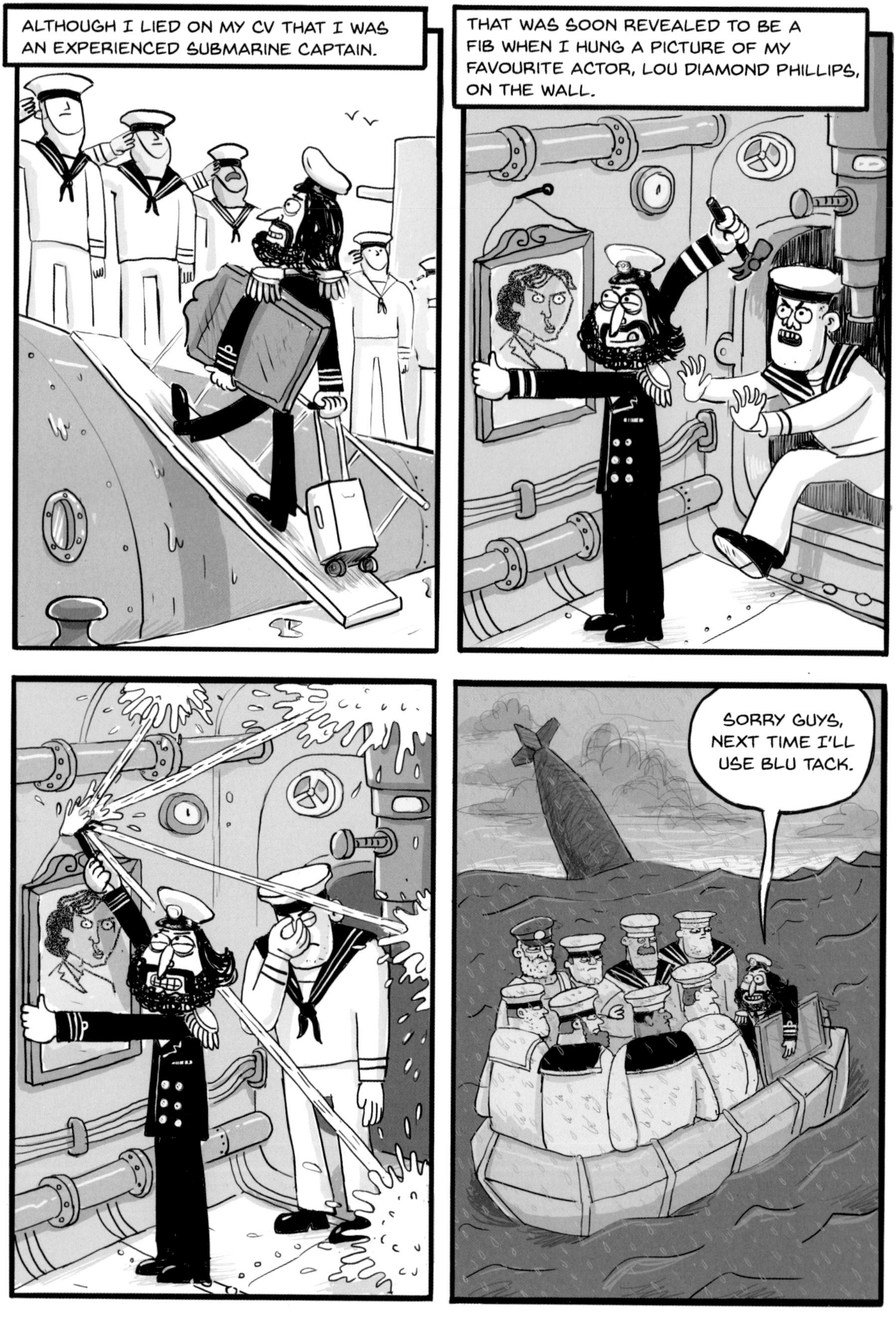
ALTHOUGH I LIED ON MY CV THAT I WAS AN EXPERIENCED SUBMARINE CAPTAIN.
THAT WAS SOON REVEALED TO BE A FIB WHEN I HUNG A PICTURE OF MY FAVOURITE ACTOR, LOU DIAMOND PHILLIPS, ON THE WALL.
SORRY GUYS, NEXT TIME I'LL USE BLU TACK.

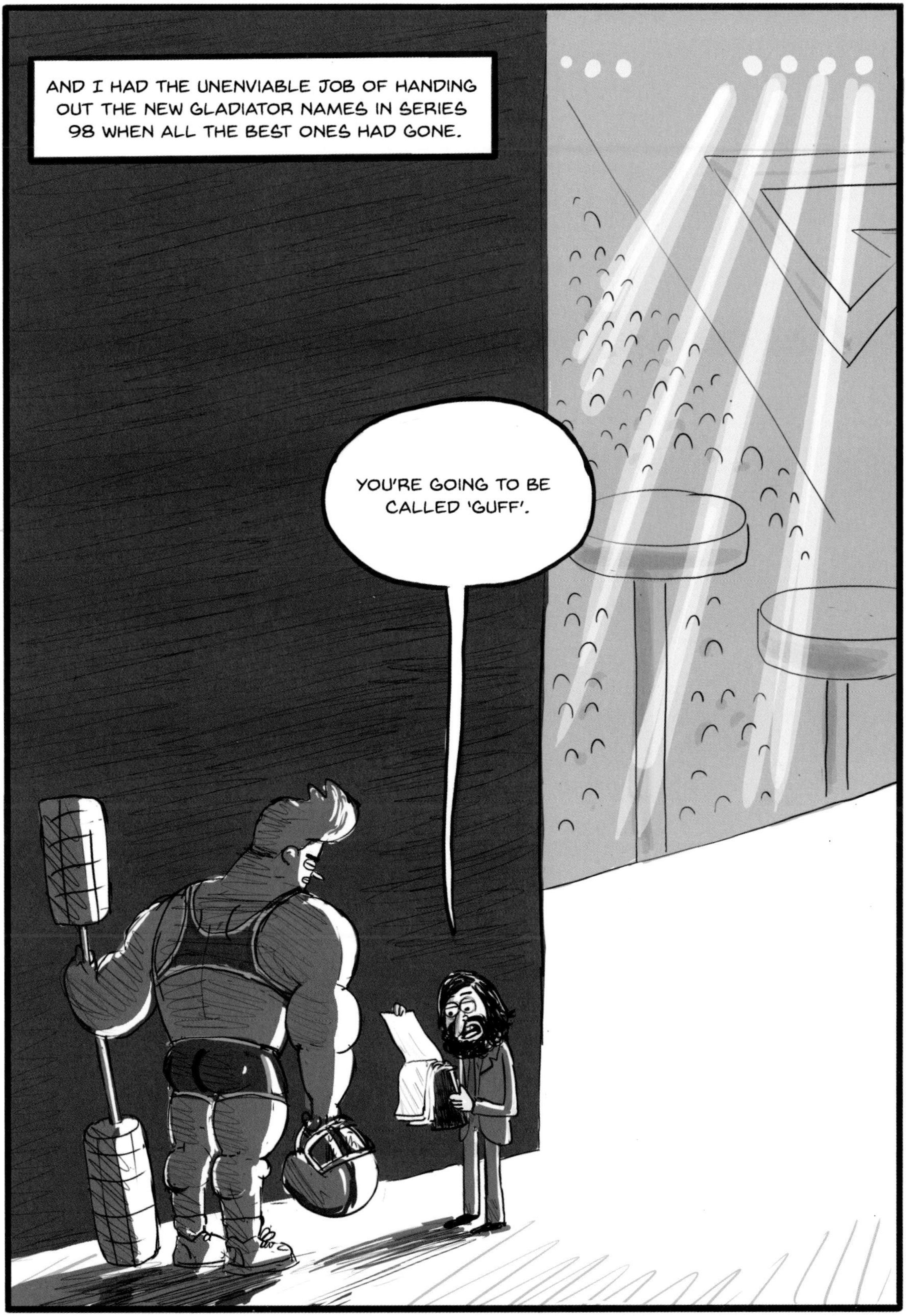
AND I HAD THE UNENVIABLE JOB OF HANDING OUT THE NEW GLADIATOR NAMES IN SERIES 98 WHEN ALL THE BEST ONES HAD GONE.
YOU'RE GOING TO BE CALLED 'GUFF'.

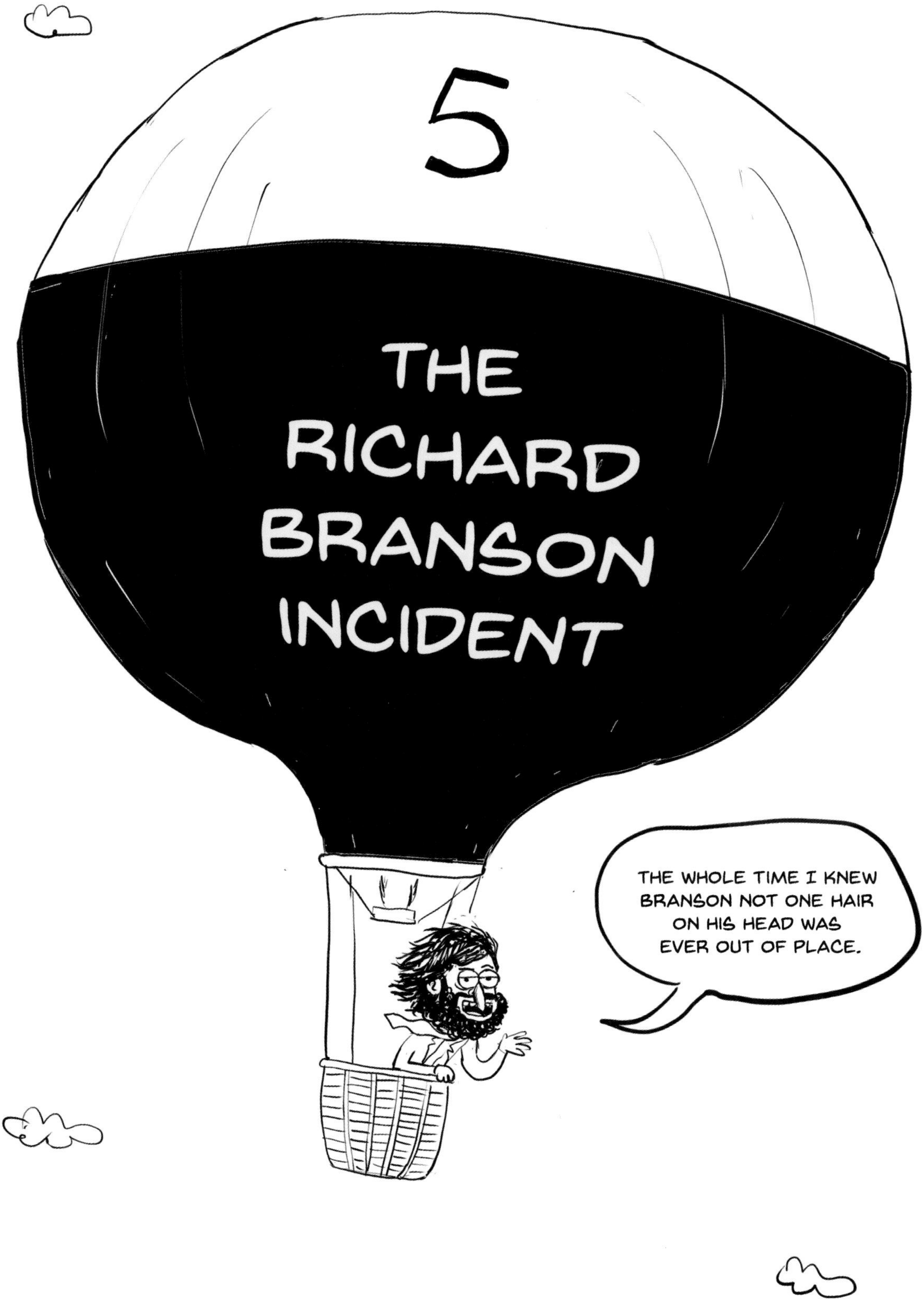
5
THE RICHARD BRANSON INCIDENT
THE WHOLE TIME I KNEW BRANSON NOT ONE HAIR ON HIS HEAD WAS EVER OUT OF PLACE.

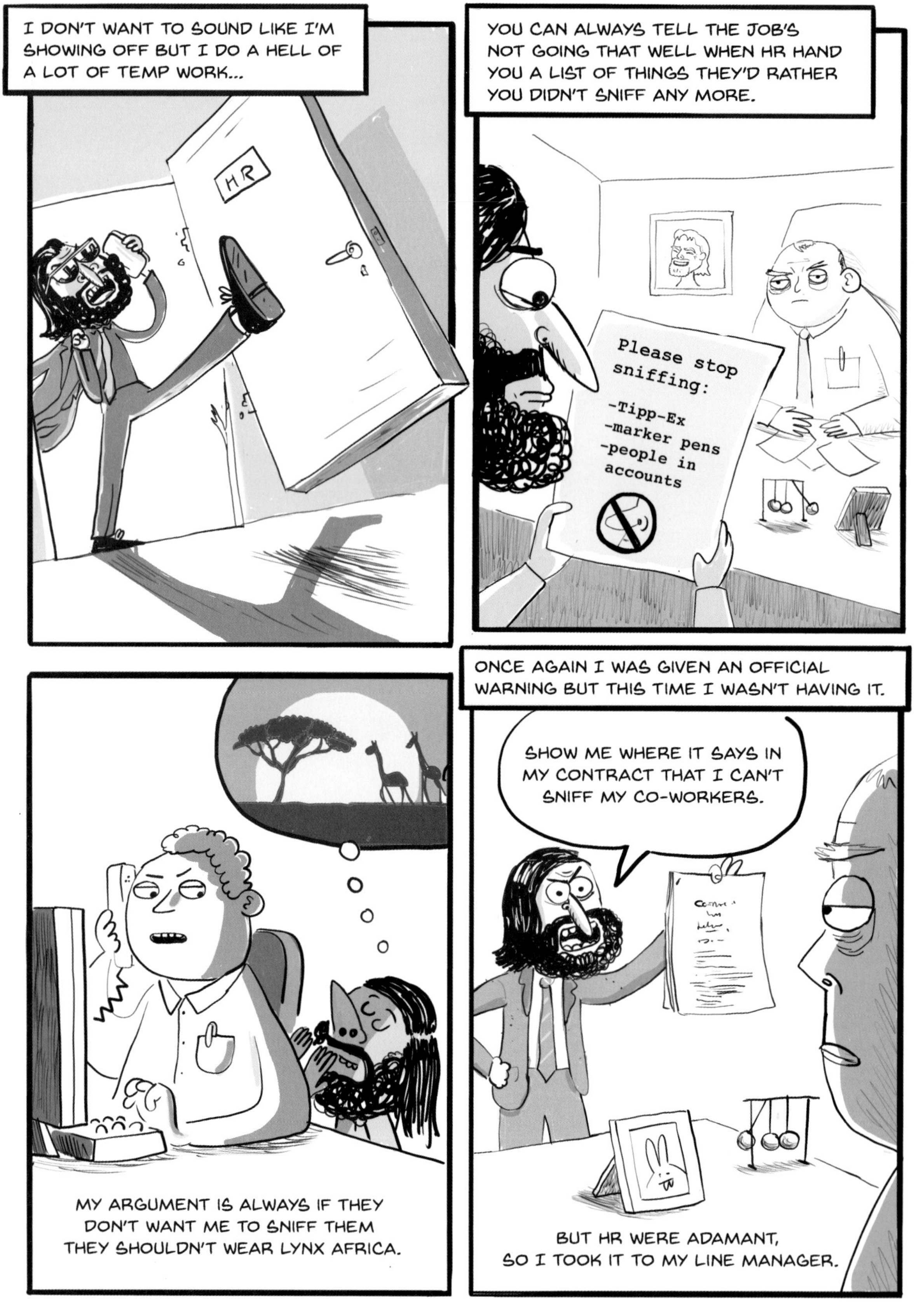
I DON'T WANT TO SOUND LIKE I'M SHOWING OFF BUT I DO A HELL OF A LOT OF TEMP WORK...
HR
YOU CAN ALWAYS TELL THE JOB'S NOT GOING THAT WELL WHEN HR HAND YOU A LIST OF THINGS THEY'D RATHER YOU DIDN'T SNIFF ANY MORE.
Please stop sniffing:
-Tipp-Ex
-marker pens
-people in accounts
MY ARGUMENT IS ALWAYS IF THEY DON'T WANT ME TO SNIFF THEM THEY SHOULDN'T WEAR LYNX AFRICA.
ONCE AGAIN I WAS GIVEN AN OFFICIAL WARNING BUT THIS TIME I WASN'T HAVING IT.
SHOW ME WHERE IT SAYS IN MY CONTRACT THAT I CAN'T SNIFF MY CO-WORKERS.
BUT HR WERE ADAMANT, SO I TOOK IT TO MY LINE MANAGER.

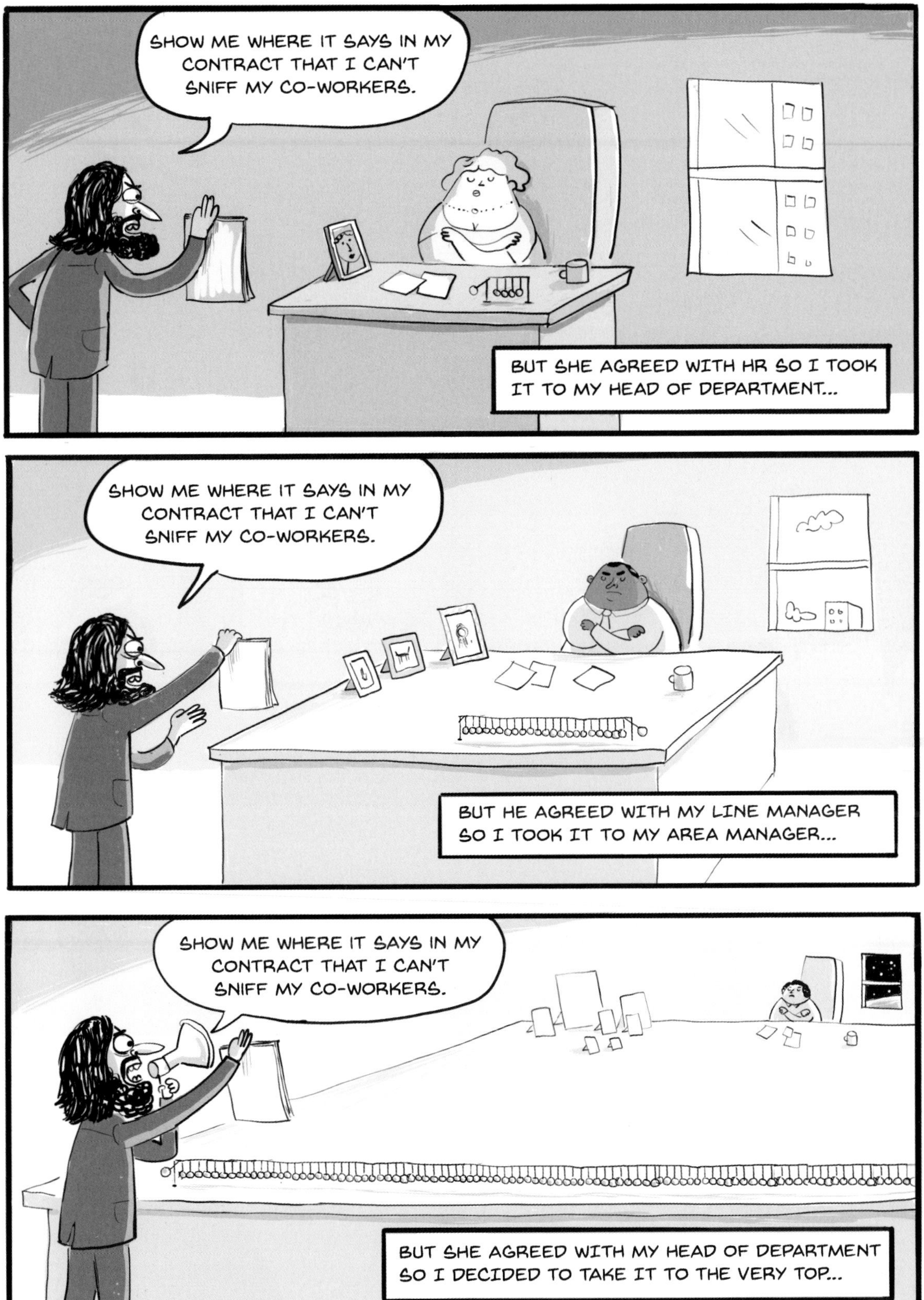
SHOW ME WHERE IT SAYS IN MY CONTRACT THAT I CAN'T SNIFF MY CO-WORKERS.
BUT SHE AGREED WITH HR SO I TOOK IT TO MY HEAD OF DEPARTMENT...
SHOW ME WHERE IT SAYS IN MY CONTRACT THAT I CAN'T SNIFF MY CO-WORKERS.
BUT HE AGREED WITH MY LINE MANAGER SO I TOOK IT TO MY AREA MANAGER...
SHOW ME WHERE IT SAYS IN MY CONTRACT THAT I CAN'T SNIFF MY CO-WORKERS.
BUT SHE AGREED WITH MY HEAD OF DEPARTMENT SO I DECIDED TO TAKE IT TO THE VERY TOP...

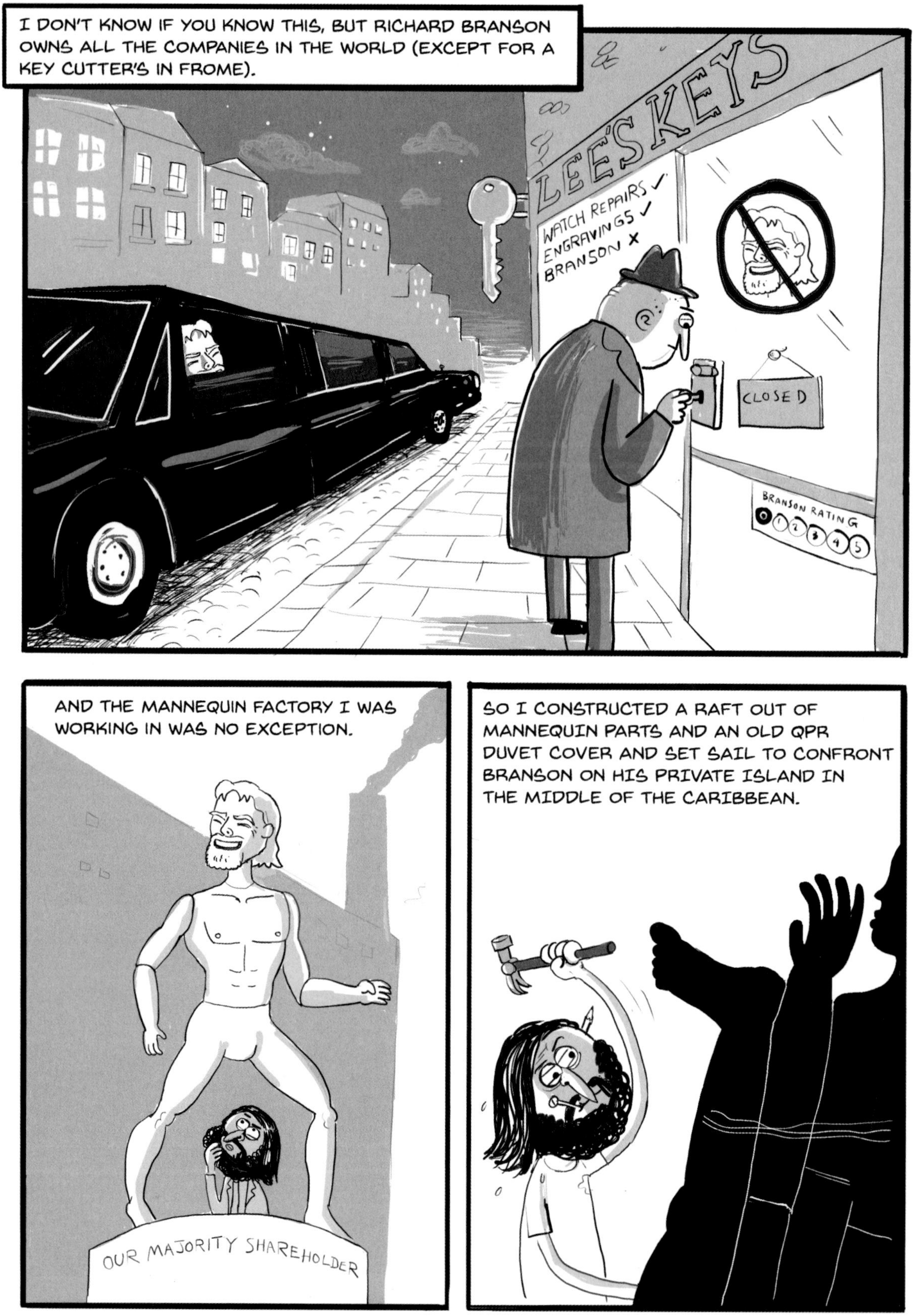
I DON'T KNOW IF YOU KNOW THIS, BUT RICHARD BRANSON OWNS ALL THE COMPANIES IN THE WORLD (EXCEPT FOR A KEY CUTTER'S IN FROME).
LEE'S KEYS
WATCH REPAIRS ✓
ENGRAVINGS ✓
BRANSON X
CLOSED
BRANSON RATING
0 1 2 3 4 5
AND THE MANNEQUIN FACTORY I WAS WORKING IN WAS NO EXCEPTION.
OUR MAJORITY SHAREHOLDER
SO I CONSTRUCTED A RAFT OUT OF MANNEQUIN PARTS AND AN OLD QPR DUVET COVER AND SET SAIL TO CONFRONT BRANSON ON HIS PRIVATE ISLAND IN THE MIDDLE OF THE CARIBBEAN.

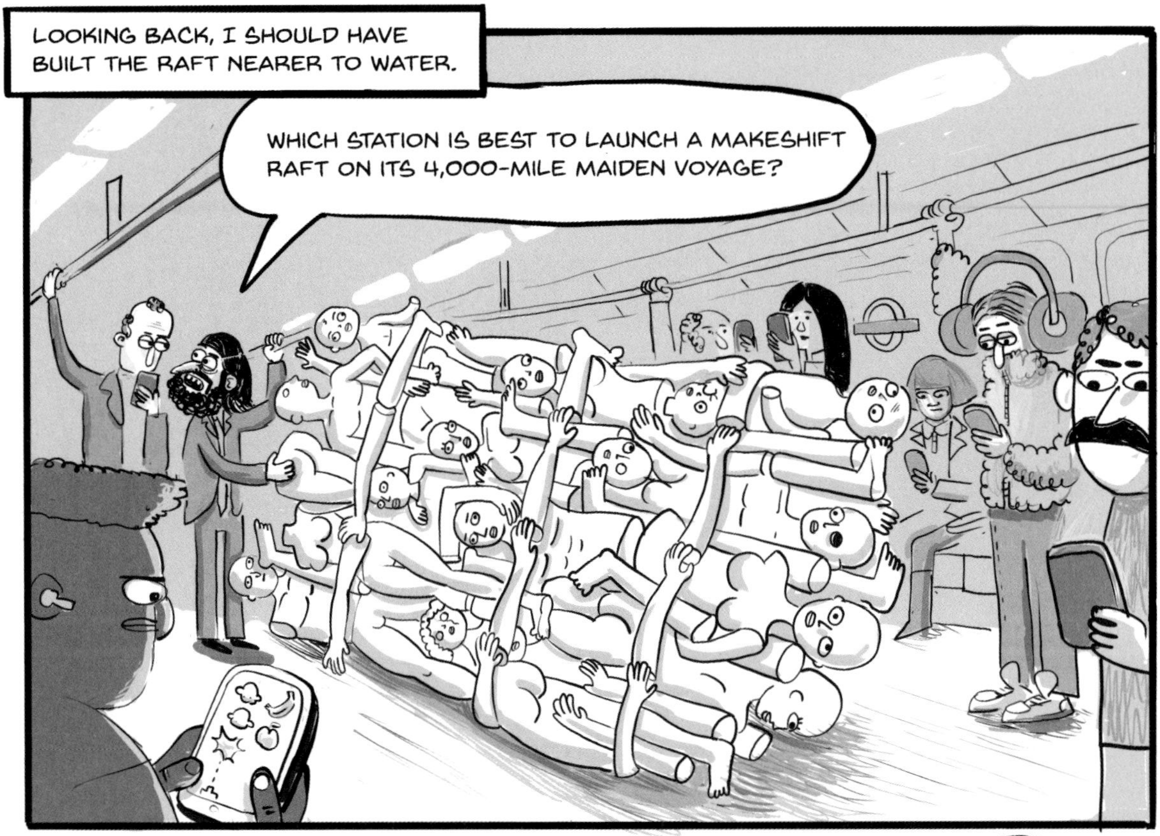
LOOKING BACK, I SHOULD HAVE BUILT THE RAFT NEARER TO WATER.
WHICH STATION IS BEST TO LAUNCH A MAKESHIFT RAFT ON ITS 4,000-MILE MAIDEN VOYAGE?

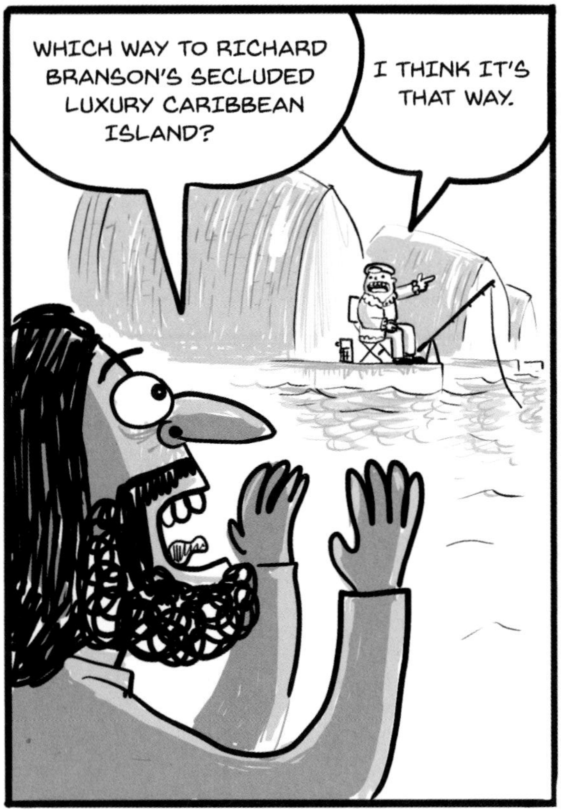
WHICH WAY TO RICHARD BRANSON'S SECLUDED LUXURY CARIBBEAN ISLAND?
I THINK IT'S THAT WAY.

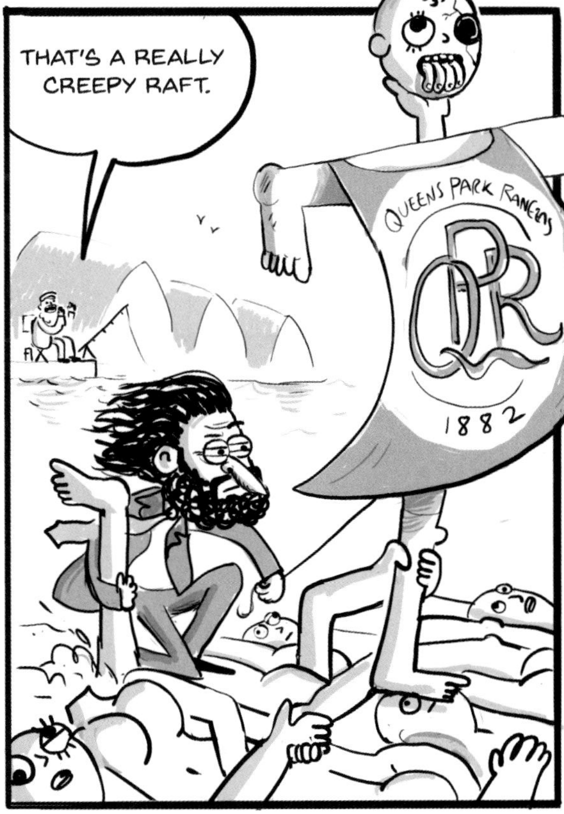
THAT'S A REALLY CREEPY RAFT.
QUEENS PARK RANGERS
QPR
1882

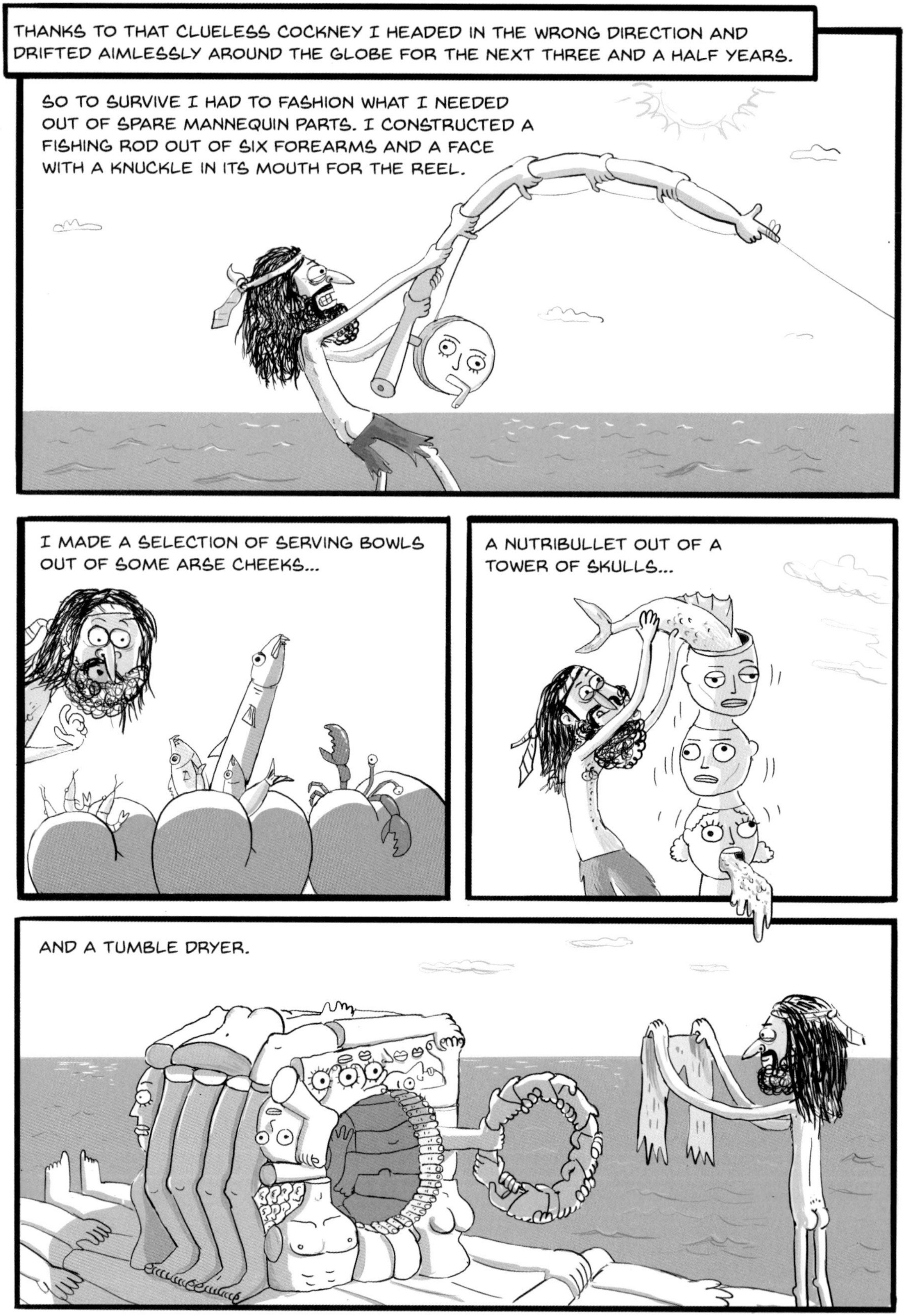
THANKS TO THAT CLUELESS COCKNEY I HEADED IN THE WRONG DIRECTION AND DRIFTED AIMLESSLY AROUND THE GLOBE FOR THE NEXT THREE AND A HALF YEARS.
SO TO SURVIVE I HAD TO FASHION WHAT I NEEDED OUT OF SPARE MANNEQUIN PARTS. I CONSTRUCTED A FISHING ROD OUT OF SIX FOREARMS AND A FACE WITH A KNUCKLE IN ITS MOUTH FOR THE REEL.
I MADE A SELECTION OF SERVING BOWLS OUT OF SOME ARSE CHEEKS...
A NUTRIBULLET OUT OF A TOWER OF SKULLS...
AND A TUMBLE DRYER.

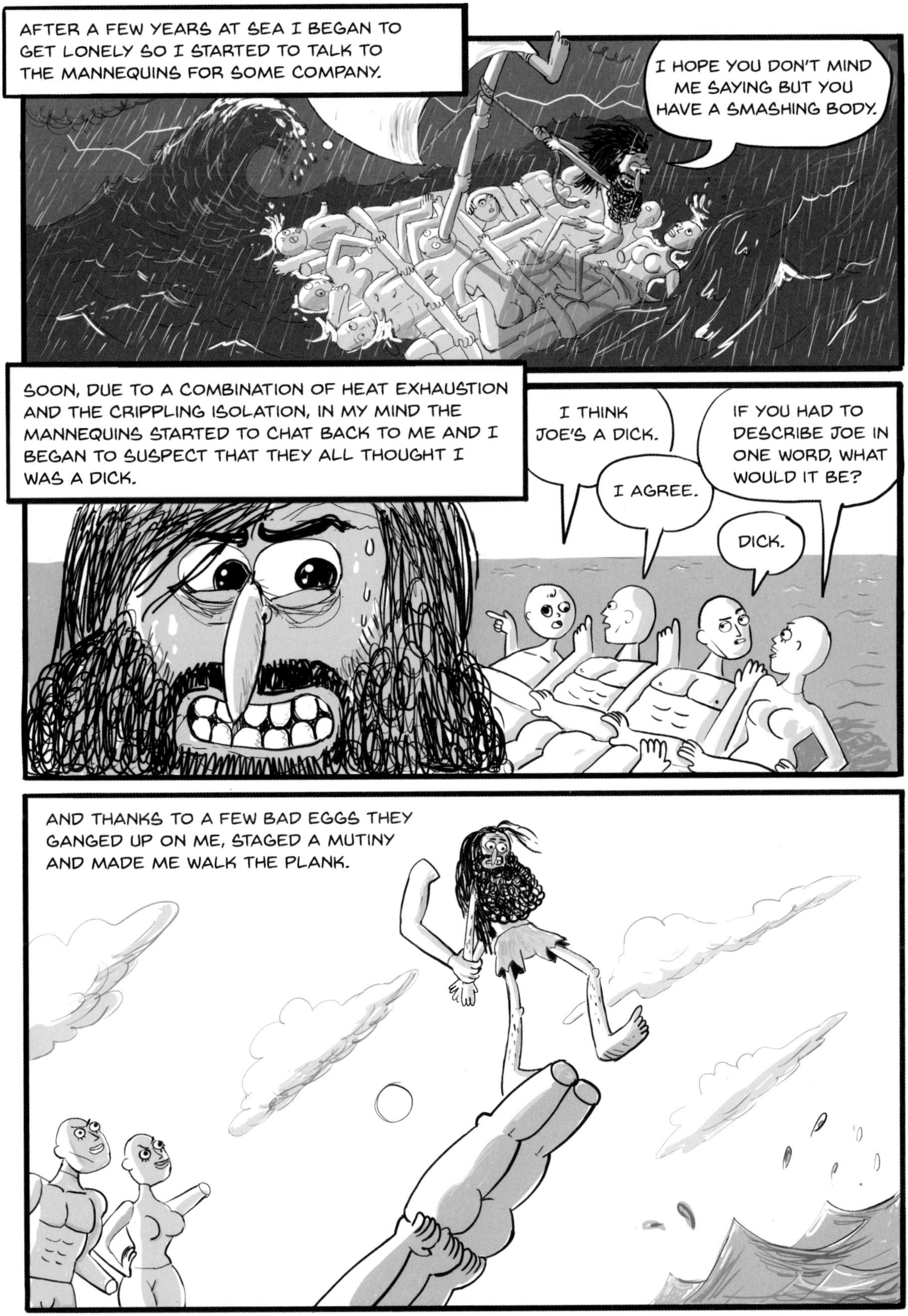
AFTER A FEW YEARS AT SEA I BEGAN TO GET LONELY SO I STARTED TO TALK TO THE MANNEQUINS FOR SOME COMPANY.
I HOPE YOU DON'T MIND ME SAYING BUT YOU HAVE A SMASHING BODY.
SOON, DUE TO A COMBINATION OF HEAT EXHAUSTION AND THE CRIPPLING ISOLATION, IN MY MIND THE MANNEQUINS STARTED TO CHAT BACK TO ME AND I BEGAN TO SUSPECT THAT THEY ALL THOUGHT I WAS A DICK.
I THINK JOE'S A DICK.
I AGREE.
IF YOU HAD TO DESCRIBE JOE IN ONE WORD, WHAT WOULD IT BE?
DICK.
AND THANKS TO A FEW BAD EGGS THEY GANGED UP ON ME, STAGED A MUTINY AND MADE ME WALK THE PLANK.

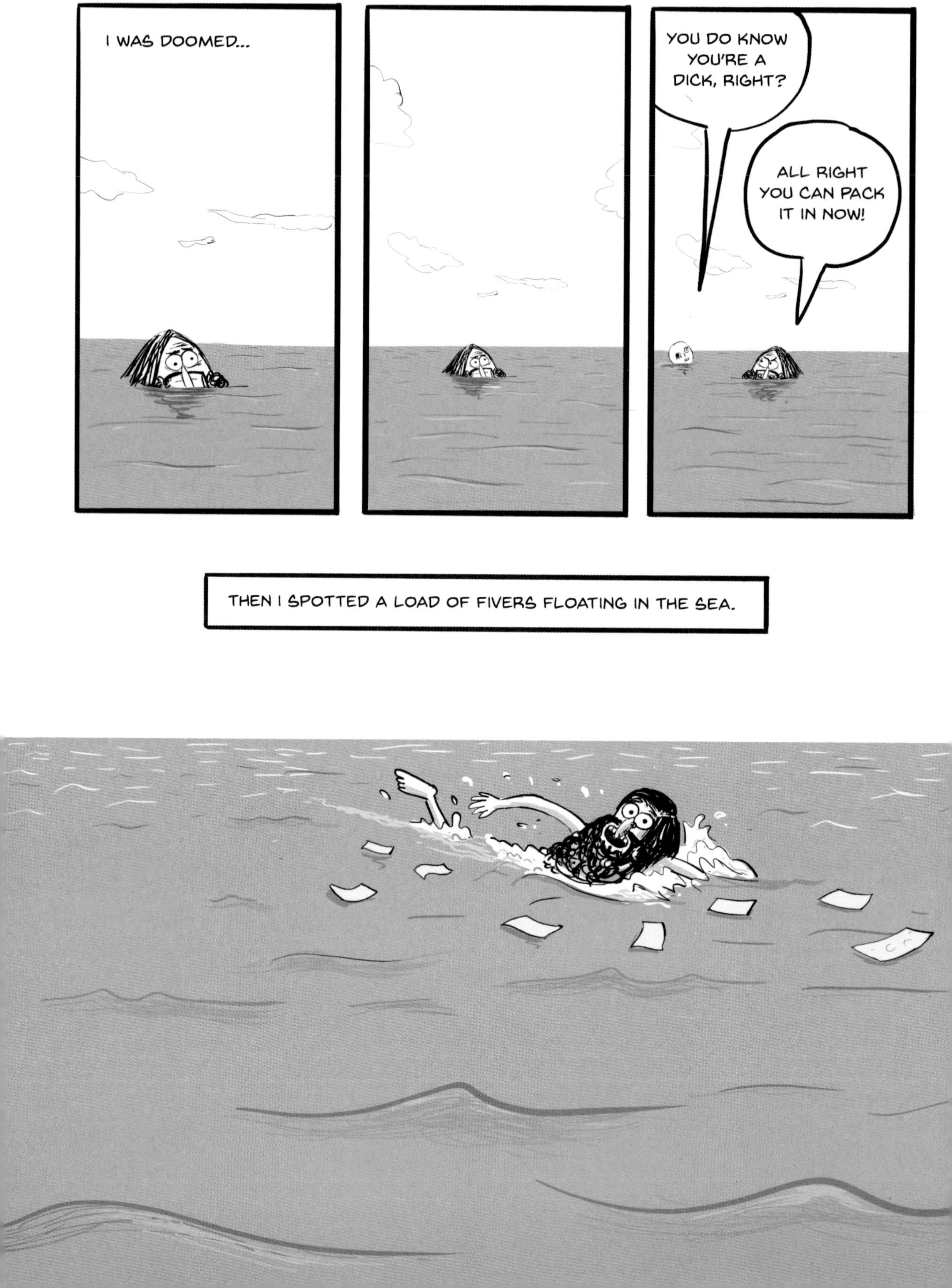
I WAS DOOMED...
YOU DO KNOW YOU'RE A DICK, RIGHT?
ALL RIGHT YOU CAN PACK IT IN NOW!
THEN I SPOTTED A LOAD OF FIVERS FLOATING IN THE SEA.

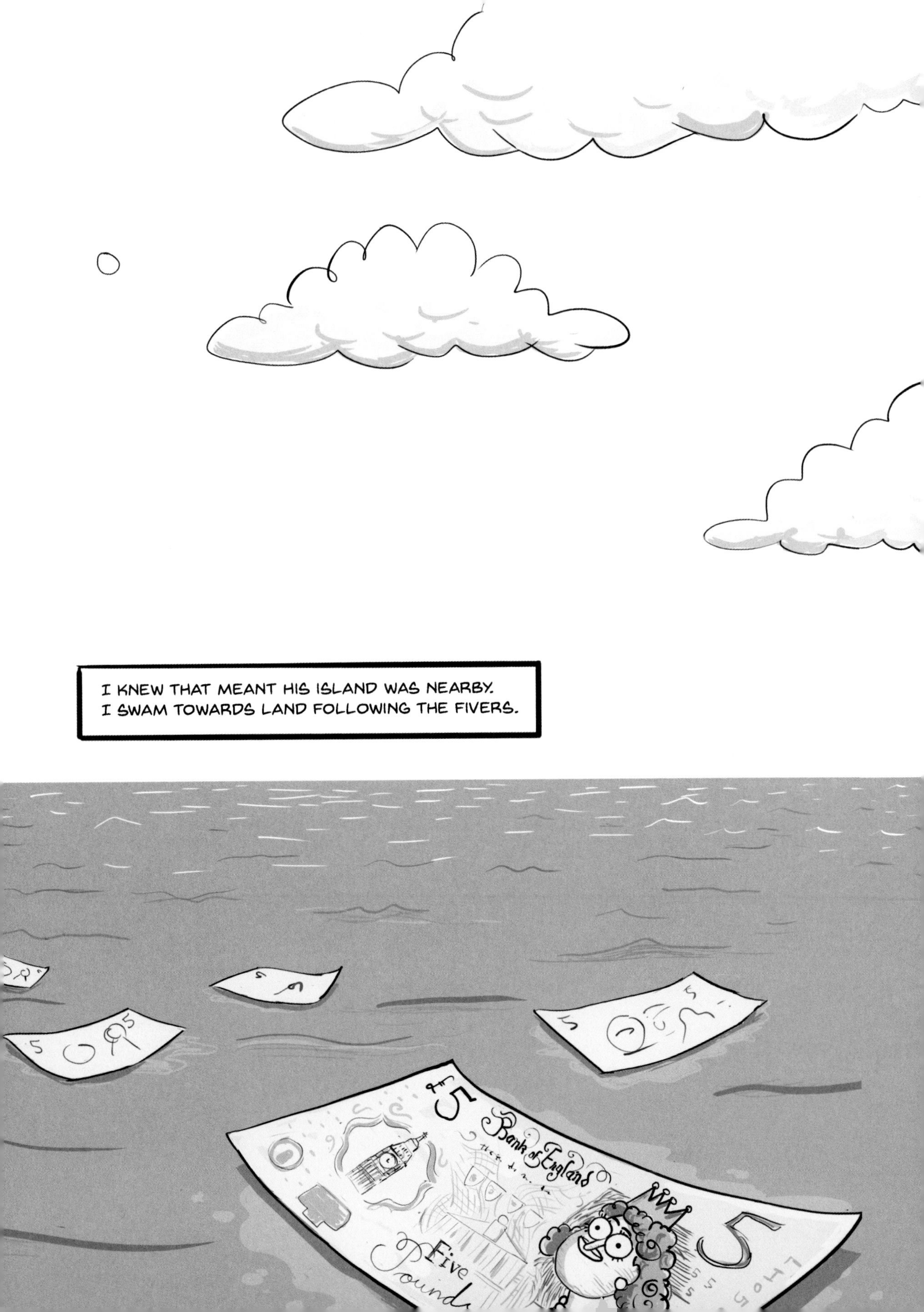
I KNEW THAT MEANT HIS ISLAND WAS NEARBY.
I SWAM TOWARDS LAND FOLLOWING THE FIVERS.
£5
Bank of England
Five

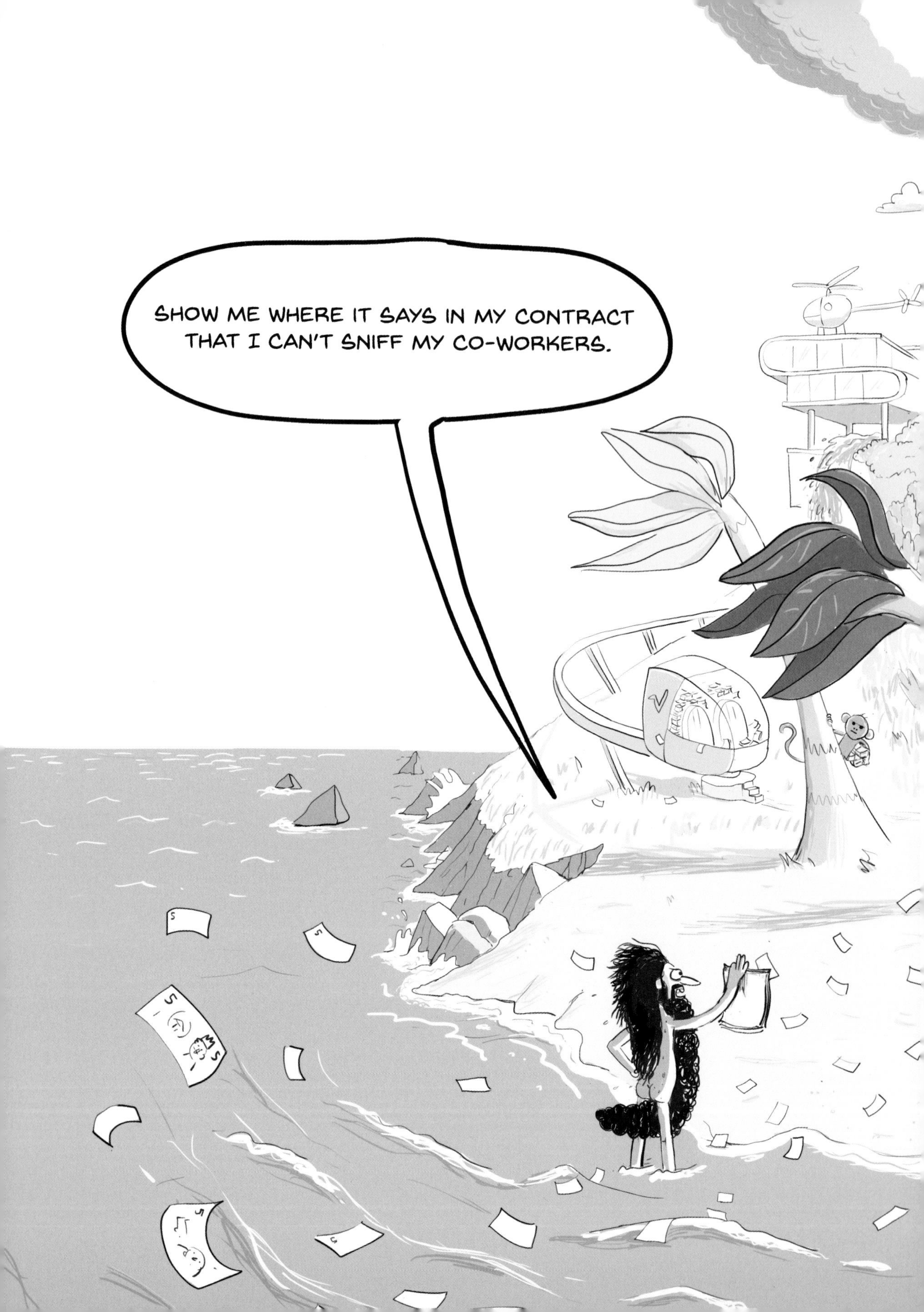
SHOW ME WHERE IT SAYS IN MY CONTRACT THAT I CAN'T SNIFF MY CO-WORKERS.

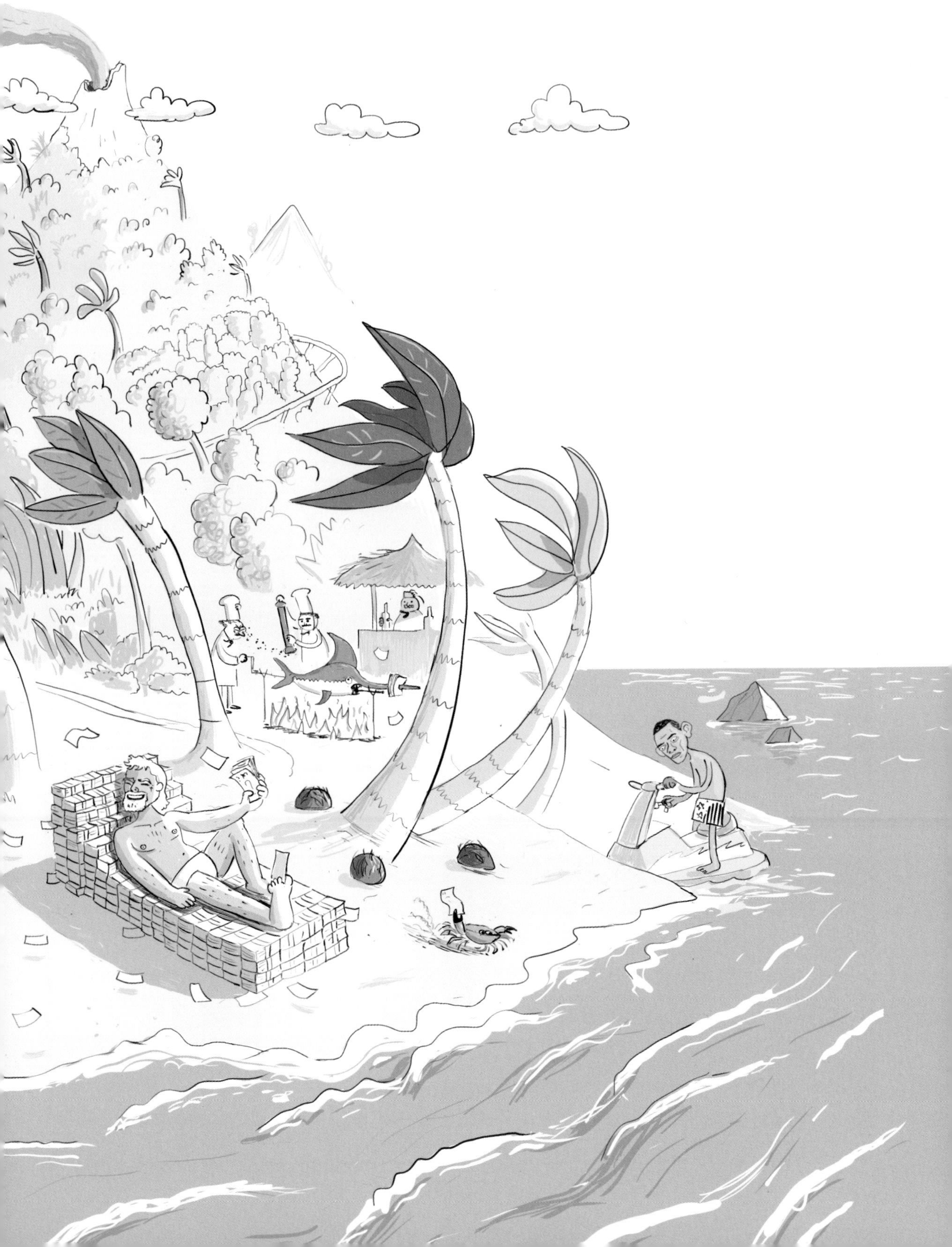

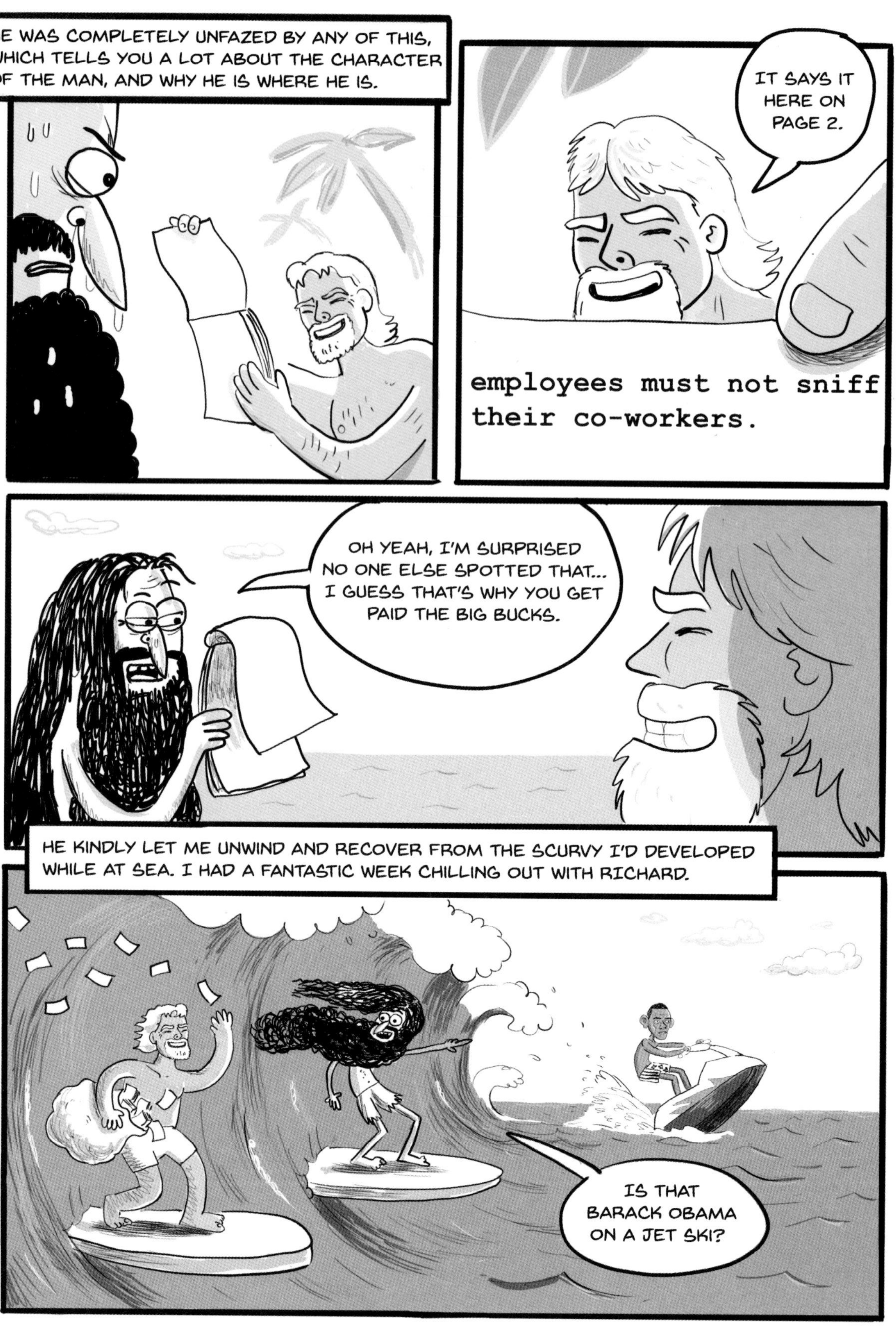

HE WAS COMPLETELY UNFAZED BY ANY OF THIS, WHICH TELLS YOU A LOT ABOUT THE CHARACTER OF THE MAN, AND WHY HE IS WHERE HE IS.
IT SAYS IT HERE ON PAGE 2.
employees must not sniff their co-workers.
OH YEAH, I'M SURPRISED NO ONE ELSE SPOTTED THAT... I GUESS THAT'S WHY YOU GET PAID THE BIG BUCKS.
HE KINDLY LET ME UNWIND AND RECOVER FROM THE SCURVY I'D DEVELOPED WHILE AT SEA. I HAD A FANTASTIC WEEK CHILLING OUT WITH RICHARD.
IS THAT BARACK OBAMA ON A JET SKI?

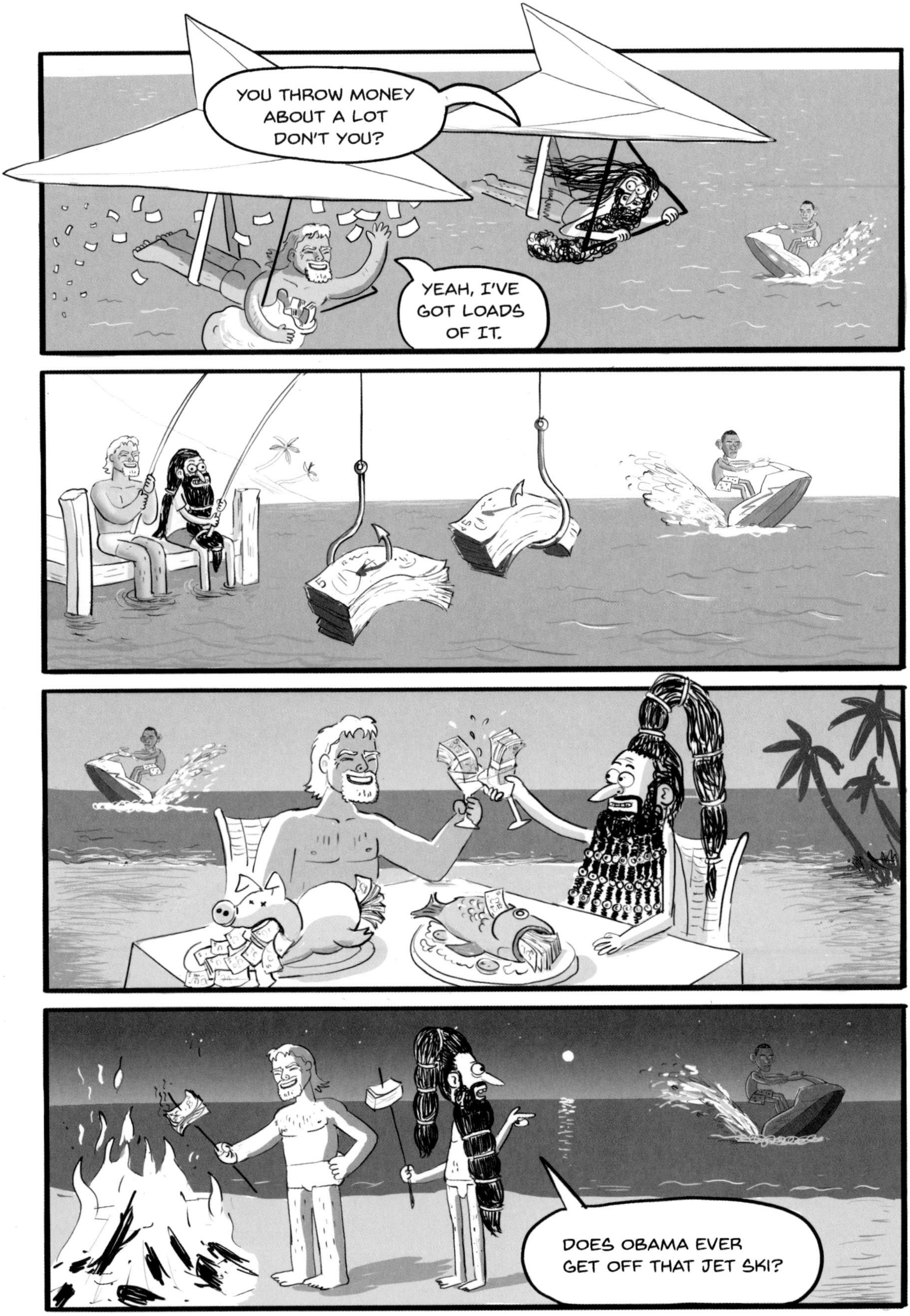
YOU THROW MONEY ABOUT A LOT DON'T YOU?
YEAH, I'VE GOT LOADS OF IT.
DOES OBAMA EVER GET OFF THAT JET SKI?

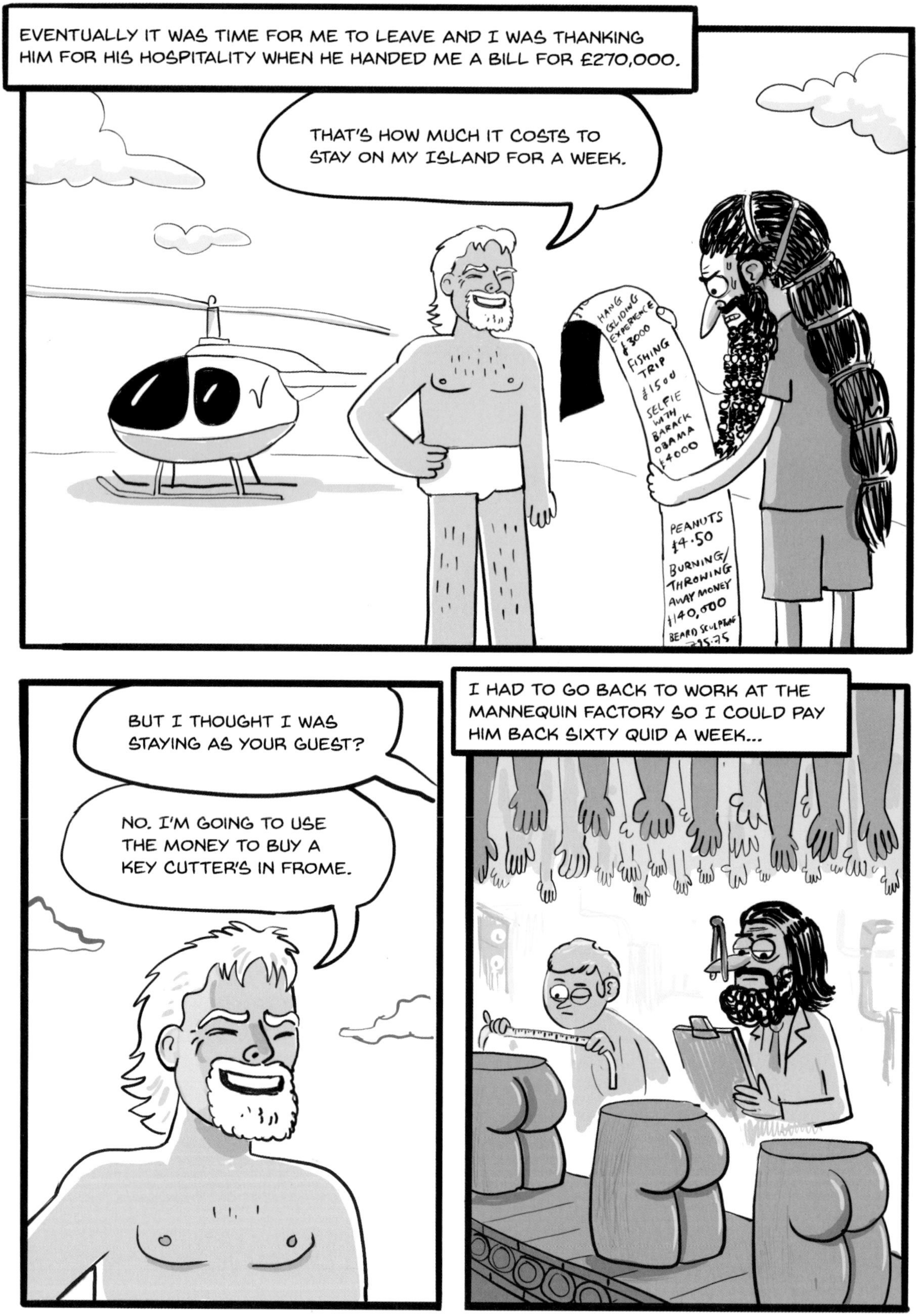
EVENTUALLY IT WAS TIME FOR ME TO LEAVE AND I WAS THANKING HIM FOR HIS HOSPITALITY WHEN HE HANDED ME A BILL FOR £270,000.
THAT'S HOW MUCH IT COSTS TO STAY ON MY ISLAND FOR A WEEK.
HANG GLIDING EXPERIENCE £3000
FISHING TRIP £1500
SELFIE WITH BARACK OBAMA £4000
PEANUTS £4.50
BURNING/THROWING AWAY MONEY £140,000
BEARD SCULPTING
BUT I THOUGHT I WAS STAYING AS YOUR GUEST?
NO. I'M GOING TO USE THE MONEY TO BUY A KEY CUTTER'S IN FROME.
I HAD TO GO BACK TO WORK AT THE MANNEQUIN FACTORY SO I COULD PAY HIM BACK SIXTY QUID A WEEK...

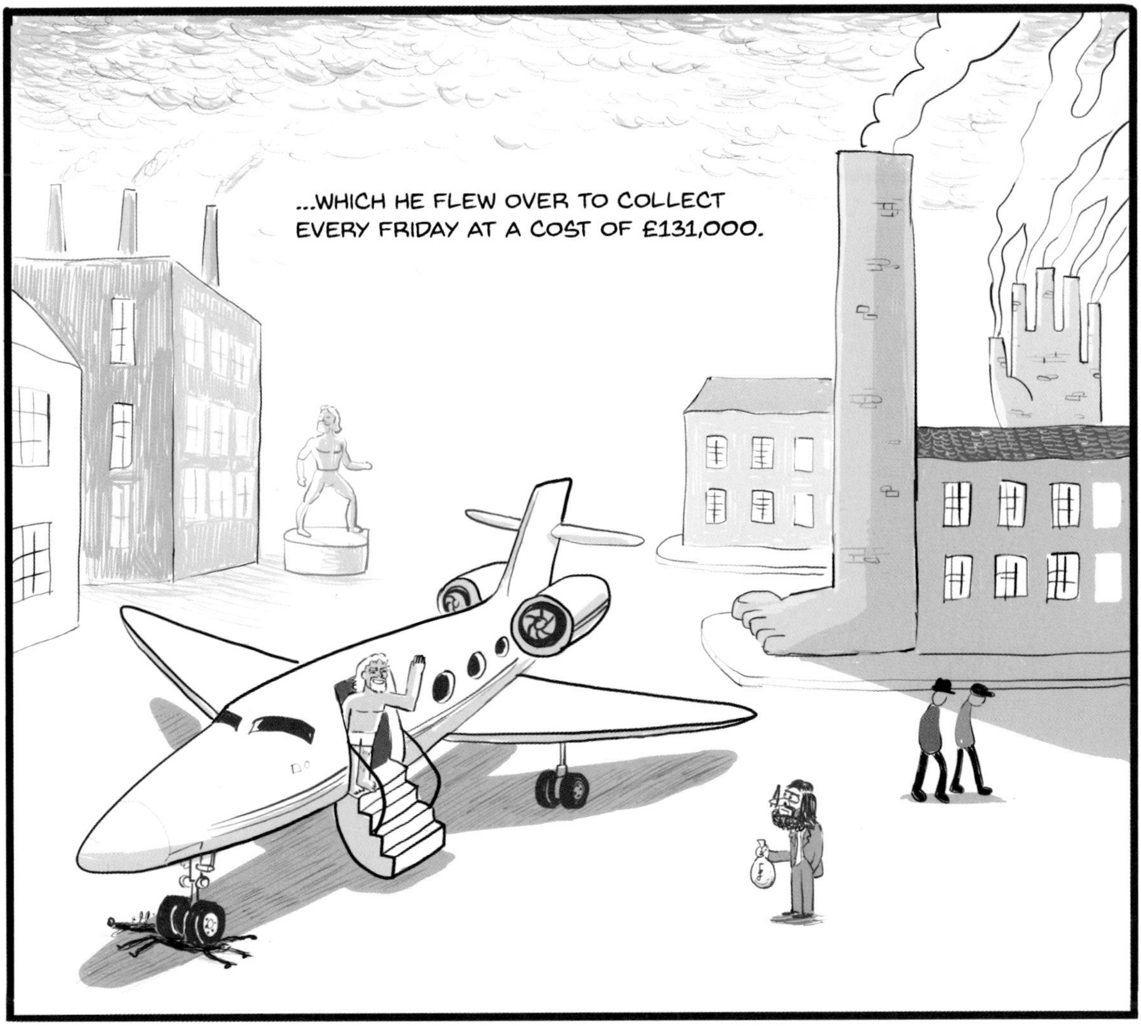
...WHICH HE FLEW OVER TO COLLECT
EVERY FRIDAY AT A COST OF £131,000.

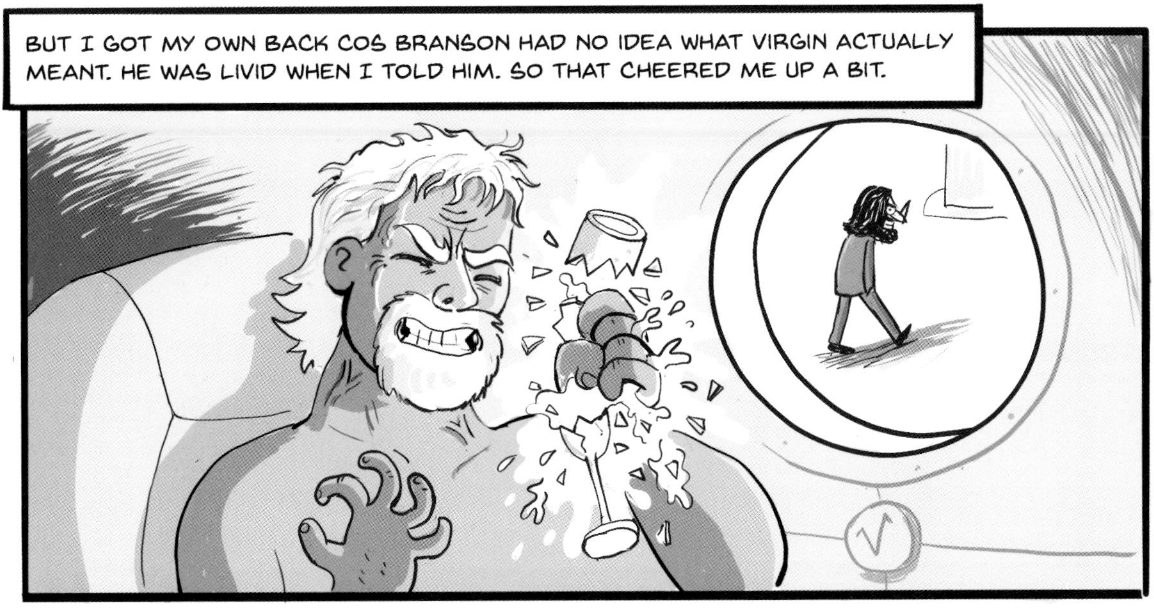
BUT I GOT MY OWN BACK COS BRANSON HAD NO IDEA WHAT VIRGIN ACTUALLY MEANT. HE WAS LIVID WHEN I TOLD HIM. SO THAT CHEERED ME UP A BIT.

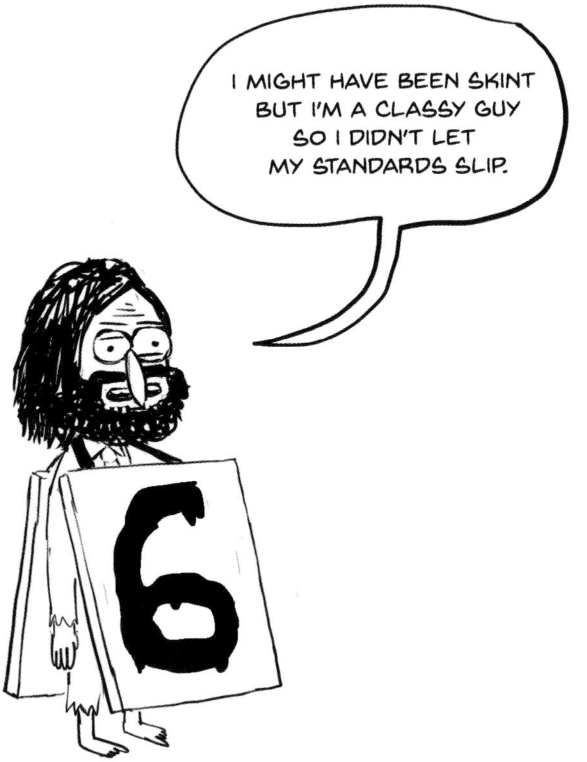
I MIGHT HAVE BEEN SKINT BUT I'M A CLASSY GUY SO I DIDN'T LET MY STANDARDS SLIP.
6

HARD TIMES

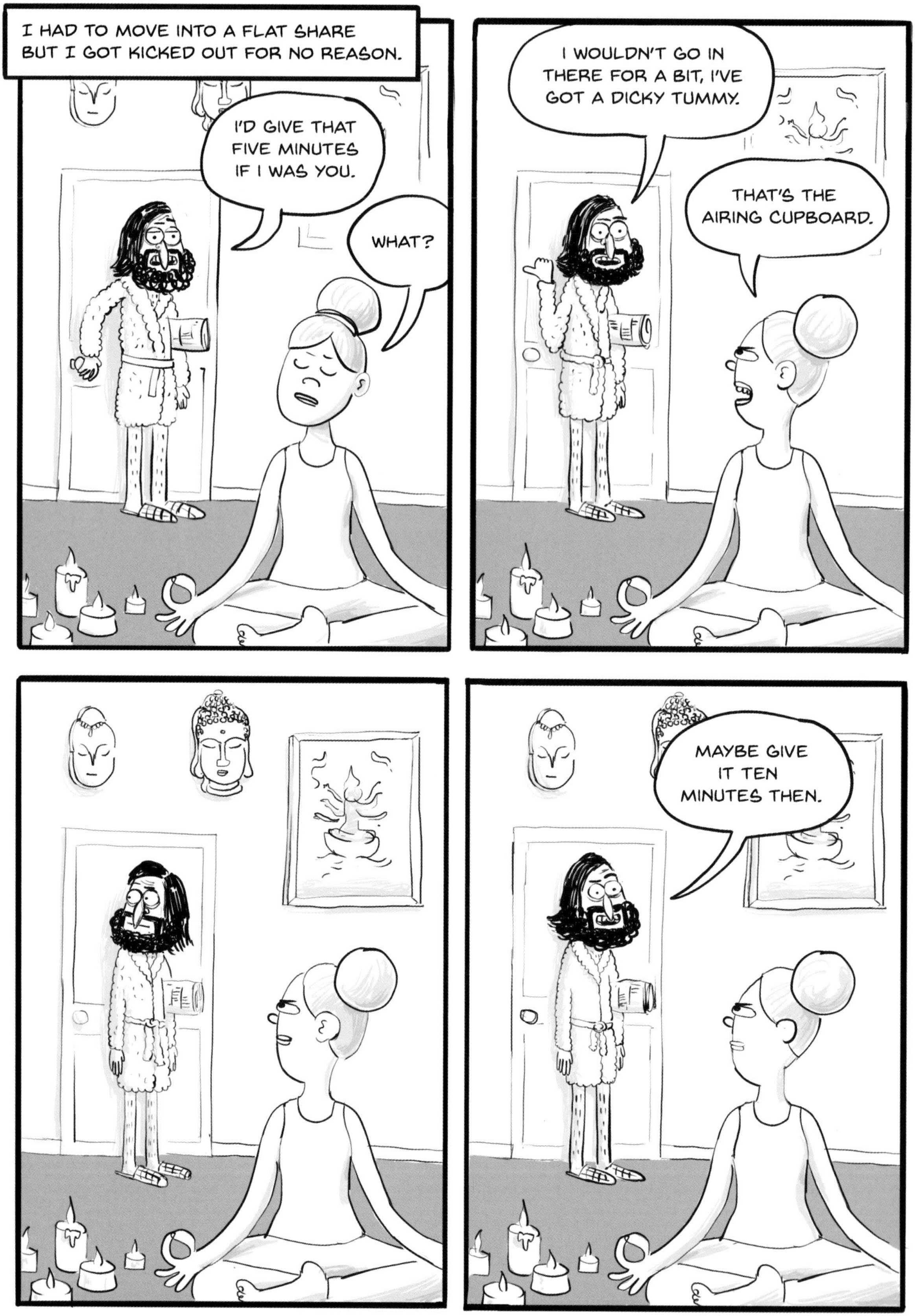
I HAD TO MOVE INTO A FLAT SHARE BUT I GOT KICKED OUT FOR NO REASON.
I'D GIVE THAT FIVE MINUTES IF I WAS YOU.
WHAT?
I WOULDN'T GO IN THERE FOR A BIT, I'VE GOT A DICKY TUMMY.
THAT'S THE AIRING CUPBOARD.
MAYBE GIVE IT TEN MINUTES THEN.

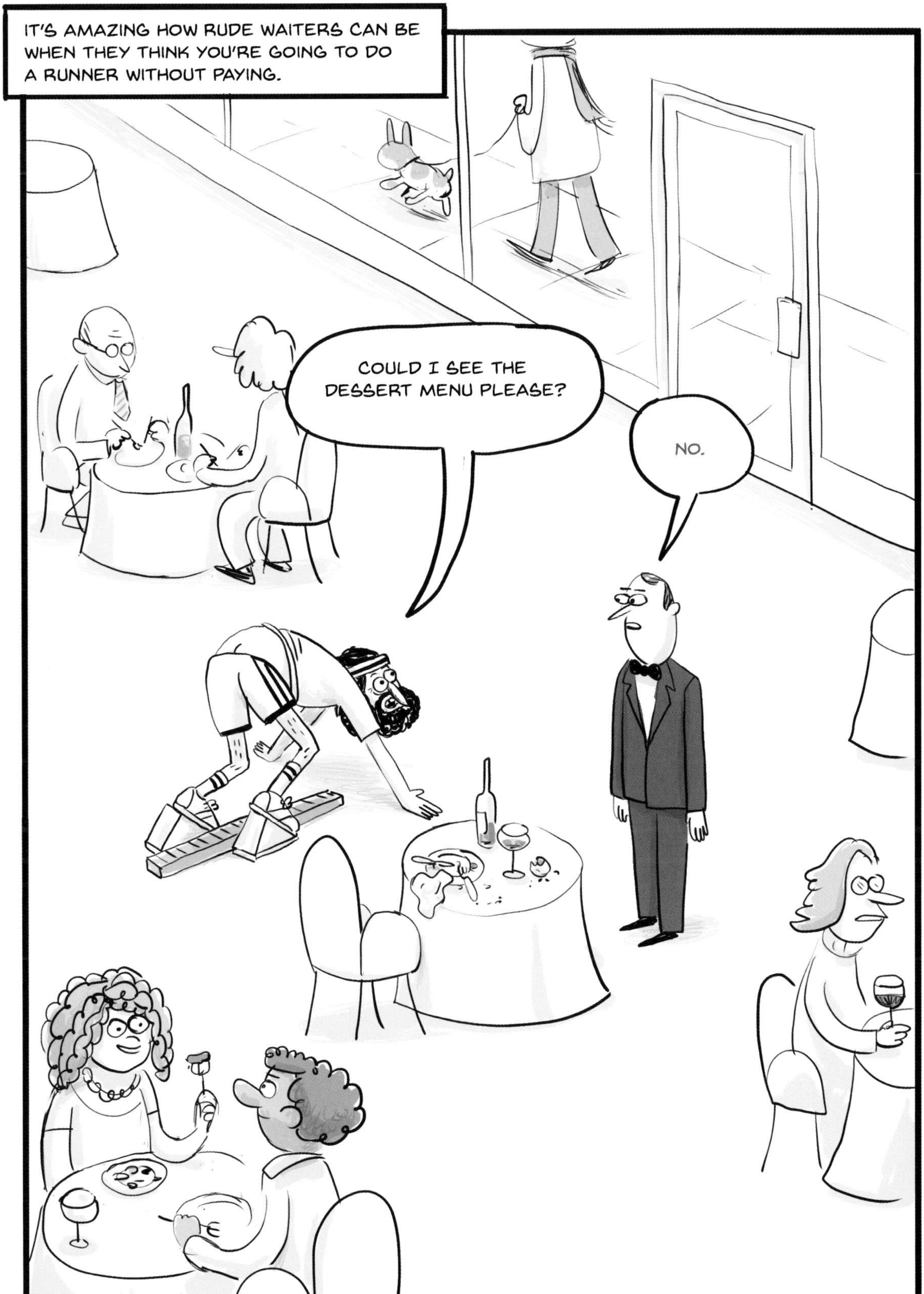
IT'S AMAZING HOW RUDE WAITERS CAN BE WHEN THEY THINK YOU'RE GOING TO DO A RUNNER WITHOUT PAYING.
COULD I SEE THE DESSERT MENU PLEASE?
NO.

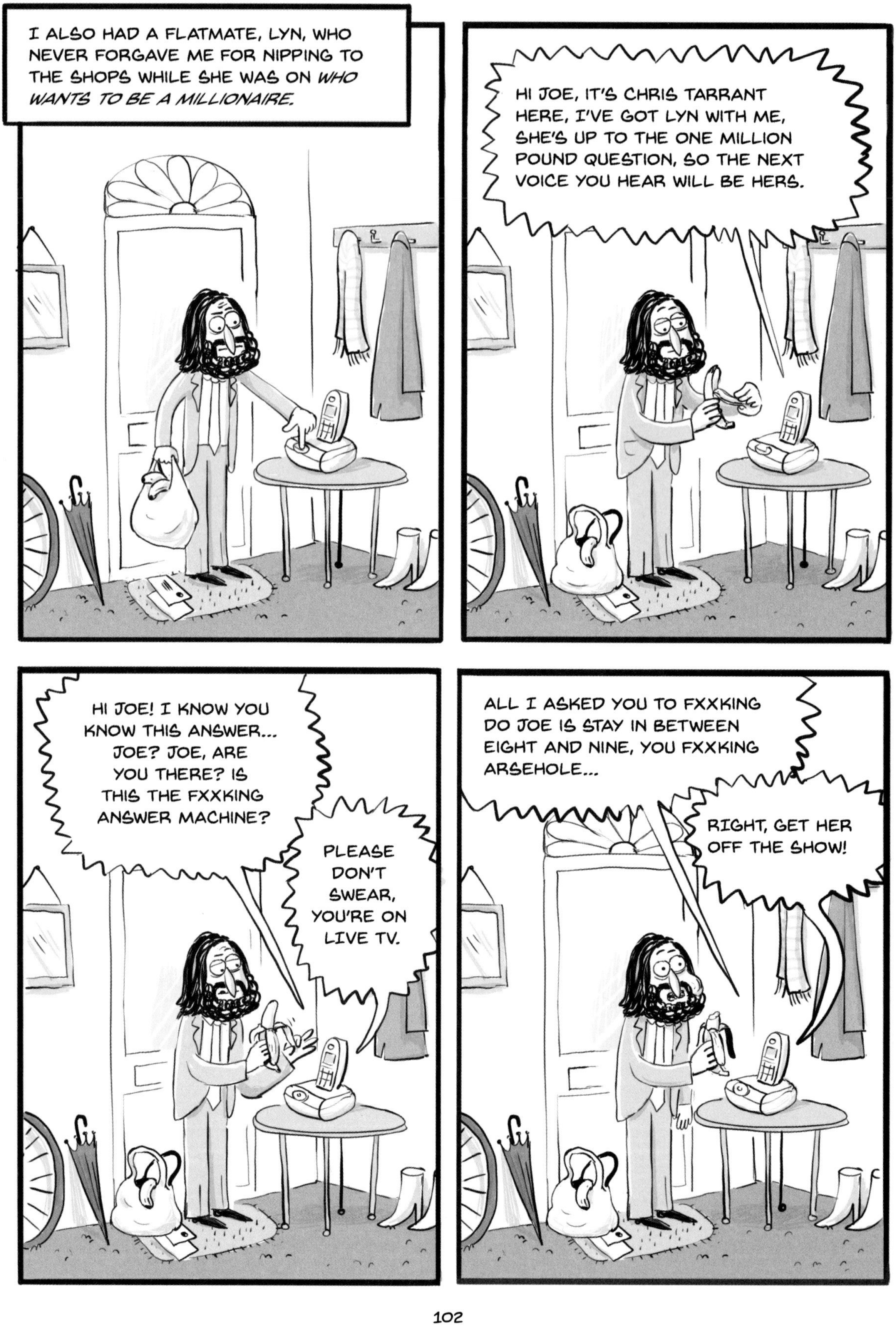
I ALSO HAD A FLATMATE, LYN, WHO NEVER FORGAVE ME FOR NIPPING TO THE SHOPS WHILE SHE WAS ON *WHO WANTS TO BE A MILLIONAIRE.*
HI JOE, IT'S CHRIS TARRANT HERE, I'VE GOT LYN WITH ME, SHE'S UP TO THE ONE MILLION POUND QUESTION, SO THE NEXT VOICE YOU HEAR WILL BE HERS.
HI JOE! I KNOW YOU KNOW THIS ANSWER... JOE? JOE, ARE YOU THERE? IS THIS THE FXXKING ANSWER MACHINE?
PLEASE DON'T SWEAR, YOU'RE ON LIVE TV.
ALL I ASKED YOU TO FXXKING DO JOE IS STAY IN BETWEEN EIGHT AND NINE, YOU FXXKING ARSEHOLE...
RIGHT, GET HER OFF THE SHOW!

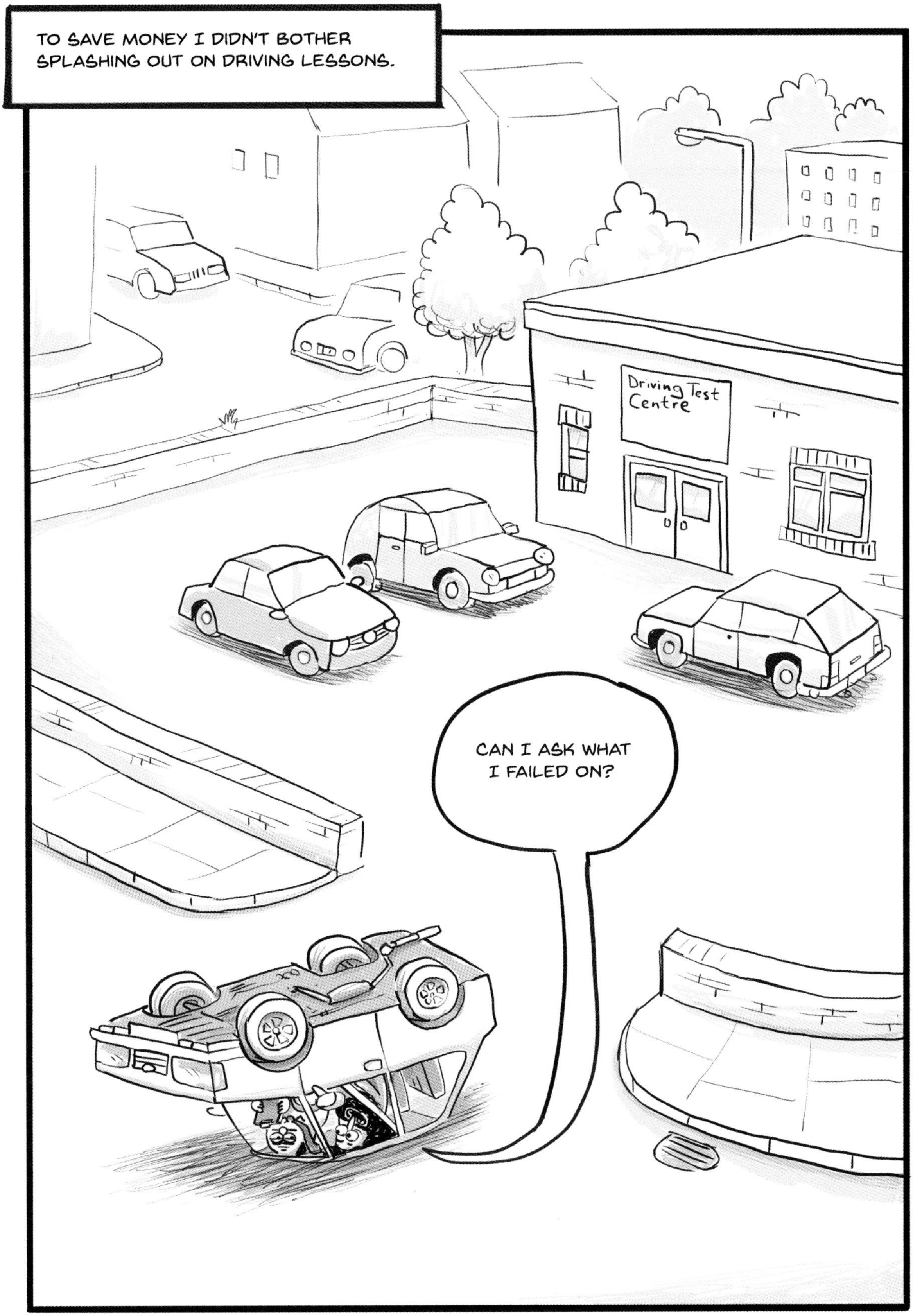
TO SAVE MONEY I DIDN'T BOTHER SPLASHING OUT ON DRIVING LESSONS.
Driving Test Centre
CAN I ASK WHAT I FAILED ON?

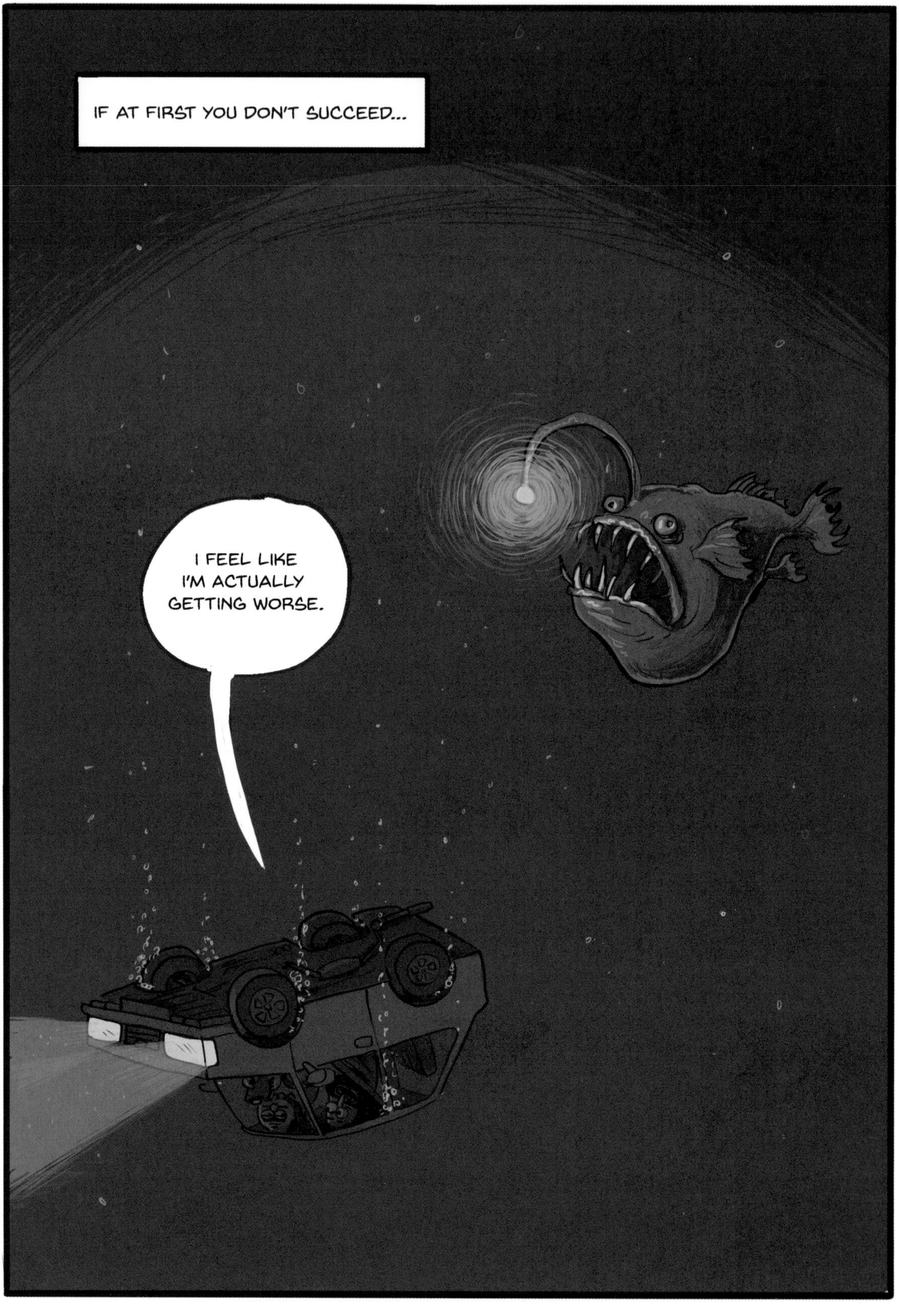
IF AT FIRST YOU DON'T SUCCEED...
I FEEL LIKE I'M ACTUALLY GETTING WORSE.

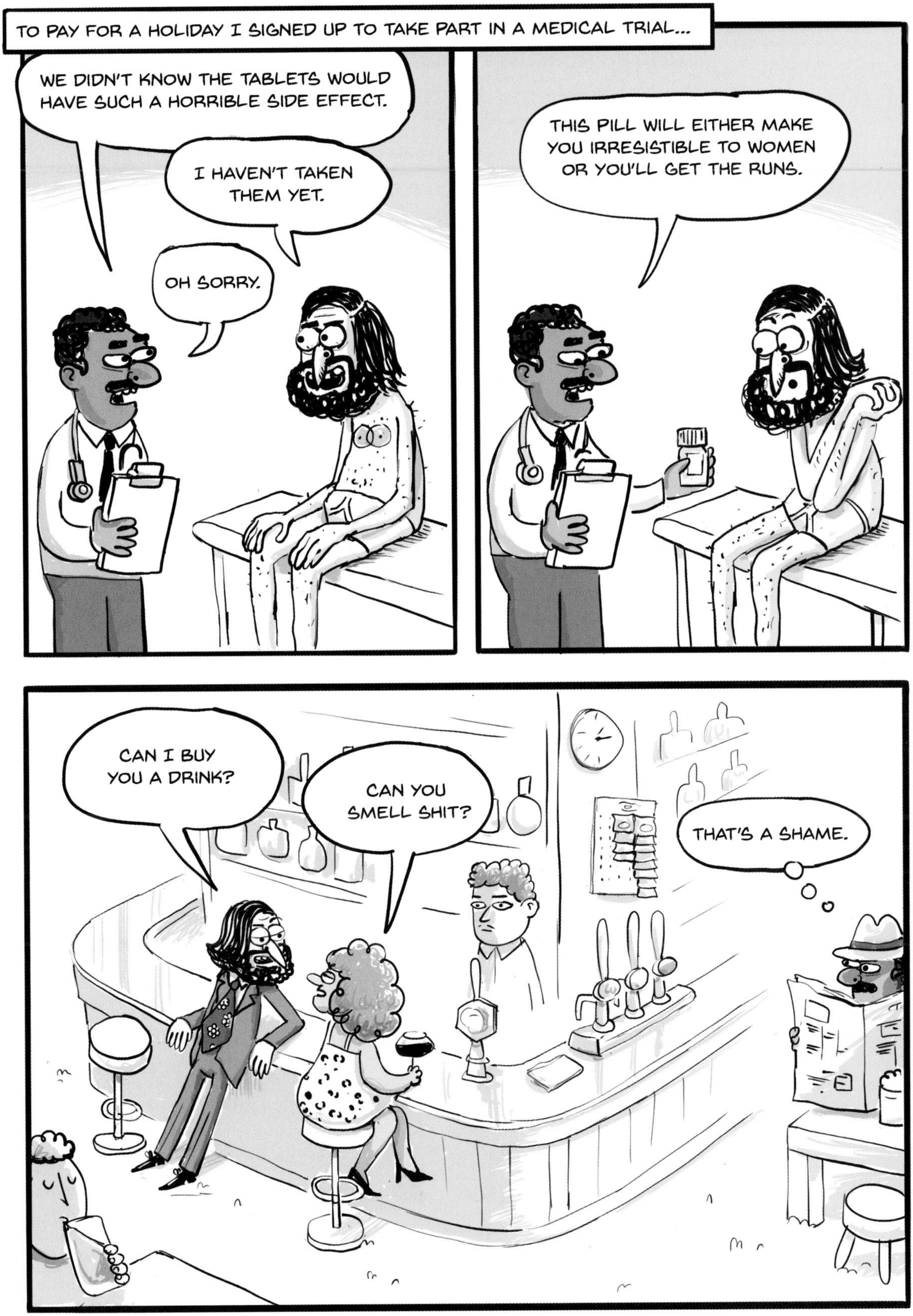
TO PAY FOR A HOLIDAY I SIGNED UP TO TAKE PART IN A MEDICAL TRIAL...
WE DIDN'T KNOW THE TABLETS WOULD HAVE SUCH A HORRIBLE SIDE EFFECT.
I HAVEN'T TAKEN THEM YET.
OH SORRY.
THIS PILL WILL EITHER MAKE YOU IRRESISTIBLE TO WOMEN OR YOU'LL GET THE RUNS.
CAN I BUY YOU A DRINK?
CAN YOU SMELL SHIT?
THAT'S A SHAME.

ANOTHER SIDE EFFECT OF THE MEDICAL TRIALS WAS THAT I WAS INVISIBLE FOR THE FOLLOWING FORTNIGHT, WHICH RUINED MY HOLIDAY SNAPS.

HERE'S ONE OF ME LOUNGING BY THE POOL.

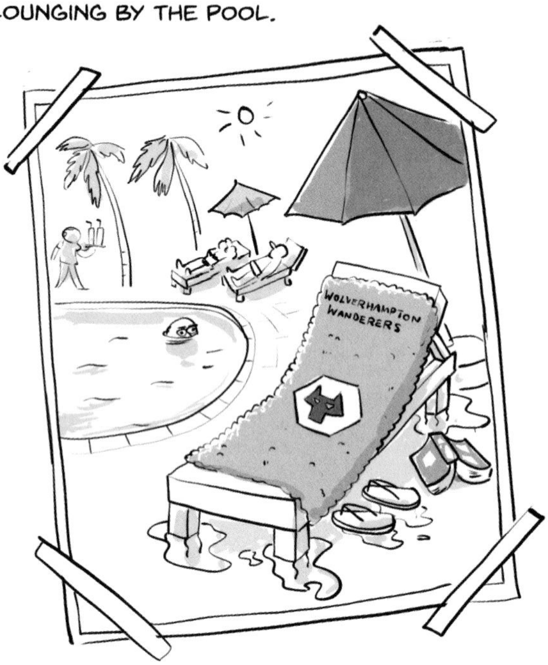
WOLVERHAMPTON WANDERERS

HERE'S ME DRINKING A SPARKLY COCKTAIL.

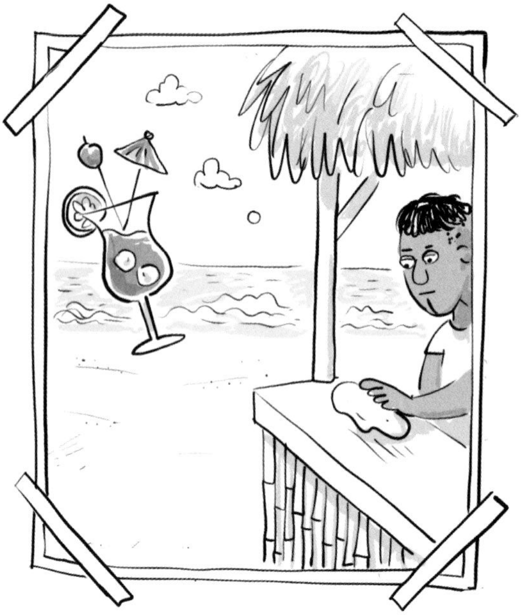

HERE'S ME WITH MY ARM ROUND THE WAITER, RAUL.

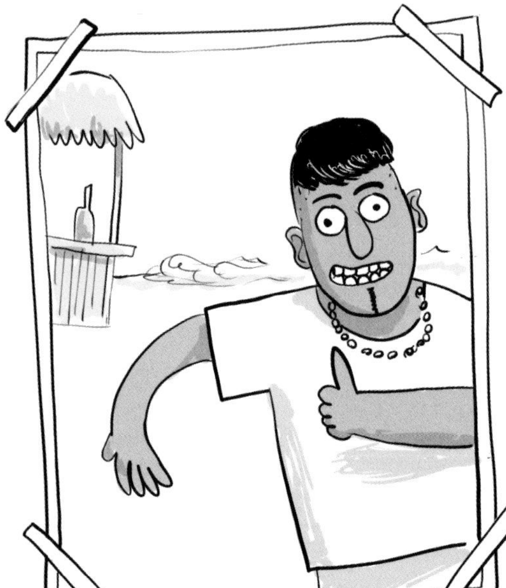

HERE'S ME FEEDING A HORSE.

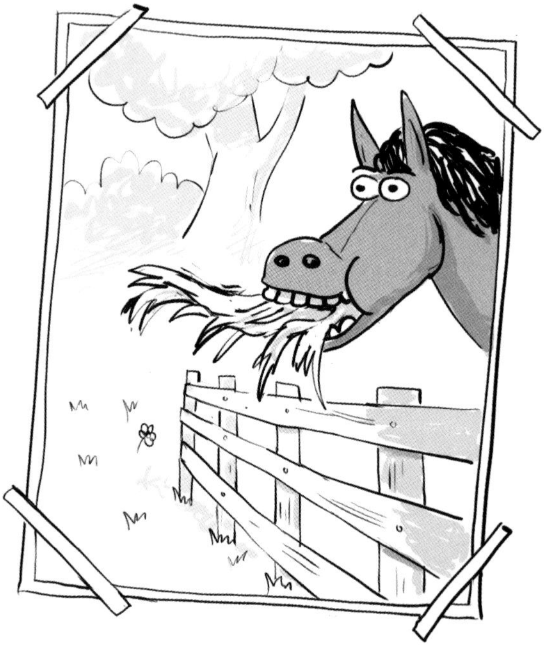

HERE'S ME WITH MY HEAD THROUGH
ONE OF THOSE FUNNY THINGS.

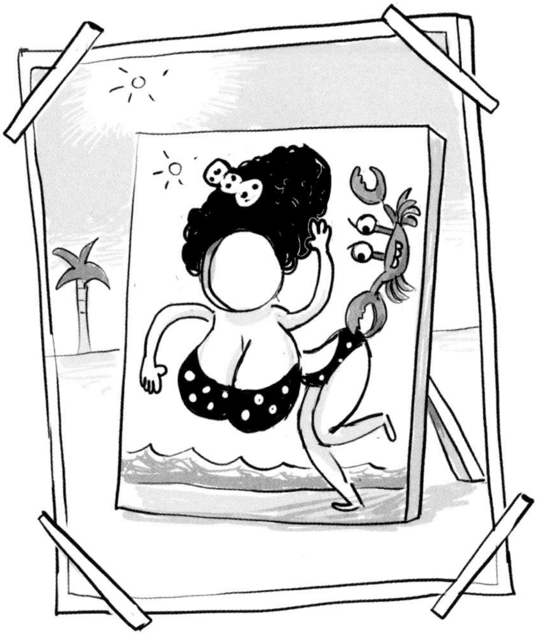

HERE'S ME DOING A POSE SO
IT LOOKS LIKE I'M HOLDING UP THE
LEANING TOWER OF PISA.

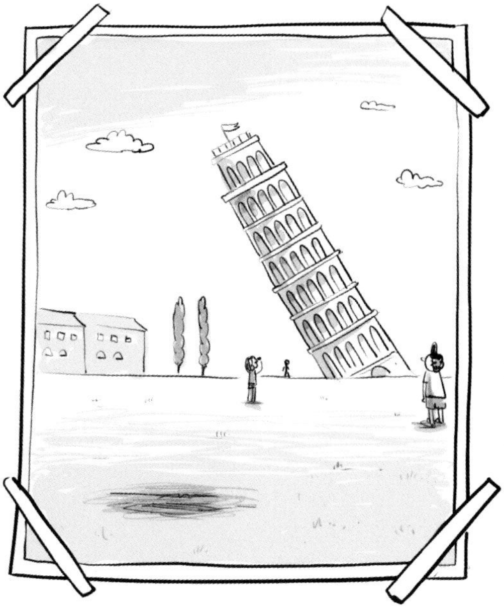

HERE'S THE MOMENT A
SEAGULL LANDED ON MY HEAD.

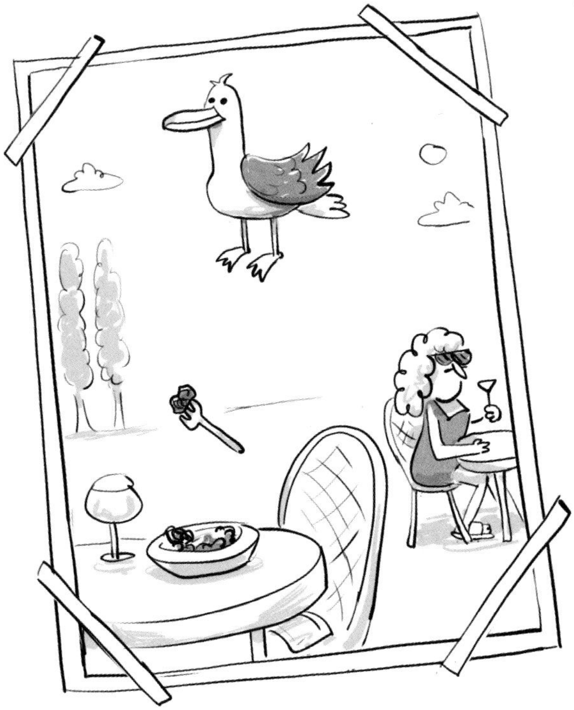

HERE'S ONE I ACCIDENTALLY TOOK
OF MYSELF SITTING ON THE TOILET.

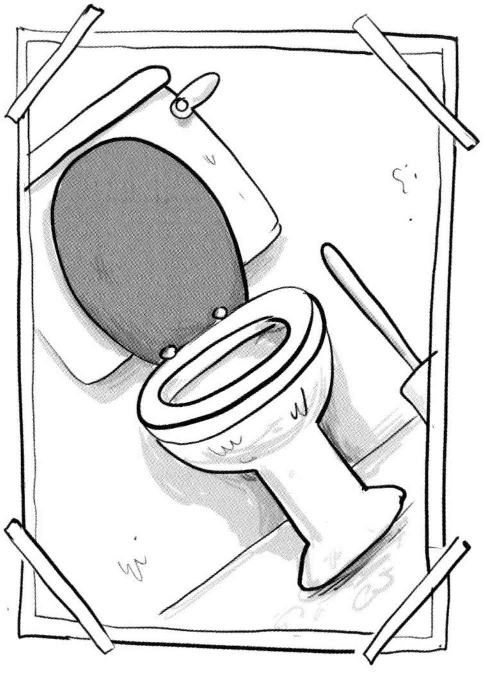

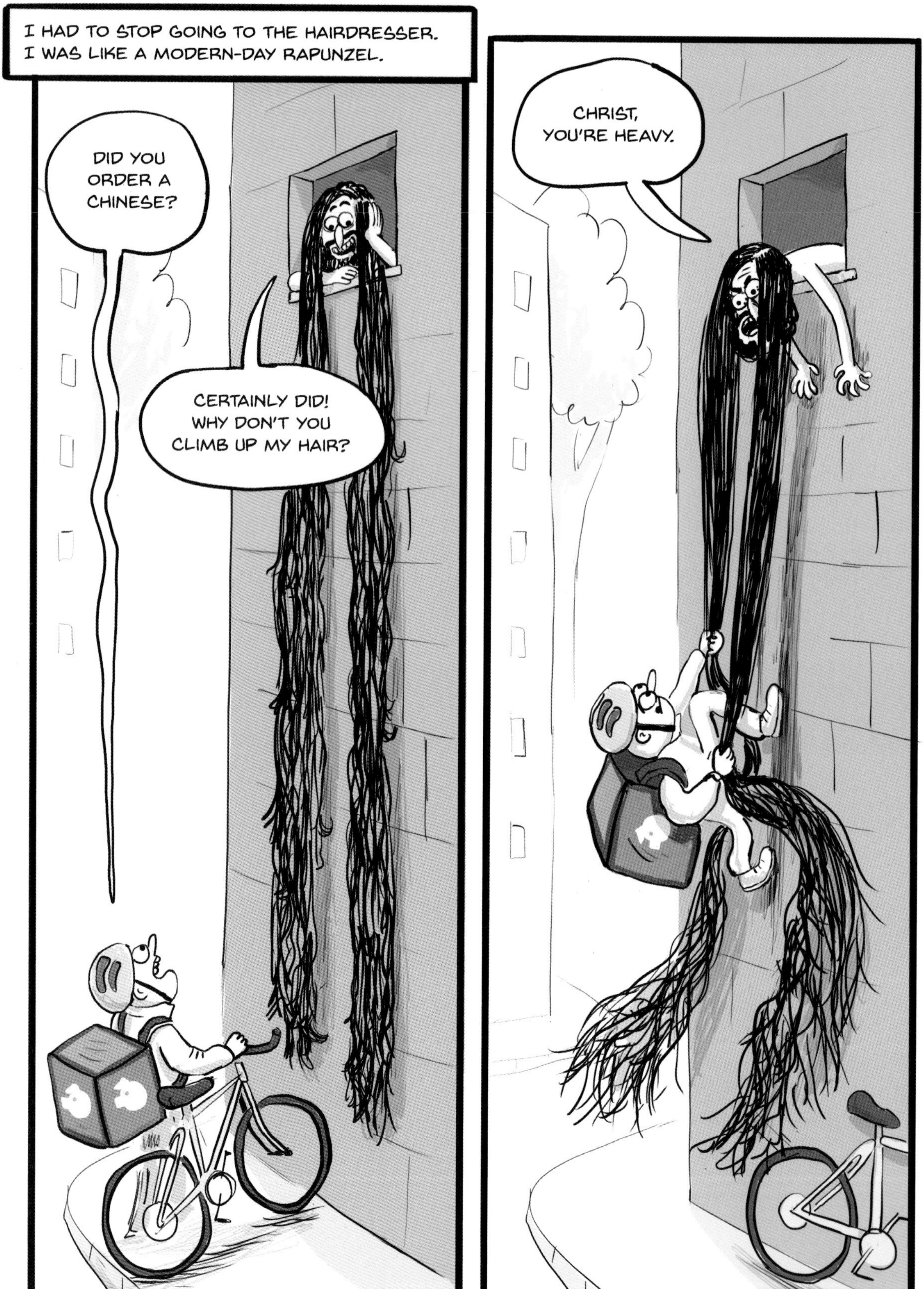
I HAD TO STOP GOING TO THE HAIRDRESSER. I WAS LIKE A MODERN-DAY RAPUNZEL.
DID YOU ORDER A CHINESE?
CERTAINLY DID! WHY DON'T YOU CLIMB UP MY HAIR?
CHRIST, YOU'RE HEAVY.

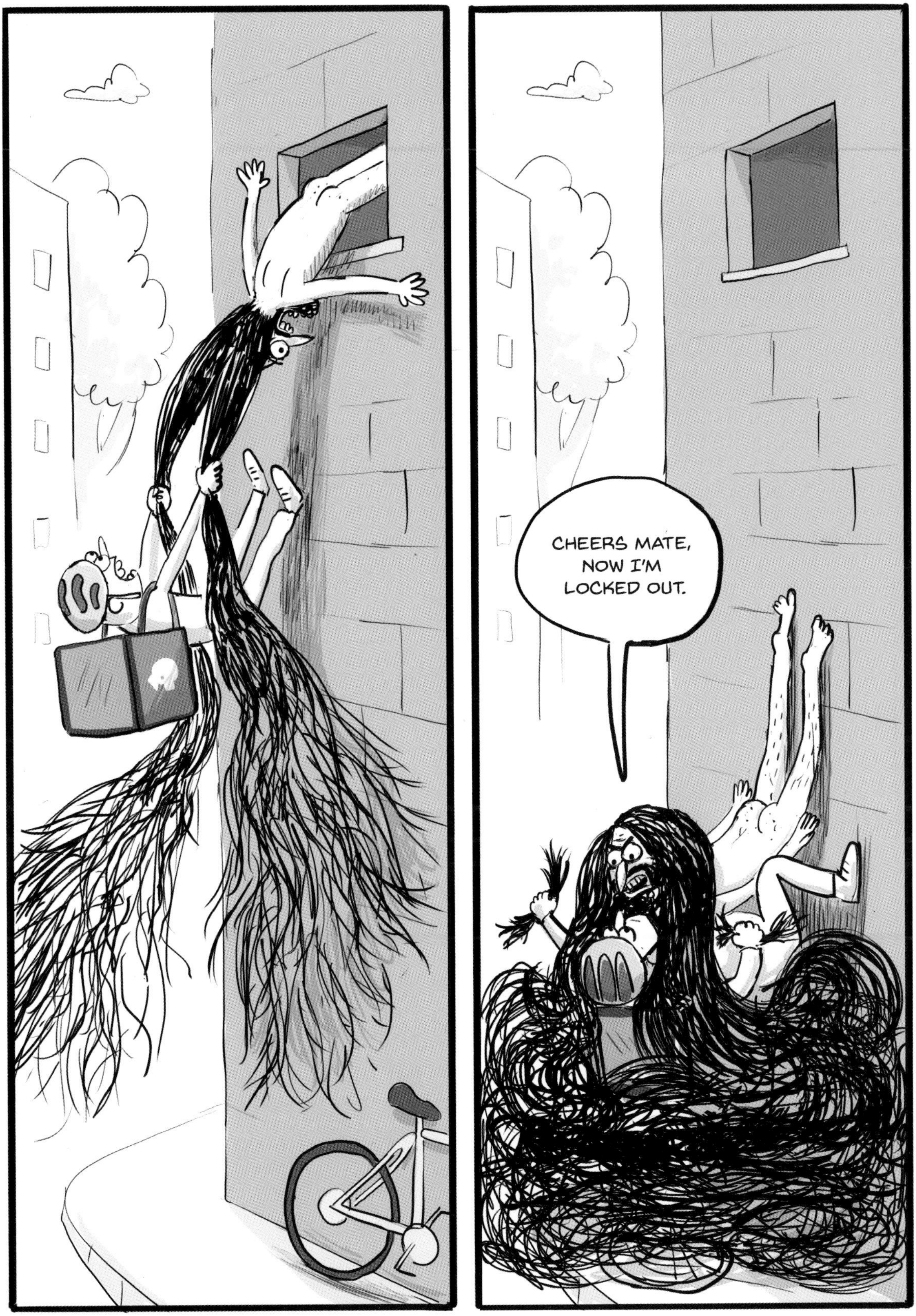
CHEERS MATE, NOW I'M LOCKED OUT.

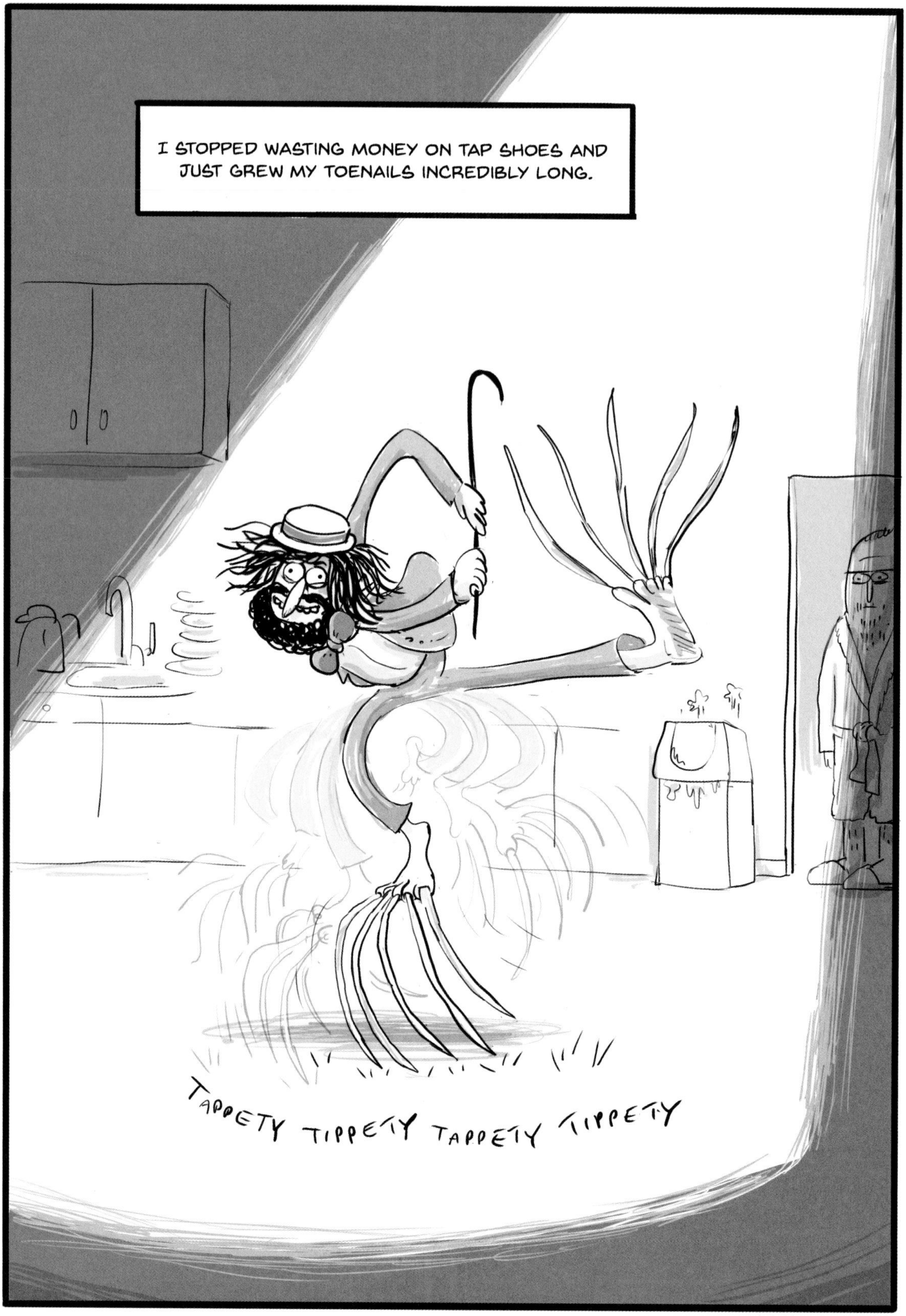
I STOPPED WASTING MONEY ON TAP SHOES AND JUST GREW MY TOENAILS INCREDIBLY LONG.
TAPPETY TIPPETY TAPPETY TIPPETY

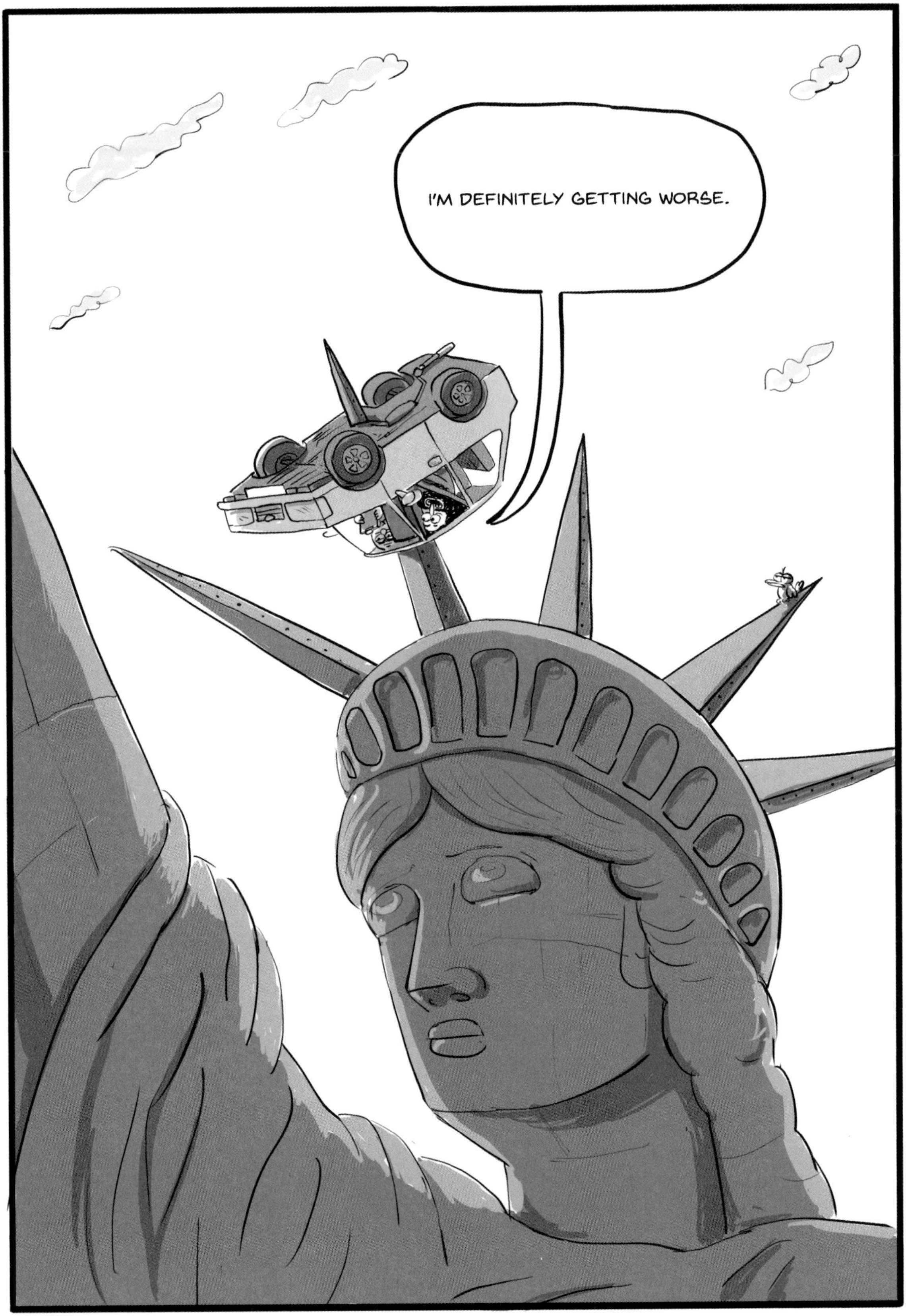
I'M DEFINITELY GETTING WORSE.

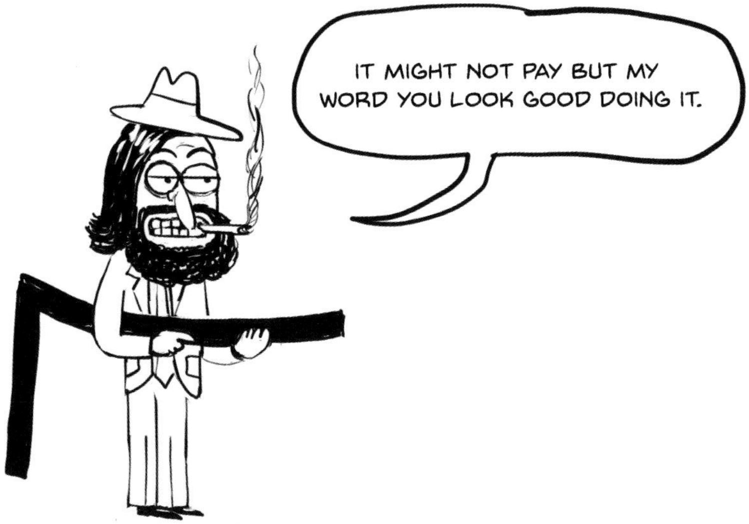
IT MIGHT NOT PAY BUT MY WORD YOU LOOK GOOD DOING IT.

CRIME DOESN'T PAY

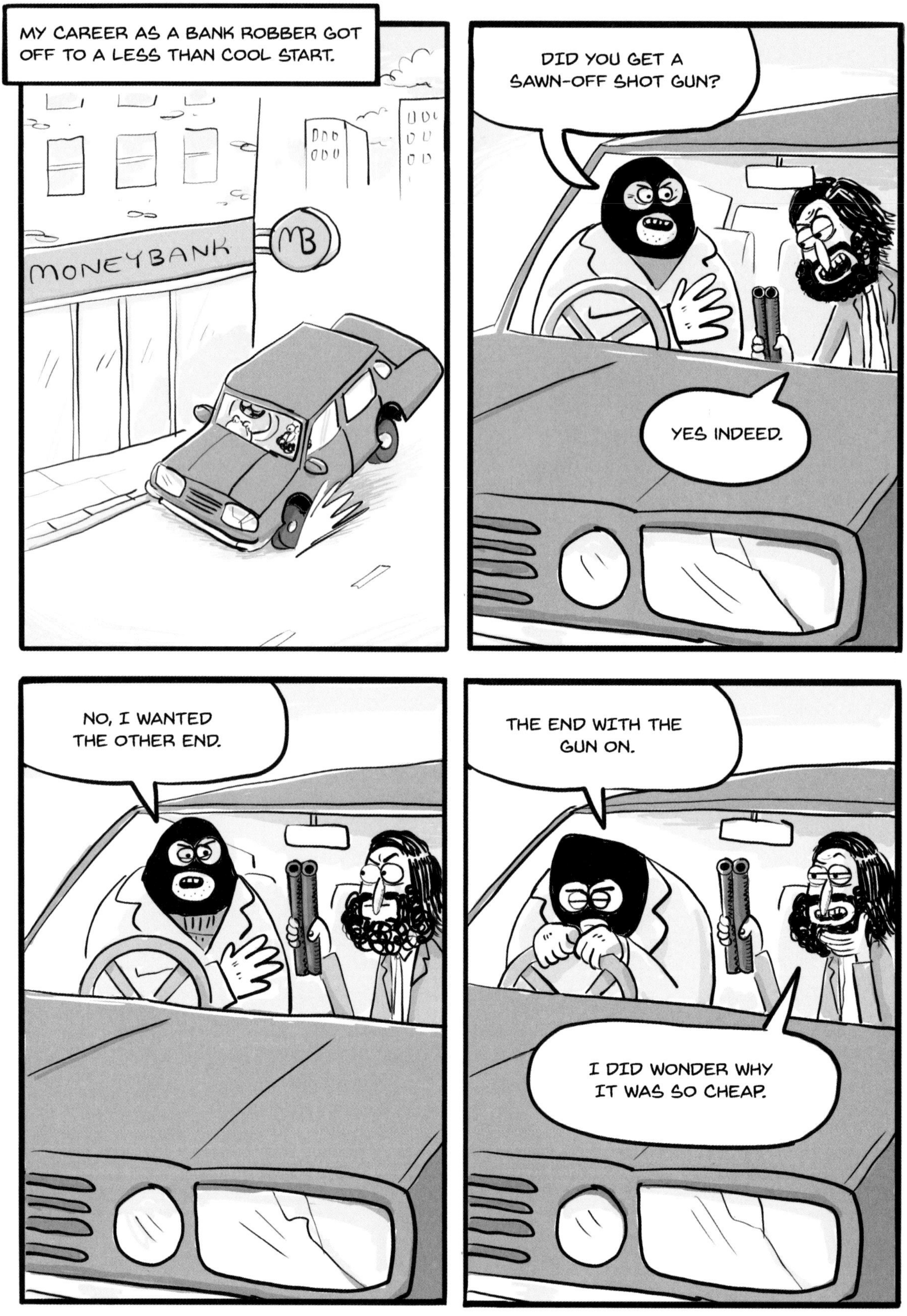
MY CAREER AS A BANK ROBBER GOT OFF TO A LESS THAN COOL START.
MONEYBANK
MB
DID YOU GET A SAWN-OFF SHOT GUN?
YES INDEED.
NO, I WANTED THE OTHER END.
THE END WITH THE GUN ON.
I DID WONDER WHY IT WAS SO CHEAP.

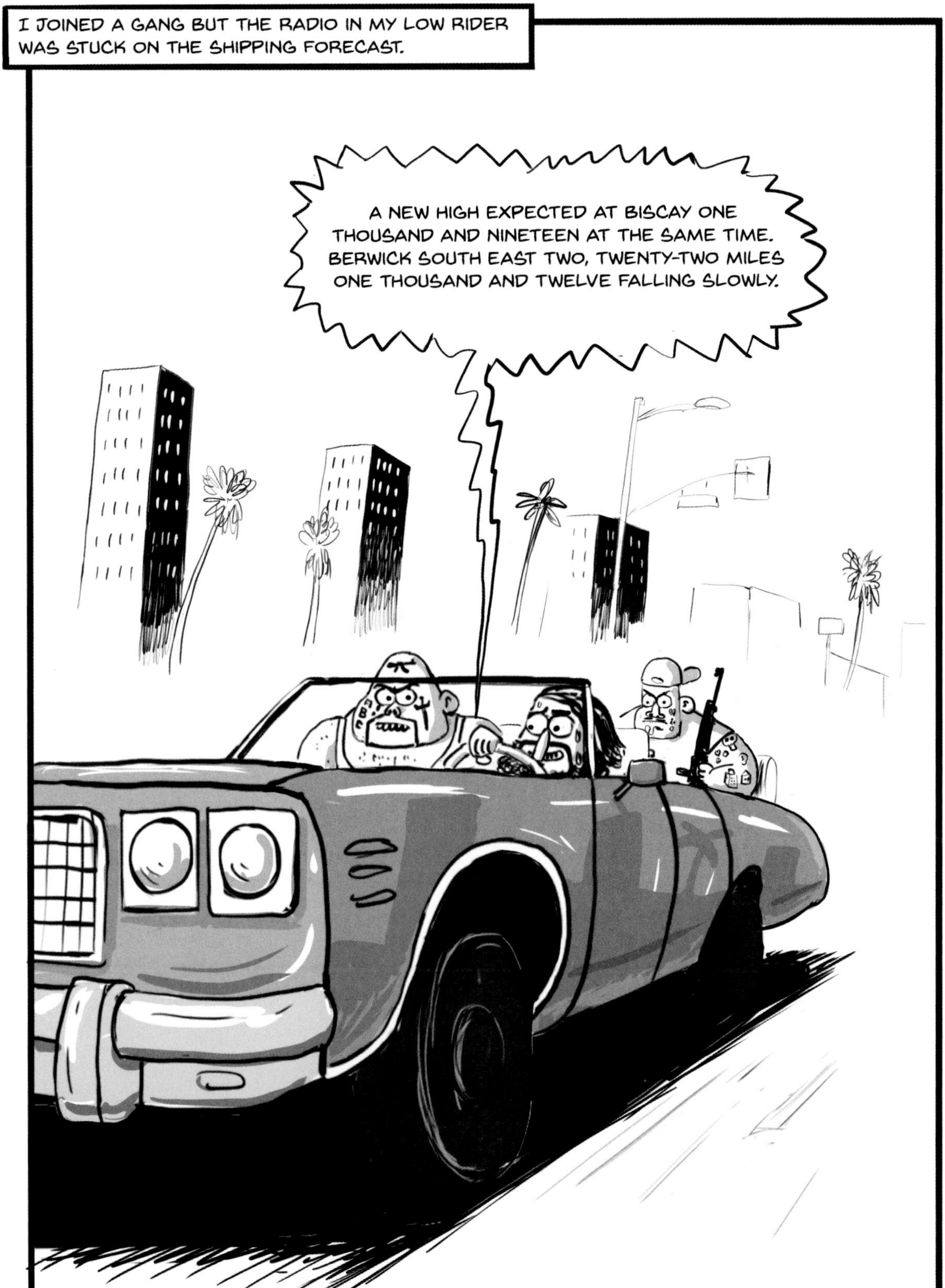
I JOINED A GANG BUT THE RADIO IN MY LOW RIDER WAS STUCK ON THE SHIPPING FORECAST.
A NEW HIGH EXPECTED AT BISCAY ONE THOUSAND AND NINETEEN AT THE SAME TIME. BERWICK SOUTH EAST TWO, TWENTY-TWO MILES ONE THOUSAND AND TWELVE FALLING SLOWLY.

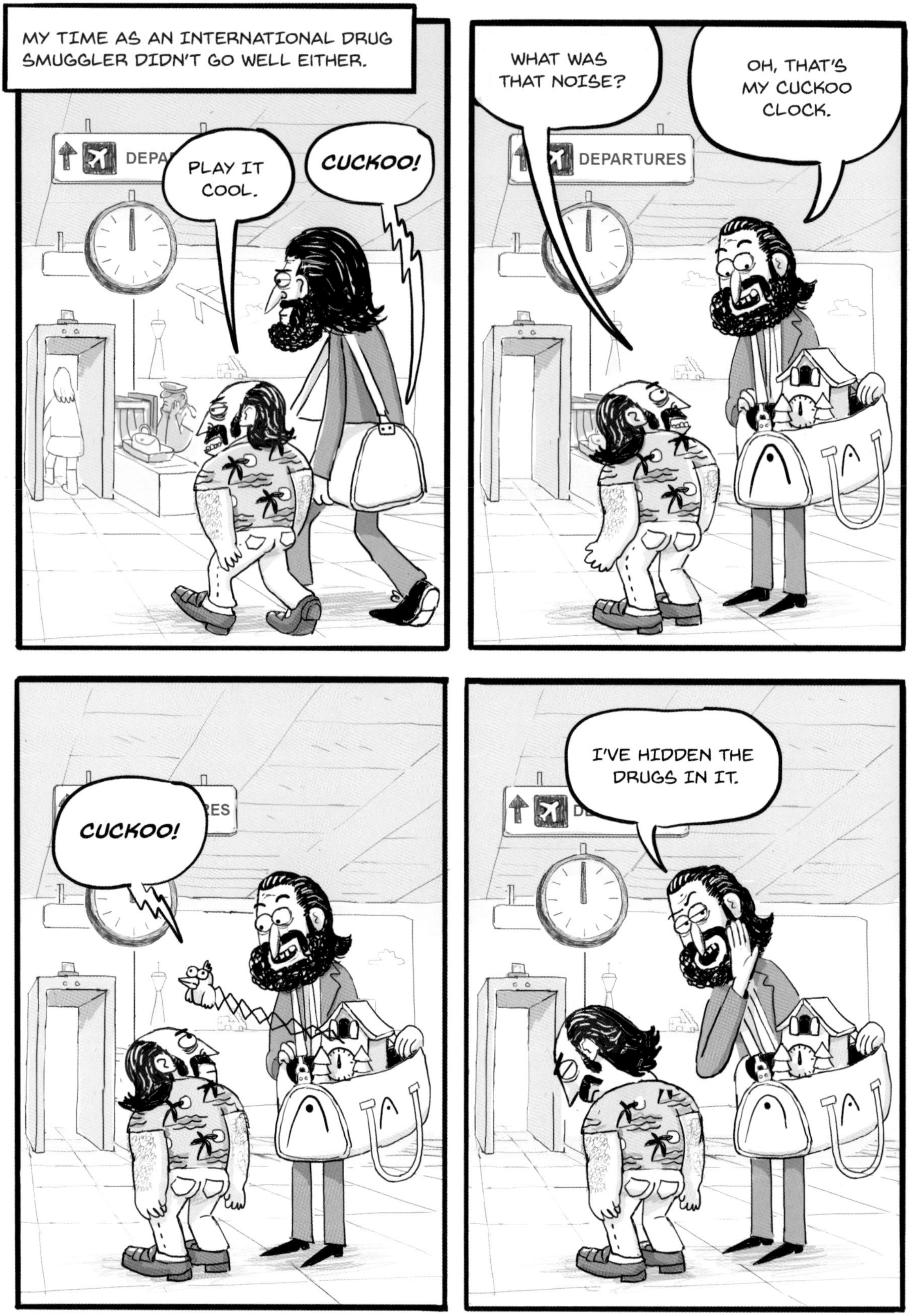
MY TIME AS AN INTERNATIONAL DRUG SMUGGLER DIDN'T GO WELL EITHER.
DEPAR
PLAY IT COOL.
CUCKOO!
WHAT WAS THAT NOISE?
OH, THAT'S MY CUCKOO CLOCK.
DEPARTURES
CUCKOO!
RES
I'VE HIDDEN THE DRUGS IN IT.
DE

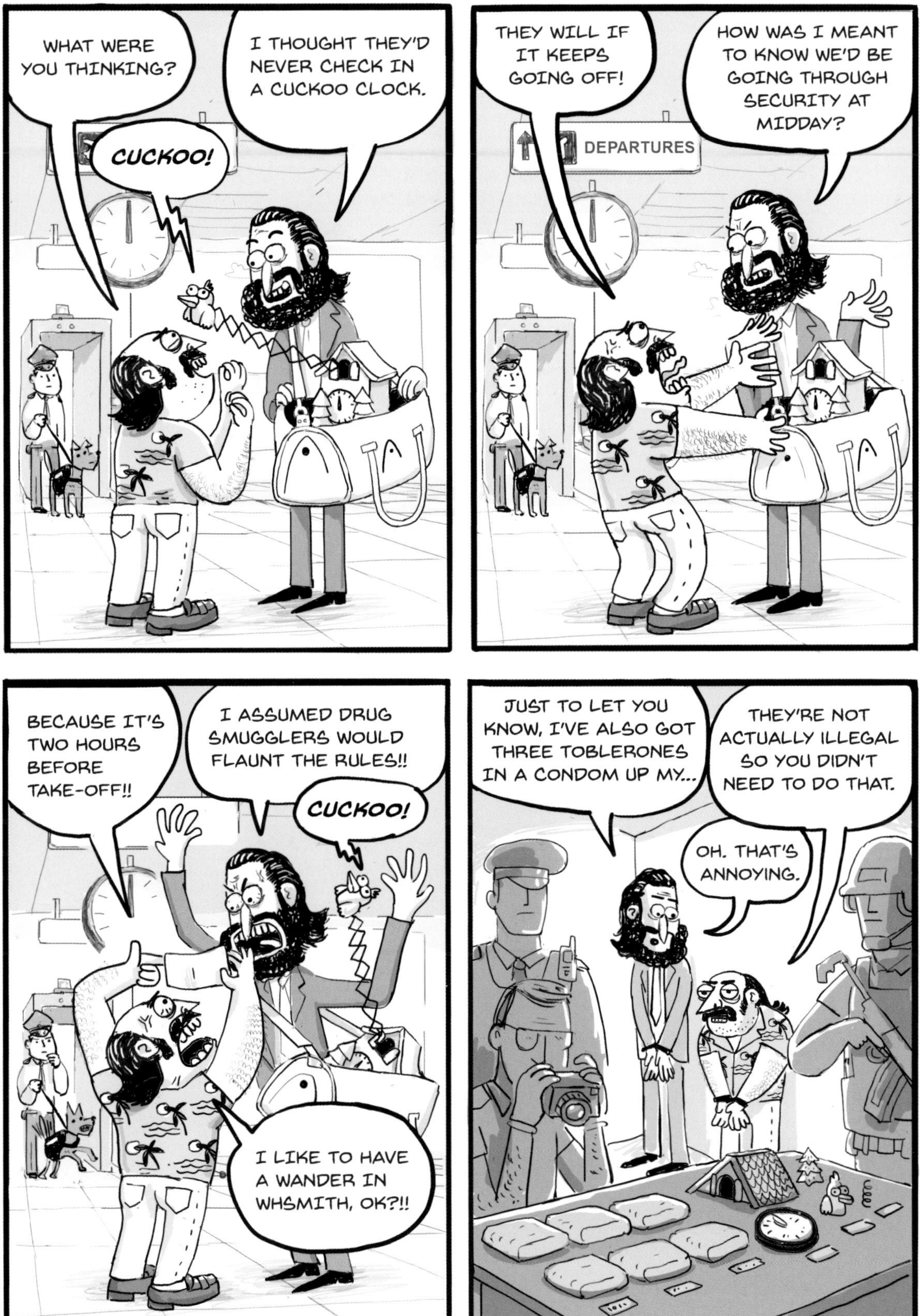
WHAT WERE YOU THINKING?
I THOUGHT THEY'D NEVER CHECK IN A CUCKOO CLOCK.
CUCKOO!
THEY WILL IF IT KEEPS GOING OFF!
HOW WAS I MEANT TO KNOW WE'D BE GOING THROUGH SECURITY AT MIDDAY?
DEPARTURES
BECAUSE IT'S TWO HOURS BEFORE TAKE-OFF!!
I ASSUMED DRUG SMUGGLERS WOULD FLAUNT THE RULES!!
CUCKOO!
I LIKE TO HAVE A WANDER IN WHSMITH, OK?!!
JUST TO LET YOU KNOW, I'VE ALSO GOT THREE TOBLERONES IN A CONDOM UP MY...
THEY'RE NOT ACTUALLY ILLEGAL SO YOU DIDN'T NEED TO DO THAT.
OH. THAT'S ANNOYING.

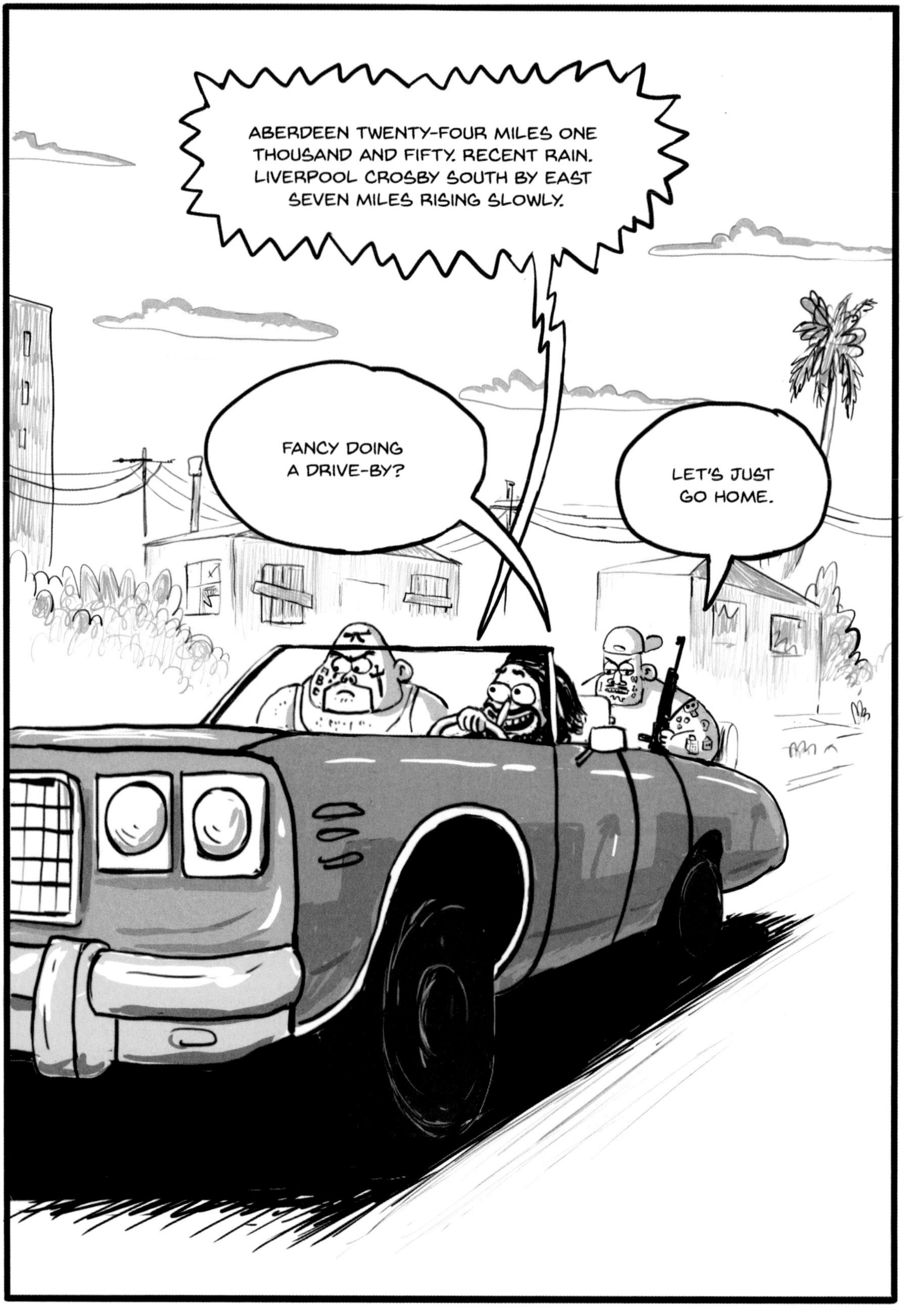
ABERDEEN TWENTY-FOUR MILES ONE THOUSAND AND FIFTY. RECENT RAIN. LIVERPOOL CROSBY SOUTH BY EAST SEVEN MILES RISING SLOWLY.
FANCY DOING A DRIVE-BY?
LET'S JUST GO HOME.

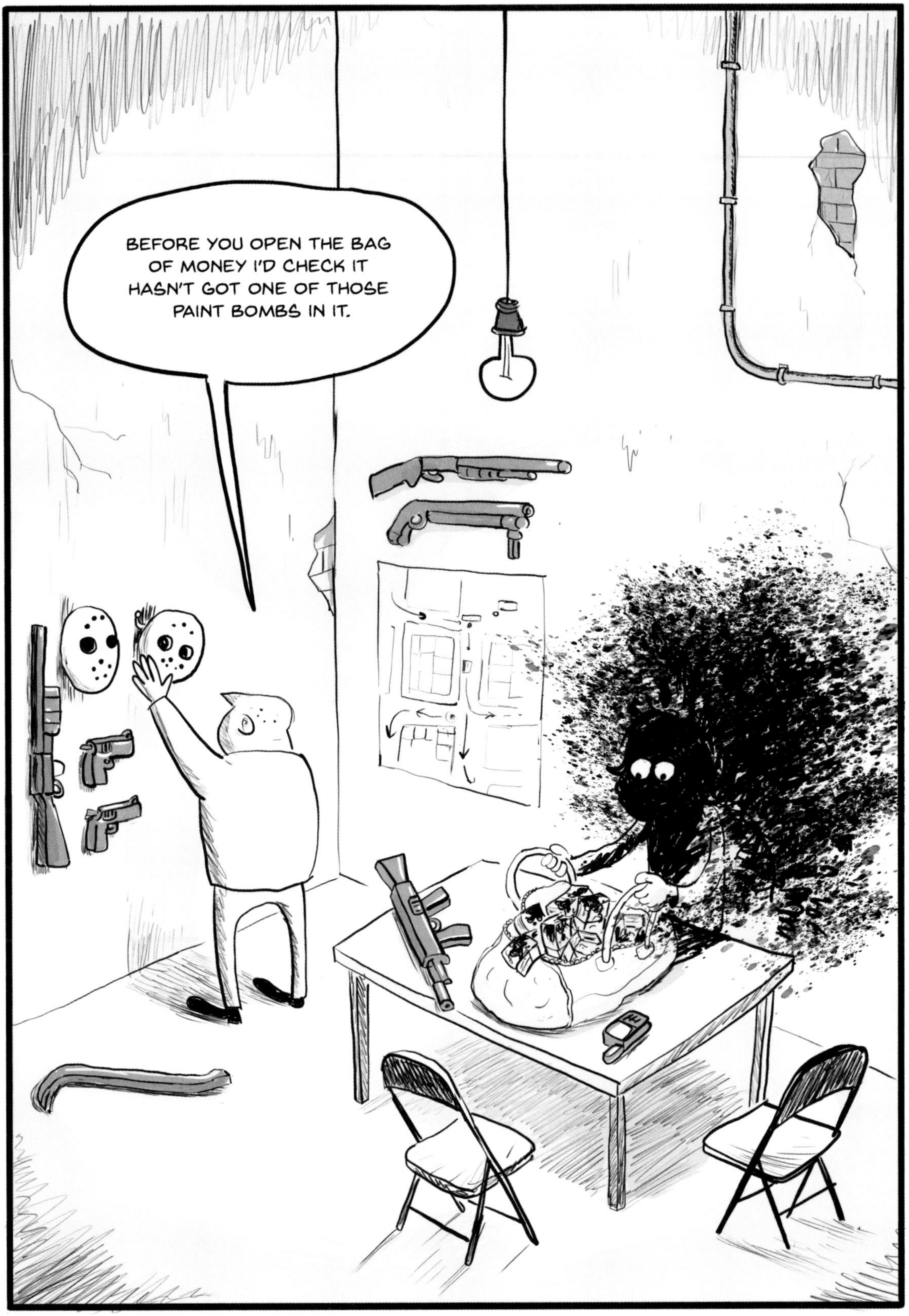
BEFORE YOU OPEN THE BAG OF MONEY I'D CHECK IT HASN'T GOT ONE OF THOSE PAINT BOMBS IN IT.

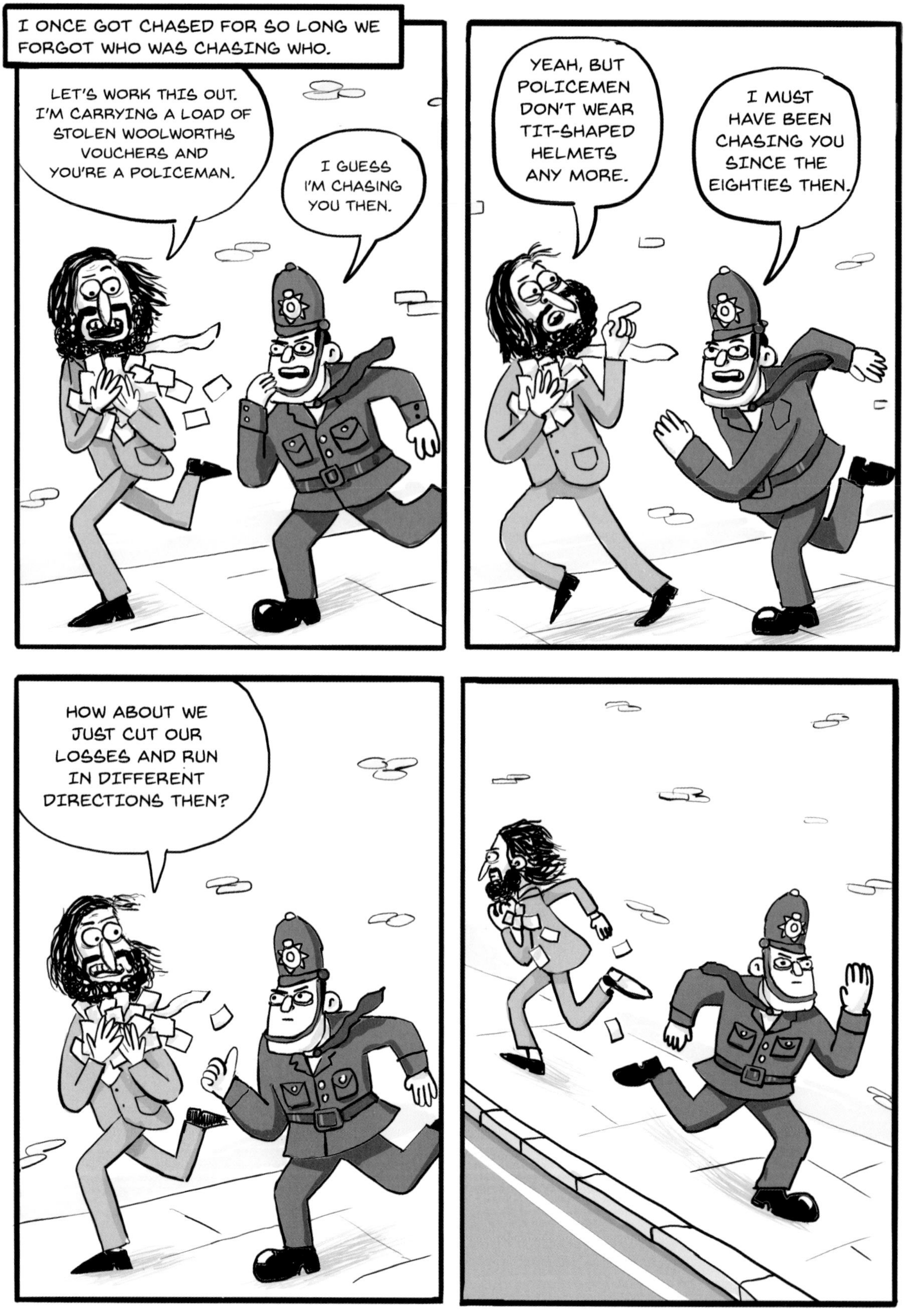
I ONCE GOT CHASED FOR SO LONG WE FORGOT WHO WAS CHASING WHO.
LET'S WORK THIS OUT. I'M CARRYING A LOAD OF STOLEN WOOLWORTHS VOUCHERS AND YOU'RE A POLICEMAN.
I GUESS I'M CHASING YOU THEN.
YEAH, BUT POLICEMEN DON'T WEAR TIT-SHAPED HELMETS ANY MORE.
I MUST HAVE BEEN CHASING YOU SINCE THE EIGHTIES THEN.
HOW ABOUT WE JUST CUT OUR LOSSES AND RUN IN DIFFERENT DIRECTIONS THEN?

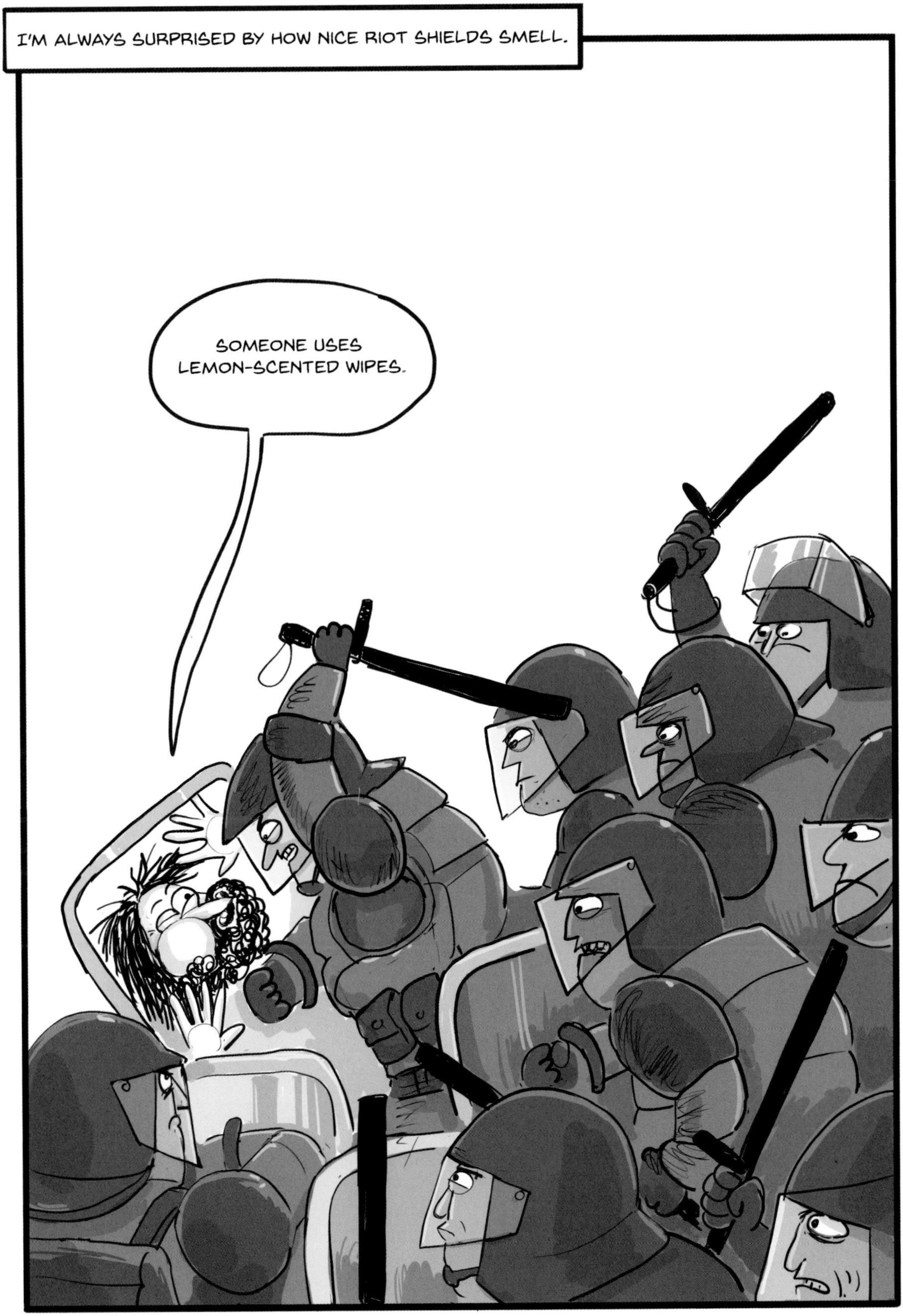
I'M ALWAYS SURPRISED BY HOW NICE RIOT SHIELDS SMELL.
SOMEONE USES LEMON-SCENTED WIPES.

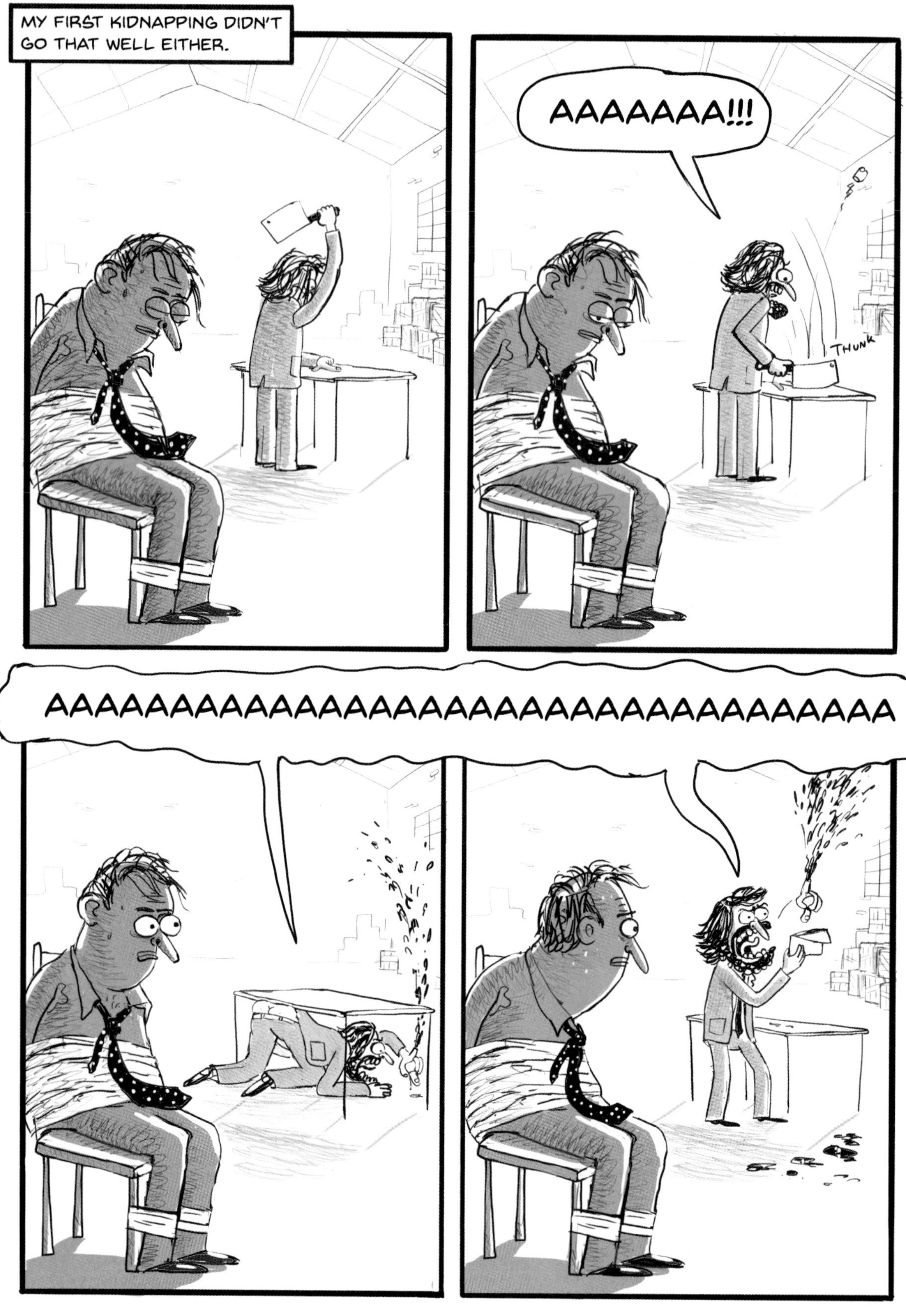
MY FIRST KIDNAPPING DIDN'T GO THAT WELL EITHER.
AAAAAAA!!!
THUNK
AAAAAAAAAAAAAAAAAAAAAAAAAAAAAAAAAAA

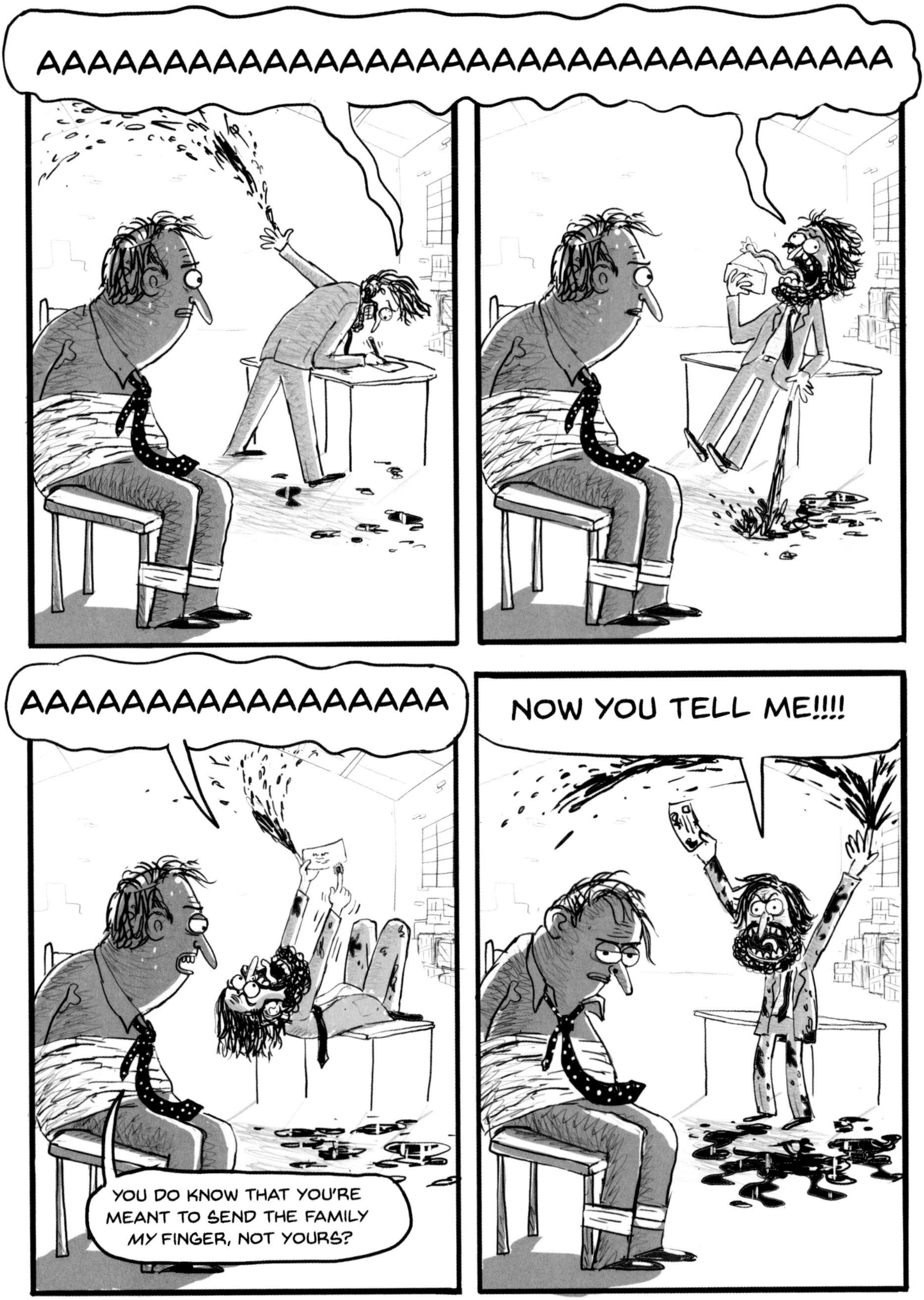
AAAAAAAAAAAAAAAAAAAAAAAAAAAAAAAAAA
AAAAAAAAAAAAAAAAA
YOU DO KNOW THAT YOU'RE MEANT TO SEND THE FAMILY MY FINGER, NOT YOURS?
NOW YOU TELL ME!!!!

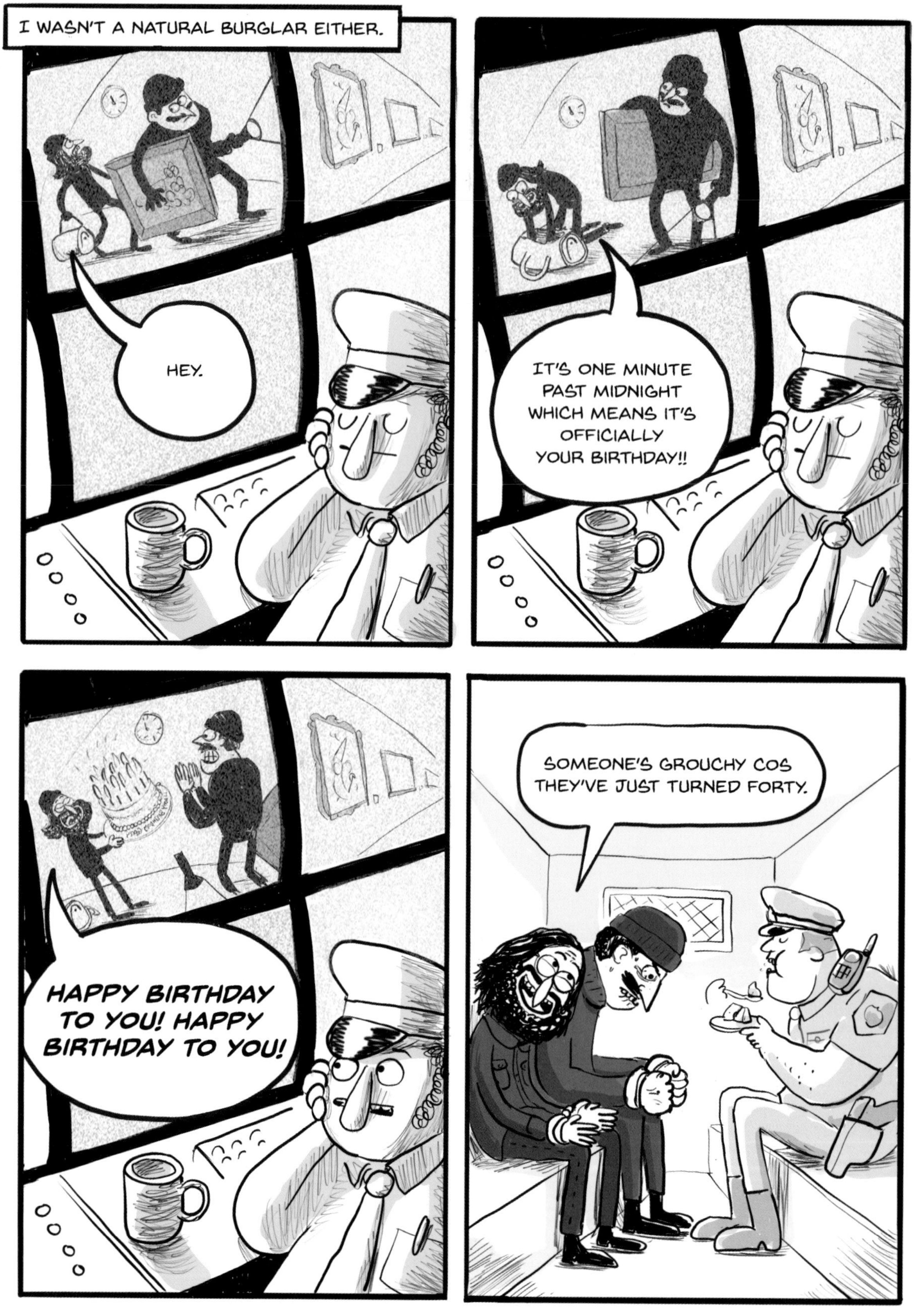

I WASN'T A NATURAL BURGLAR EITHER.
HEY.
IT'S ONE MINUTE PAST MIDNIGHT WHICH MEANS IT'S OFFICIALLY YOUR BIRTHDAY!!
HAPPY BIRTHDAY TO YOU! HAPPY BIRTHDAY TO YOU!
SOMEONE'S GROUCHY COS THEY'VE JUST TURNED FORTY.

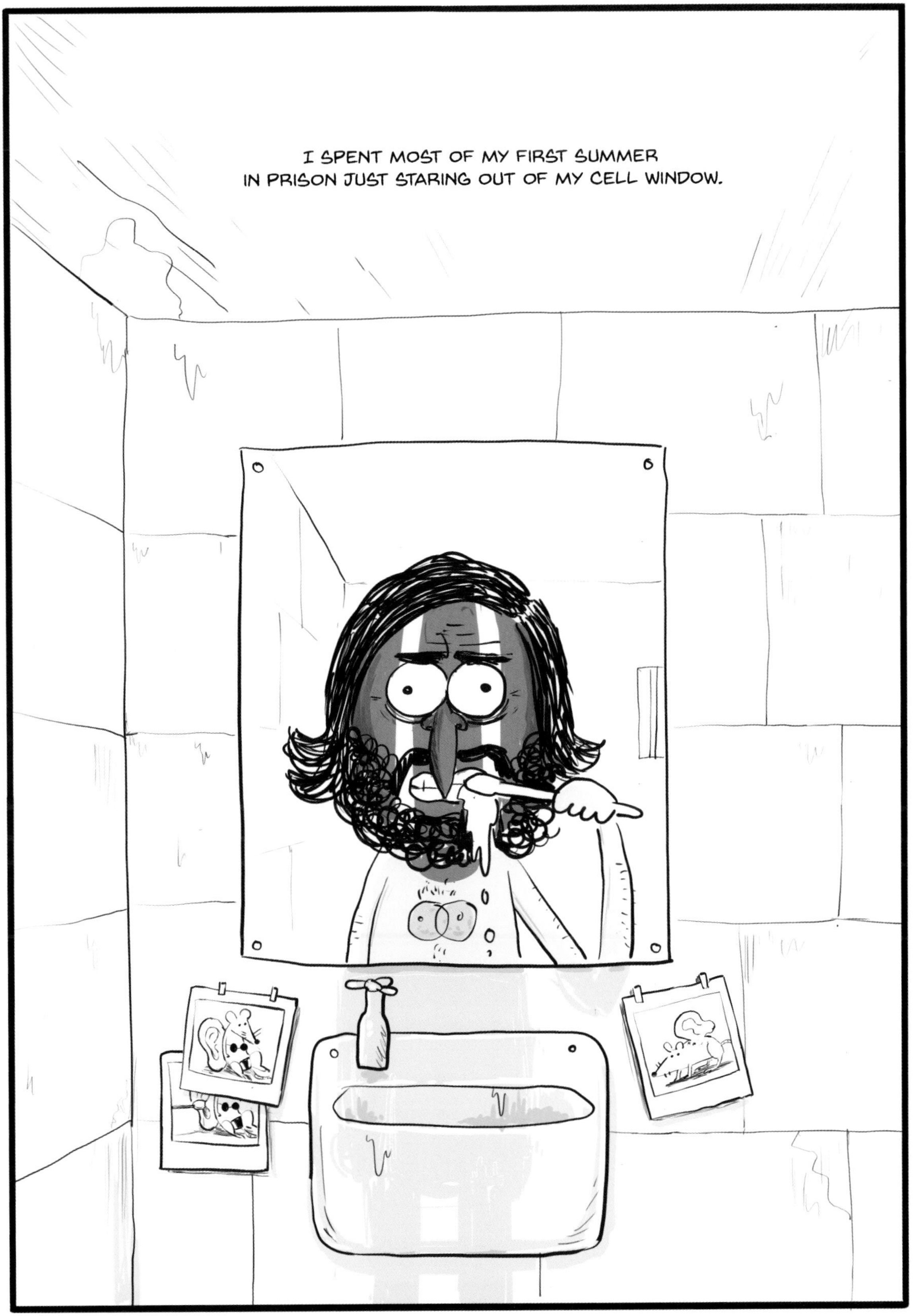
I SPENT MOST OF MY FIRST SUMMER
IN PRISON JUST STARING OUT OF MY CELL WINDOW.

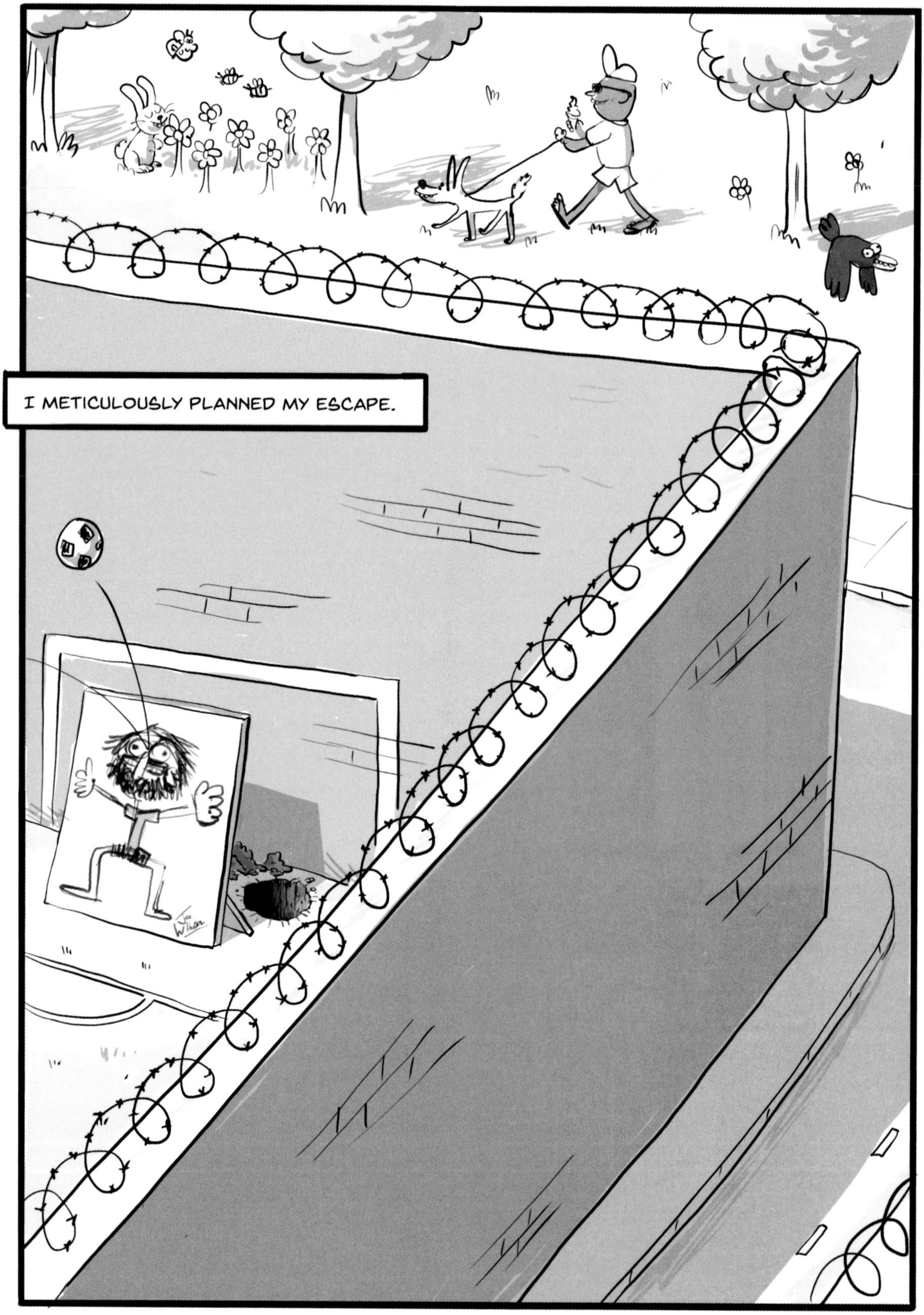
I METICULOUSLY PLANNED MY ESCAPE.

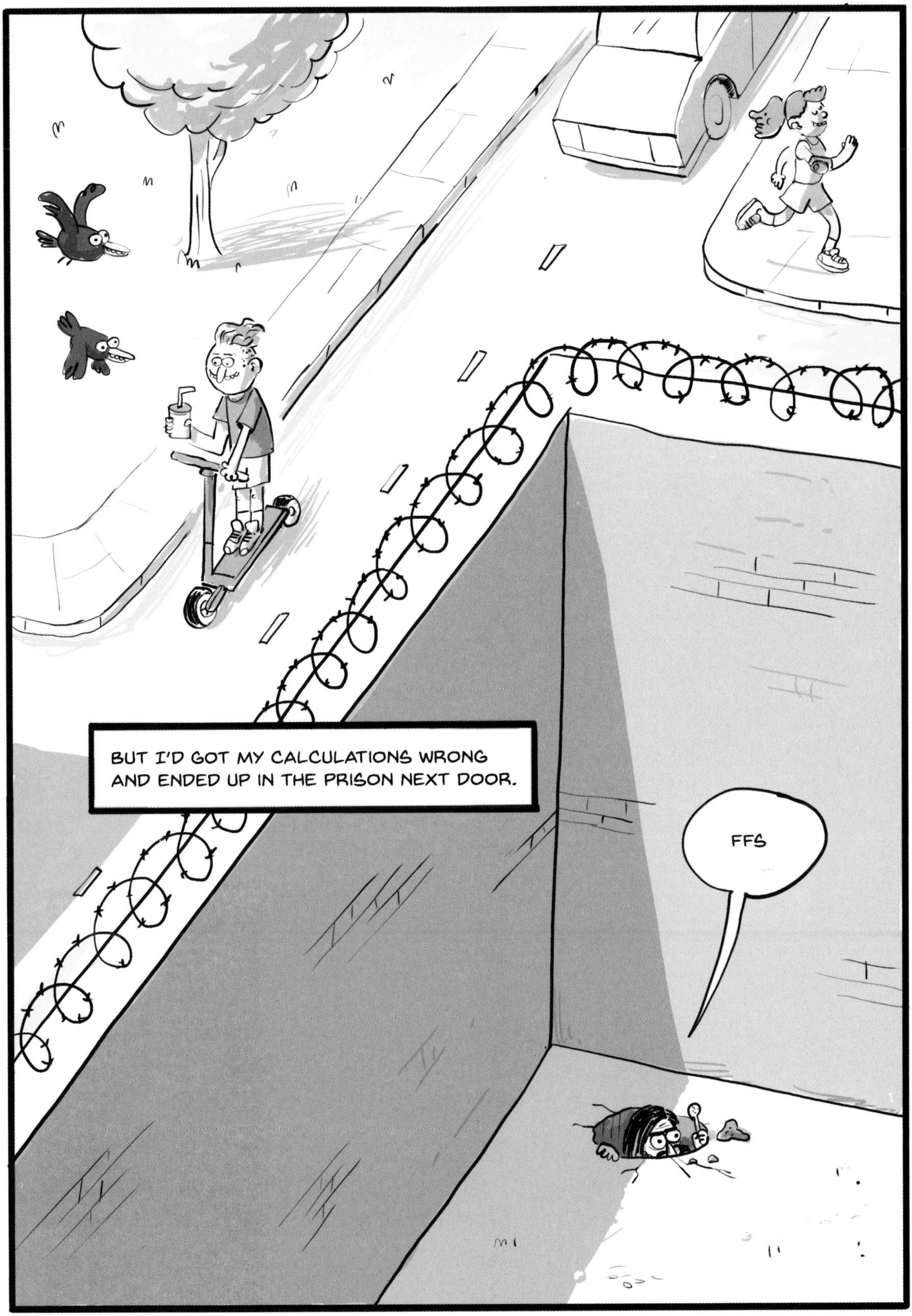
BUT I'D GOT MY CALCULATIONS WRONG AND ENDED UP IN THE PRISON NEXT DOOR.
FFS

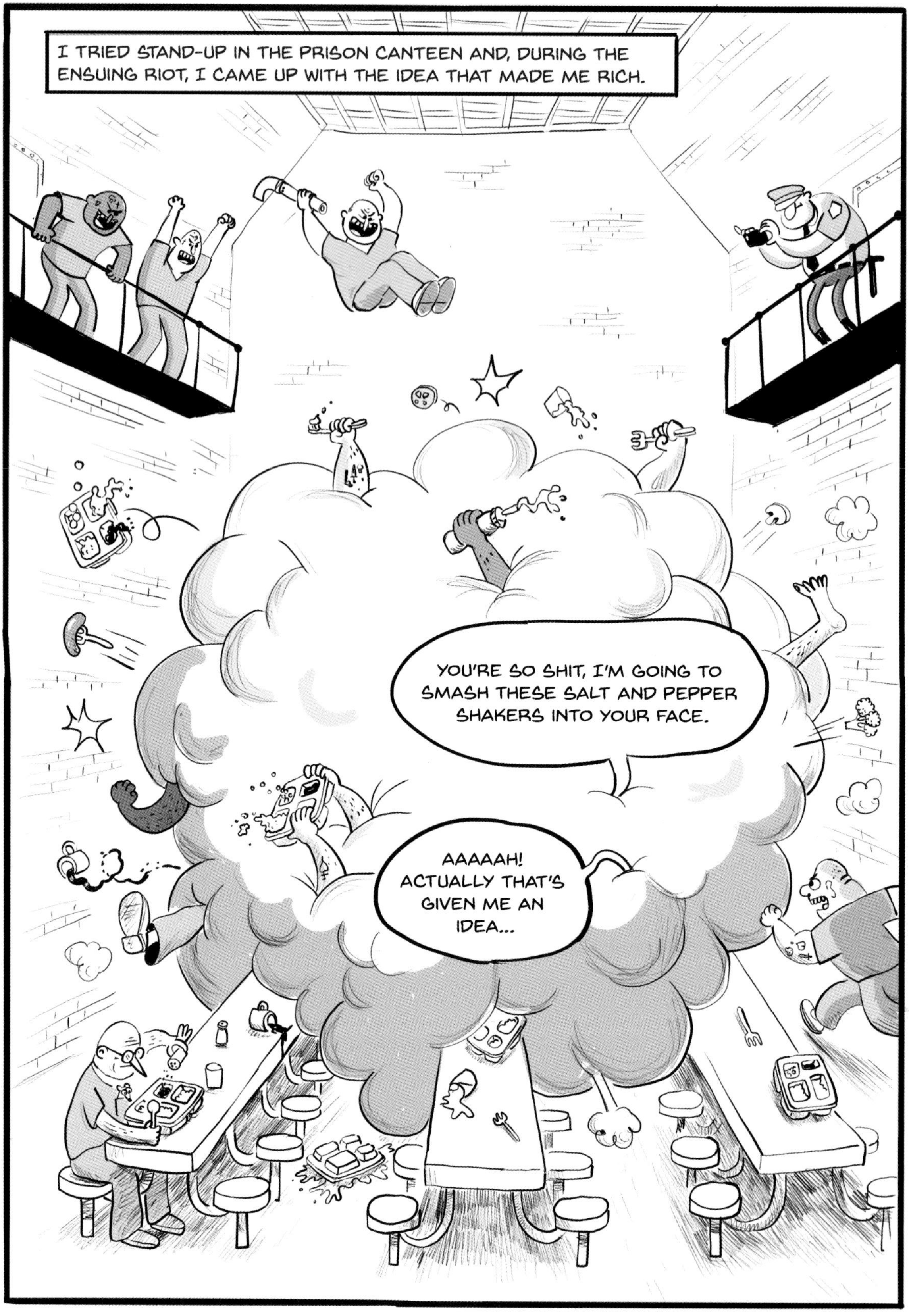
I TRIED STAND-UP IN THE PRISON CANTEEN AND, DURING THE ENSUING RIOT, I CAME UP WITH THE IDEA THAT MADE ME RICH.
YOU'RE SO SHIT, I'M GOING TO SMASH THESE SALT AND PEPPER SHAKERS INTO YOUR FACE.
AAAAAH! ACTUALLY THAT'S GIVEN ME AN IDEA...

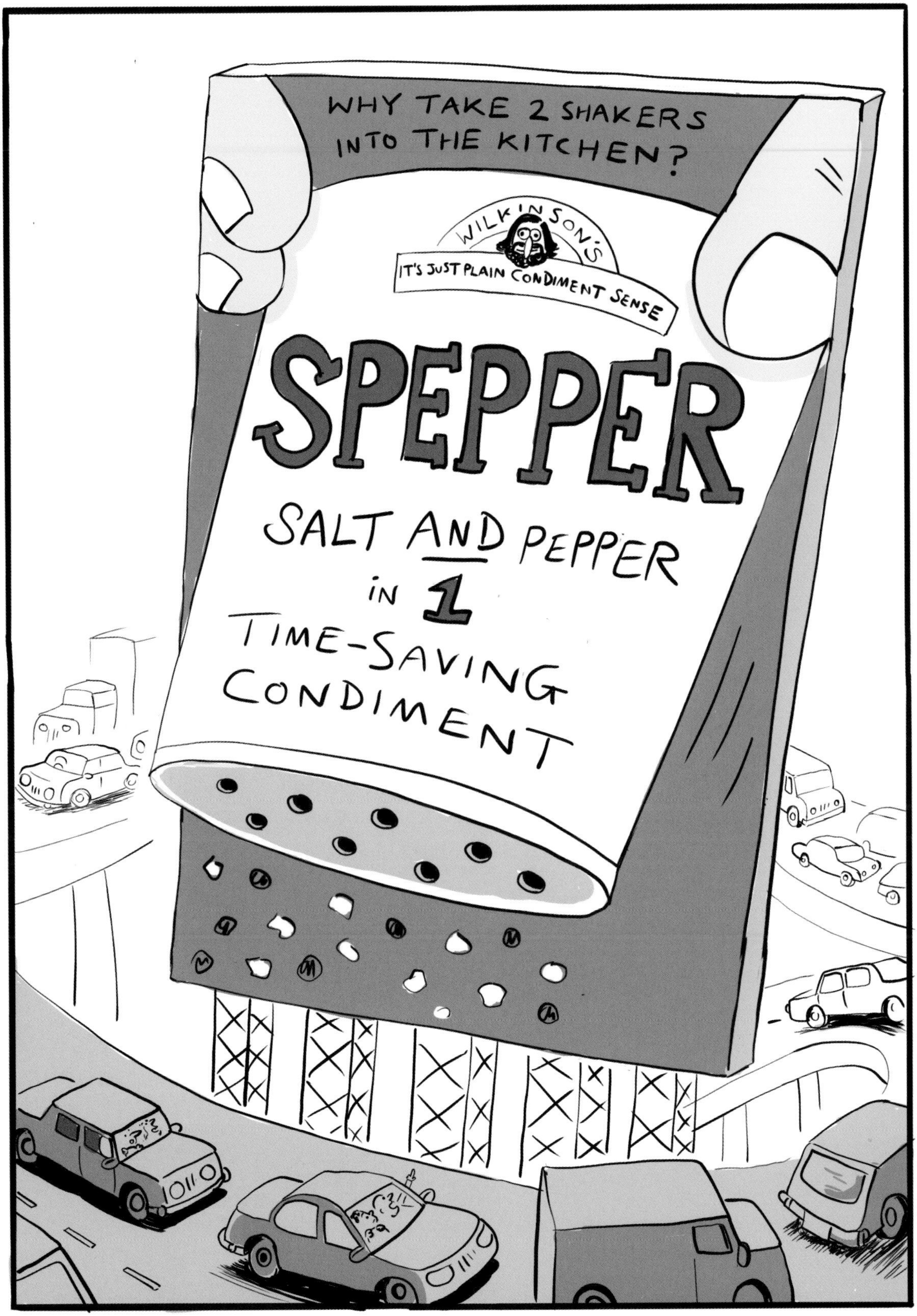
WHY TAKE 2 SHAKERS INTO THE KITCHEN?
WILKINSON'S
IT'S JUST PLAIN CONDIMENT SENSE
SPEPPER
SALT AND PEPPER in 1 TIME-SAVING CONDIMENT

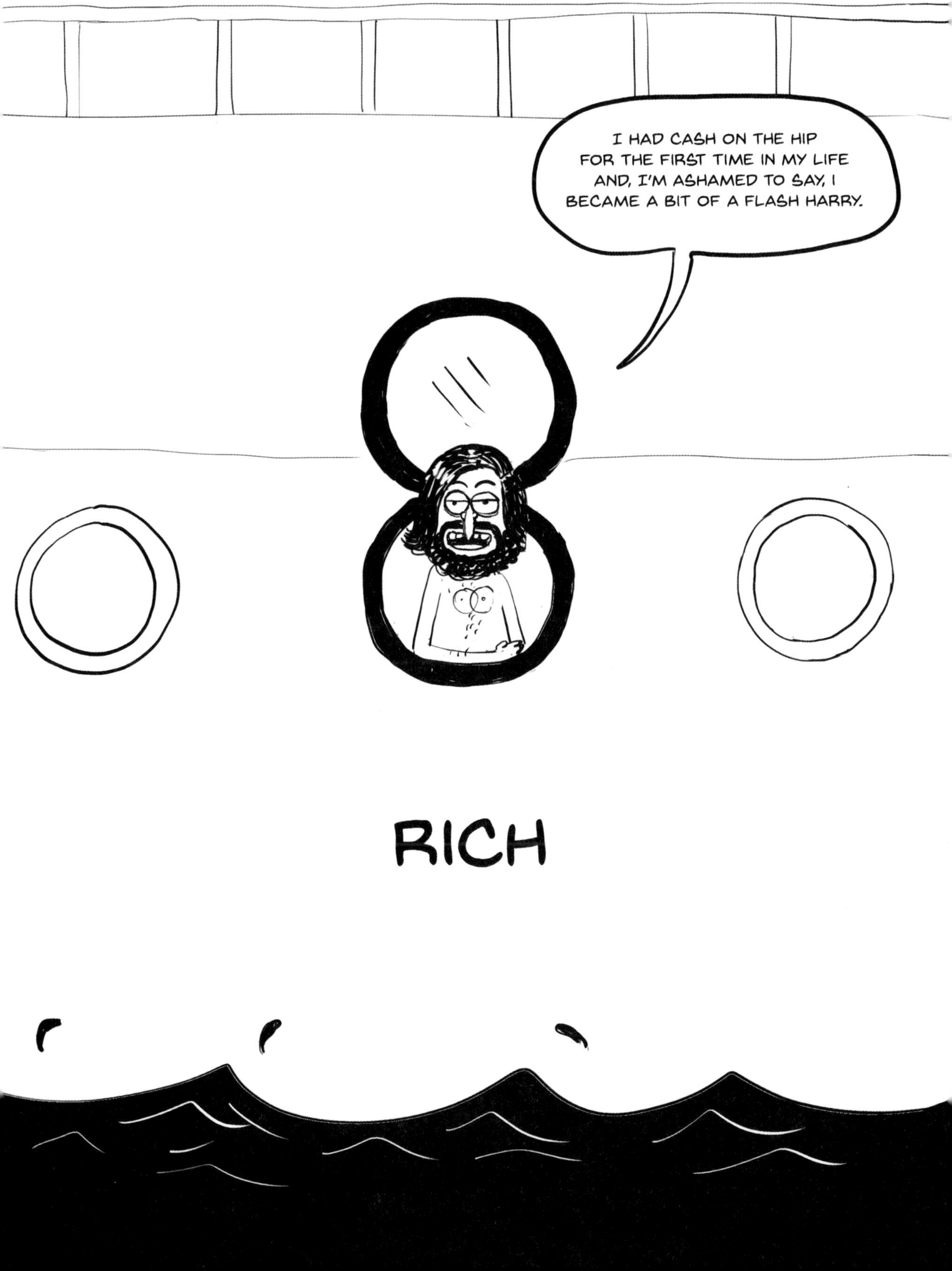
I HAD CASH ON THE HIP FOR THE FIRST TIME IN MY LIFE AND, I'M ASHAMED TO SAY, I BECAME A BIT OF A FLASH HARRY.
RICH

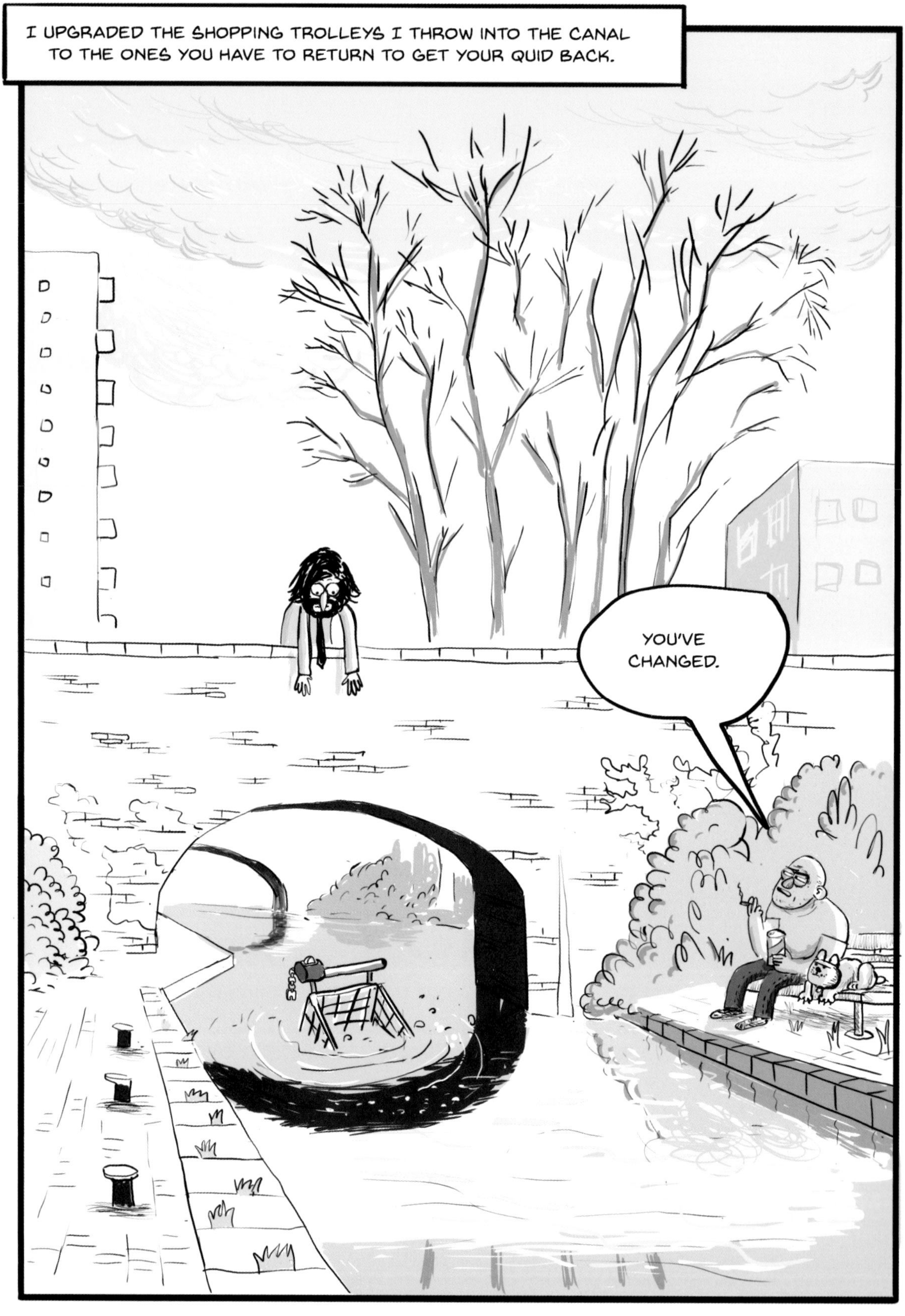
I UPGRADED THE SHOPPING TROLLEYS I THROW INTO THE CANAL TO THE ONES YOU HAVE TO RETURN TO GET YOUR QUID BACK.
YOU'VE CHANGED.

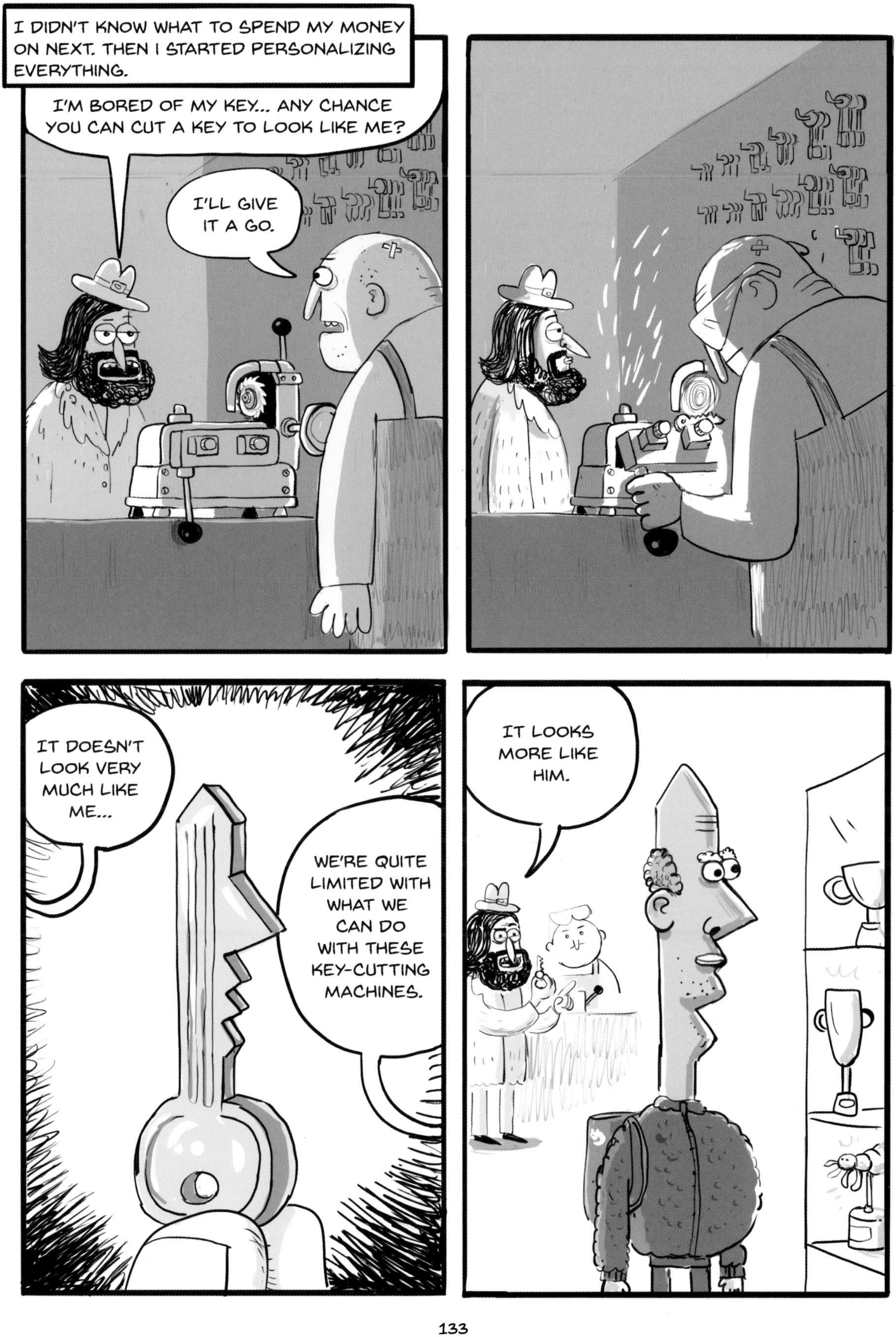
I DIDN'T KNOW WHAT TO SPEND MY MONEY ON NEXT. THEN I STARTED PERSONALIZING EVERYTHING.
I'M BORED OF MY KEY... ANY CHANCE YOU CAN CUT A KEY TO LOOK LIKE ME?
I'LL GIVE IT A GO.
IT DOESN'T LOOK VERY MUCH LIKE ME...
WE'RE QUITE LIMITED WITH WHAT WE CAN DO WITH THESE KEY-CUTTING MACHINES.
IT LOOKS MORE LIKE HIM.

I STARTED TO SPEND WAY TOO MUCH MONEY ON FIBREGLASS.

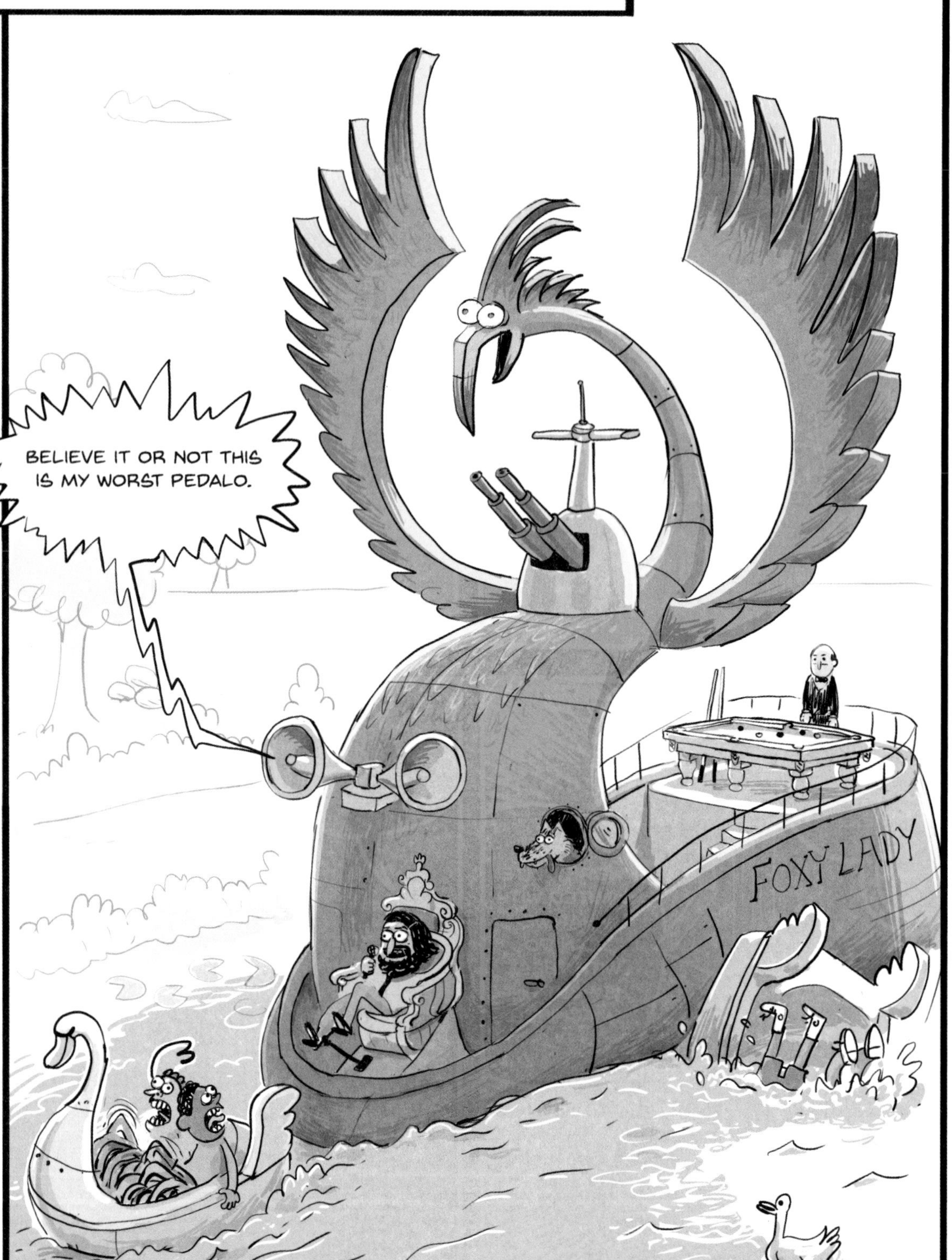
BELIEVE IT OR NOT THIS IS MY WORST PEDALO.
FOXY LADY

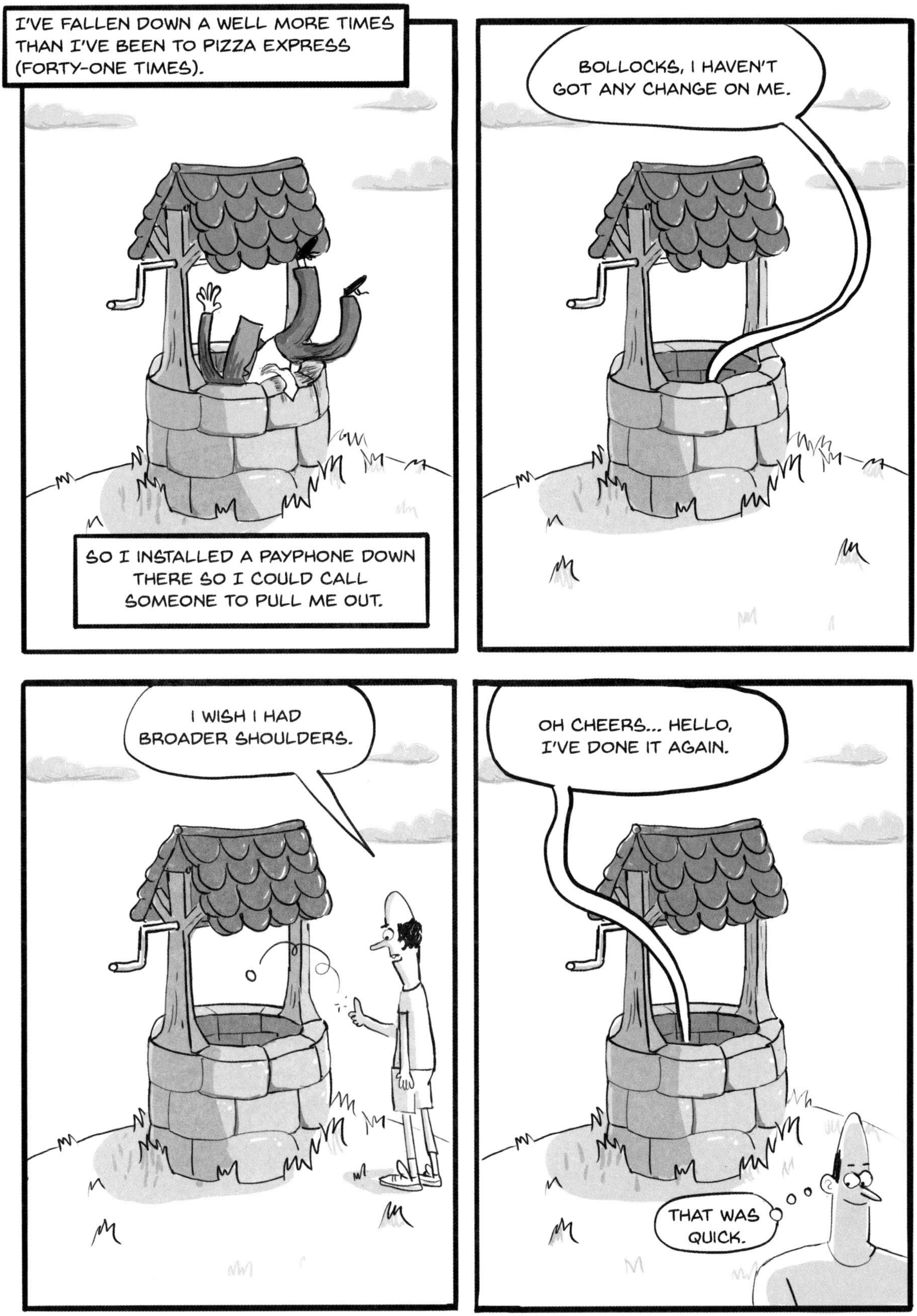
I'VE FALLEN DOWN A WELL MORE TIMES THAN I'VE BEEN TO PIZZA EXPRESS (FORTY-ONE TIMES).
SO I INSTALLED A PAYPHONE DOWN THERE SO I COULD CALL SOMEONE TO PULL ME OUT.
BOLLOCKS, I HAVEN'T GOT ANY CHANGE ON ME.
I WISH I HAD BROADER SHOULDERS.
OH CHEERS... HELLO, I'VE DONE IT AGAIN.
THAT WAS QUICK.

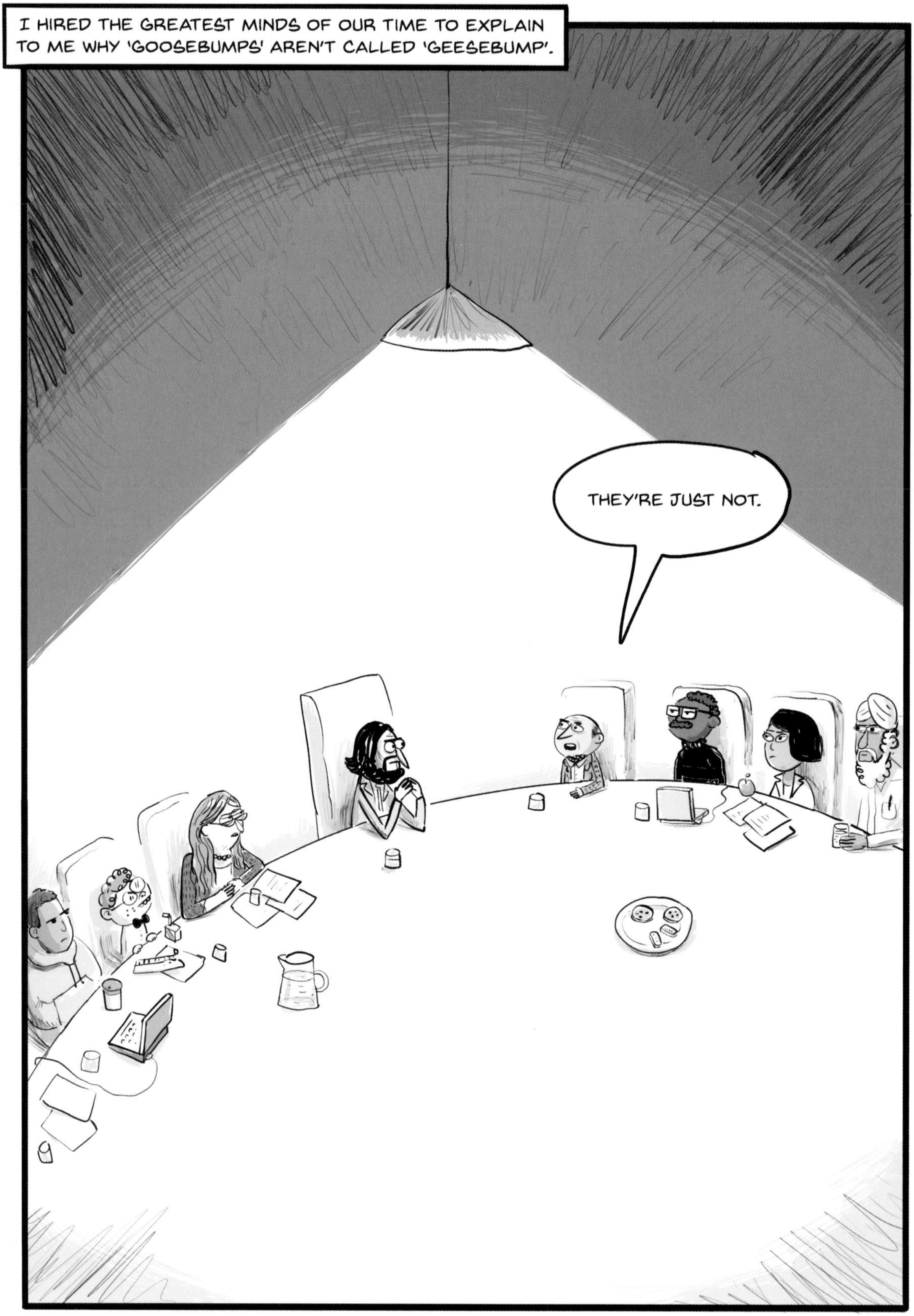
I HIRED THE GREATEST MINDS OF OUR TIME TO EXPLAIN TO ME WHY 'GOOSEBUMPS' AREN'T CALLED 'GEESEBUMP'.
THEY'RE JUST NOT.

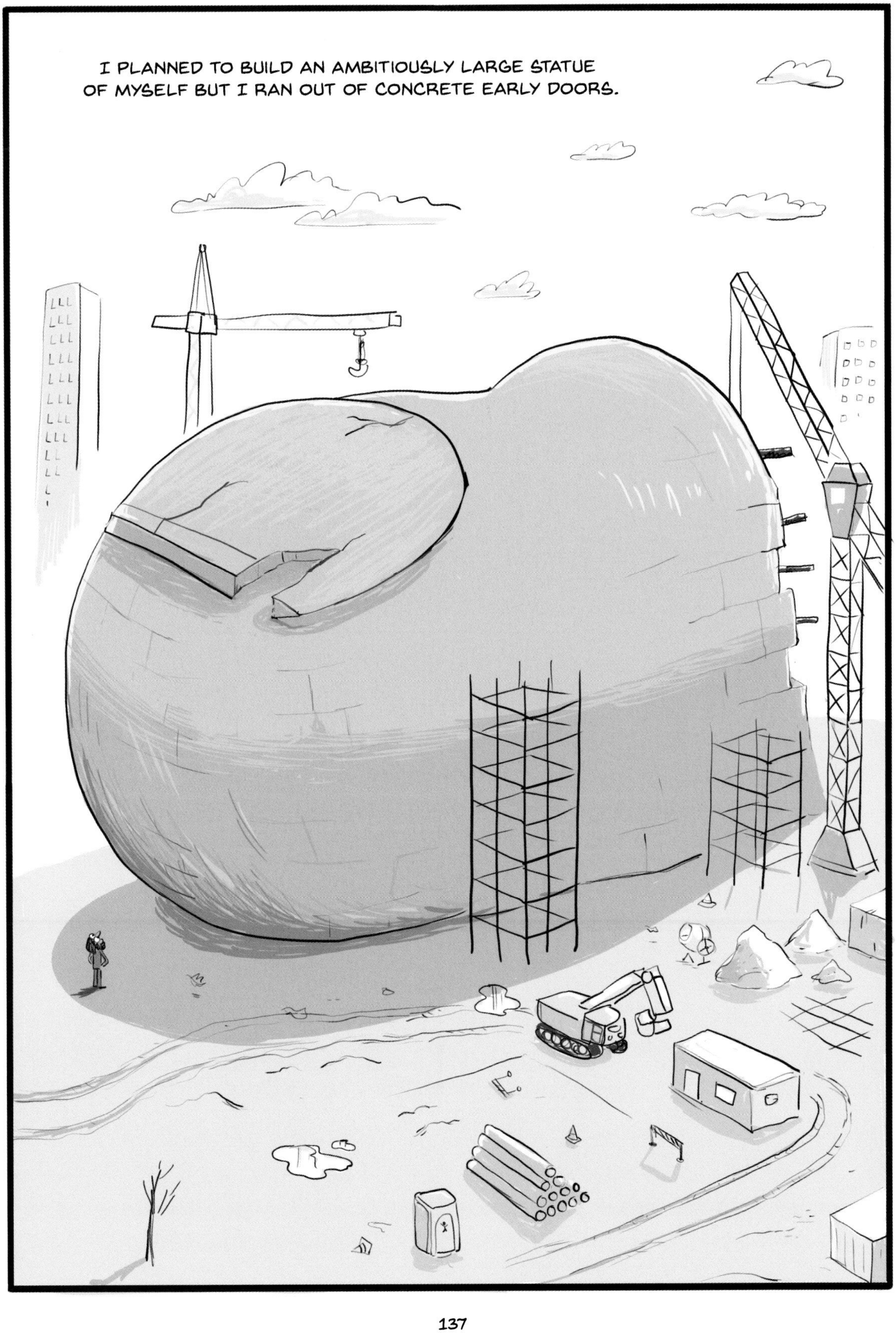
I PLANNED TO BUILD AN AMBITIOUSLY LARGE STATUE OF MYSELF BUT I RAN OUT OF CONCRETE EARLY DOORS.

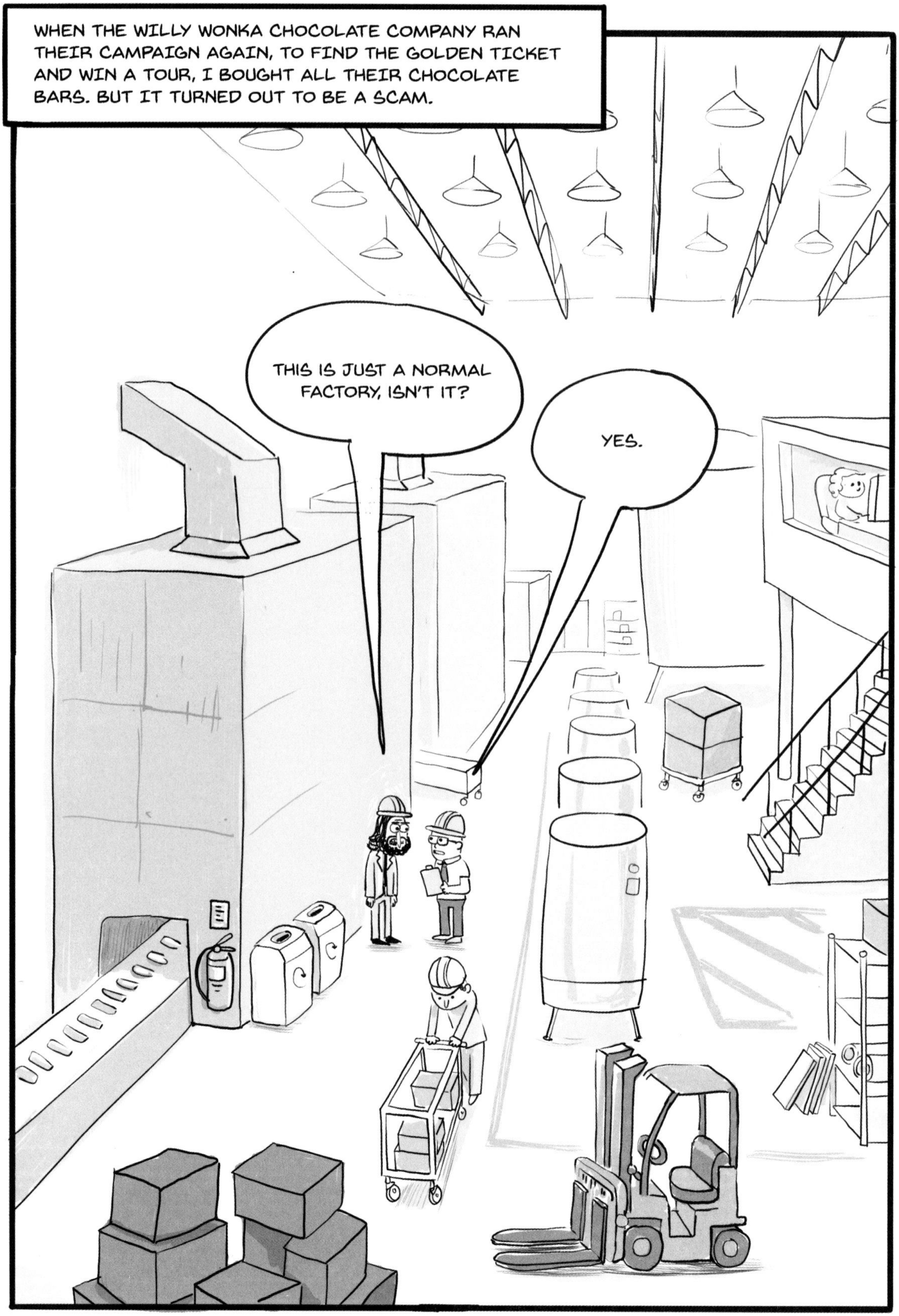
WHEN THE WILLY WONKA CHOCOLATE COMPANY RAN THEIR CAMPAIGN AGAIN, TO FIND THE GOLDEN TICKET AND WIN A TOUR, I BOUGHT ALL THEIR CHOCOLATE BARS. BUT IT TURNED OUT TO BE A SCAM.
THIS IS JUST A NORMAL FACTORY, ISN'T IT?
YES.

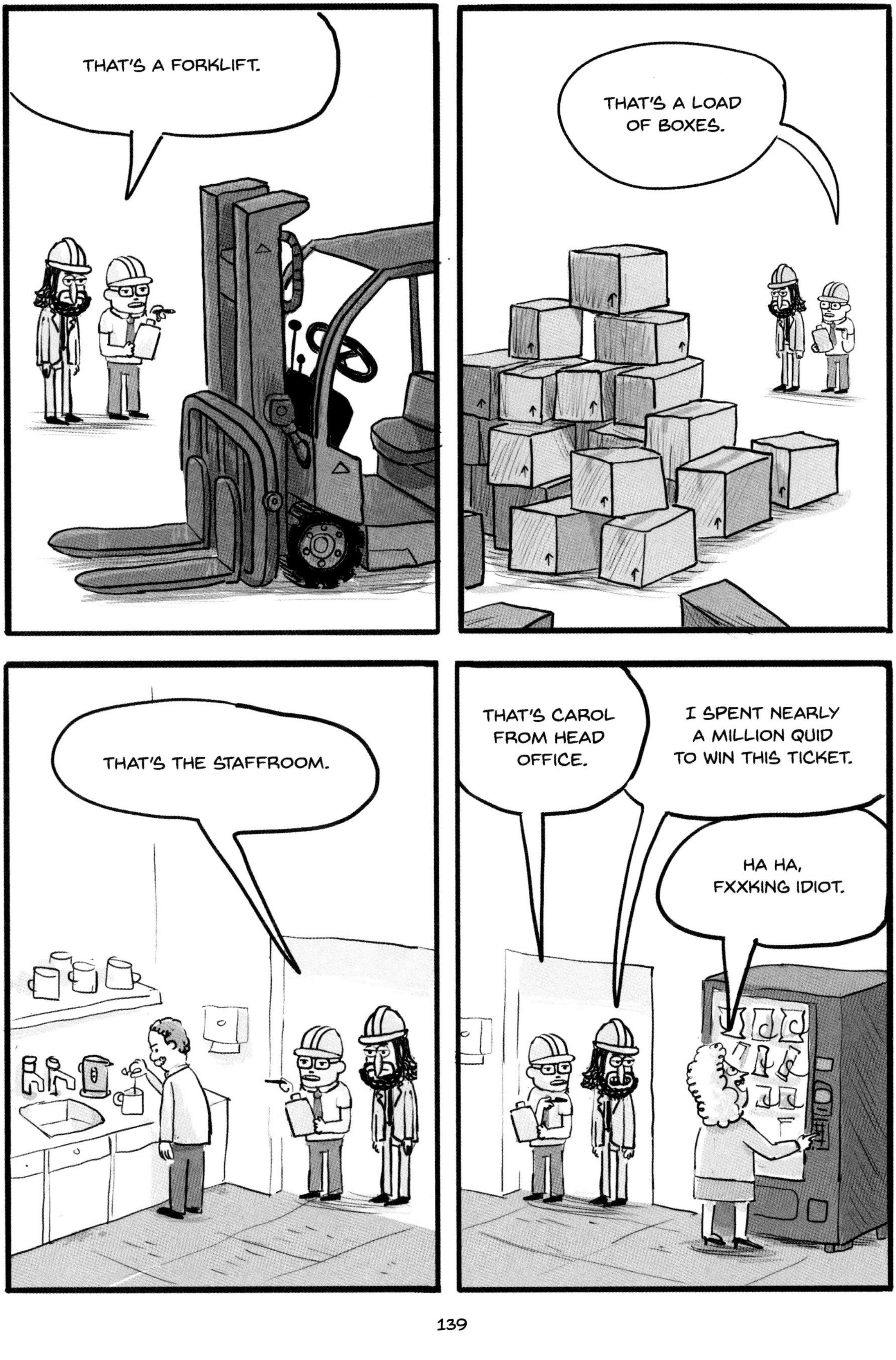
THAT'S A FORKLIFT.
THAT'S A LOAD OF BOXES.
THAT'S THE STAFFROOM.
THAT'S CAROL FROM HEAD OFFICE.
I SPENT NEARLY A MILLION QUID TO WIN THIS TICKET.
HA HA, FXXKING IDIOT.

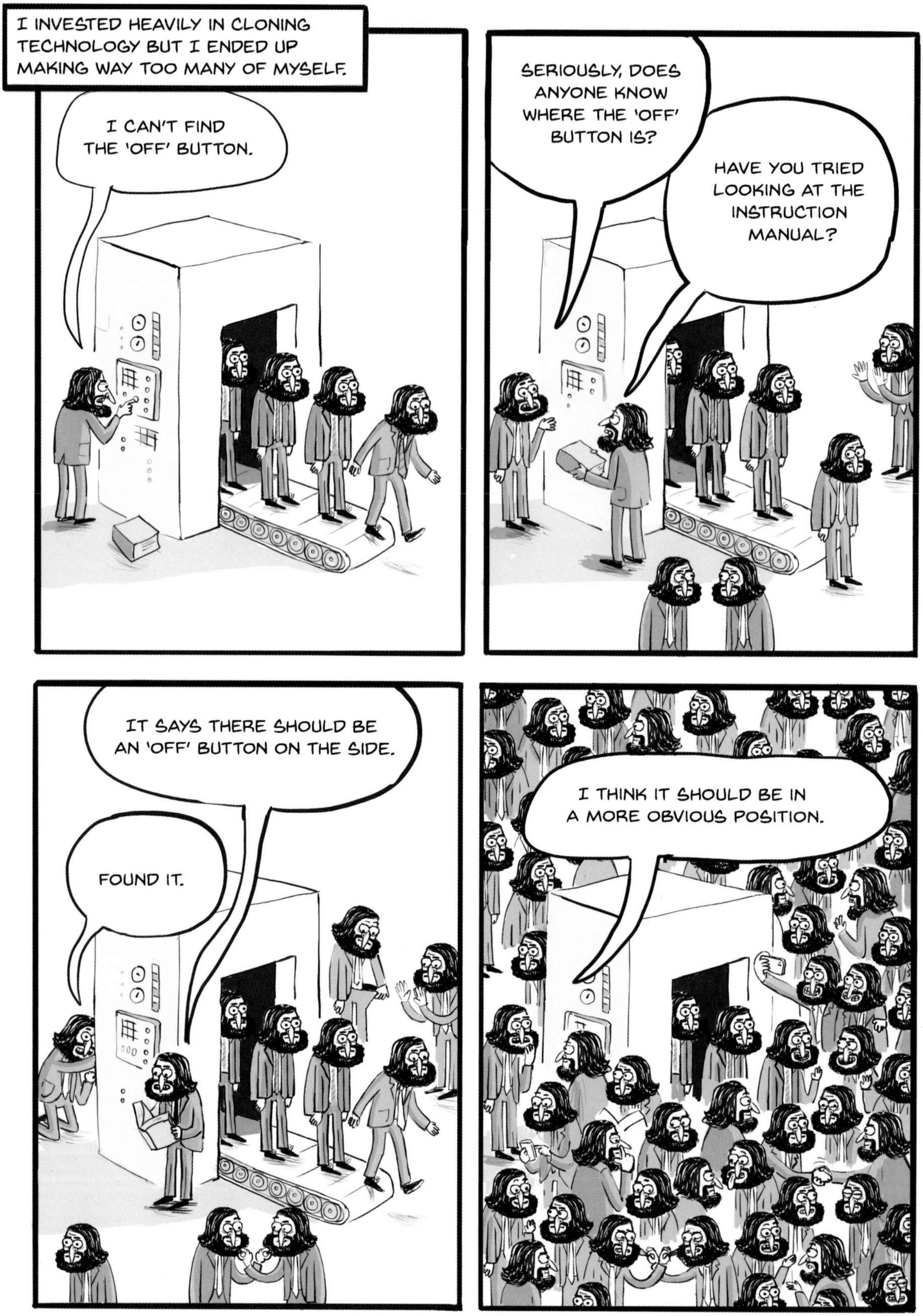
I INVESTED HEAVILY IN CLONING TECHNOLOGY BUT I ENDED UP MAKING WAY TOO MANY OF MYSELF.
I CAN'T FIND THE 'OFF' BUTTON.
SERIOUSLY, DOES ANYONE KNOW WHERE THE 'OFF' BUTTON IS?
HAVE YOU TRIED LOOKING AT THE INSTRUCTION MANUAL?
IT SAYS THERE SHOULD BE AN 'OFF' BUTTON ON THE SIDE.
FOUND IT.
I THINK IT SHOULD BE IN A MORE OBVIOUS POSITION.

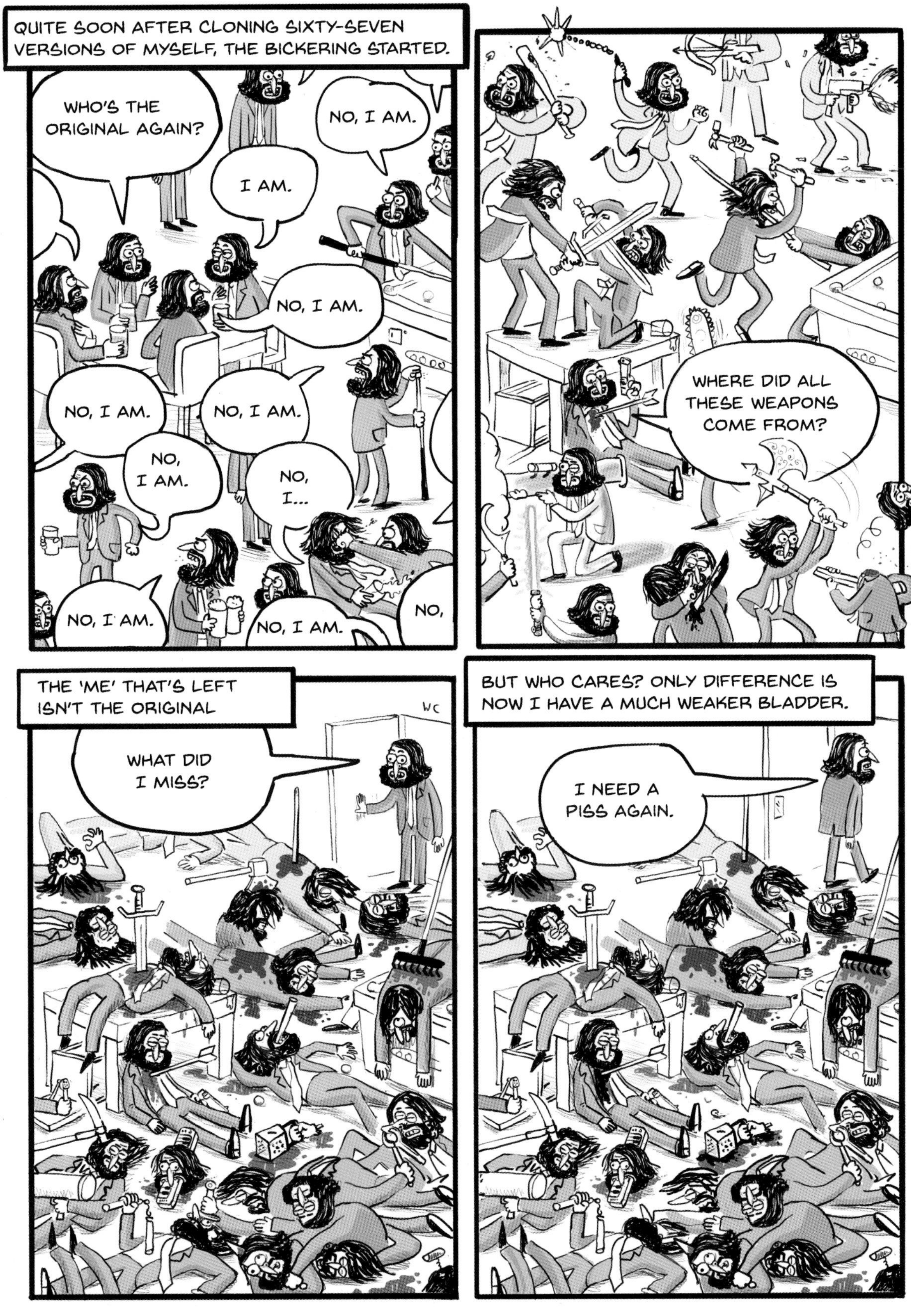
QUITE SOON AFTER CLONING SIXTY-SEVEN VERSIONS OF MYSELF, THE BICKERING STARTED.
WHO'S THE ORIGINAL AGAIN?
NO, I AM.
I AM.
NO, I AM.
NO, I AM.
NO, I AM.
NO, I AM.
NO, I...
NO, I AM.
NO, I AM.
NO,
WHERE DID ALL THESE WEAPONS COME FROM?
THE 'ME' THAT'S LEFT ISN'T THE ORIGINAL
WC
WHAT DID I MISS?
BUT WHO CARES? ONLY DIFFERENCE IS NOW I HAVE A MUCH WEAKER BLADDER.
I NEED A PISS AGAIN.

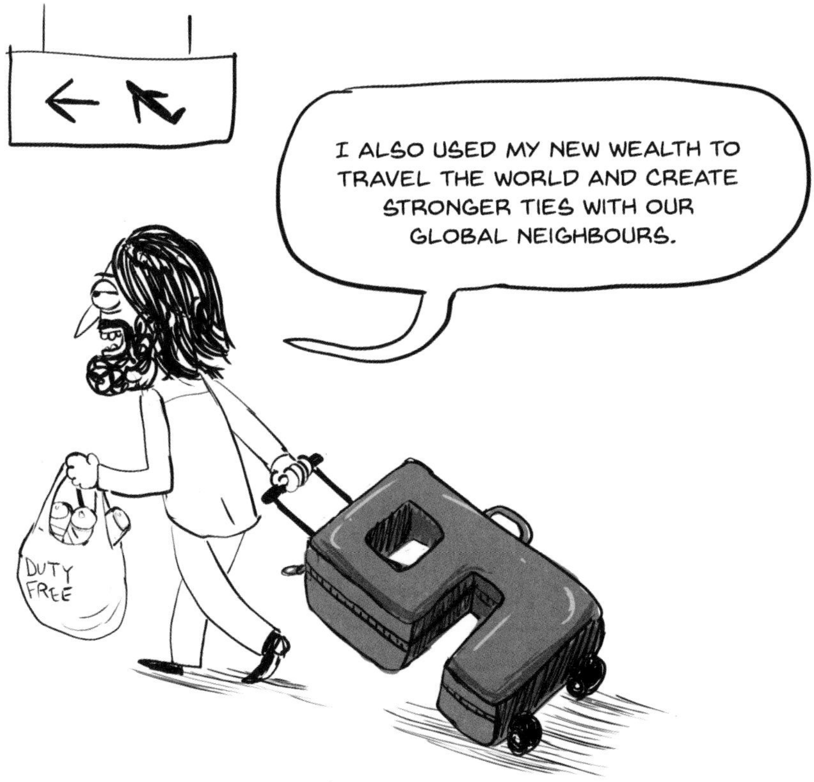
I ALSO USED MY NEW WEALTH TO TRAVEL THE WORLD AND CREATE STRONGER TIES WITH OUR GLOBAL NEIGHBOURS.
DUTY FREE

EXPERIENCING OTHER CULTURES

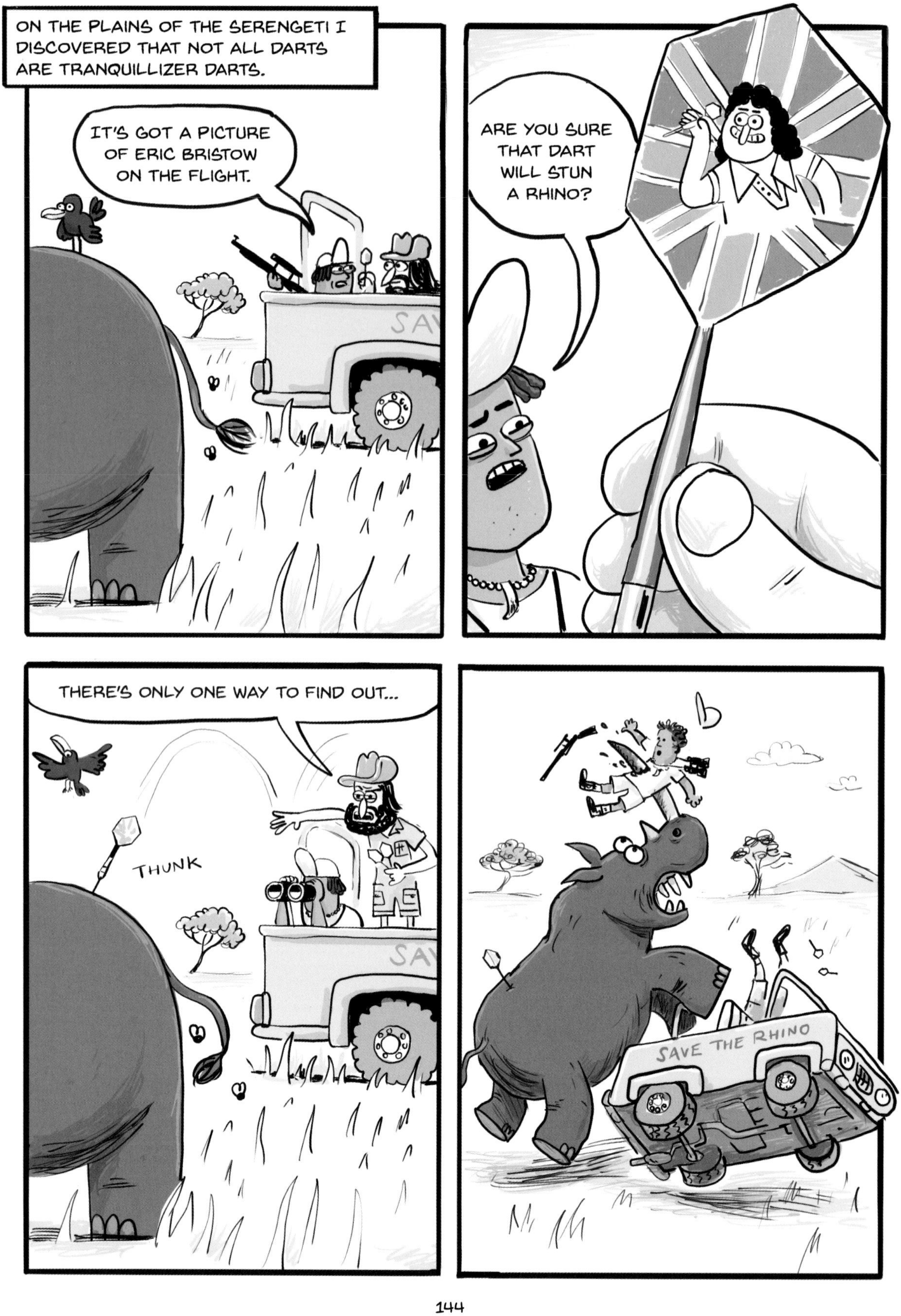

ON THE PLAINS OF THE SERENGETI I DISCOVERED THAT NOT ALL DARTS ARE TRANQUILLIZER DARTS.
IT'S GOT A PICTURE OF ERIC BRISTOW ON THE FLIGHT.
ARE YOU SURE THAT DART WILL STUN A RHINO?
THERE'S ONLY ONE WAY TO FIND OUT...
THUNK
SAVE THE RHINO

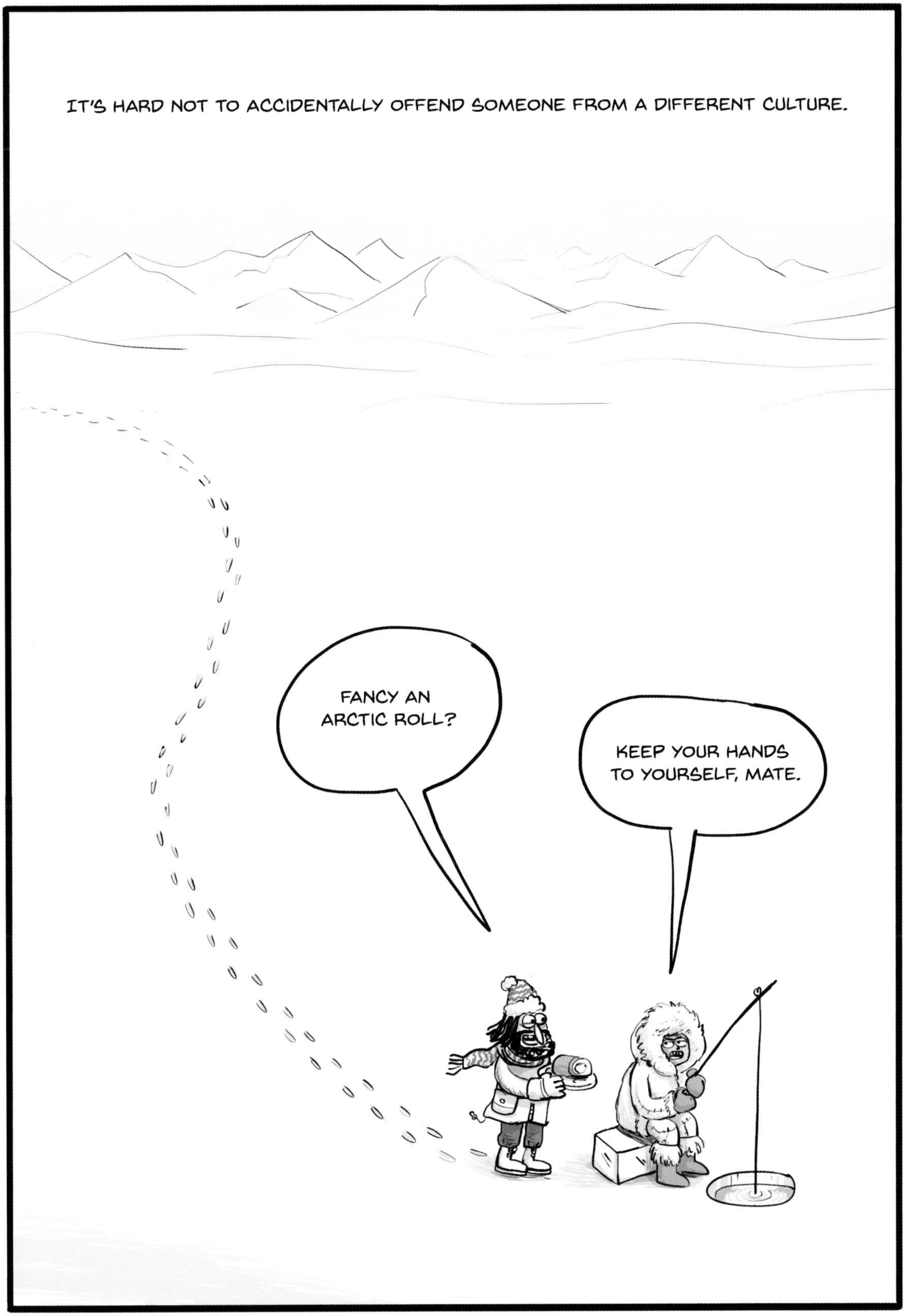
IT'S HARD NOT TO ACCIDENTALLY OFFEND SOMEONE FROM A DIFFERENT CULTURE.
FANCY AN ARCTIC ROLL?
KEEP YOUR HANDS TO YOURSELF, MATE.

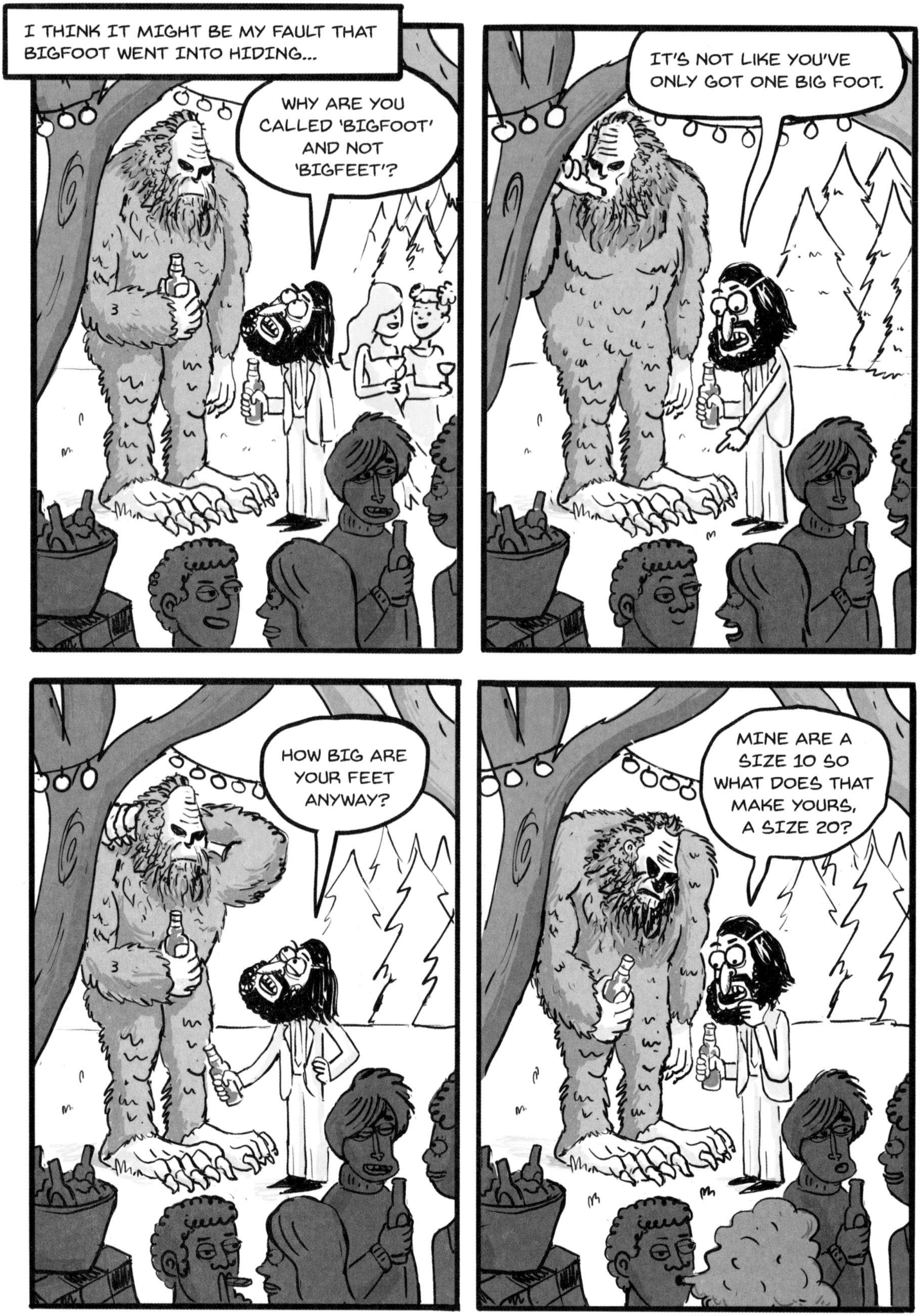
I THINK IT MIGHT BE MY FAULT THAT BIGFOOT WENT INTO HIDING...
WHY ARE YOU CALLED 'BIGFOOT' AND NOT 'BIGFEET'?
IT'S NOT LIKE YOU'VE ONLY GOT ONE BIG FOOT.
HOW BIG ARE YOUR FEET ANYWAY?
MINE ARE A SIZE 10 SO WHAT DOES THAT MAKE YOURS, A SIZE 20?

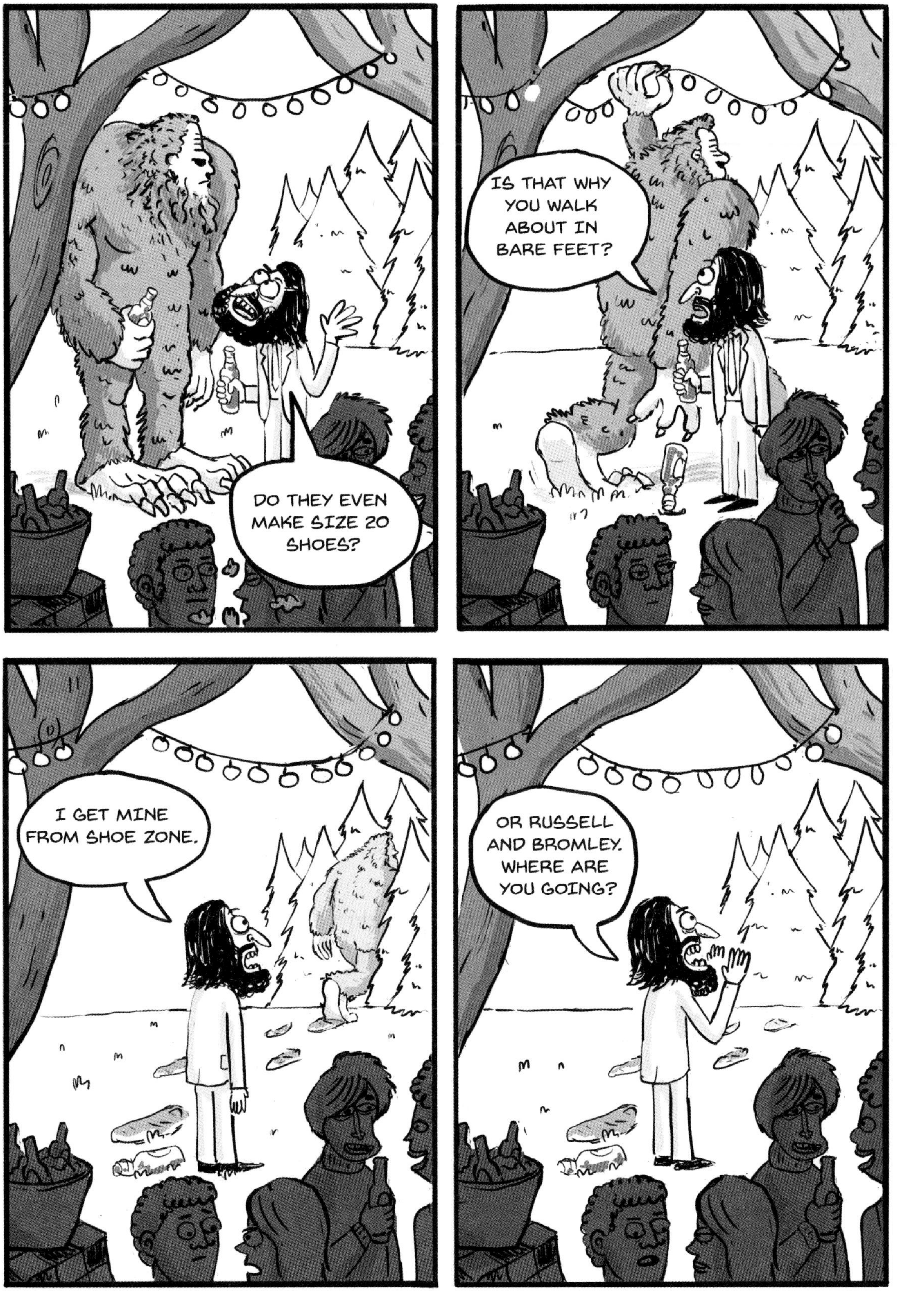
DO THEY EVEN MAKE SIZE 20 SHOES?
IS THAT WHY YOU WALK ABOUT IN BARE FEET?
I GET MINE FROM SHOE ZONE.
OR RUSSELL AND BROMLEY. WHERE ARE YOU GOING?

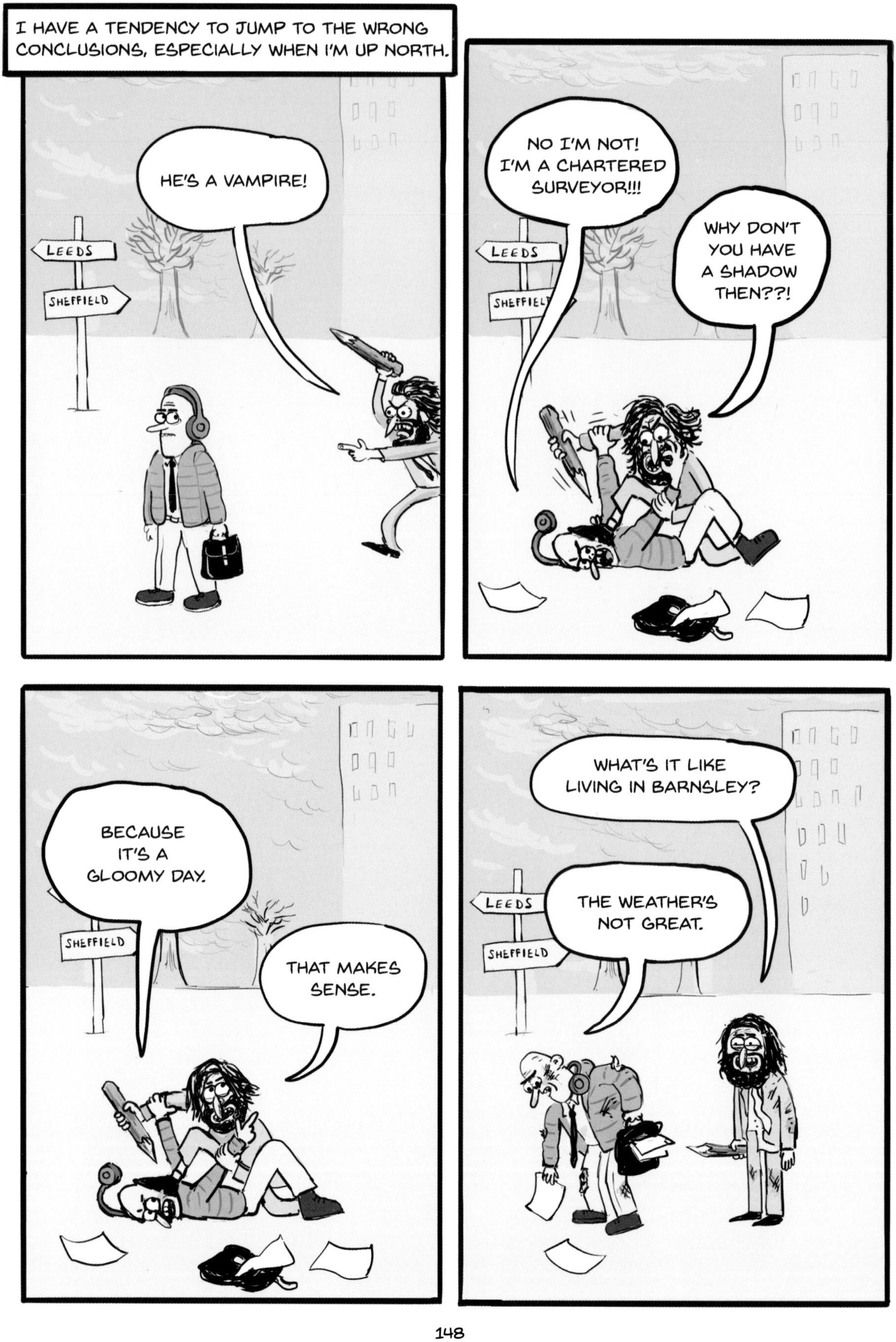
I HAVE A TENDENCY TO JUMP TO THE WRONG CONCLUSIONS, ESPECIALLY WHEN I'M UP NORTH.
LEEDS
SHEFFIELD
HE'S A VAMPIRE!
NO I'M NOT! I'M A CHARTERED SURVEYOR!!!
WHY DON'T YOU HAVE A SHADOW THEN??!
BECAUSE IT'S A GLOOMY DAY.
THAT MAKES SENSE.
WHAT'S IT LIKE LIVING IN BARNSLEY?
THE WEATHER'S NOT GREAT.

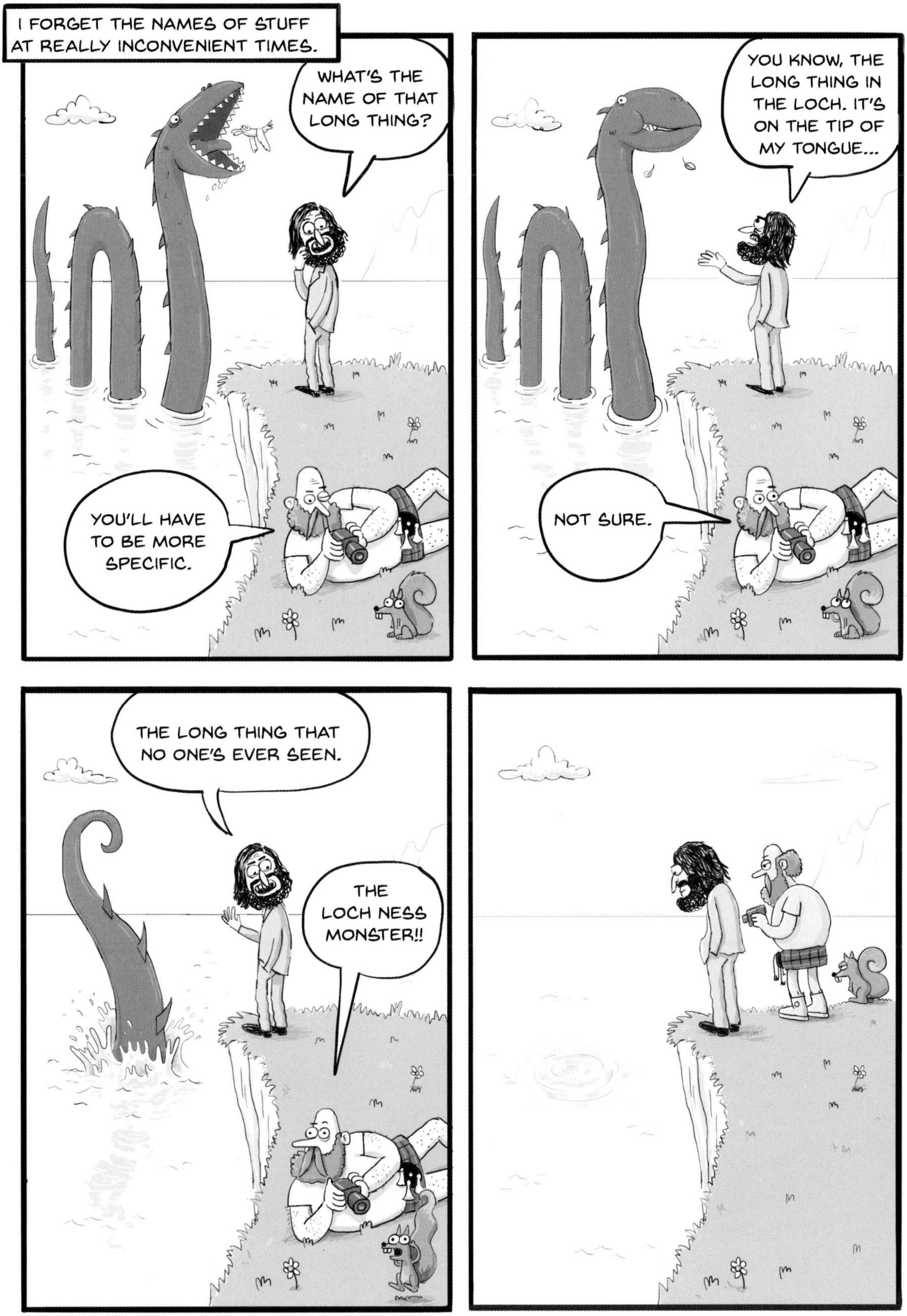
I FORGET THE NAMES OF STUFF AT REALLY INCONVENIENT TIMES.
WHAT'S THE NAME OF THAT LONG THING?
YOU'LL HAVE TO BE MORE SPECIFIC.
YOU KNOW, THE LONG THING IN THE LOCH. IT'S ON THE TIP OF MY TONGUE...
NOT SURE.
THE LONG THING THAT NO ONE'S EVER SEEN.
THE LOCH NESS MONSTER!!

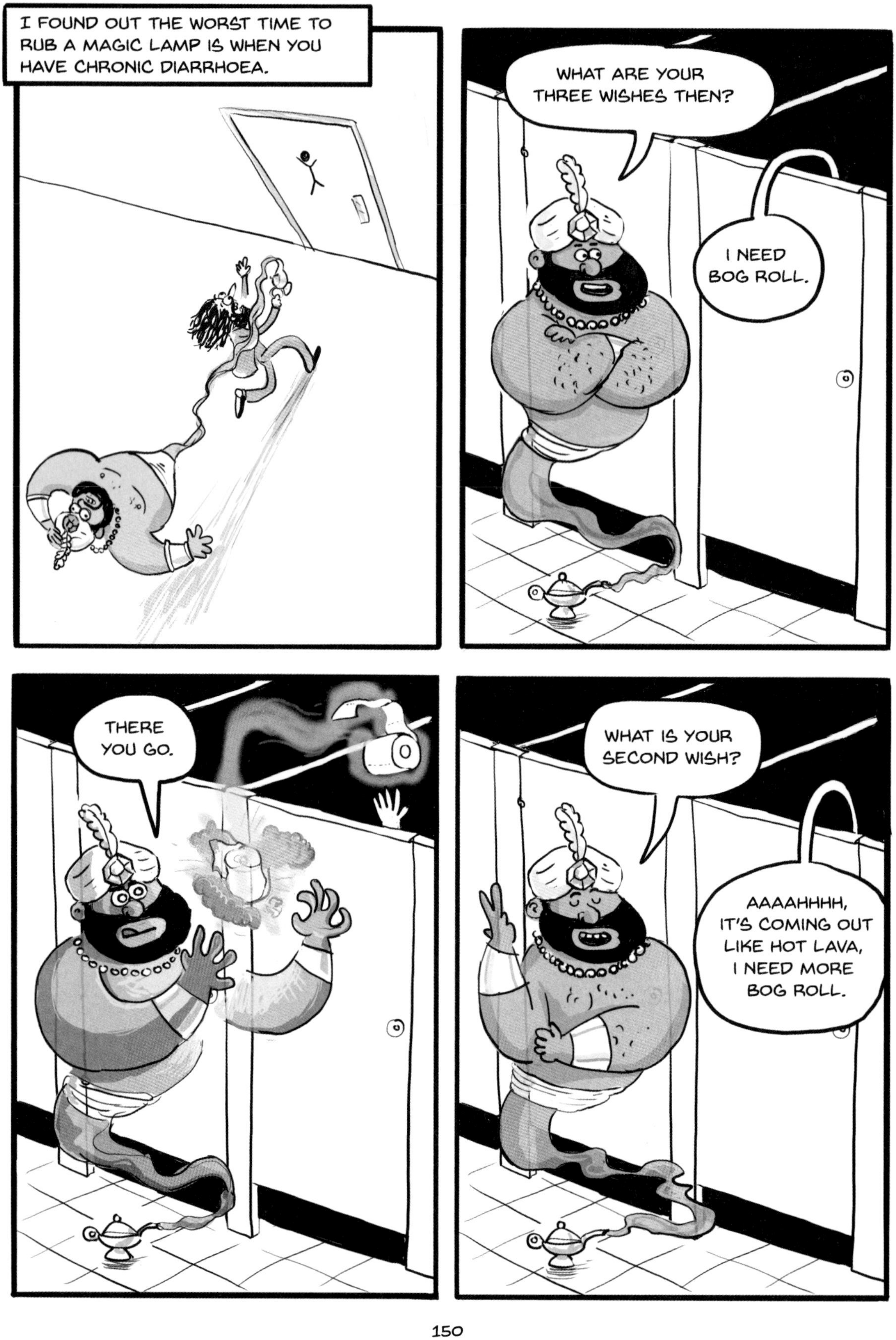
I FOUND OUT THE WORST TIME TO RUB A MAGIC LAMP IS WHEN YOU HAVE CHRONIC DIARRHOEA.
WHAT ARE YOUR THREE WISHES THEN?
I NEED BOG ROLL.
THERE YOU GO.
WHAT IS YOUR SECOND WISH?
AAAAHHHH, IT'S COMING OUT LIKE HOT LAVA, I NEED MORE BOG ROLL.

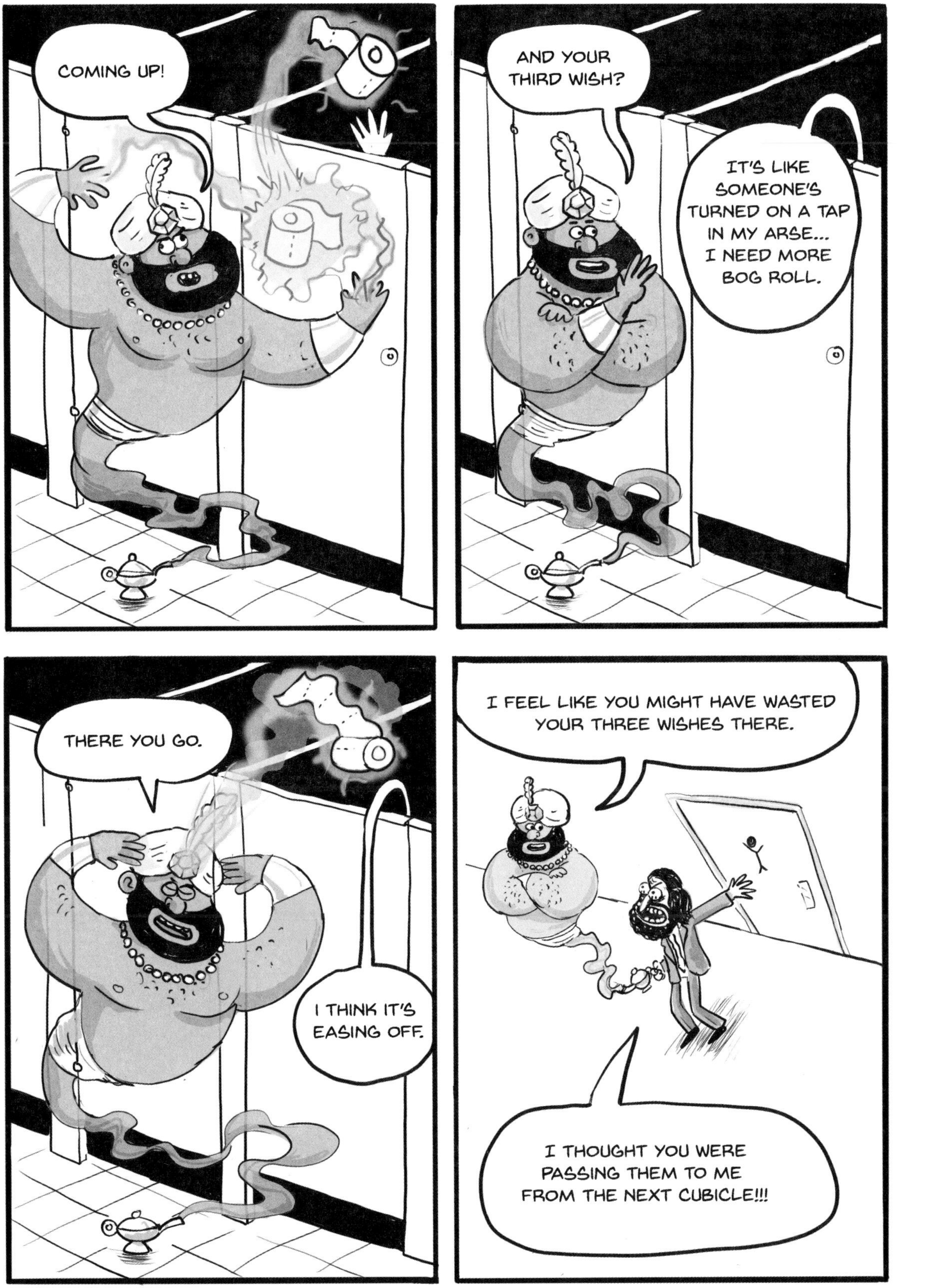
COMING UP!
AND YOUR THIRD WISH?
IT'S LIKE SOMEONE'S TURNED ON A TAP IN MY ARSE... I NEED MORE BOG ROLL.
THERE YOU GO.
I THINK IT'S EASING OFF.
I FEEL LIKE YOU MIGHT HAVE WASTED YOUR THREE WISHES THERE.
I THOUGHT YOU WERE PASSING THEM TO ME FROM THE NEXT CUBICLE!!!

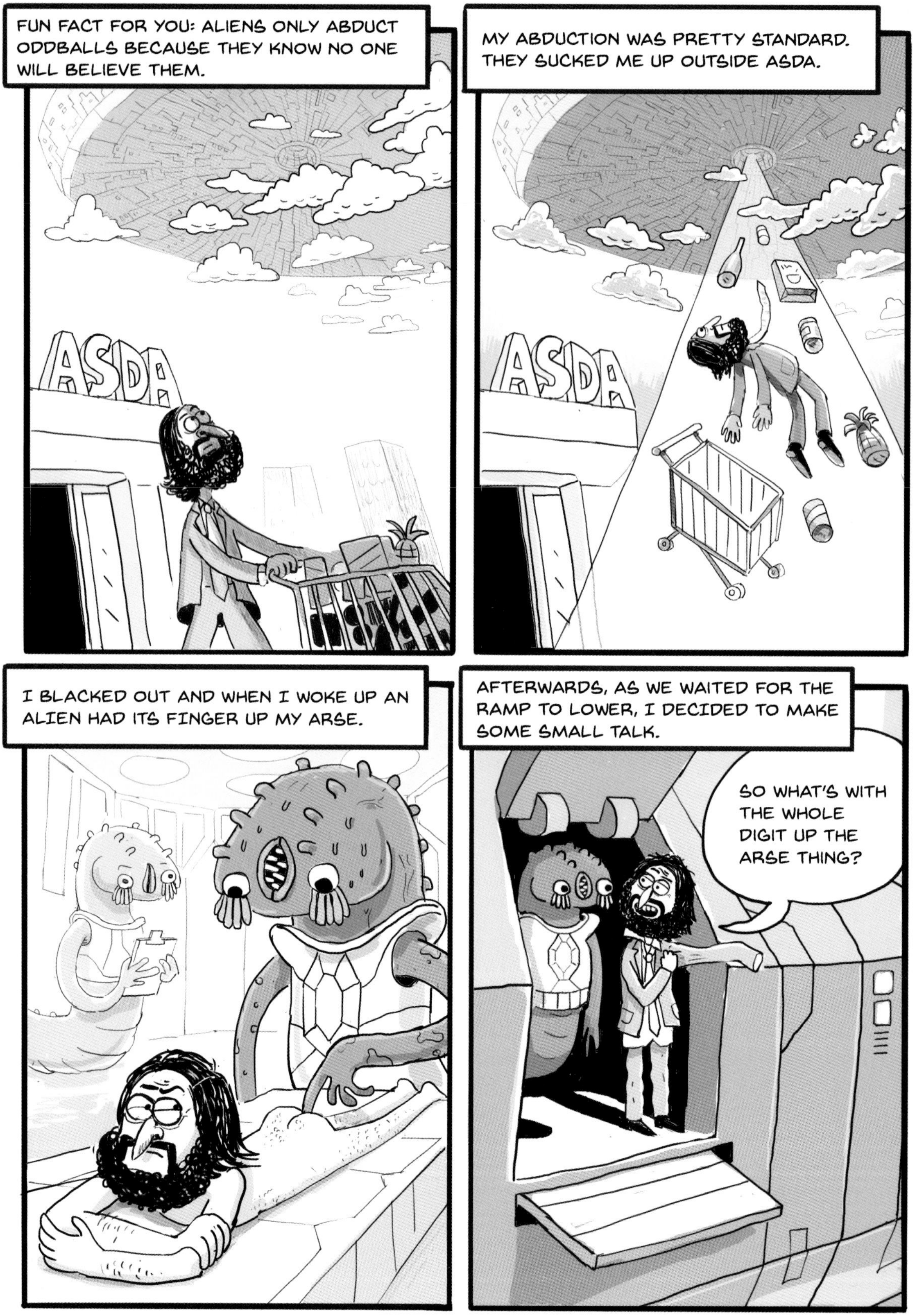
FUN FACT FOR YOU: ALIENS ONLY ABDUCT ODDBALLS BECAUSE THEY KNOW NO ONE WILL BELIEVE THEM.
ASDA
MY ABDUCTION WAS PRETTY STANDARD. THEY SUCKED ME UP OUTSIDE ASDA.
ASDA
I BLACKED OUT AND WHEN I WOKE UP AN ALIEN HAD ITS FINGER UP MY ARSE.
AFTERWARDS, AS WE WAITED FOR THE RAMP TO LOWER, I DECIDED TO MAKE SOME SMALL TALK.
SO WHAT'S WITH THE WHOLE DIGIT UP THE ARSE THING?

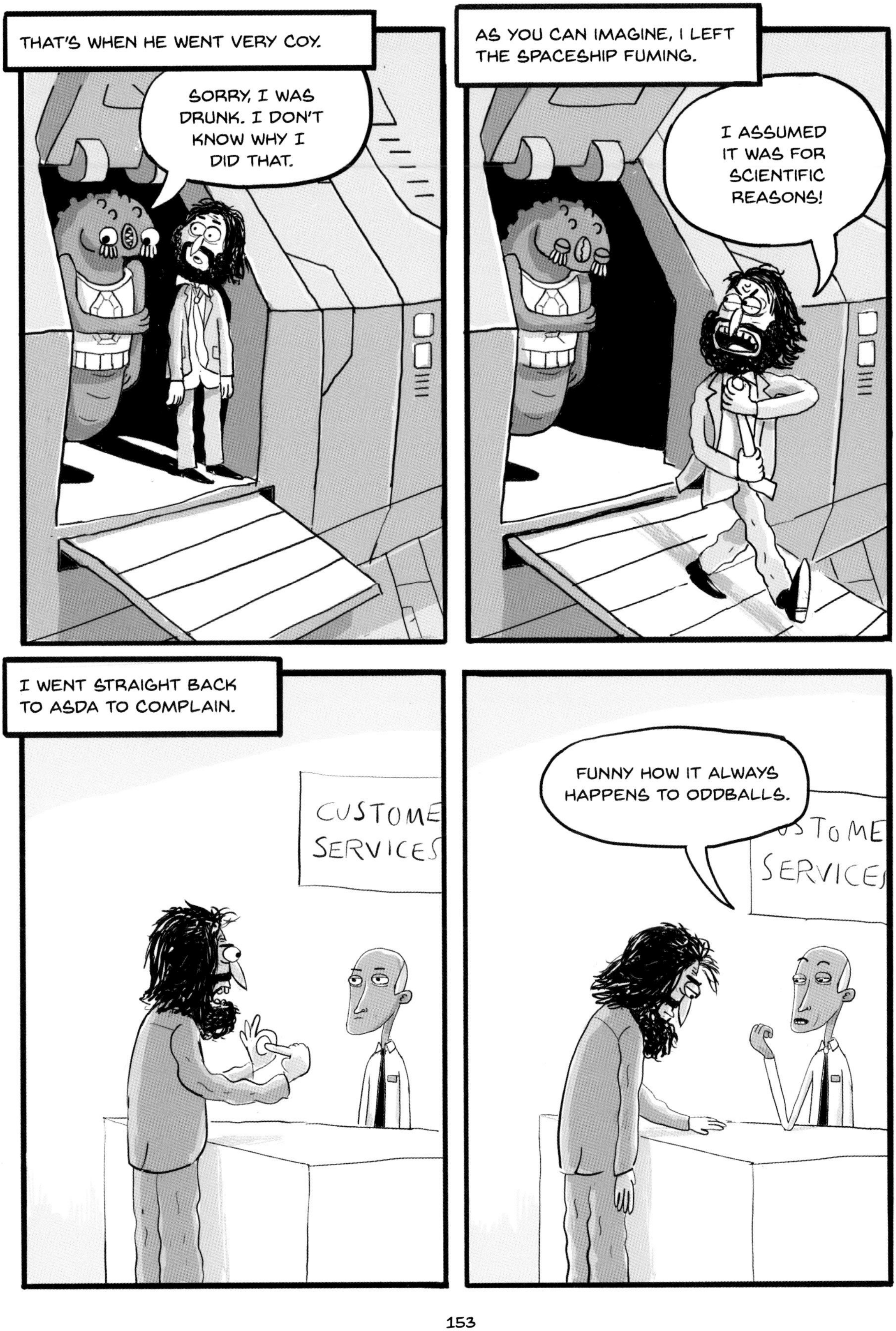
THAT'S WHEN HE WENT VERY COY.
SORRY, I WAS DRUNK. I DON'T KNOW WHY I DID THAT.
AS YOU CAN IMAGINE, I LEFT THE SPACESHIP FUMING.
I ASSUMED IT WAS FOR SCIENTIFIC REASONS!
I WENT STRAIGHT BACK TO ASDA TO COMPLAIN.
CUSTOME SERVICES
FUNNY HOW IT ALWAYS HAPPENS TO ODDBALLS.

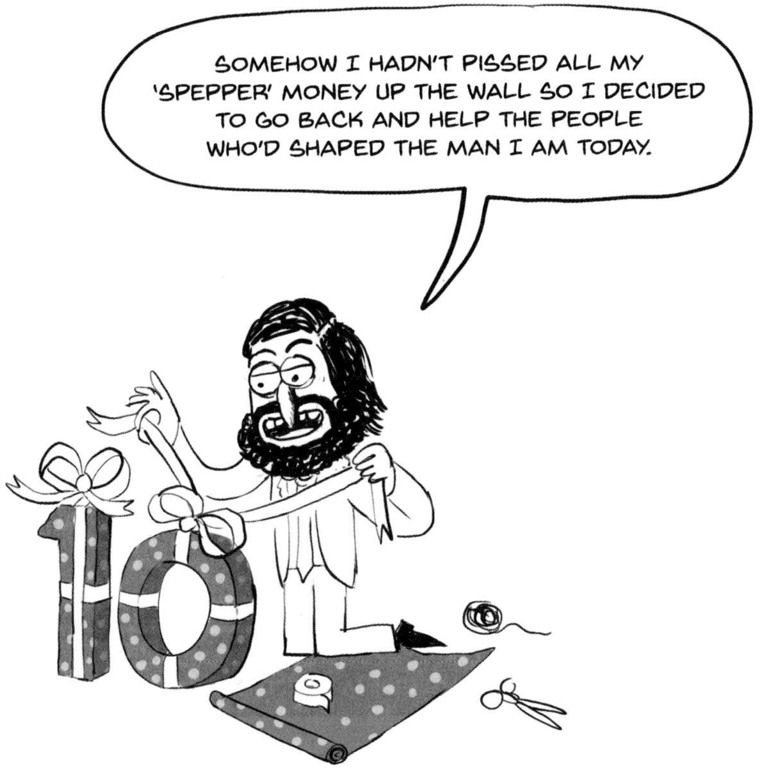
SOMEHOW I HADN'T PISSED ALL MY 'SPEPPER' MONEY UP THE WALL SO I DECIDED TO GO BACK AND HELP THE PEOPLE WHO'D SHAPED THE MAN I AM TODAY.

GIVING SOMETHING BACK

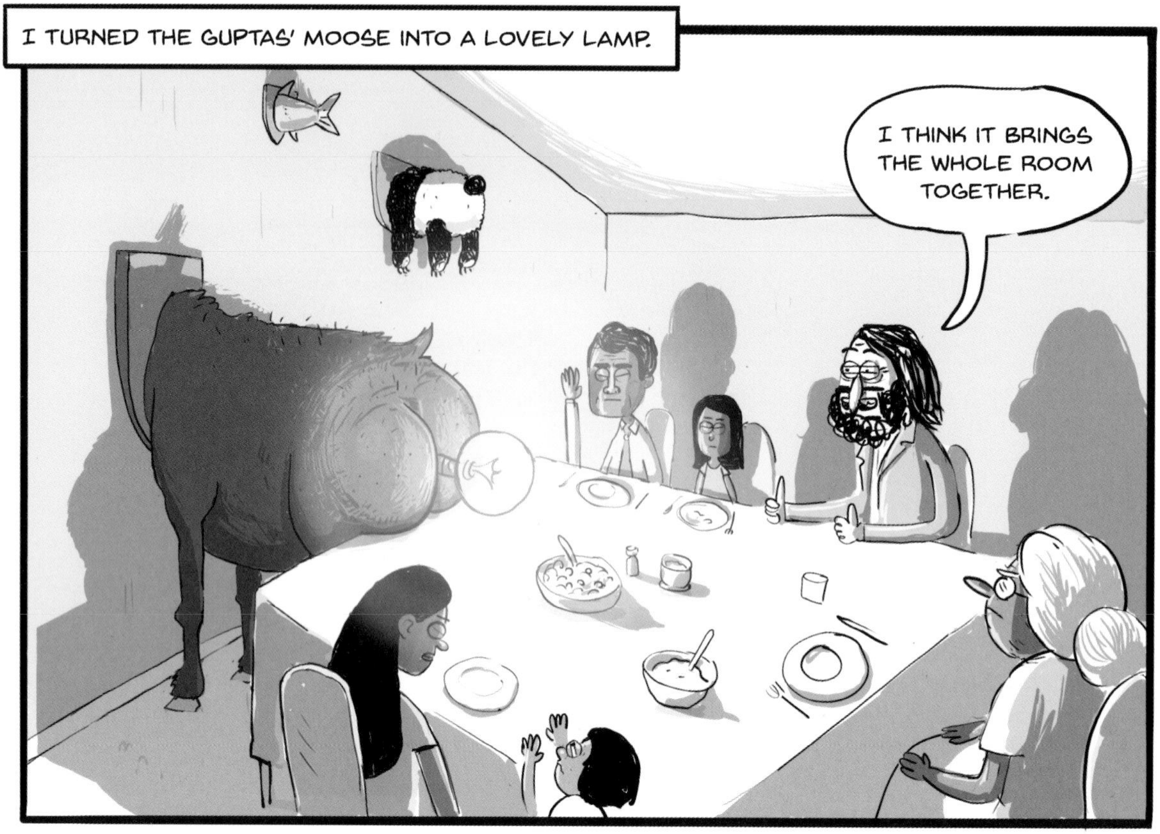
I TURNED THE GUPTAS' MOOSE INTO A LOVELY LAMP.
I THINK IT BRINGS THE WHOLE ROOM TOGETHER.

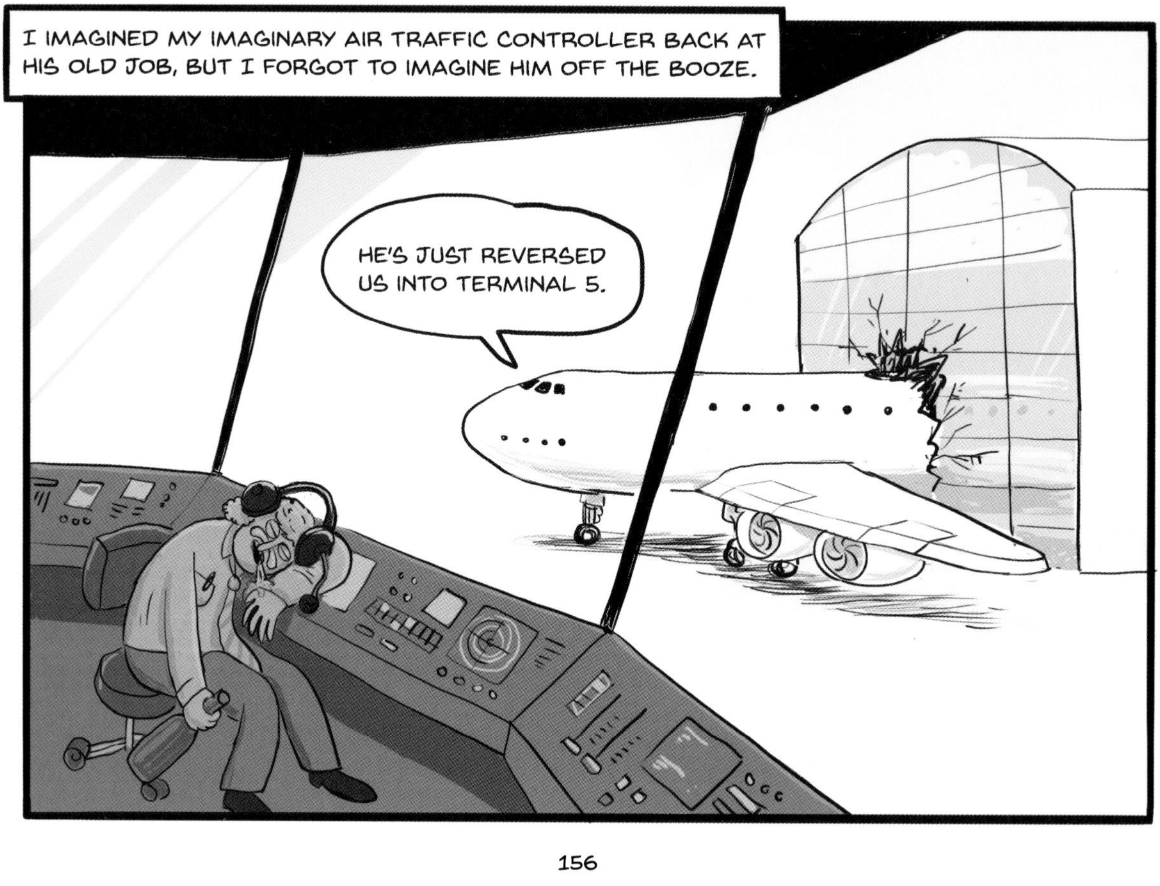
I IMAGINED MY IMAGINARY AIR TRAFFIC CONTROLLER BACK AT HIS OLD JOB, BUT I FORGOT TO IMAGINE HIM OFF THE BOOZE.
HE'S JUST REVERSED US INTO TERMINAL 5.

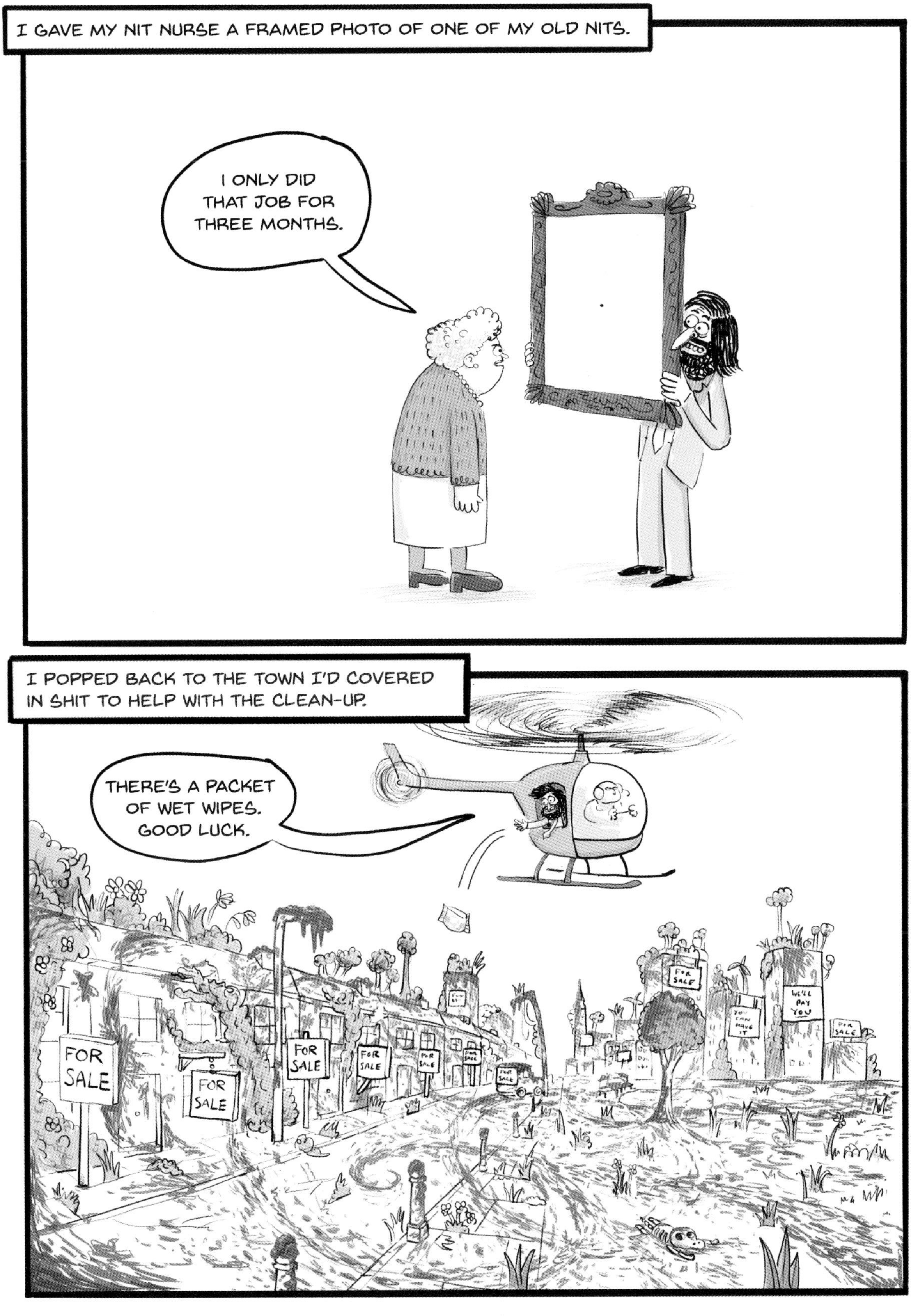
I GAVE MY NIT NURSE A FRAMED PHOTO OF ONE OF MY OLD NITS.
I ONLY DID THAT JOB FOR THREE MONTHS.
I POPPED BACK TO THE TOWN I'D COVERED IN SHIT TO HELP WITH THE CLEAN-UP.
THERE'S A PACKET OF WET WIPES. GOOD LUCK.
FOR SALE
FOR SALE
FOR SALE
FOR SALE
FOR SALE
WE'LL PAY YOU

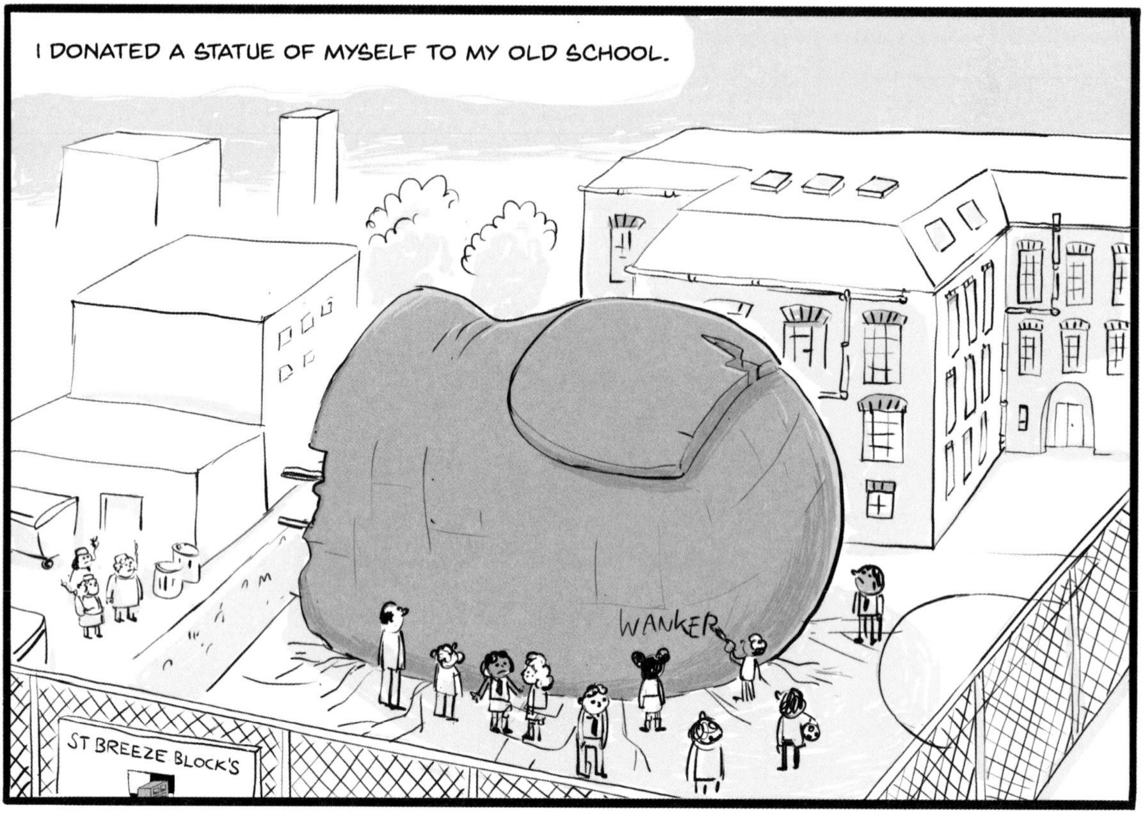
I DONATED A STATUE OF MYSELF TO MY OLD SCHOOL.
WANKER
ST BREEZE BLOCK'S

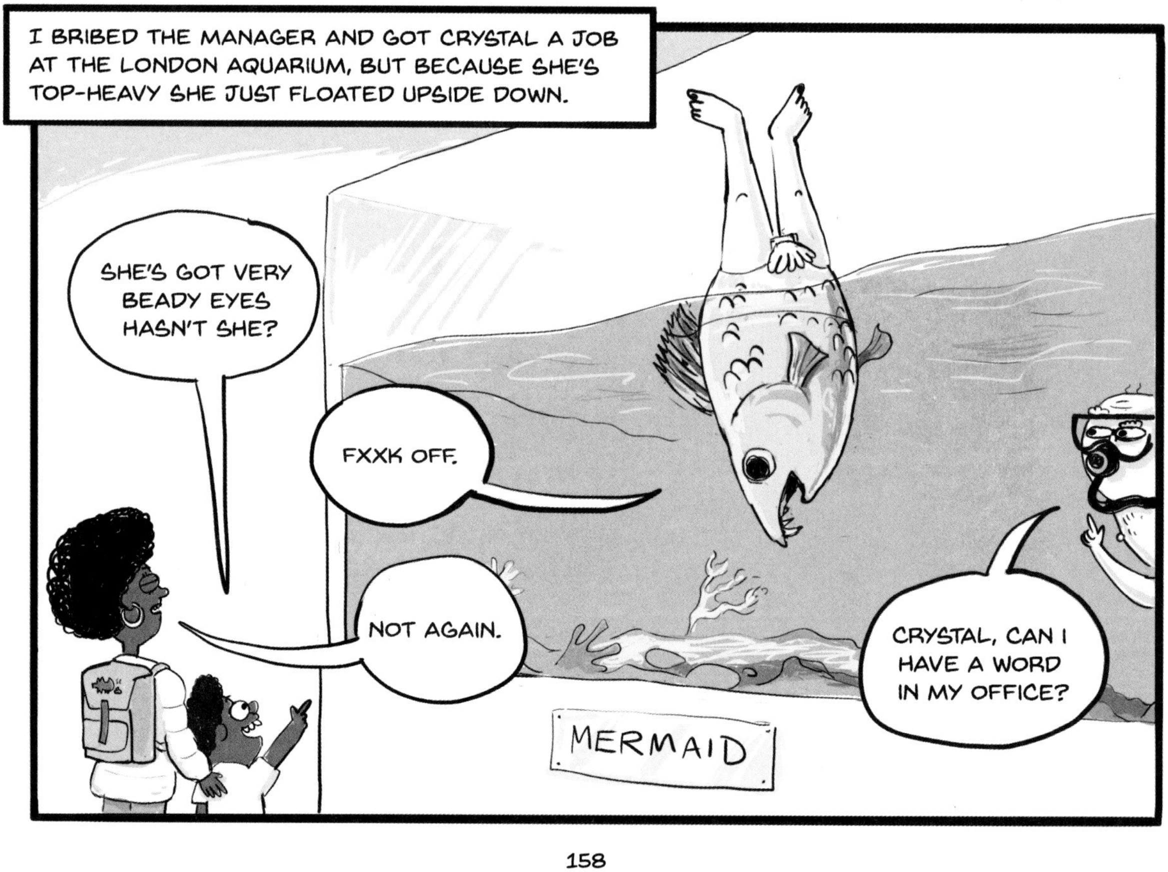
I BRIBED THE MANAGER AND GOT CRYSTAL A JOB AT THE LONDON AQUARIUM, BUT BECAUSE SHE'S TOP-HEAVY SHE JUST FLOATED UPSIDE DOWN.
SHE'S GOT VERY BEADY EYES HASN'T SHE?
FXXK OFF.
NOT AGAIN.
CRYSTAL, CAN I HAVE A WORD IN MY OFFICE?
MERMAID

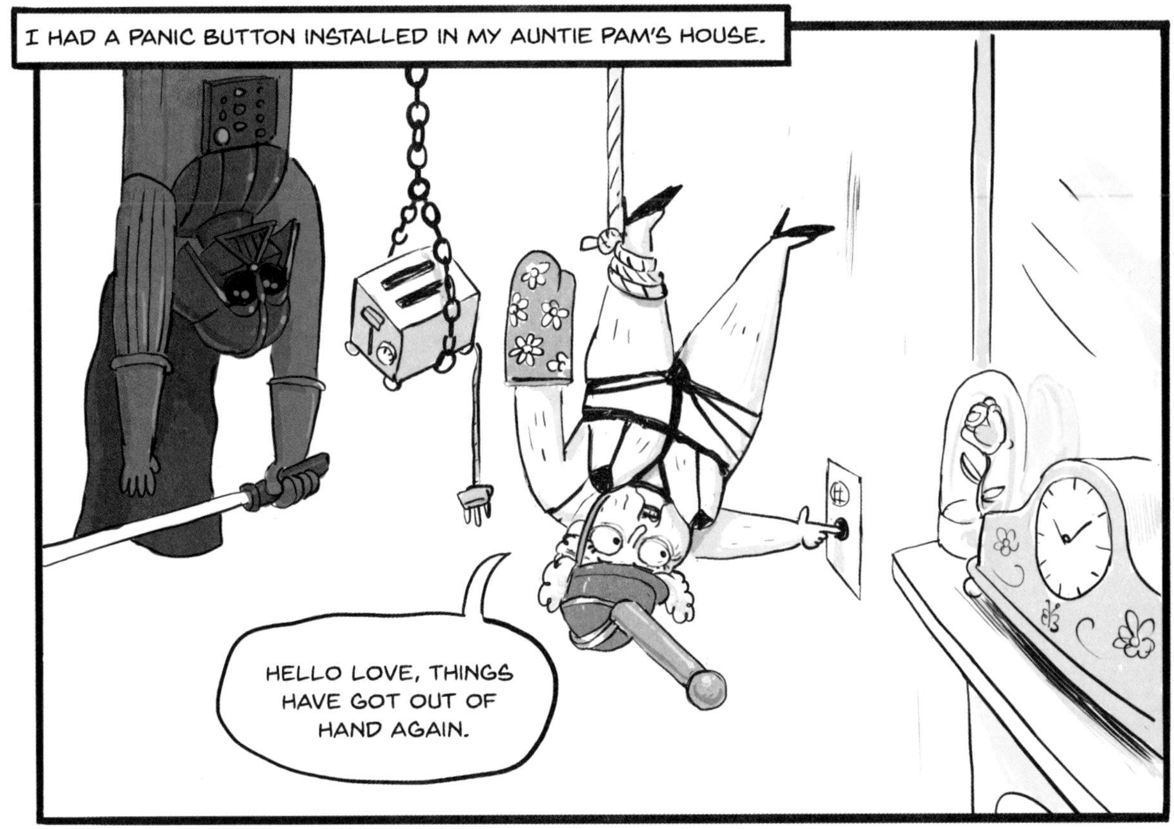
I HAD A PANIC BUTTON INSTALLED IN MY AUNTIE PAM'S HOUSE.
HELLO LOVE, THINGS HAVE GOT OUT OF HAND AGAIN.

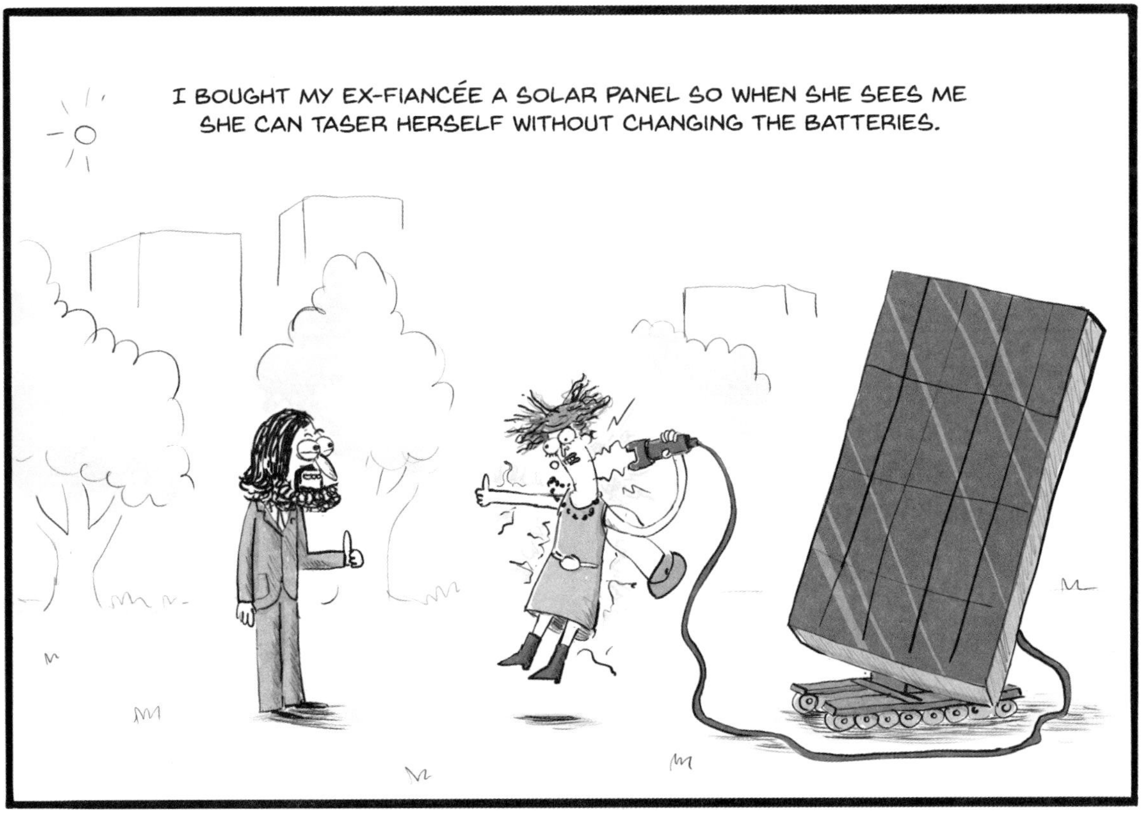
I BOUGHT MY EX-FIANCÉE A SOLAR PANEL SO WHEN SHE SEES ME SHE CAN TASER HERSELF WITHOUT CHANGING THE BATTERIES.

AS A THANK YOU FOR MY THREE WISHES I HAD SKY SPORTS INSTALLED IN THE GENIE'S LANTERN.

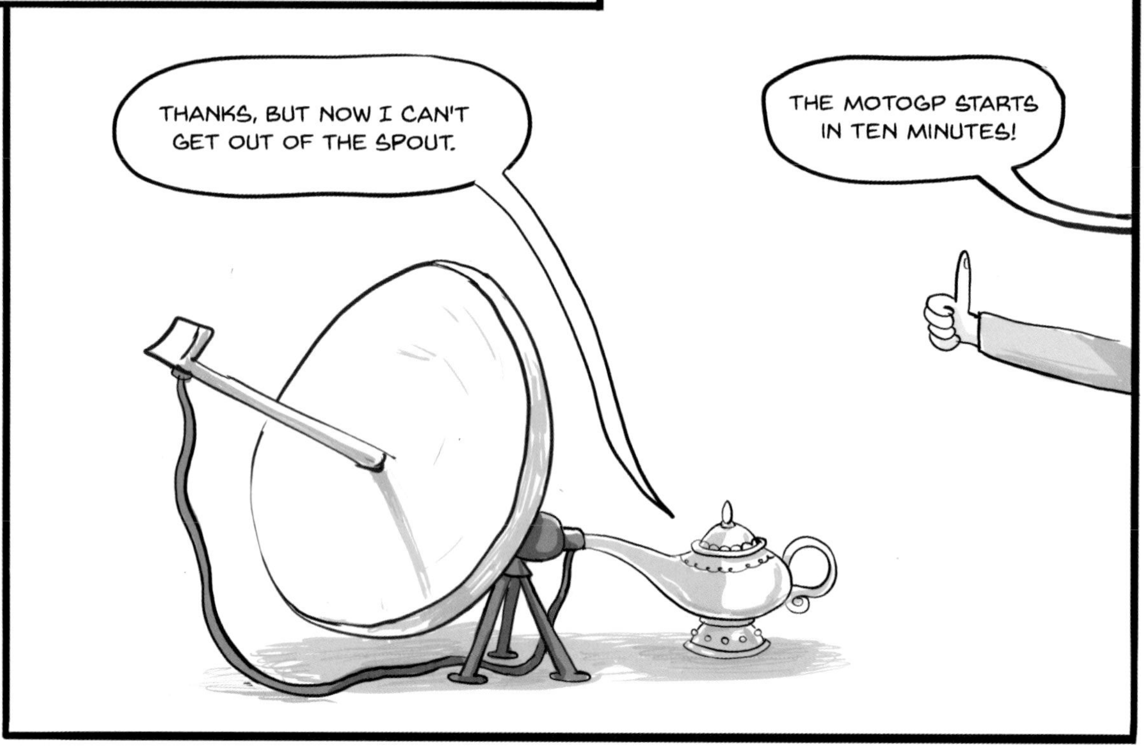
THANKS, BUT NOW I CAN'T GET OUT OF THE SPOUT.
THE MOTOGP STARTS IN TEN MINUTES!

I BOUGHT THE ALIEN A SUBSCRIPTION TO AAA.

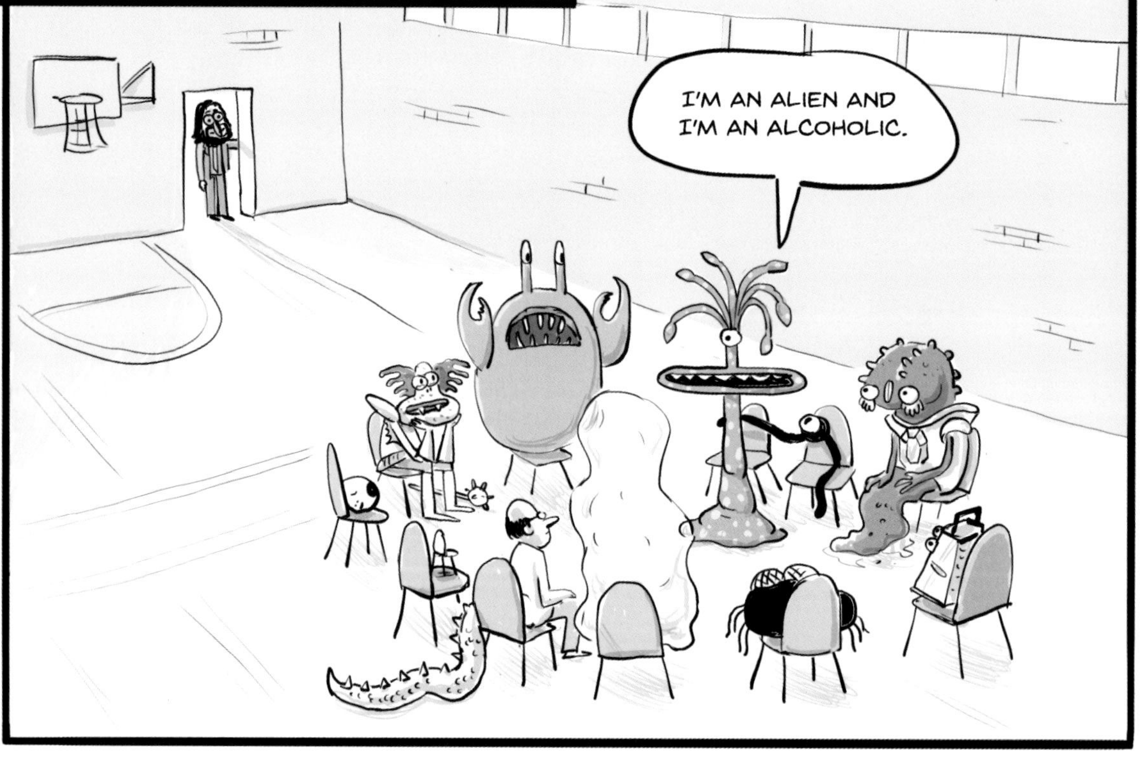
I'M AN ALIEN AND I'M AN ALCOHOLIC.

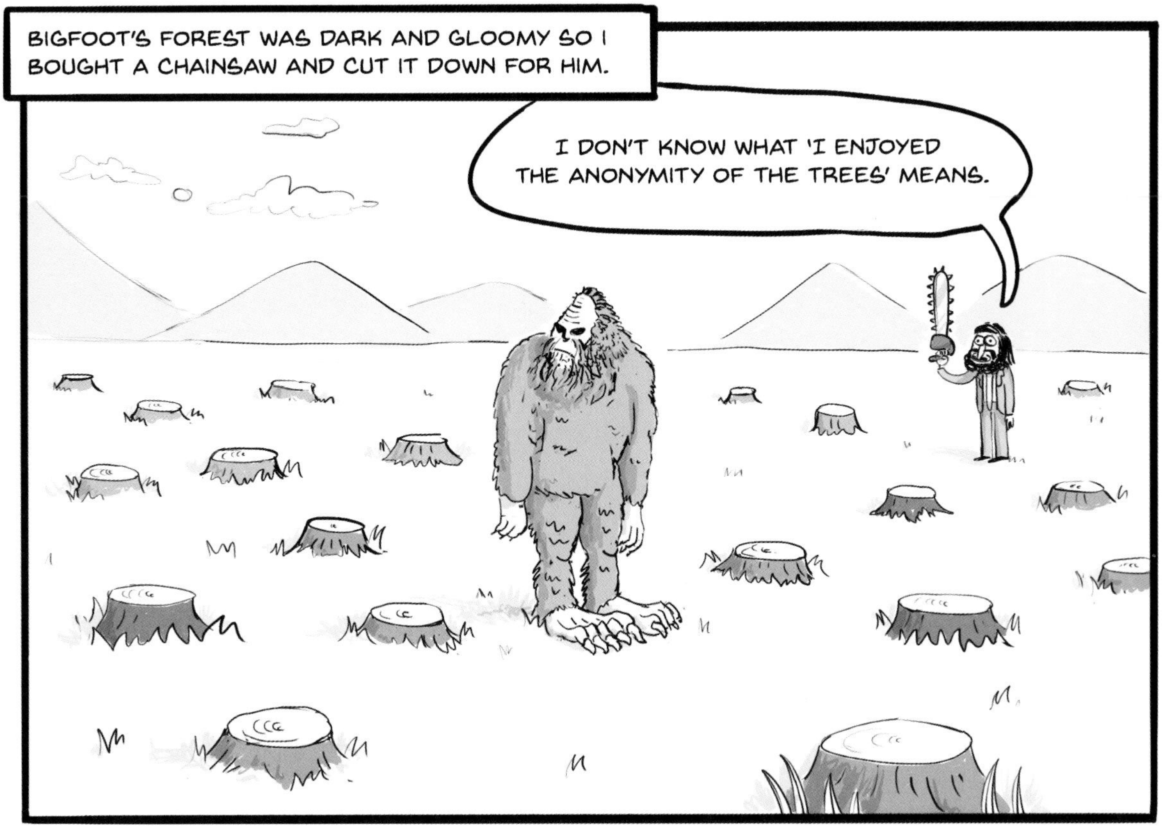
BIGFOOT'S FOREST WAS DARK AND GLOOMY SO I BOUGHT A CHAINSAW AND CUT IT DOWN FOR HIM.
I DON'T KNOW WHAT 'I ENJOYED THE ANONYMITY OF THE TREES' MEANS.

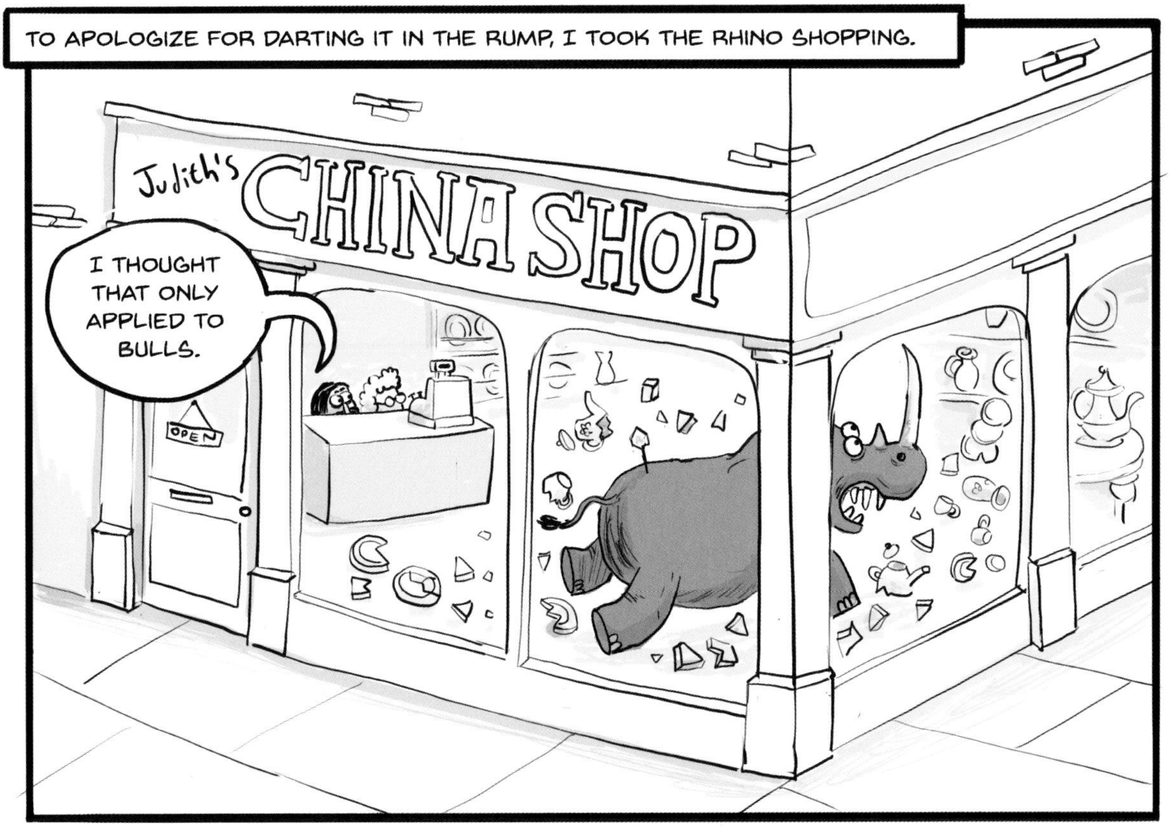
TO APOLOGIZE FOR DARTING IT IN THE RUMP, I TOOK THE RHINO SHOPPING.
Judith's CHINA SHOP
I THOUGHT THAT ONLY APPLIED TO BULLS.
OPEN

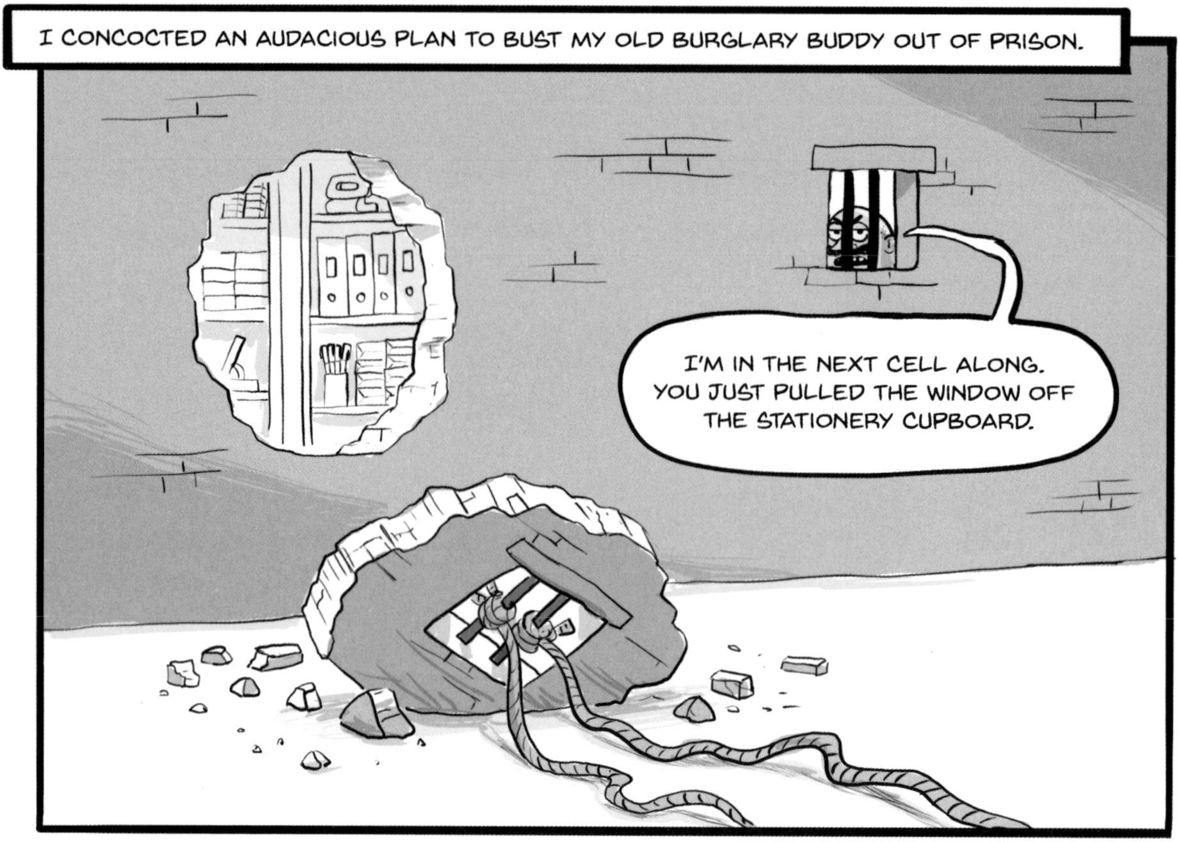
I CONCOCTED AN AUDACIOUS PLAN TO BUST MY OLD BURGLARY BUDDY OUT OF PRISON.
I'M IN THE NEXT CELL ALONG. YOU JUST PULLED THE WINDOW OFF THE STATIONERY CUPBOARD.

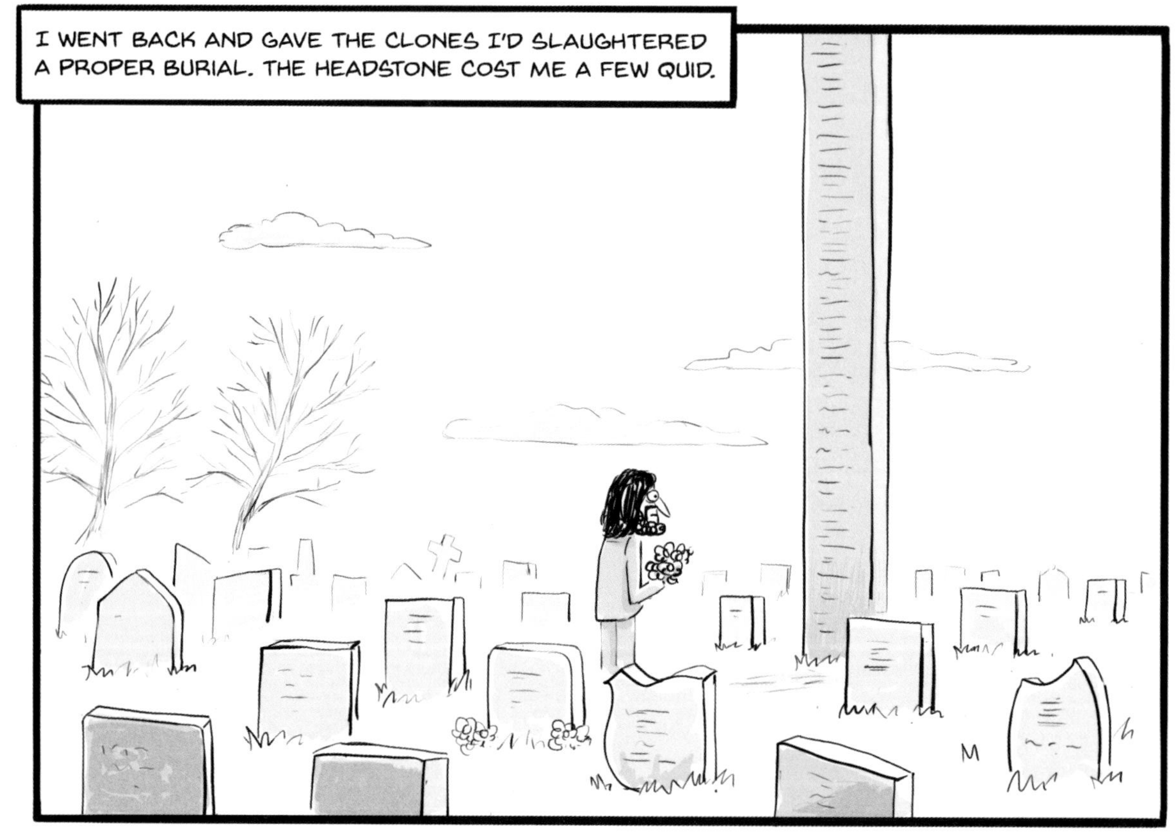
I WENT BACK AND GAVE THE CLONES I'D SLAUGHTERED A PROPER BURIAL. THE HEADSTONE COST ME A FEW QUID.

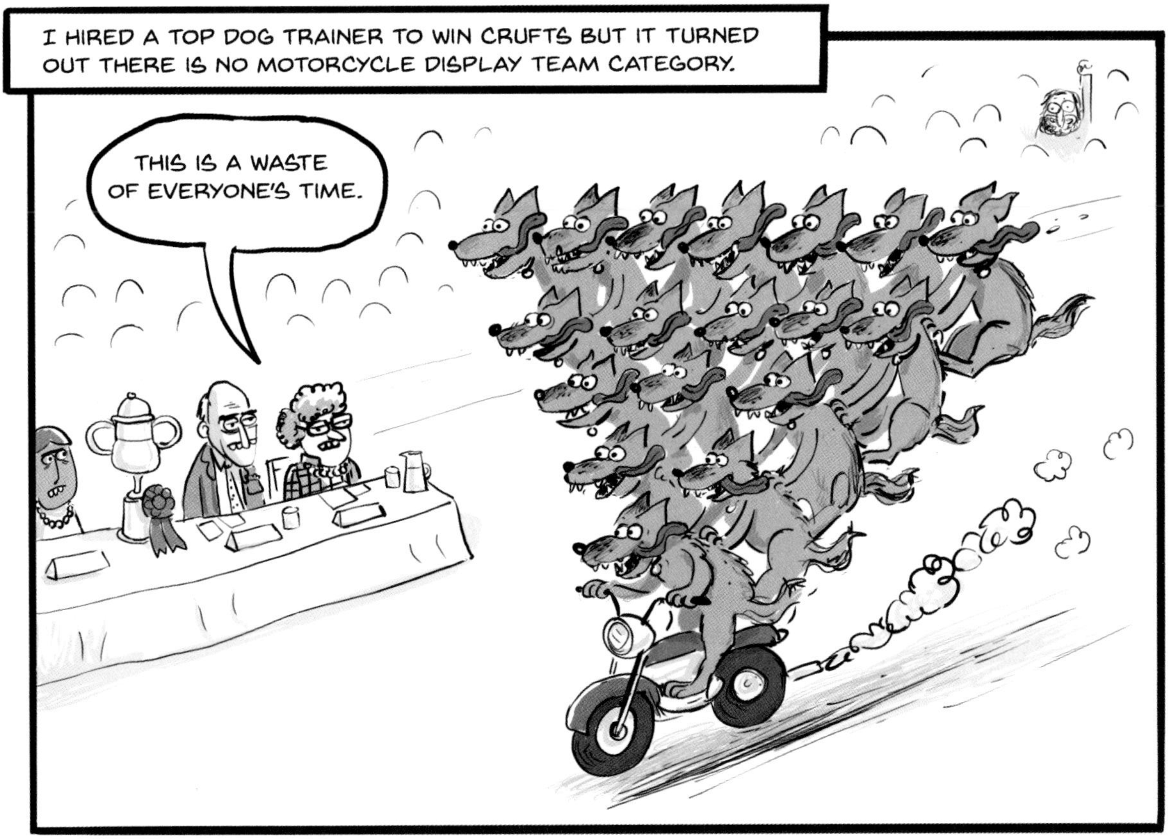
I HIRED A TOP DOG TRAINER TO WIN CRUFTS BUT IT TURNED OUT THERE IS NO MOTORCYCLE DISPLAY TEAM CATEGORY.
THIS IS A WASTE OF EVERYONE'S TIME.

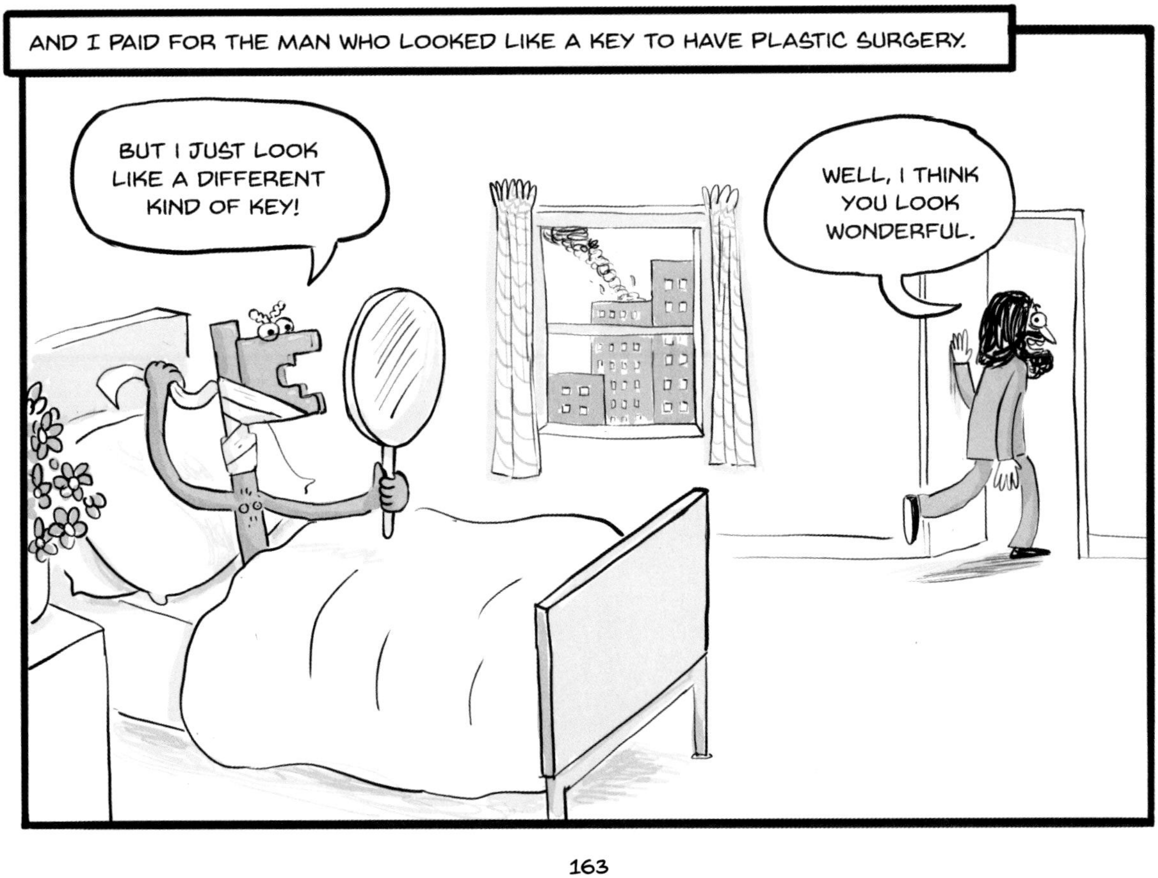
AND I PAID FOR THE MAN WHO LOOKED LIKE A KEY TO HAVE PLASTIC SURGERY.
BUT I JUST LOOK LIKE A DIFFERENT KIND OF KEY!
WELL, I THINK YOU LOOK WONDERFUL.

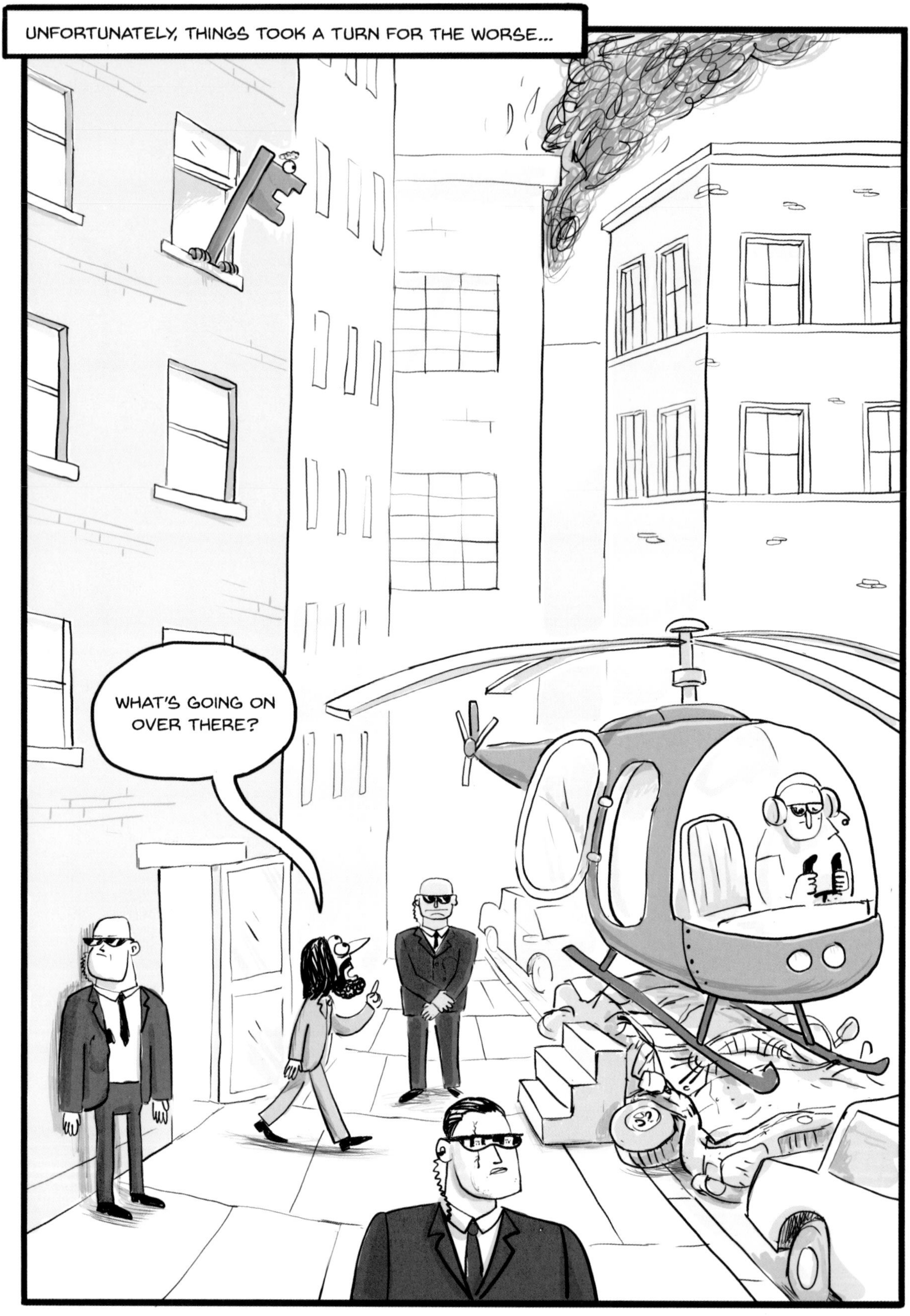
UNFORTUNATELY, THINGS TOOK A TURN FOR THE WORSE...
WHAT'S GOING ON OVER THERE?

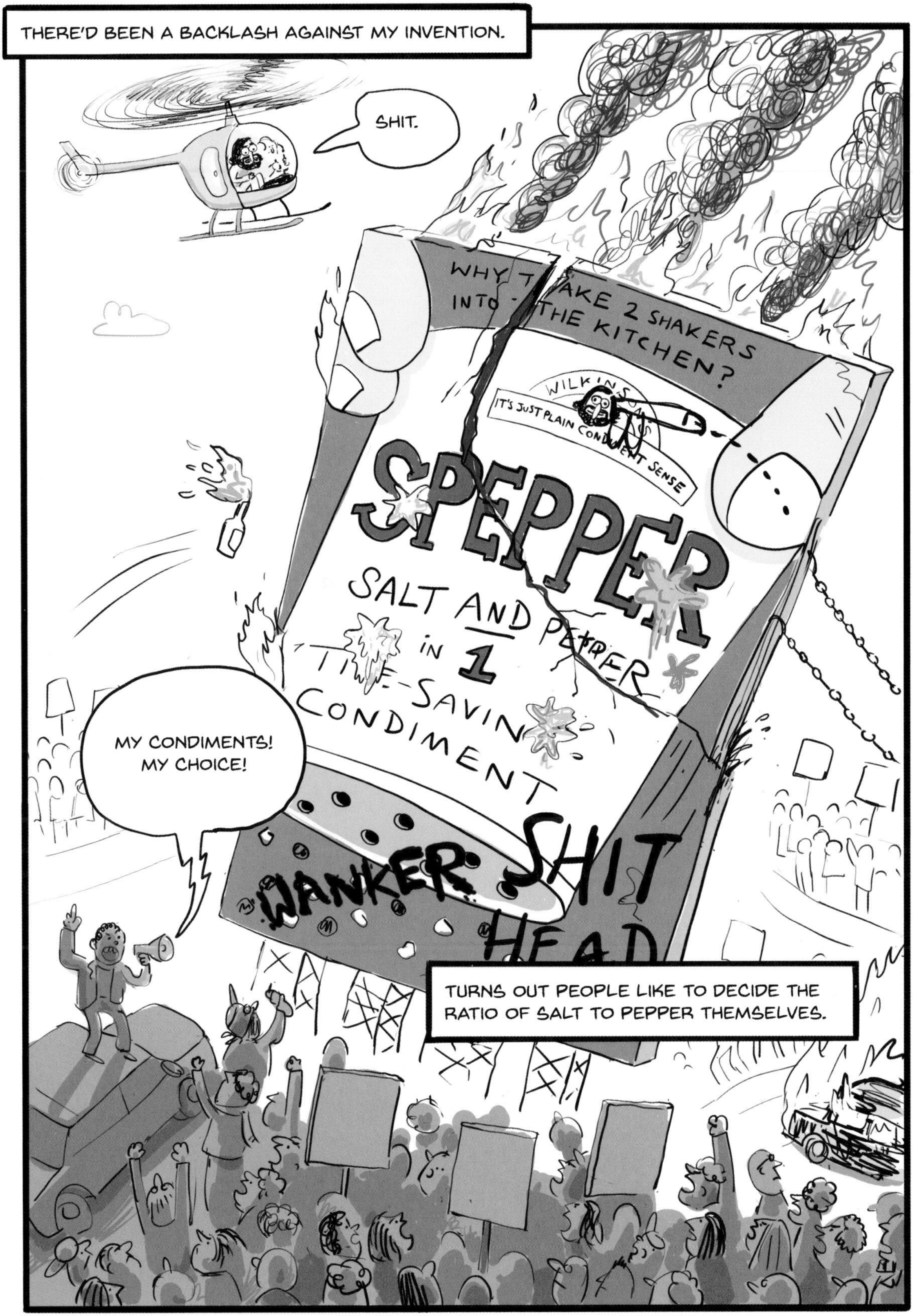
THERE'D BEEN A BACKLASH AGAINST MY INVENTION.
SHIT.
WHY TAKE 2 SHAKERS INTO THE KITCHEN?
IT'S JUST PLAIN CONDIMENT SENSE
SPEPPER
SALT AND PEPPER IN 1
CONDIMENT
MY CONDIMENTS! MY CHOICE!
WANKER
SHIT HEAD
TURNS OUT PEOPLE LIKE TO DECIDE THE RATIO OF SALT TO PEPPER THEMSELVES.

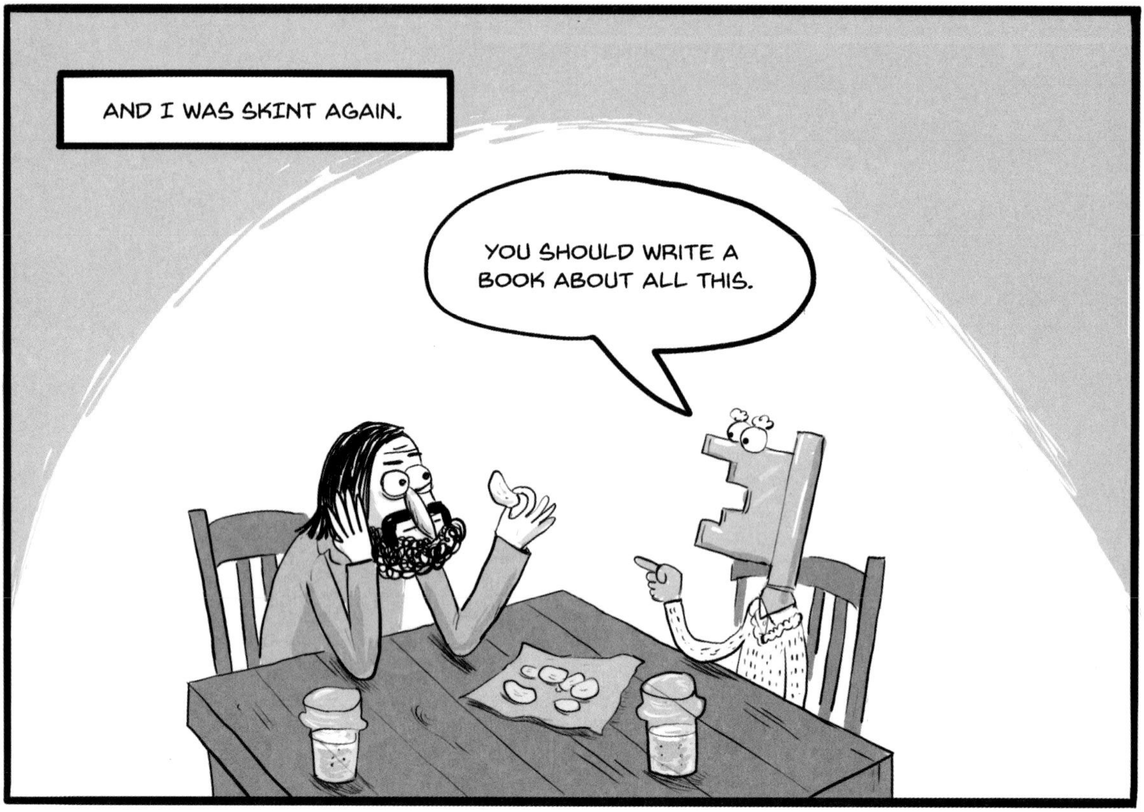
AND I WAS SKINT AGAIN.
YOU SHOULD WRITE A BOOK ABOUT ALL THIS.

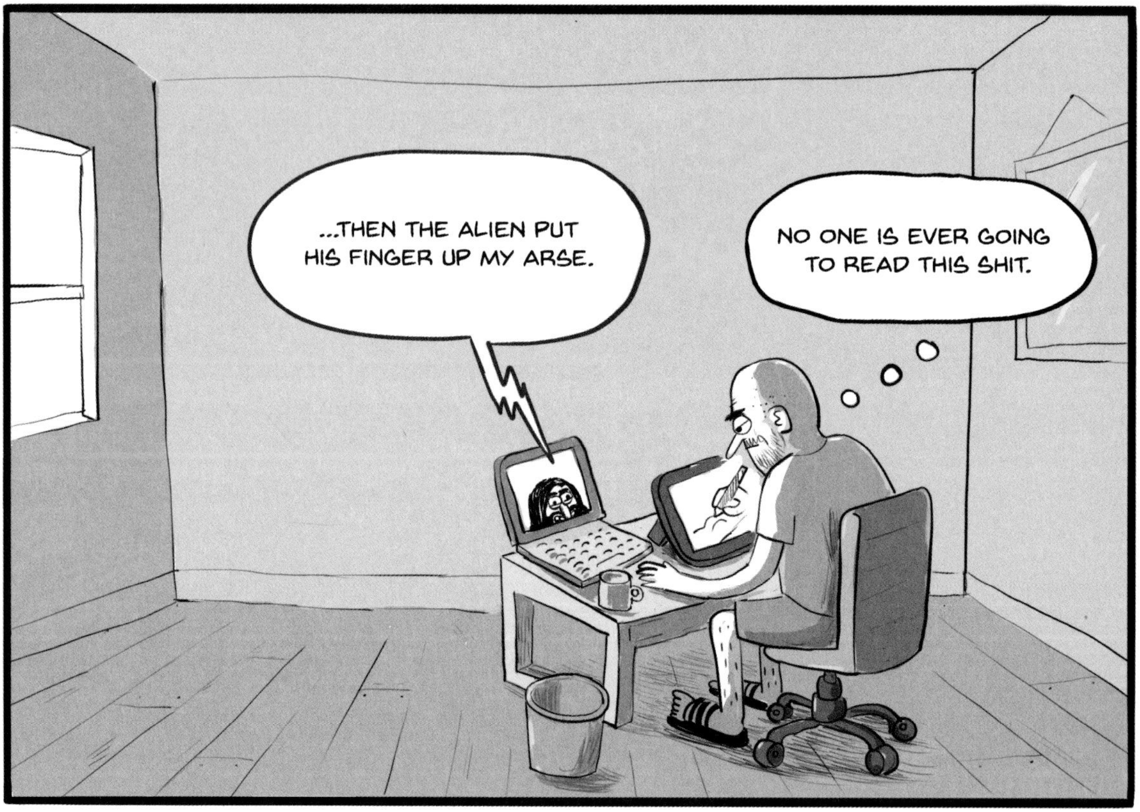
...THEN THE ALIEN PUT HIS FINGER UP MY ARSE.
NO ONE IS EVER GOING TO READ THIS SHIT.

The End

ACKNOWLEDGEMENTS

I'D LIKE TO THANK ALL MY ALSATIANS, ESPECIALLY DRAGØR.
I DON'T THINK I'D BE HERE TODAY IF IT WASN'T FOR YOUR CONTINUED LOVE AND SUPPORT.

I'D ALSO LIKE TO THANK MINTY — YOU'VE HELPED ME MORE THAN YOU WILL EVER KNOW. FOR LETTING ME BECOME THE MAN I AM TODAY.

I'D ALSO LIKE TO THANK FOXY LADY. I'VE WATCHED YOUR LEADERSHIP FROM AFAR. YOU ARE THE INSPIRATION AND FOUNDATION FOR THIS BOOK.

I'D ALSO LIKE TO THANK THE ANGLE GRINDER. I'LL NEVER FORGET OUR TIME IN DELHI.

I'D ALSO LIKE TO THANK RITA. YOU WERE MY EDITOR, MENTOR AND (HEAVEN HELP YOU) MY BEST FRIEND.

I'D ALSO LIKE TO THANK SUE. IT TAKES A VILLAGE TO RAISE A CHILD. YOU ARE MY VILLAGE.

I'D ALSO LIKE TO THANK BOB. YOU ENCOURAGED ME TO INDULGE MYSELF IN MEDIEVAL WEAPONRY. WE SPENT MANY A LONG CAR JOURNEY CREATING EPIC TALES OF SWORD-WIELDING HEROINES.

I'D ALSO LIKE TO THANK MIKE PATTERSON FOR CHECKING THE SPELING FOR ME.

I'D ALSO LIKE TO THANK TURPS. THIS BOOK IS THE BRAINCHILD OF A WET WEDNESDAY AFTERNOON CHAT WE HAD THINKING ABOUT THE STRUGGLES OF OUR YOUNGER SELVES AND LOOKING FORWARD TO HELPING GENERATIONS OF YOUNG DOG OWNERS STILL TO COME.

I'D ALSO LIKE TO THANK BATTERY ACID FOR YOUR HONESTY, PATIENCE AND BRAVERY. EVERYTHING GOOD IN MY LIFE IS BECAUSE OF YOUR LOVE AND CARE.

I'D ALSO LIKE TO THANK BIG VAL FOR REGULARLY REJECTING MY FIRST IDEAS THUS FORCING ME INTO DEEPER THOUGHT.

I'D ALSO LIKE TO THANK MERTHYR TYDFIL. NEW WRITERS WILL STUDY YOU LONG AFTER YOU ARE NO LONGER WITH US.

I'D ALSO LIKE TO THANK LUCIFER FOR EMPOWERING ME AND SO MANY OTHERS WITH YOUR GREATNESS.

I'D ALSO LIKE TO THANK GUNPOWDER FOR GUIDING ME THROUGH THE PROCESS OF HOW TO BE A NON-AWARD-WINNING WRITER.

I'D ALSO LIKE TO THANK BERNIE NOLAN AND HER RESEARCH TEAM. WITHOUT YOU THERE IS NO BOOK.

I'D ALSO LIKE TO THANK DASHER. YOU TAUGHT ME THAT DESPITE WHAT WE CONSIDER CONVINCING THEORETICAL AND EMPIRICAL EVIDENCE, A CYCLE TIME-BASED ACCOUNT IS LESS VALID THAN A PREFERRED ACTIVATION AND MICRO-LAPSES THEORY.

I'D ALSO LIKE TO THANK COURTNEY. I WROTE THIS FOR YOU BUT WHEN I BEGAN IT I HAD NOT REALIZED THAT ALSATIANS GROW QUICKER THAN BOOKS.

I'D ALSO LIKE TO THANK THE MUSCLES FROM BRUSSELS. YOU STUCK WITH ME THROUGH THIS WHOLE EPIC ROLLERCOASTER. I WOULDN'T TRADE YOU FOR ALL THE GLITTER IN THE WORLD.

SOURCES

WELCOME TO WEAVING: THE MODERN GUIDE BY LINDSEY CAMPBELL

HANDWEAVER'S PATTERN BOOK: THE ESSENTIAL ILLUSTRATED GUIDE TO OVER 600 FABRIC WEAVES BY ANNE DIXON

WEAVING AN OTHERWISE: IN-RELATIONS METHODOLOGICAL PRACTICE EDITED BY AMANDA R. TACHINE AND Z. NICOLAZZO

LEARNING TO WEAVE BY DEBORAH CHANDLER

A HANDBOOK OF WEAVES: 1875 ILLUSTRATIONS BY G. H. OELSNER

THREADS OF LIFE: A HISTORY OF THE WORLD THROUGH THE EYE OF A NEEDLE BY CLARE HUNTER

PERTH: ITS WEAVERS AND WEAVING AND THE WEAVER INCORPORATION OF PERTH BY PETER BAXTER

WEAVING AS AN ART FORM: A PERSONAL STATEMENT BY THEO MOORMAN

THE COMPLETE BASKET-MAKING BOOK WEAVING TECHNICAL WITH NATURAL MATERIAL BY REIKO SASAKI

ABOUT THE AUTHOR

JOE WILKINSON IS A REGULAR FIGURE ON KENT'S SUNDAY MORNING CAR BOOT SALE SCENE, BOTH AS A VENDOR AND A PATRON. HE'S RIDDEN SEVERAL BICYCLES AND CAN PUT HIS FIST IN HIS MOUTH. HE'S NEVER OWNED, READ OR WRITTEN A BOOK IN HIS LIFE.

HE IS ALSO AN AWARD-WINNING COMEDIAN AND HAS BEEN A FIXTURE ON OUR TELEVISION SCREENS FOR OVER A DECADE. MAKING REGULAR APPEARANCES ON SHOWS SUCH AS *8 OUT OF 10 CATS DOES COUNTDOWN*, *HAVE I GOT NEWS FOR YOU* AND *NEVER MIND THE BUZZCOCKS*, HE IS REGARDED AS ONE OF THE FINEST AND MOST SURREAL COMEDIANS ON THE CIRCUIT.

AS AN ACTOR, HE HAS STARRED IN HIT SHOWS SUCH AS *HIM & HER*, *MIRANDA*, *DEREK*, *AFTERLIFE*, *SEX EDUCATION*, *THE COCKFIELDS* AND *ROVERS*.

ABOUT THE ILLUSTRATOR

HENRY PAKER IS AN AWARD-WINNING COMEDIAN, WRITER AND ILLUSTRATOR. HE CO-WRITES AND STARS IN THE BBC RADIO 4 SITCOM *REINCARNATHAN* AND THE SKETCH SHOW *SMALL SCENES*. HE IS CO-HOST OF THE *THREE BEAN SALAD* PODCAST.

HE ILLUSTRATES ADAM KAY'S CHILDREN'S BOOKS, INCLUDING THE SUNDAY TIMES BESTSELLER *KAY'S MARVELLOUS MEDICINE* AND *KAY'S BRILLIANT BRAINS* FOR *WORLD BOOK DAY*. THEY HAVE ALSO JUST COLLABORATED ON THEIR FIRST PICTURE BOOK, *AMY GETS EATEN*. HENRY HAS ILLUSTRATED TWO HUMOUR BOOKS, *WHY STEVE WAS LATE* AND *DON'T ARM WRESTLE A PIRATE*.

HENRY SPLITS HIS TIME BETWEEN BEING AWAKE AND BEING ASLEEP.

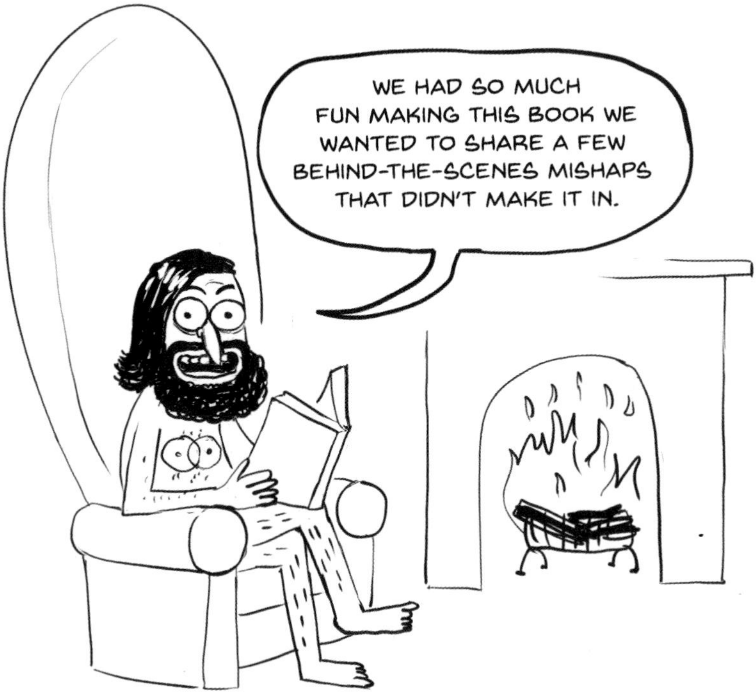
WE HAD SO MUCH FUN MAKING THIS BOOK WE WANTED TO SHARE A FEW BEHIND-THE-SCENES MISHAPS THAT DIDN'T MAKE IT IN.

BLOOPERS

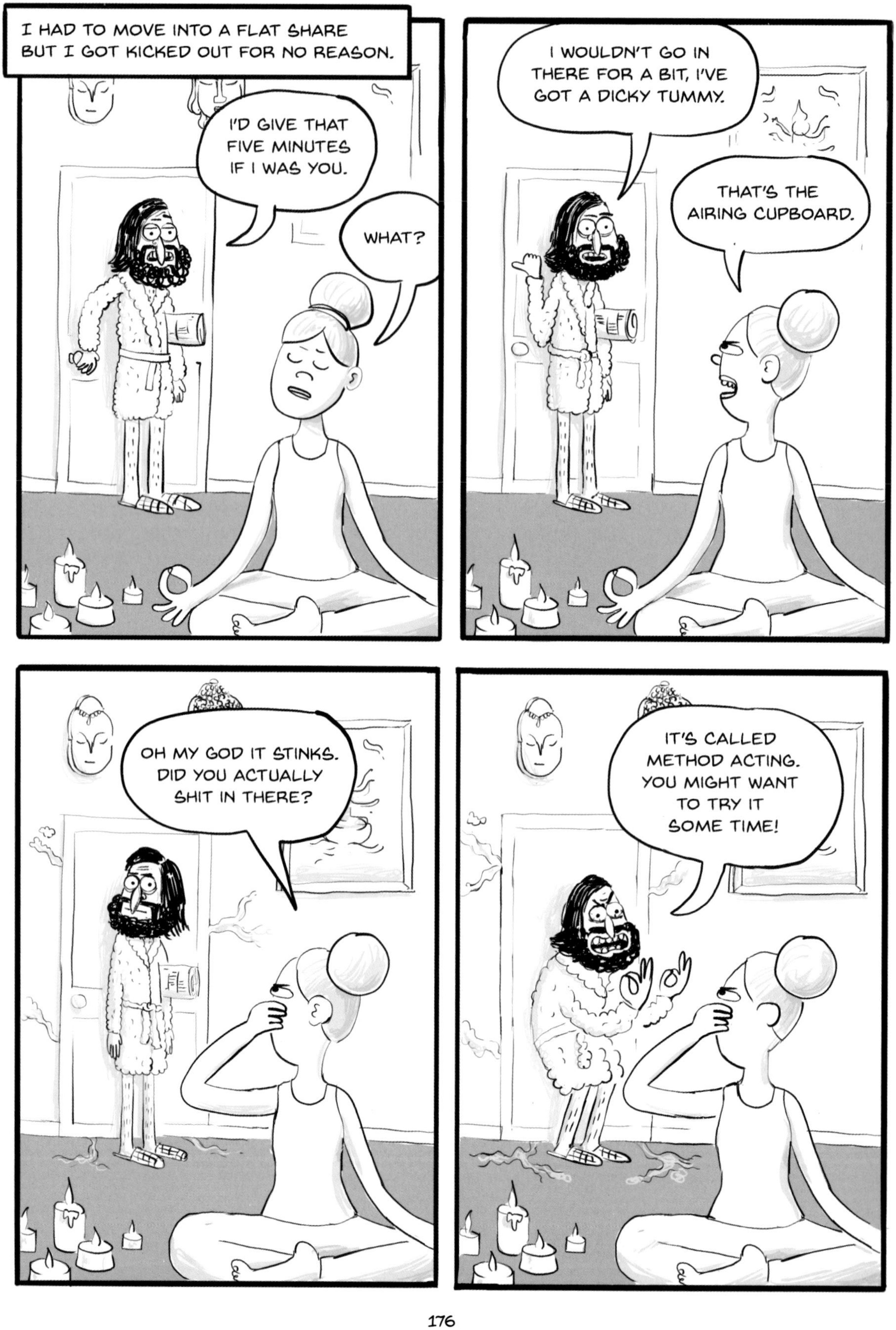
I HAD TO MOVE INTO A FLAT SHARE BUT I GOT KICKED OUT FOR NO REASON.
I'D GIVE THAT FIVE MINUTES IF I WAS YOU.
WHAT?
I WOULDN'T GO IN THERE FOR A BIT, I'VE GOT A DICKY TUMMY.
THAT'S THE AIRING CUPBOARD.
OH MY GOD IT STINKS. DID YOU ACTUALLY SHIT IN THERE?
IT'S CALLED METHOD ACTING. YOU MIGHT WANT TO TRY IT SOME TIME!

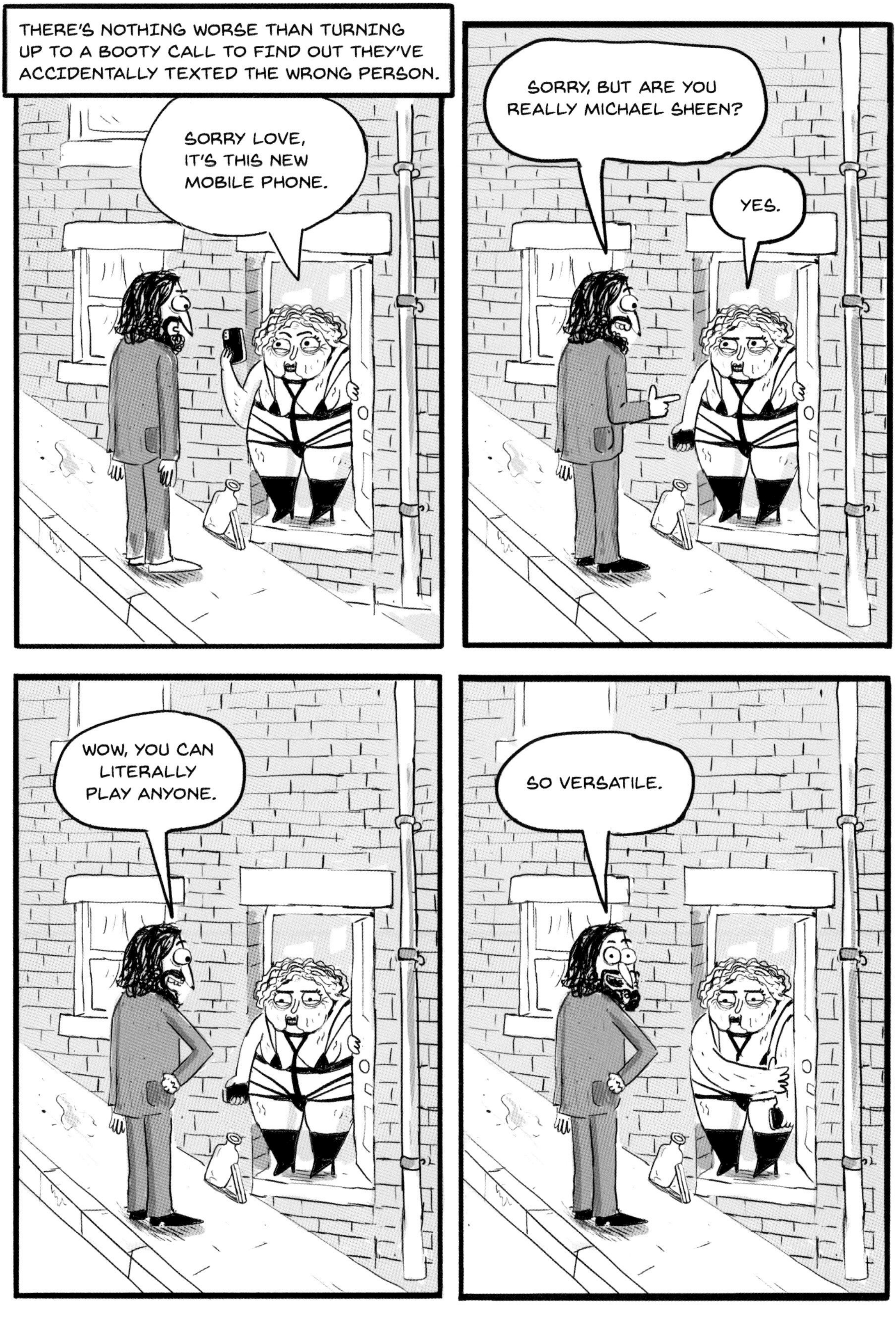
THERE'S NOTHING WORSE THAN TURNING UP TO A BOOTY CALL TO FIND OUT THEY'VE ACCIDENTALLY TEXTED THE WRONG PERSON.
SORRY LOVE, IT'S THIS NEW MOBILE PHONE.
SORRY, BUT ARE YOU REALLY MICHAEL SHEEN?
YES.
WOW, YOU CAN LITERALLY PLAY ANYONE.
SO VERSATILE.

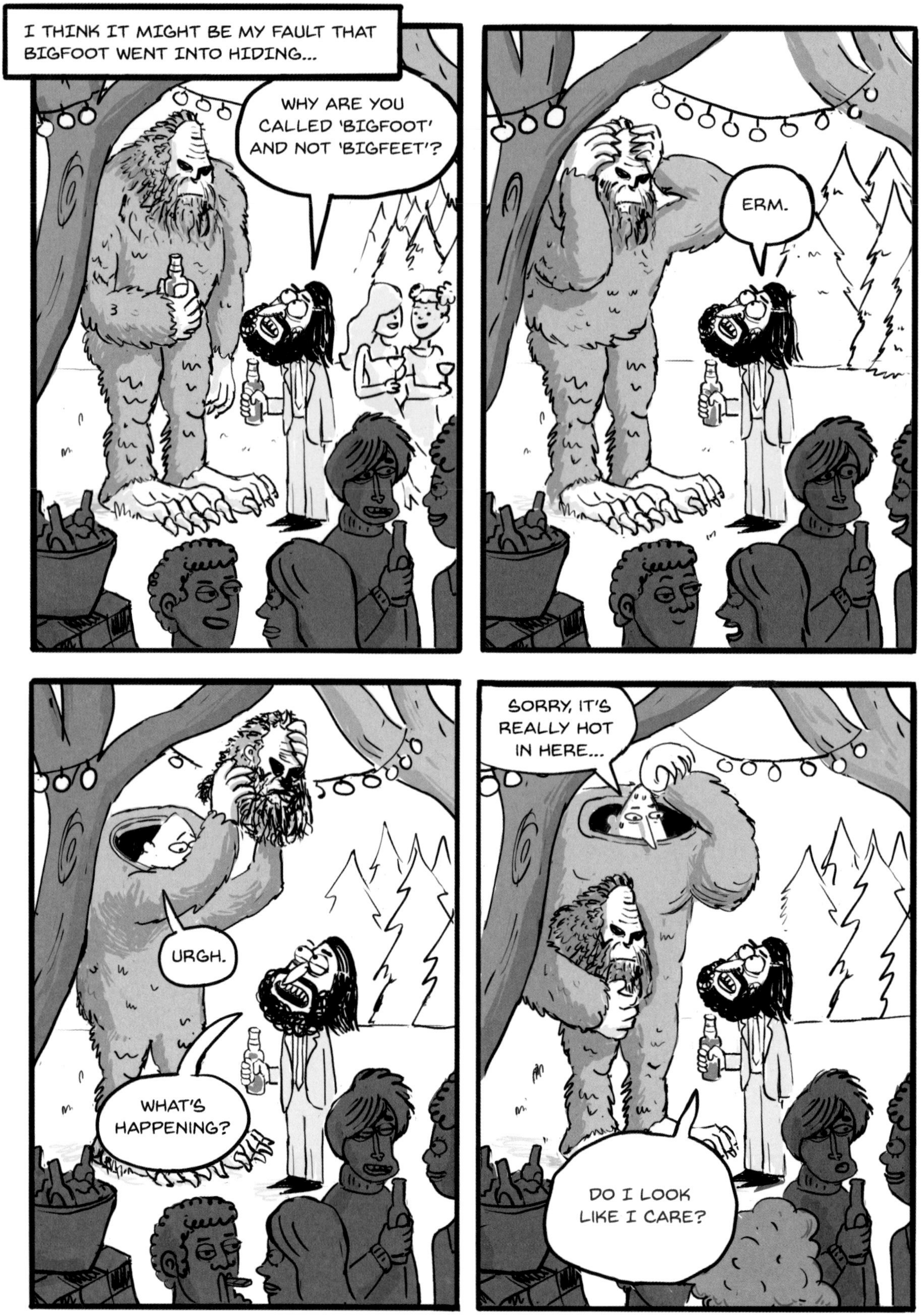
I THINK IT MIGHT BE MY FAULT THAT BIGFOOT WENT INTO HIDING...
WHY ARE YOU CALLED 'BIGFOOT' AND NOT 'BIGFEET'?
ERM.
URGH.
WHAT'S HAPPENING?
SORRY, IT'S REALLY HOT IN HERE...
DO I LOOK LIKE I CARE?

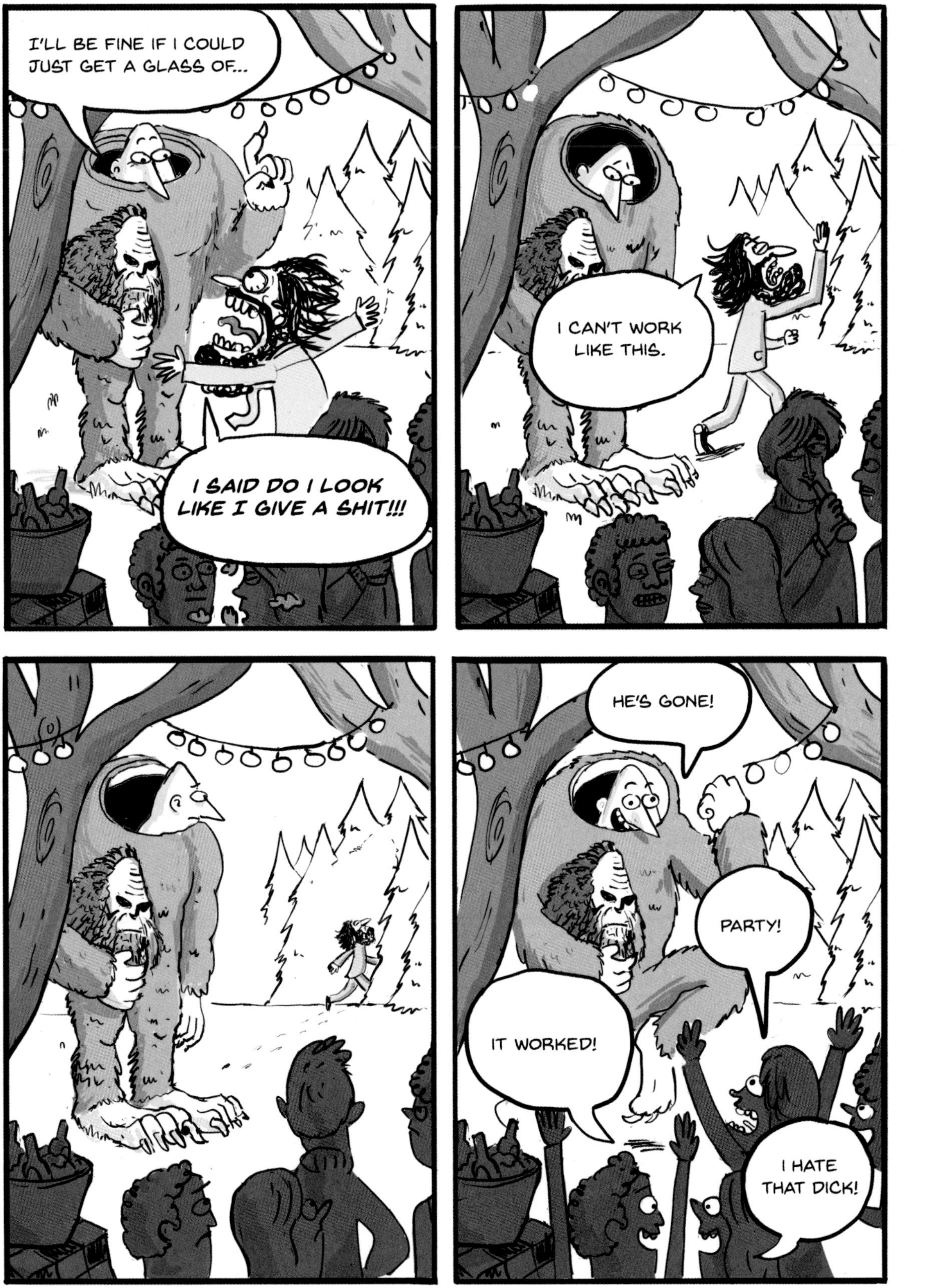
I'LL BE FINE IF I COULD JUST GET A GLASS OF...
I SAID DO I LOOK LIKE I GIVE A SHIT!!!
I CAN'T WORK LIKE THIS.
HE'S GONE!
PARTY!
IT WORKED!
I HATE THAT DICK!

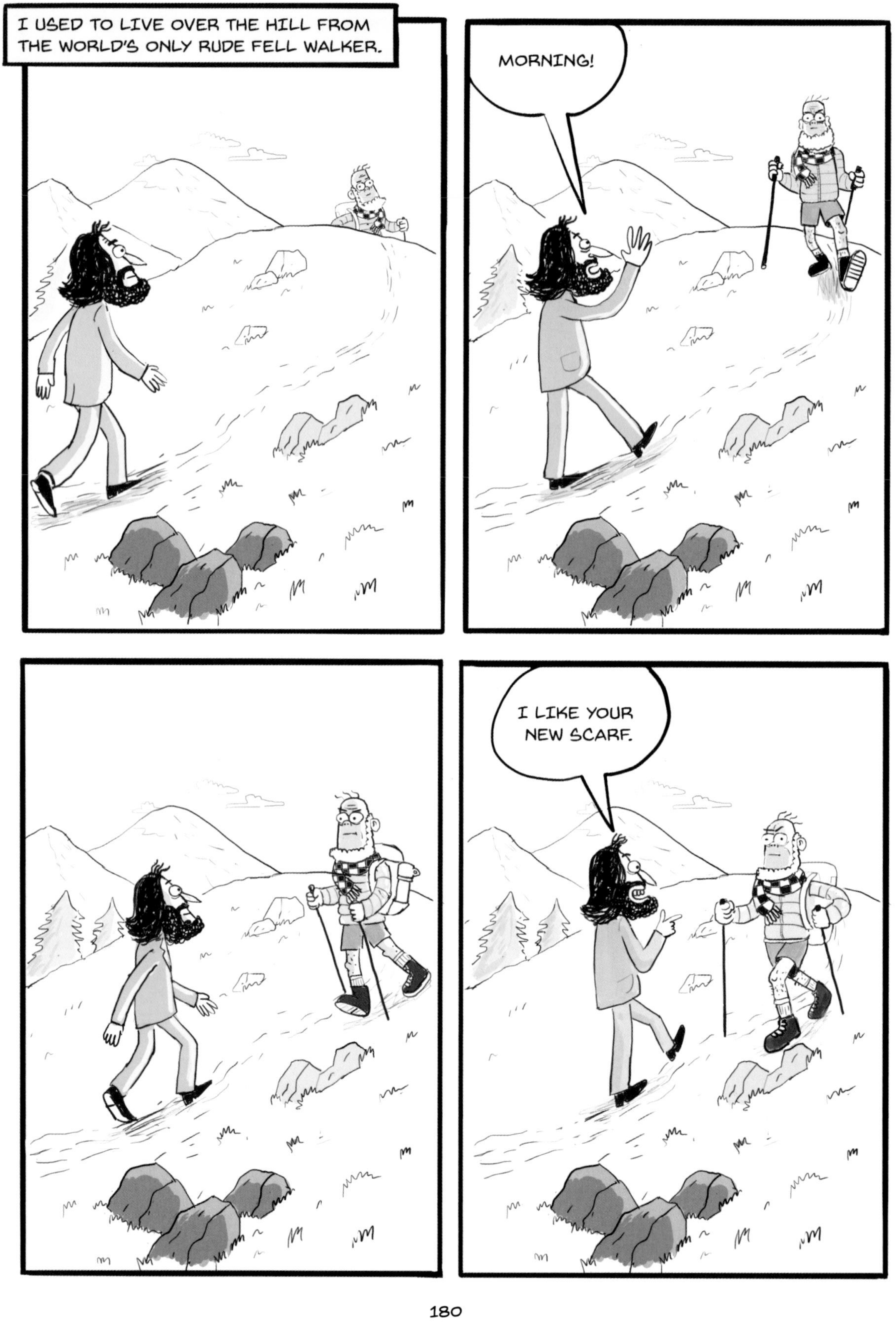
I USED TO LIVE OVER THE HILL FROM THE WORLD'S ONLY RUDE FELL WALKER.
MORNING!
I LIKE YOUR NEW SCARF.

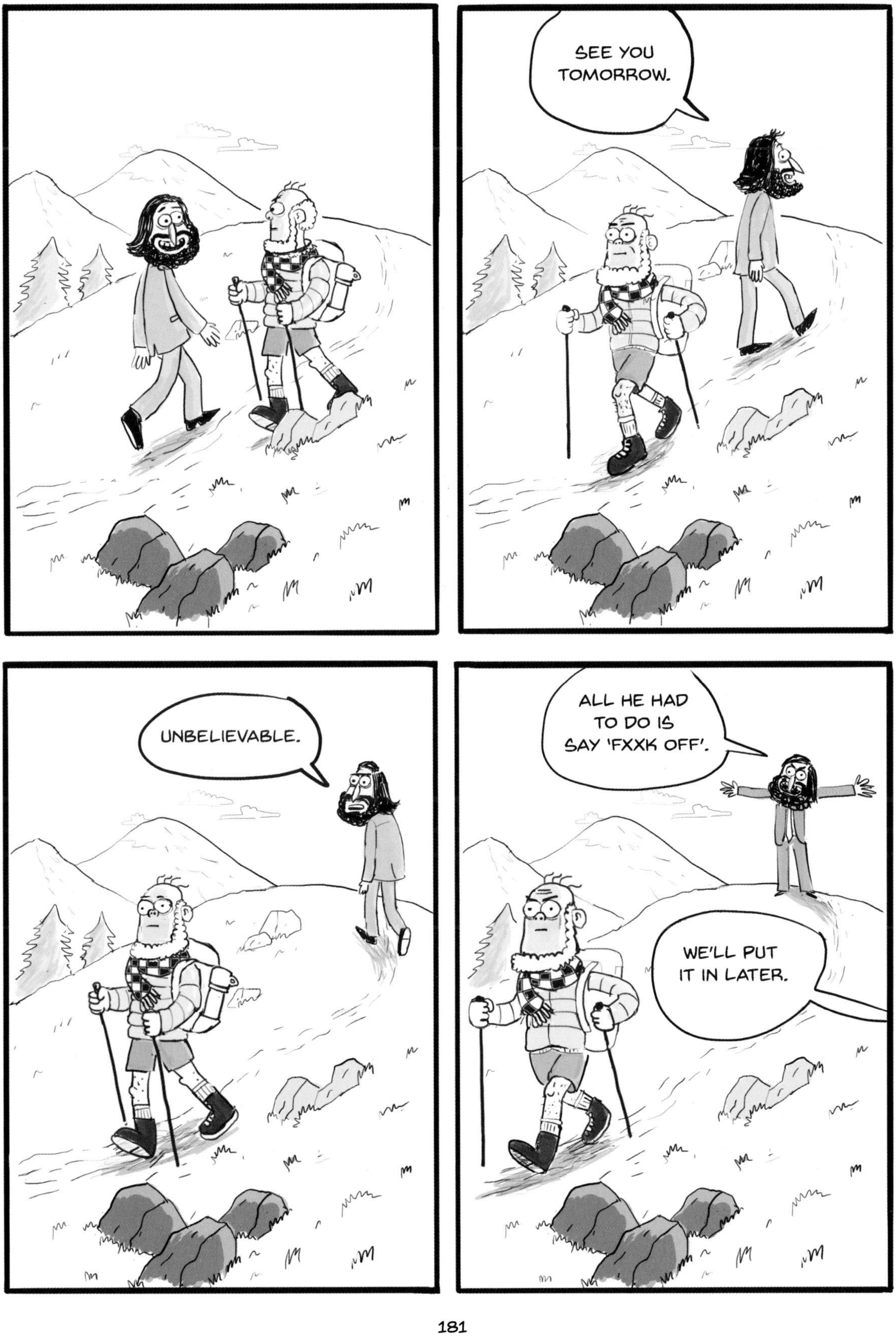
SEE YOU TOMORROW.
UNBELIEVABLE.
ALL HE HAD TO DO IS SAY 'FXXK OFF'.
WE'LL PUT IT IN LATER.

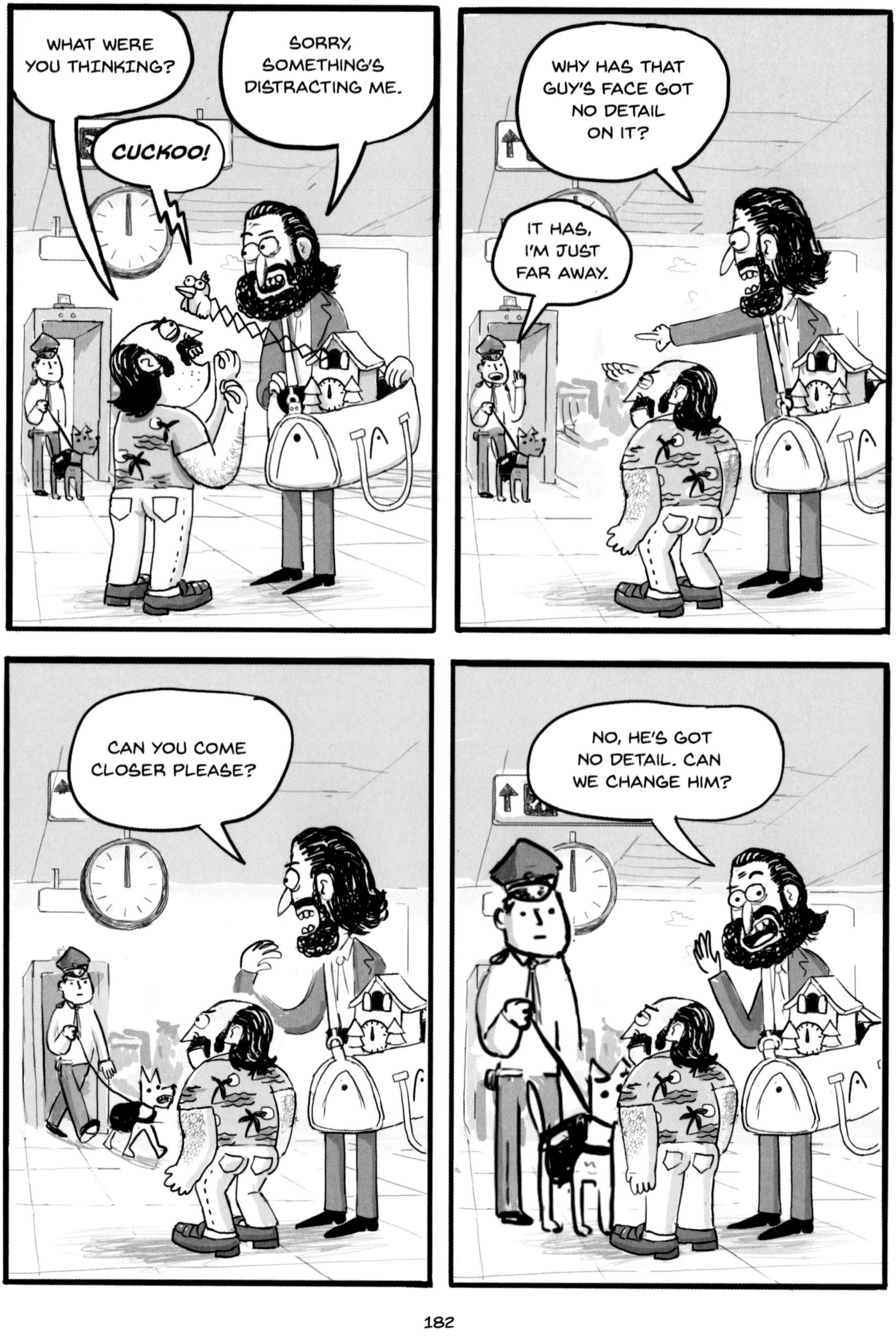
WHAT WERE YOU THINKING?
SORRY, SOMETHING'S DISTRACTING ME.
CUCKOO!
WHY HAS THAT GUY'S FACE GOT NO DETAIL ON IT?
IT HAS, I'M JUST FAR AWAY.
CAN YOU COME CLOSER PLEASE?
NO, HE'S GOT NO DETAIL. CAN WE CHANGE HIM?

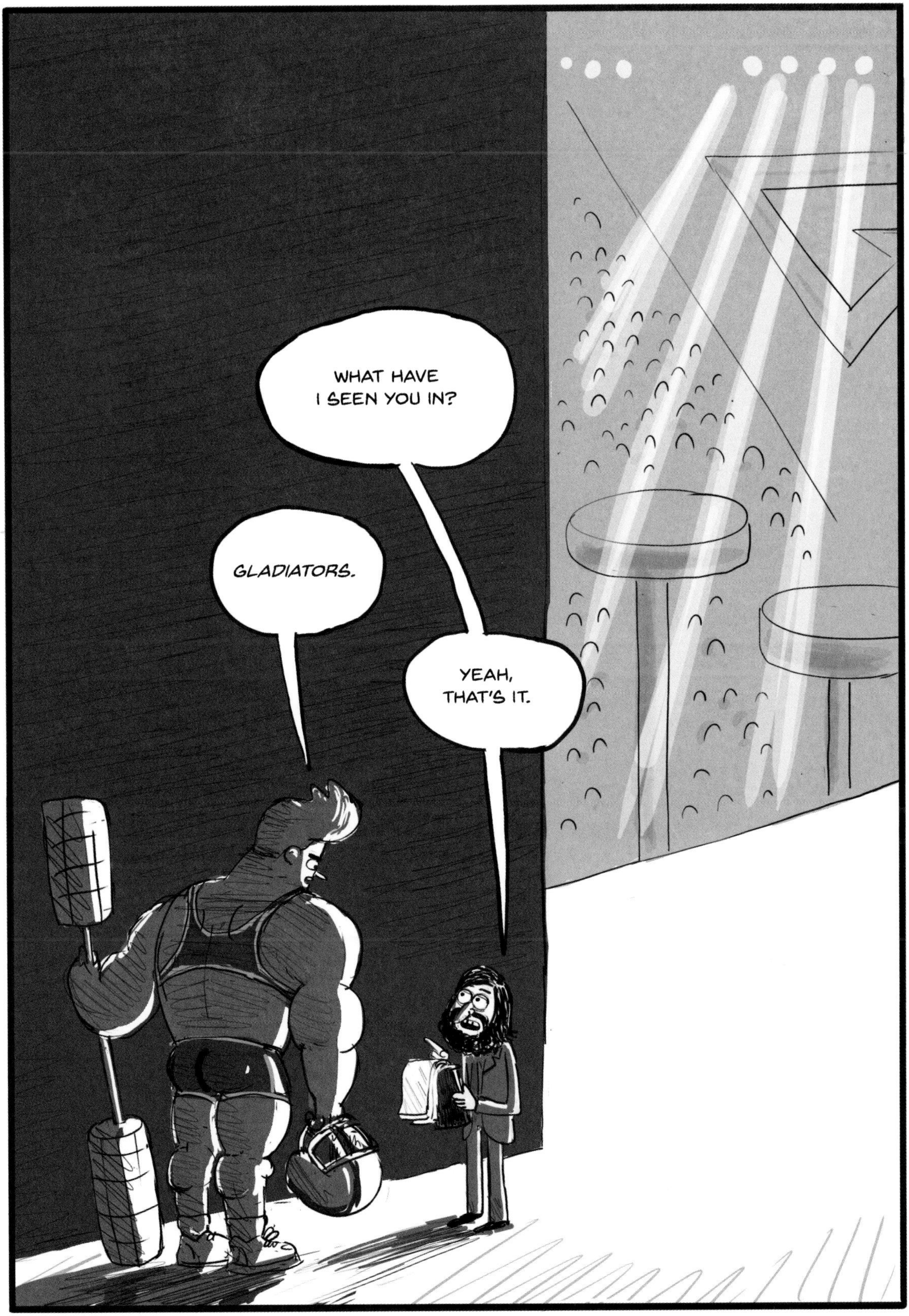
WHAT HAVE I SEEN YOU IN?
GLADIATORS.
YEAH, THAT'S IT.

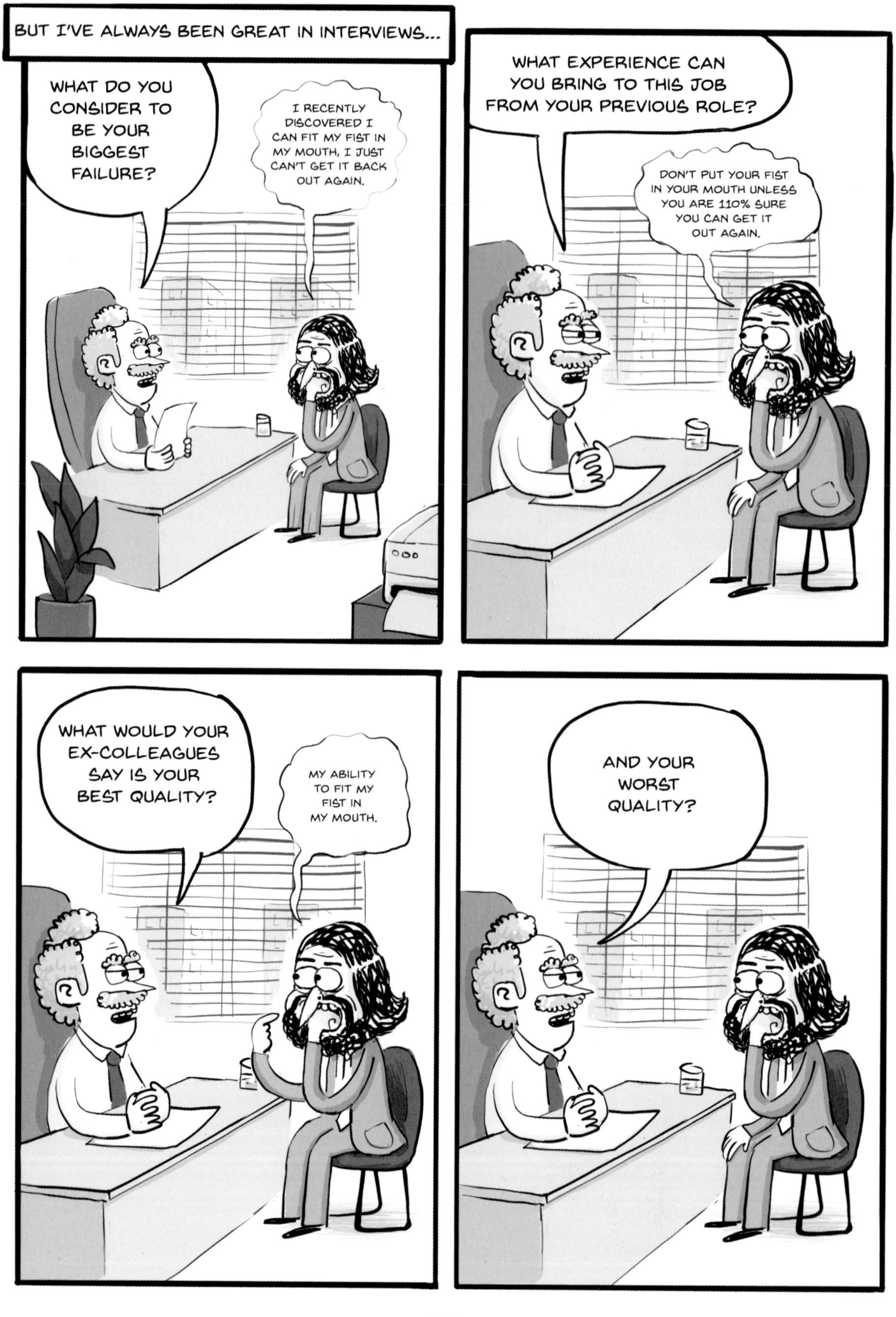
BUT I'VE ALWAYS BEEN GREAT IN INTERVIEWS...
WHAT DO YOU CONSIDER TO BE YOUR BIGGEST FAILURE?
I RECENTLY DISCOVERED I CAN FIT MY FIST IN MY MOUTH, I JUST CAN'T GET IT BACK OUT AGAIN.
WHAT EXPERIENCE CAN YOU BRING TO THIS JOB FROM YOUR PREVIOUS ROLE?
DON'T PUT YOUR FIST IN YOUR MOUTH UNLESS YOU ARE 110% SURE YOU CAN GET IT OUT AGAIN.
WHAT WOULD YOUR EX-COLLEAGUES SAY IS YOUR BEST QUALITY?
MY ABILITY TO FIT MY FIST IN MY MOUTH.
AND YOUR WORST QUALITY?

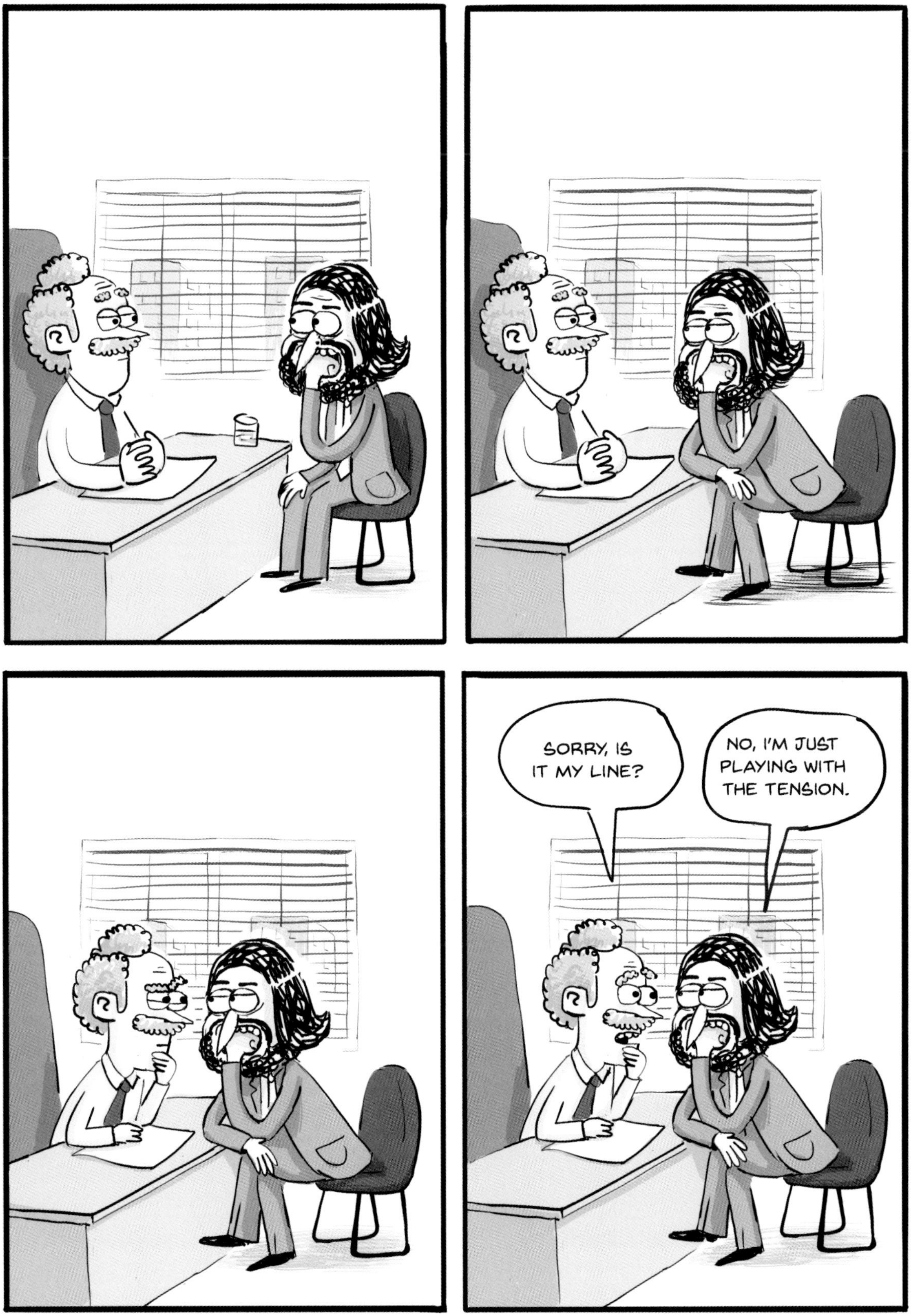
SORRY, IS IT MY LINE?
NO, I'M JUST PLAYING WITH THE TENSION.

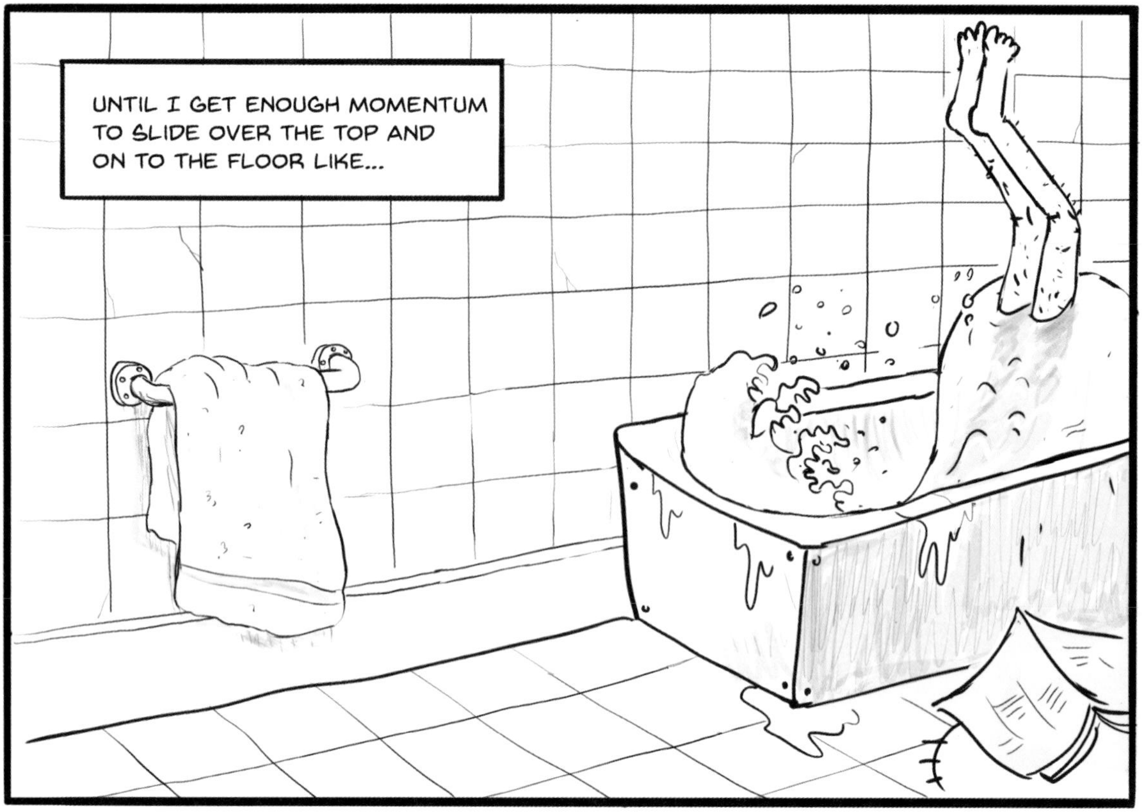
UNTIL I GET ENOUGH MOMENTUM TO SLIDE OVER THE TOP AND ON TO THE FLOOR LIKE...

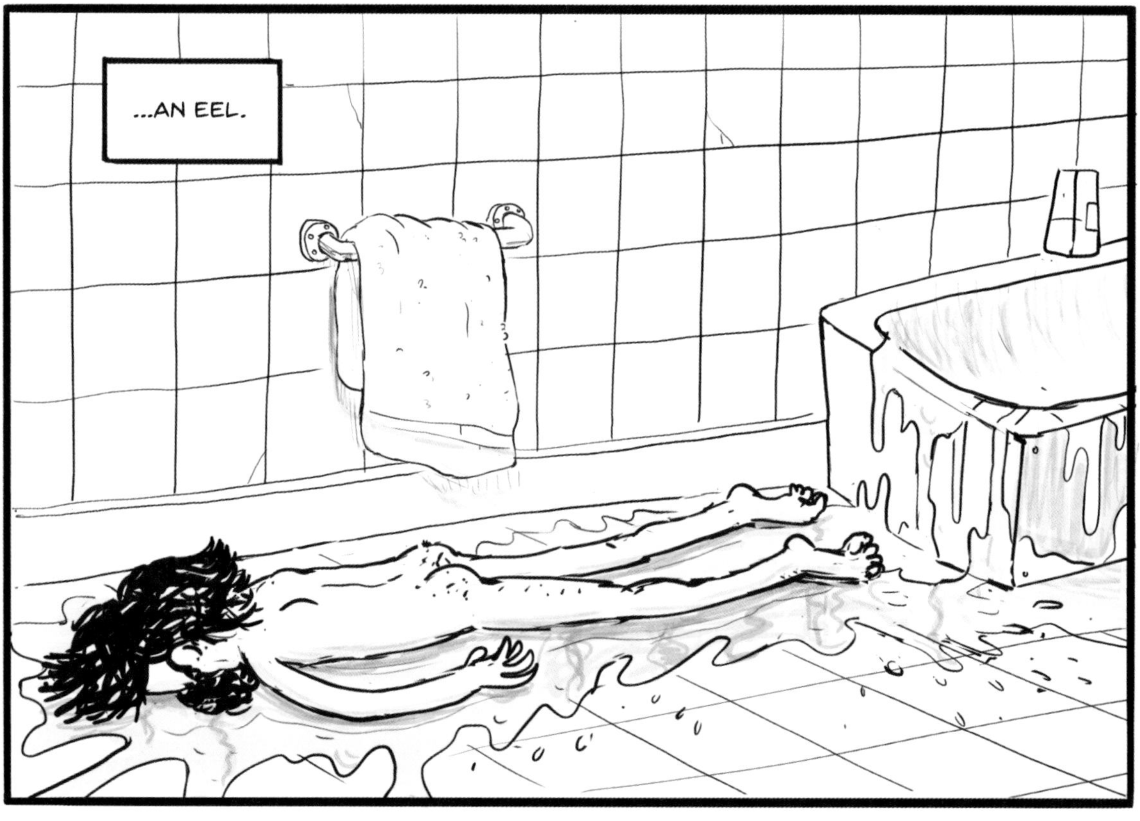
...AN EEL.

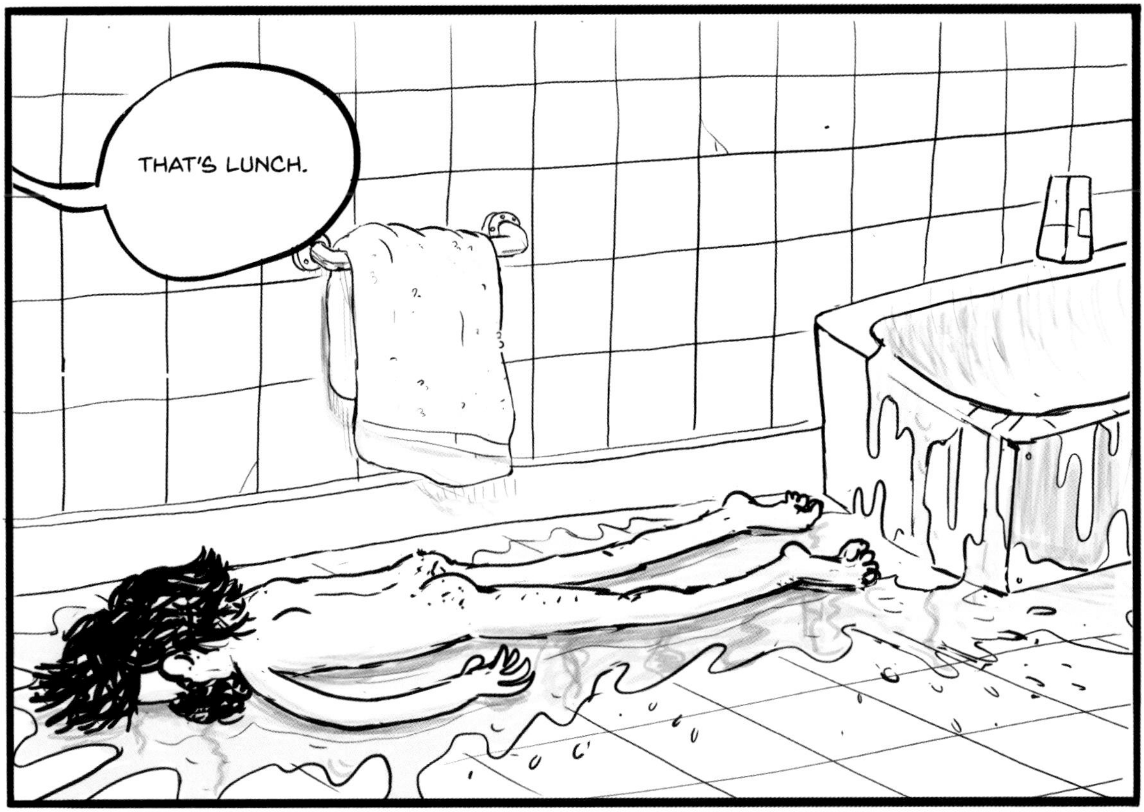
THAT'S LUNCH.

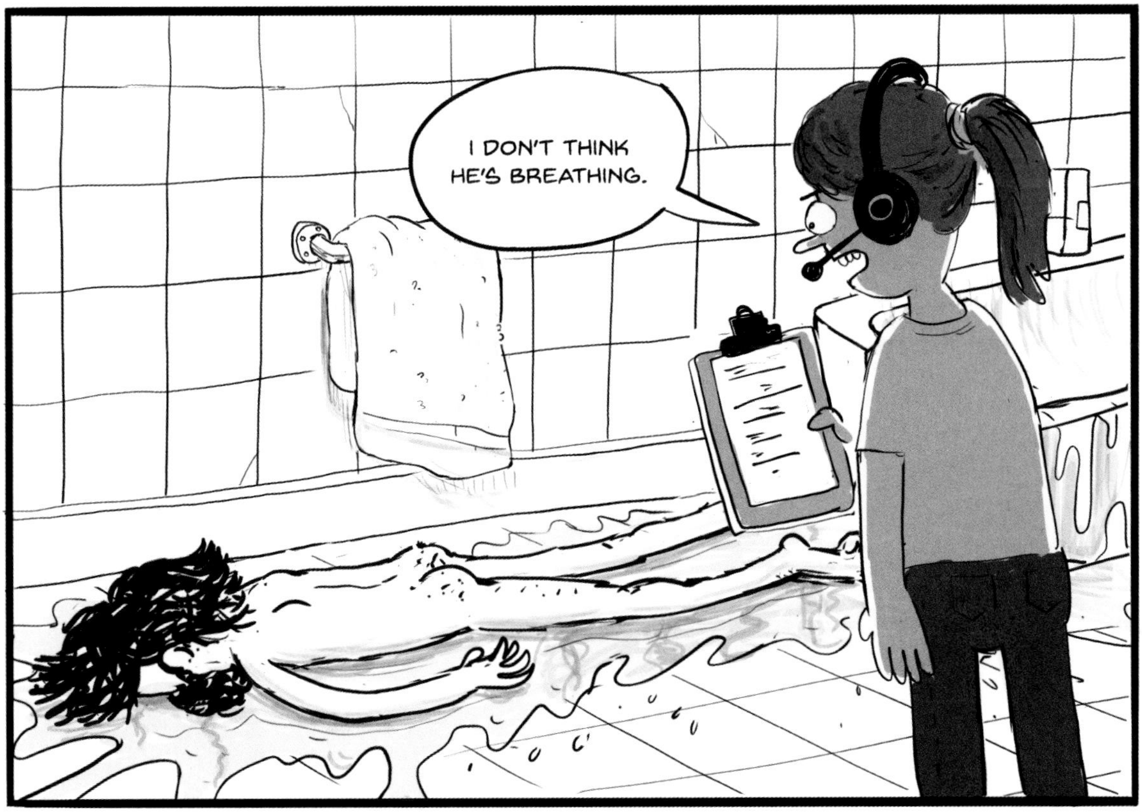
I DON'T THINK HE'S BREATHING.

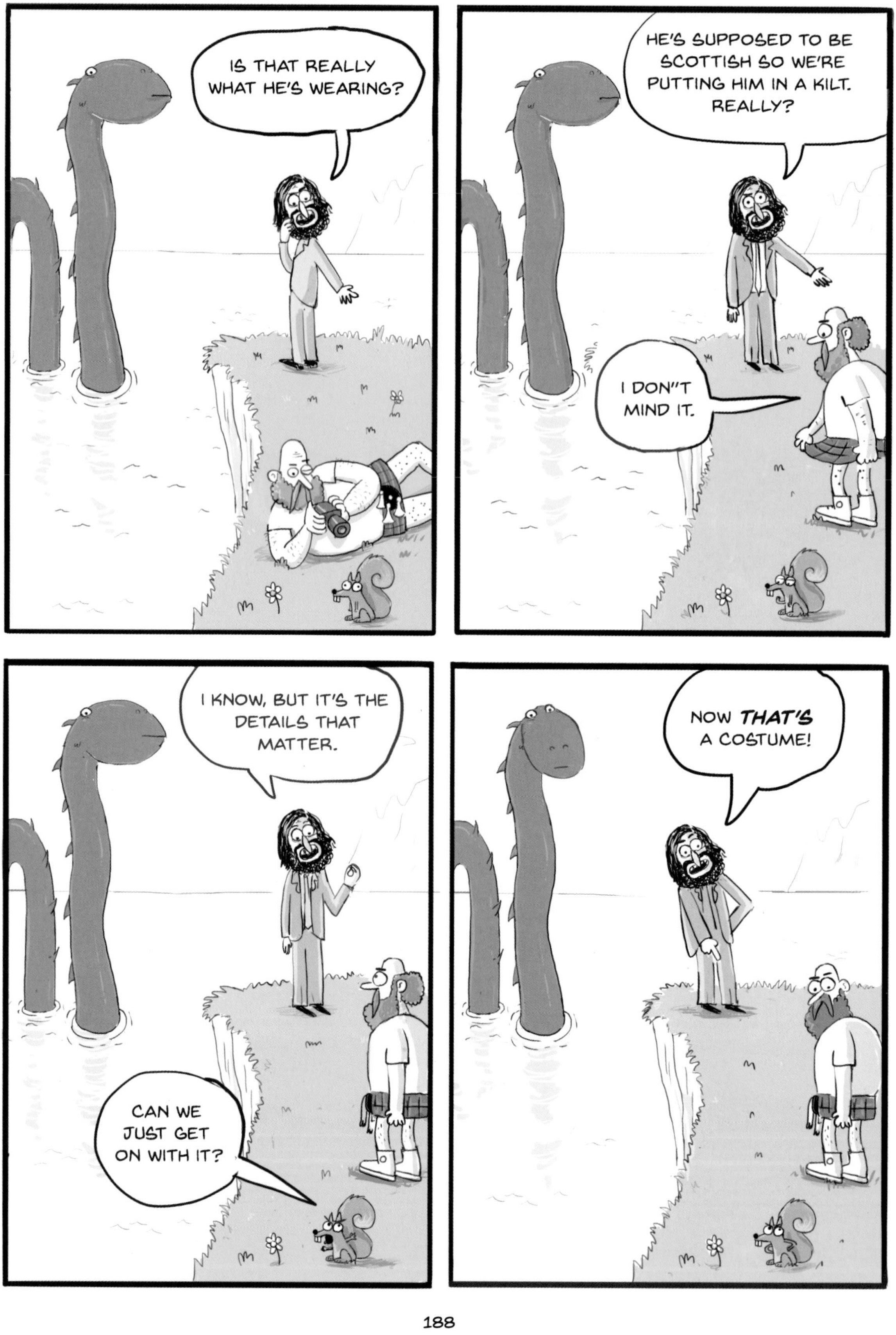
IS THAT REALLY WHAT HE'S WEARING?
HE'S SUPPOSED TO BE SCOTTISH SO WE'RE PUTTING HIM IN A KILT. REALLY?
I DON''T MIND IT.
I KNOW, BUT IT'S THE DETAILS THAT MATTER.
CAN WE JUST GET ON WITH IT?
NOW ***THAT'S*** A COSTUME!

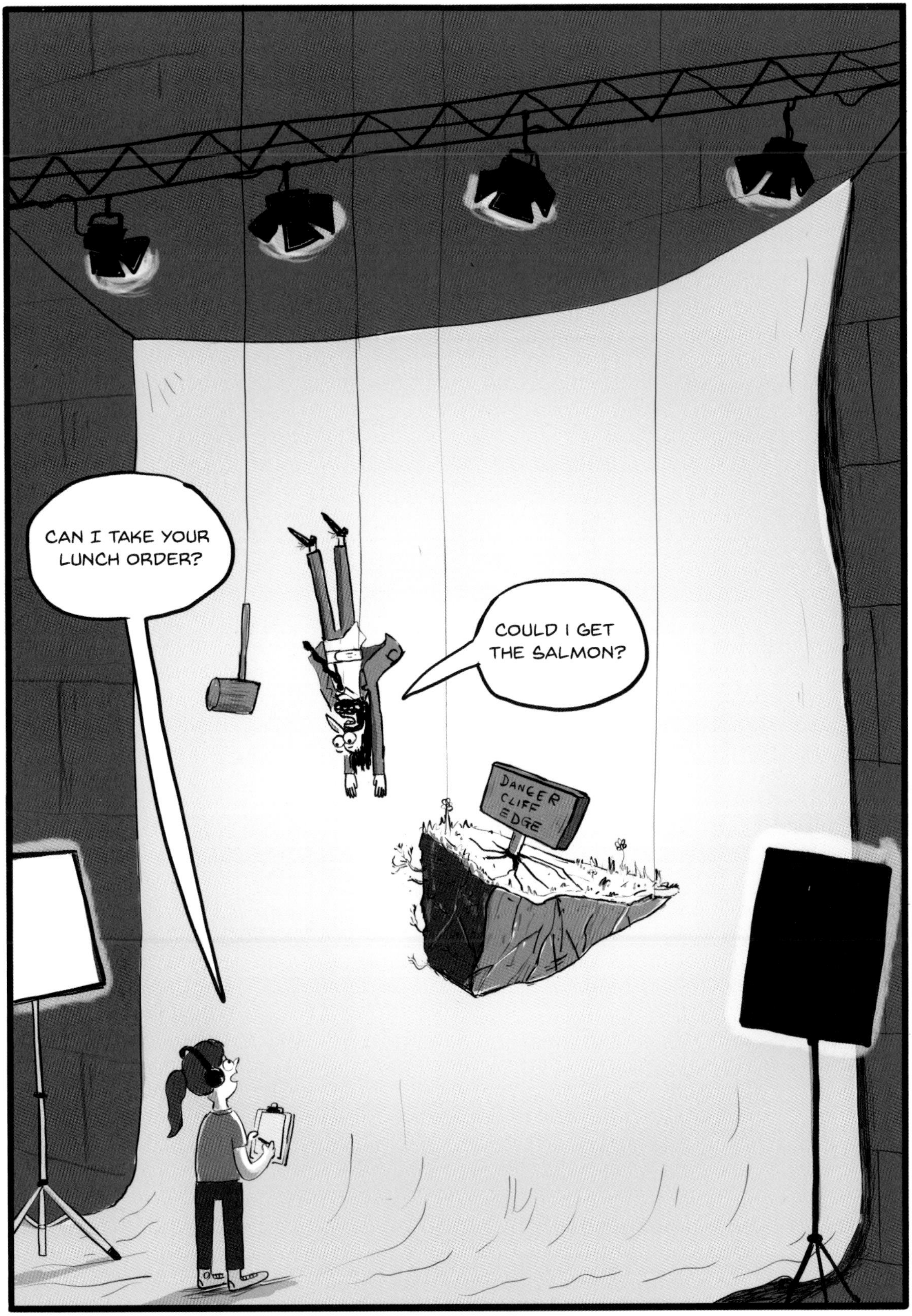
CAN I TAKE YOUR LUNCH ORDER?
COULD I GET THE SALMON?
DANGER CLIFF EDGE